Descendants of Troy
Readings in the Humanities

PRELIMINARY EDITION

Edited by Sergio La Porta

"Don't worry. Prophesy to the best of your knowledge.
I swear by Apollo, to whom you pray when you reveal
The gods' secrets to the Greeks, Calchas, that while I live
And look upon this earth, no one will lay a hand
On you here beside these hollow ships, no, not even
Agamemnon, who boasts he is the best of the Achaeans."

And Calchas, the perfect prophet, taking courage:

"The god finds no fault with vow or sacrifice.
It is for his priest, whom Agamemnon dishonored
And would not allow to ransom his daughter,
That Apollo deals and will deal death from afar.
He will not lift this foul plague from the Greeks
Until we return the dancing-eyed girl to her father
Unransomed, unbought, and make formal sacrifice
On Chryse. Only then might we appease the god."

He finished speaking and sat down. Then up rose
Atreus' son, the warlord Agamemnon,
Furious, anger like twin black thunderheads seething
In his lungs, and his eyes flickered with fire
As he looked Calchas up and down, and said:

"You damn soothsayer!
You've never given me a good omen yet.
You take some kind of perverse pleasure in prophesying
Doom, don't you? Not a single favorable omen ever!
Nothing good ever happens! And now you stand here
Uttering oracles before the Greeks, telling us
That your great ballistic god is giving us all this trouble
Because I was unwilling to accept the ransom
For Chryses' daughter but preferred instead to keep her
In my tent! And why shouldn't I? I like her better than
My wife Clytemnestra. She's no worse than her
When it comes to looks, body, mind, or ability.
Still, I'll give her back, if that's what's best.
I don't want to see the army destroyed like this.
But I want another prize ready for me right away.

I'm not going to be the only Greek without a prize,
It wouldn't be right. And you all see where mine is going."

And Achilles, strong, swift, and godlike:

"And where do you think, son of Atreus,
You greedy glory-hound, the magnanimous Greeks
Are going to get another prize for you?
Do you think we have some kind of stockpile in reserve?
Every town in the area has been sacked and the stuff all divided.
You want the men to count it all back and redistribute it?
All right, you give the girl back to the god. The army
Will repay you three and four times over—when and if
Zeus allows us to rip Troy down to its foundations."

The warlord Agamemnon responded:

"You may be a good man in a fight, Achilles,
And look like a god, but don't try to put one over on me—
It won't work. So while you have your prize,
You want me to sit tight and do without?
Give the girl back, just like that? Now maybe
If the army, in a generous spirit, voted me
Some suitable prize of their own choice, something fair—
But if it doesn't, I'll just go take something myself,
Your prize perhaps, or Ajax's, or Odysseus',
And whoever she belongs to, it'll stick in his throat.

But we can think about that later.
Right now we launch
A black ship on the bright salt water, get a crew aboard,
Load on a hundred bulls, and have Chryseis board her too,
My girl with her lovely cheeks. And we'll want a good man
For captain, Ajax or Idomeneus or godlike Odysseus—
Or maybe you, son of Peleus, our most formidable hero—
To offer sacrifice and appease the Arch-Destroyer for us."

Achilles looked him up and down and said:

"You sorry, profiteering excuse for a commander!

How are you going to get any Greek warrior
To follow you into battle again? You know,
I don't have any quarrel with the Trojans,
They didn't do anything to *me* to make me
Come over here and fight, didn't run off *my* cattle or horses
Or ruin *my* farmland back home in Phthia, not with all
The shadowy mountains and moaning seas between.
It's for *you*, dogface, for your precious pleasure—
And Menelaus' honor—that we came here,
A fact you don't have the decency even to mention!
And now you're threatening to take away the prize
That I sweated for and the Greeks gave me.
I never get a prize equal to yours when the army
Captures one of the Trojan strongholds.
No, I do all the dirty work with my own hands,
And when the battle's over and we divide the loot
You get the lion's share and I go back to the ships
With some pitiful little thing, so worn out from fighting
I don't have the strength left even to complain.
Well, I'm going back to Phthia now. Far better
To head home with my curved ships than stay here,
Unhonored myself and piling up a fortune for you."

The warlord Agamemnon responded:

"Go ahead and desert, if that's what you want!
I'm not going to beg you to stay. There are plenty of others
Who will honor me, not least of all Zeus the Counselor.
To me, you're the most hateful king under heaven,
A born troublemaker. You actually *like* fighting and war.
If you're all that strong, it's just a gift from some god.
So why don't you go home with your ships and lord it over
Your precious Myrmidons. I couldn't care less about you
Or your famous temper. But I'll tell you this:
Since Phoebus Apollo is taking away my Chryseis,
Whom I'm sending back aboard ship with my friends,
I'm coming to your hut and taking Briseis,
Your own beautiful prize, so that you will see just how much
Stronger I am than you, and the next person will wince
At the thought of opposing me as an equal."

Achilles' chest was a rough knot of pain
Twisting around his heart: should he
Draw the sharp sword that hung by his thigh,
Scatter the ranks and gut Agamemnon,
Or control his temper, repress his rage?
He was mulling it over, inching the great sword
From its sheath, when out of the blue
Athena came, sent by the white-armed goddess
Hera, who loved and watched over both men.
She stood behind Achilles and grabbed his sandy hair,
Visible only to him: not another soul saw her.
Awestruck, Achilles turned around, recognizing
Pallas Athena at once—it was her eyes—
And words flew from his mouth like winging birds:

"Daughter of Zeus! Why have you come here?
To see Agamemnon's arrogance, no doubt.
I'll tell you where I place my bets, Goddess:
Sudden death for this outrageous behavior."

Athena's eyes glared through the sea's salt haze.

"I came to see if I could check this temper of yours,
Sent from heaven by the white-armed goddess
Hera, who loves and watches over both of you men.
Now come on, drop this quarrel, don't draw your sword.
Tell him off instead. And I'll tell you,
Achilles, how things will be: You're going to get
Three times as many magnificent gifts
Because of his arrogance. Just listen to us and be patient."

Achilles, the great runner, responded:

"When you two speak, Goddess, a man has to listen
No matter how angry. It's better that way.
Obey the gods and they hear you when you pray."

With that he ground his heavy hand
Onto the silver hilt and pushed the great sword
Back into its sheath. Athena's speech

Had been well-timed. She was on her way
To Olympus by now, to the halls of Zeus
And the other immortals, while Achilles
Tore into Agamemnon again:

"You bloated drunk,
With a dog's eyes and a rabbit's heart!
You've never had the guts to buckle on armor in battle
Or come out with the best fighting Greeks
On any campaign! Afraid to look Death in the eye,
Agamemnon? It's far more profitable
To hang back in the army's rear—isn't it?—
Confiscating prizes from any Greek who talks back
And bleeding your people dry. There's not a real man
Under your command, or this latest atrocity
Would be your last, son of Atreus.
Now get this straight. I swear a formal oath:
By this scepter, which will never sprout leaf
Or branch again since it was cut from its stock
In the mountains, which will bloom no more
Now that bronze has pared off leaf and bark,
And which now the sons of the Greeks hold in their hands
At council, upholding Zeus' laws—
By this scepter I swear:
When every last Greek desperately misses Achilles,
Your remorse won't do any good then,
When Hector the man-killer swats you down like flies.
And you will eat your heart out
Because you failed to honor the best Greek of all."

Those were his words, and he slammed the scepter,
Studded with gold, to the ground and sat down.

Opposite him, Agamemnon fumed.
Then Nestor
Stood up, sweet-worded Nestor, the orator from Pylos
With a voice high-toned and liquid as honey.
He had seen two generations of men pass away
In sandy Pylos and was now king in the third.
He was full of good will in the speech he made:

"It's a sad day for Greece, a sad day.
Priam and Priam's sons would be happy indeed,
And the rest of the Trojans too, glad in their hearts,
If they learned all this about you two fighting,
Our two best men in council and in battle.
Now you listen to me, both of you. You are both
Younger than I am, and I've associated with men
Better than you, and they didn't treat me lightly.
I've never seen men like those, and never will,
The likes of Peirithous and Dryas, a shepherd to his people,
Caineus and Exadius and godlike Polyphemus,
And Aegeus' son, Theseus, who could have passed for a god,
The strongest men who ever lived on earth, the strongest,
And they fought with the strongest, with wild things
From the mountains, and beat the daylights out of them.
I was their companion, although I came from Pylos,
From the ends of the earth—they sent for me themselves.
And I held my own fighting with them. You couldn't find
A mortal on earth who could fight with them now.
And when I talked in council, they took my advice.
So should you two now: taking advice is a good thing.
Agamemnon, for all your nobility, do not take his girl.
Leave her be: the army originally gave her to him as a prize.
Nor should you, son of Peleus, want to lock horns with a king.
A scepter-holding king has honor beyond the rest of men,
Power and glory given by Zeus himself.
You are stronger, and it is a goddess who bore you.
But he is more powerful, since he rules over more.
Son of Atreus, cease your anger. And I appeal
Personally to Achilles to control his temper, since he is,
For all Greeks, a mighty bulwark in this evil war."

And Agamemnon, the warlord:

"Yes, old man, everything you've said is absolutely right.
But this man wants to be ahead of everyone else,
He wants to rule everyone, give orders to everyone,
Lord it over everyone, and he's not going to get away with it.
If the gods eternal made him a spearman, does that mean
They gave him permission to be insolent as well?"

And Achilles, breaking in on him:

"Ha, and think of the names people would call me
If I bowed and scraped every time you opened your mouth.
Try that on somebody else, but not on me.
I'll tell you this, and you can stick it in your gut:
I'm not going to put up a fight on account of the girl.
You, all of you, gave her to me and you can all take her back.
But anything else of mine in my black sailing ship
You keep your goddamn hands off, you hear?
Try it. Let everybody here see how fast
Your black blood boils up around my spear."

So it was a stand-off, their battle of words,
And the assembly beside the Greek ships dissolved.
Achilles went back to the huts by his ships
With Patroclus and his men. Agamemnon had a fast ship
Hauled down to the sea, picked twenty oarsmen,
Loaded on a hundred bulls due to the god, and had Chryses'
daughter,
His fair-cheeked girl, go aboard also. Odysseus captained,
And when they were all on board, the ship headed out to sea.

Onshore, Agamemnon ordered a purification.
The troops scrubbed down and poured the filth
Into the sea.Then they sacrificed to Apollo
Oxen and goats by the hundreds on the barren shore.
The smoky savor swirled up to the sky.

That was the order of the day. But Agamemnon
Did not forget his spiteful threat against Achilles.
He summoned Talthybius and Eurybates,
Faithful retainers who served as his heralds:

"Go to the hut of Achilles, son of Peleus;
Bring back the girl, fair-cheeked Briseis.
If he won't give her up, I'll come myself
With my men and take her—and freeze his heart cold."

It was not the sort of mission a herald would relish.

The pair trailed along the barren seashore
Until they came to the Myrmidons' ships and encampment.
They found Achilles sitting outside his hut
Beside his black ship. He was not glad to see them.
They stood respectfully silent, in awe of this king,
And it was Achilles who was moved to address them first:

"Welcome, heralds, the gods' messengers and men's.
Come closer. You're not to blame, Agamemnon is,
Who sent you here for the girl, Briseis.
Patroclus,
Bring the girl out and give her to these gentlemen.
You two are witnesses before the blessed gods,
Before mortal men and that hard-hearted king,
If ever I'm needed to protect the others
From being hacked to bits. His mind is murky with anger,
And he doesn't have the sense to look ahead and behind
To see how the Greeks might defend their ships."

Thus Achilles.
Patroclus obeyed his beloved friend
And brought Briseis, cheeks flushed, out of the tent
And gave her to the heralds, who led her away.
She went unwillingly.
Then Achilles, in tears,
Withdrew from his friends and sat down far away
On the foaming white seashore, staring out
At the endless sea. Stretching out his hands,
He prayed over and over to his beloved mother:

"Mother, since you bore me for a short life only,
Olympian Zeus was supposed to grant me honor.
Well, he hasn't given me any at all. Agamemnon
Has taken away my prize and dishonored me."

His voice, choked with tears, was heard by his mother
As she sat in the sea-depths beside her old father.
She rose up from the white-capped sea like a mist,
And settling herself beside her weeping child
She stroked him with her hand and talked to him:

"Why are you crying, son? What's wrong?
Don't keep it inside. Tell me so we'll both know."

And Achilles, with a deep groan:

"You already know. Why do I have to tell you?
We went after Thebes, Eëtion's sacred town,
Sacked it and brought the plunder back here.
The army divided everything up and chose
For Agamemnon fair-cheeked Chryseis.
Then her father, Chryses, a priest of Apollo,
Came to our army's ships on the beachhead,
Hauling a fortune for his daughter's ransom.
He displayed Apollo's sacral ribbons
On a golden staff and made a formal plea
To the entire Greek army, but especially
The commanders, Atreus' two sons.
You could hear the troops murmuring,
'Respect the priest and take the ransom.'
But Agamemnon wouldn't hear of it
And dismissed Chryses with a rough speech.
The old man went back angry, and Apollo
Heard his beloved priest's prayer.
He hit the Greeks hard, and the troops
Were falling over dead, the god's arrows
Raining down all through the Greek camp.
A prophet told us the Arch-Destroyer's will,
And I demanded the god be appeased.
Agamemnon got angry, stood up
And threatened me, and made good his threat.
The high command sent the girl on a fast ship
Back to Chryse with gifts for Apollo,
And heralds led away my girl, Briseis,
Whom the army had given to me.
Now you have to help me, if you can.
  Go to Olympus
And call in the debt that Zeus owes you.
I remember often hearing you tell
In my father's house how you alone managed,

Of all the immortals, to save Zeus' neck
When the other Olympians wanted to bind him—
Hera and Poseidon and Pallas Athena.
You came and loosened him from his chains,
And you lured to Olympus' summit the giant
With a hundred hands whom the gods call
Briareus but men call Aegaeon, stronger
Even than his own father Uranus, and he
Sat hulking in front of cloud-black Zeus,
Proud of his prowess, and scared all the gods
Who were trying to put the son of Cronus in chains.
  Remind Zeus of this, sit holding his knees,
See if he is willing to help the Trojans
Hem the Greeks in between the fleet and the sea.
Once they start being killed, the Greeks may
Appreciate Agamemnon for what he is,
And the wide-ruling son of Atreus will see
What a fool he's been because he did not honor
The best of all the fighting Achaeans."

And Thetis, now weeping herself:

  "O my poor child. I bore you for sorrow,
Nursed you for grief. Why? You should be
Spending your time here by your ships
Happily and untroubled by tears,
Since life is short for you, all too brief.
Now you're destined for both an early death
And misery beyond compare. It was for this
I gave birth to you in your father's palace
Under an evil star.
                I'll go to snow-bound Olympus
And tell all this to the Lord of Lightning.
I hope he listens. You stay here, though,
Beside your ships and let the Greeks feel
Your spite; withdraw completely from the war.
Zeus left yesterday for the River Ocean
On his way to a feast with the Ethiopians.
All the gods went with him. He'll return

To Olympus twelve days from now,
And I'll go then to his bronze threshold
And plead with him. I think I'll persuade him."

And she left him there, angry and heartsick
At being forced to give up the silken-waisted girl.

Meanwhile, Odysseus was putting in
At Chryse with his sacred cargo on board.
When they were well within the deepwater harbor
They furled the sail and stowed it in the ship's hold,
Slackened the forestays and lowered the mast,
Working quickly, then rowed her to a mooring, where
They dropped anchor and made the stern cables fast.
The crew disembarked on the seabeach
And unloaded the bulls for Apollo the Archer.
Then Chryses' daughter stepped off the seagoing vessel,
And Odysseus led her to an altar
And placed her in her father's hands, saying:

"Chryses, King Agamemnon has sent me here
To return your child and offer to Phoebus
Formal sacrifice on behalf of the Greeks.
So may we appease Lord Apollo, and may he
Lift the afflictions he has sent upon us."

Chryses received his daughter tenderly.

Moving quickly, they lined the hundred oxen
Around the massive altar, a glorious offering,
Washed their hands and sprinkled on the victims
Sacrificial barley. On behalf of the Greeks
Chryses lifted his hands and prayed aloud:

"Hear me, Silverbow, Protector of Chryse,
Lord of Holy Cilla, Master of Tenedos,
As once before you heard my prayer,
Did me honor, and smote the Greeks mightily,
So now also grant me this prayer:
Lift the plague

From the Greeks and save them from death."

Thus the old priest, and Apollo heard him.

After the prayers and the strewing of barley
They slaughtered and flayed the oxen,
Jointed the thighbones and wrapped them
In a layer of fat with cuts of meat on top.
The old man roasted them over charcoal
And doused them with wine. Younger men
Stood by with five-tined forks in their hands.
When the thigh pieces were charred and they had
Tasted the tripe, they cut the rest into strips,
Skewered it on spits and roasted it skillfully.
When they were done and the feast was ready,
Feast they did, and no one lacked an equal share.
When they had all had enough to eat and drink,
The young men topped off mixing bowls with wine
And served it in goblets to all the guests.
All day long these young Greeks propitiated
The god with dancing, singing to Apollo
A paean as they danced, and the god was pleased.
When the sun went down and darkness came on,
They went to sleep by the ship's stern-cables.

Dawn came early, a palmetto of rose,
Time to make sail for the wide beachhead camp.
They set up mast and spread the white canvas,
And the following wind, sent by Apollo,
Boomed in the mainsail. An indigo wave
Hissed off the bow as the ship surged on,
Leaving a wake as she held on course through the billows.

When they reached the beachhead they hauled the black ship
High on the sand and jammed in the long chocks;
Then the crew scattered to their own huts and ships.

All this time Achilles, the son of Peleus in the line of Zeus,
Nursed his anger, the great runner idle by his fleet's fast hulls.
He was not to be seen in council, that arena for glory,

Nor in combat. He sat tight in camp consumed with grief,
His great heart yearning for the battle cry and war.

Twelve days went by. Dawn.
The gods returned to Olympus,
Zeus at their head.
Thetis did not forget
Her son's requests. She rose from the sea
And up through the air to the great sky
And found Cronus' wide-seeing son
Sitting in isolation on the highest peak
Of the rugged Olympic massif.
She settled beside him, and touched his knees
With her left hand, his beard with her right,
And made her plea to the Lord of Sky:

"Father Zeus, if I have ever helped you
In word or deed among the immortals,
Grant me this prayer:
Honor my son, doomed to die young
And yet dishonored by King Agamemnon,
Who stole his prize, a personal affront.
Do justice by him, Lord of Olympus.
Give the Trojans the upper hand until the Greeks
Grant my son the honor he deserves."

Zeus made no reply but sat a long time
In silence, clouds scudding around him.
Thetis held fast to his knees and asked again:

"Give me a clear yes or no. Either nod in assent
Or refuse me. Why should you care if I know
How negligible a goddess I am in your eyes."

This provoked a troubled, gloomy response:

"This is disastrous. You're going to force me
Into conflict with Hera. I can just hear her now,
Cursing me and bawling me out. As it is,
She already accuses me of favoring the Trojans.

Please go back the way you came. Maybe
Hera won't notice. I'll take care of this.
And so you can have some peace of mind,
I'll say yes to you by nodding my head,
The ultimate pledge. Unambiguous,
Irreversible, and absolutely fulfilled,
Whatever I say yes to with a nod of my head."

And the Son of Cronus nodded. Black brows
Lowered, a glory of hair cascaded down from the Lord's
Immortal head, and the holy mountain trembled.

Their conference over, the two parted. The goddess
Dove into the deep sea from Olympus' snow-glare
And Zeus went to his home. The gods all
Rose from their seats at their father's entrance. Not one
Dared watch him enter without standing to greet him.
And so God entered and took his high seat.
But Hera
Had noticed his private conversation with Thetis,
The silver-footed daughter of the Old Man of the Sea,
And flew at him with cutting words:

"Who was that you were scheming with just now?
You just love devising secret plots behind my back,
Don't you? You can't bear to tell me what you're thinking,
Or you don't dare. Never have and never will."

The Father of Gods and Men answered:

"Hera, don't hope to know all my secret thoughts.
It would strain your mind even though you are my wife.
What it is proper to hear, no one, human or divine,
Will hear before you. But what I wish to conceive
Apart from the other gods, don't pry into that."

And Lady Hera, with her oxen eyes wide:

"Oh my. The awesome son of Cronus has spoken.
Pry? You know that I never pry. And you always

Cheerfully volunteer—whatever information you please.
It's just that I have this feeling that somehow
The silver-footed daughter of the Old Man of the Sea
May have won you over. She *was* sitting beside you
Up there in the mist, and she did touch your knees.
And I'm pretty sure that you agreed to honor Achilles
And destroy Greeks by the thousands beside their ships."

And Zeus, the master of cloud and storm:

"You witch! Your intuitions are always right.
But what does it get you? Nothing, except that
I like you less than ever. And so you're worse off.
If it's as you think it is, it's my business, not yours.
So sit down and shut up and do as I say.
You see these hands? All the gods on Olympus
Won't be able to help you if I ever lay them on you."

Hera lost her nerve when she heard this.
She sat down in silence, fear cramping her heart,
And gloom settled over the gods in Zeus' hall.
Hephaestus, the master artisan, broke the silence,
Out of concern for his ivory-armed mother:

"This is terrible; it's going to ruin us all.
If you two quarrel like this over mortals
It's bound to affect us gods. There'll be no more
Pleasure in our feasts if we let things turn ugly.
Mother, please, I don't have to tell you,
You have to be pleasant to our father Zeus
So he won't be angry and ruin our feast.
If the Lord of Lightning wants to blast us from our seats,
He can—that's how much stronger he is.
So apologize to him with silken-soft words,
And the Olympian in turn will be gracious to us."

He whisked up a two-handled cup, offered it
To his dear mother, and said to her:

"I know it's hard, mother, but you have to endure it.

12

I don't want to see you getting beat up, and me
Unable to help you. The Olympian can be rough.
Once before when I tried to rescue you
He flipped me by my foot off our balcony.
I fell all day and came down when the sun did
On the island of Lemnos, scarcely alive.
The Sintians had to nurse me back to health."

By the time he finished, the ivory-armed goddess
Was smiling at her son. She accepted the cup from him.
Then the lame god turned serving boy, siphoning nectar
From the mixing bowl and pouring the sweet liquor
For all of the gods, who couldn't stop laughing
At the sight of Hephaestus hustling through the halls.

And so all day long until the sun went down
They feasted to their hearts' content,
Apollo playing beautiful melodies on the lyre,
The Muses singing responsively in lovely voices.
And when the last gleams of sunset had faded,
They turned in for the night, each to a house
Built by Hephaestus, the renowned master craftsman,
The burly blacksmith with the soul of an artist.

And the Lord of Lightning, Olympian Zeus, went to his bed,
The bed he always slept in when sweet sleep overcame him.
He climbed in and slept, next to golden-throned Hera.

ILIAD 6

The battle was left to rage on the level expanse
Between Troy's two rivers. Bronze spearheads
Drove past each other as the Greek and Trojan armies
Spread like a hemorrhage across the plain.

Telamonian Ajax, the Achaean wall,
Was the first Greek to break the Trojan line
And give his comrades some daylight.
He killed Thrace's best, Acamas,
Son of Eussorus, smashing through the horn
Of his plumed helmet with his spear
And driving through until the bronze tip
Pierced the forehead's bone. Acamas' eyes went dark.

Diomedes followed up by killing Axylus,
Teuthras' son, a most hospitable man.
His comfortable home was on the road to Arisbe,
And he entertained all travellers, but not one
Came by to meet the enemy before him
And save him from death. Diomedes killed
Not only Axylus but Calesius, his driver,
Two men who would now be covered by earth.

Then Euryalus killed Opheltius and Dresus
And went on after Aesepus and Pedasus,
Twins whom the naiad Abarbarea

Bore to Bucolion, Laomedon's eldest
Though bastard son. He was with his sheep
When he made love to the nymph. She conceived,
And bore him the twins whom Euryalus
Now undid. He left their bright bodies naked.

Then Polypoetes killed Astyalus;
Odysseus got Pidytes with his spear;
And Teucer took out Aretaon, a good man.
Nestor's son Antilochus killed Ablerus;
The warlord Agamemnon killed Elatus,
Who lived in steep Pedasus on the Satnioeis;
Leitus killed Phylacus as he fled;
And Eurypylus unmanned Melanthius.

But Menelaus took Adrastus alive.
Adrastus' terrified horses became entangled
In a tamarisk as they galloped across the plain,
And, breaking the pole near the car's rim,
Bolted toward the city with the others.
Their master rolled from the car by the wheel
And fell face-first into the dust. Menelaus
Came up to him with his long-shadowed spear,
And Adrastus clasped his knees and prayed:

"Take me alive, son of Atreus, and accept
A worthy ransom from the treasure stored
In my father's palace, bronze, gold, wrought iron.
My father would lavish it all on you if he heard
I was still alive among the Achaean ships."

The speech had its intended effect.
Menelaus was about to hand him over
To be led back to the ships, but Agamemnon
Came running over to call him on it:

"Going soft, Menelaus? What does this man
Mean to you? Have the Trojans ever shown you
Any hospitality? Not one of them
Escapes sheer death at our hands, not even

The boy who is still in his mother's womb.
Every Trojan dies, unmourned and unmarked."

And so the hero changed his brother's mind
By reminding him of the ways of conduct and fate.
Menelaus shoved Adrastus aside,
And Agamemnon stabbed him in the flank.
He fell backward, and the son of Atreus
Braced his heel on his chest and pulled out the spear.

Then Nestor shouted and called to the Greeks:

"Soldiers of Greece, no lagging behind
To strip off armor from the enemy corpses
To see who comes back to the ships with the most.
Now we kill men! You will have plenty of time later
To despoil the Trojan dead on the plain."

Nestor's speech worked them up to a frenzy,
And the Trojans would have been beaten
Back to Ilion by superior force
Had not Helenus, Priam's son
And Troy's prophet, approached Aeneas and Hector:

"Aeneas and Hector, the Trojans and Lycians
Are counting on you. You two are the leaders
In every initiative in council and battle—
So make a stand here. Go through the ranks
And keep our men back from the gates,
Before they run through them and fall
Into their women's arms, making our enemies laugh.
Once you have bolstered our troops' morale,
We will stand our ground and fight the Danaans,
Tired as we are. We have our backs to the wall.
Hector, go into the city and find our mother.
Tell her to take a company of old women
To the temple of Athena on the acropolis
With the largest and loveliest robe in her house,
The one that is dearest of all to her,
And place it on the knees of braided Athena,

And promise twelve heifers to her in her temple,
Unblemished yearlings, if she will pity
The town of Troy, its wives and its children,
And if she will keep from holy Ilion
Wild Diomedes, who is raging with his spear.
I think he's the strongest of all the Achaeans.
We never even feared Achilles like this,
And they say he is half-divine. But this man
Won't stop at anything. No one can match him."

Hector took his brother's advice.
He jumped down from his chariot with his gear
And toured the ranks, a spear in each hand.
He urged them on, and with a trembling roar
The Trojans turned to face the Achaeans.
The Greeks pulled back. It looked to them
As if some god had come from the starry sky
To help the Trojans. It had been a sudden rally.
Hector shouted and called to the Trojans:

"Soldiers of Troy, and illustrious allies,
Remember to fight like the men that you are,
While I go to the city and ask the elders
Who sit in council, and our wives, to pray
To the gods and promise bulls by the hundred."

And Hector left, helmet collecting light
Above the black-hide shield whose rim tapped
His ankles and neck with each step he took.

Then Glaucus, son of Hippolochus,
Met Diomedes in no-man's-land.
Both were eager to fight, but first Tydeus' son
Made his voice heard above the battle noise:

"And which mortal hero are you? I've never seen you
Out here before on the fields of glory,
And now here you are ahead of everyone,
Ready to face my spear. Pretty bold.
I feel sorry for your parents. Of course,

You may be an immortal, down from heaven.
Far be it from me to fight an immortal god.
Not even mighty Lycurgus lived long
After he tangled with the immortals,
Driving the nurses of Dionysus
Down over the Mountain of Nysa
And making them drop their wands
As he beat them with an ox-goad. Dionysus
Was terrified and plunged into the sea,
Where Thetis received him into her bosom,
Trembling with fear at the human's threats.
Then the gods, who live easy, grew angry
With Lycurgus, and the Son of Cronus
Made him go blind, and he did not live long,
Hated as he was by the immortal gods.
No, I wouldn't want to fight an immortal.
But if you are human, and shed blood,
Step right up for a quick end to your life."

And Glaucus, Hippolochus' son:

"Great son of Tydeus, why ask about my lineage?
Human generations are like leaves in their seasons.
The wind blows them to the ground, but the tree
Sprouts new ones when spring comes again.
Men too. Their generations come and go.
But if you really do want to hear my story,
You're welcome to listen. Many men know it.
  Ephyra, in the heart of Argive horse country,
Was home to Sisyphus, the shrewdest man alive,
Sisyphus son of Aeolus. He had a son, Glaucus,
Who was the father of faultless Bellerophon,
A man of grace and courage by gift of the gods.
But Proetus, whom Zeus had made king of Argos,
Came to hate Bellerophon
And drove him out. It happened this way.
Proetus' wife, the beautiful Anteia,
Was madly in love with Bellerophon
And wanted to have him in her bed.
But she couldn't persuade him, not at all,

Because he was so virtuous and wise.
So she made up lies and spoke to the king:
'Either die yourself, Proetus, or kill Bellerophon.
He wanted to sleep with me against my will.'
The king was furious when he heard her say this.
He did not kill him—he had scruples about that—
But he sent him to Lycia with a folding tablet
On which he had scratched many evil signs,
And told him to give it to Anteia's father,
To get him killed. So off he went to Lycia,
With an immortal escort, and when he reached
The river Xanthus, the king there welcomed him
And honored him with entertainment
For nine solid days, killing an ox each day.
But when the tenth dawn spread her rosy light,
He questioned him and asked to see the tokens
He brought from Proetus, his daughter's husband.
And when he saw the evil tokens from Proetus,
He ordered him, first, to kill the Chimaera,
A raging monster, divine, inhuman—
A lion in the front, a serpent in the rear,
In the middle a goat—and breathing fire.
Bellerophon killed her, trusting signs from the gods.
Next he had to fight the glorious Solymi,
The hardest battle, he said, he ever fought,
And, third, the Amazons, women the peers of men.
As he journeyed back the king wove another wile.
He chose the best men in all wide Lycia
And laid an ambush. Not one returned home;
Blameless Bellerophon killed them all.
When the king realized his guest had divine blood,
He kept him there and gave him his daughter
And half of all his royal honor. Moreover,
The Lycians cut out for him a superb
Tract of land, plow-land and orchard.
His wife, the princess, bore him three children,
Isander, Hippolochus, and Laodameia.
Zeus in his wisdom slept with Laodameia,
And she bore him the godlike warrior Sarpedon.
But even Bellerophon lost the gods' favor

And went wandering alone over the Aleian plain.
His son Isander was slain by Ares
As he fought against the glorious Solymi,
And his daughter was killed by Artemis
Of the golden reins. But Hippolochus
Bore me, and I am proud he is my father.
He sent me to Troy with strict instructions
To be the best ever, better than all the rest,
And not to bring shame on the race of my fathers,
The noblest men in Ephyra and Lycia.
This, I am proud to say, is my lineage."

Diomedes grinned when he heard all this.
He planted his spear in the bounteous earth
And spoke gently to the Lycian prince:

"We have old ties of hospitality!
My grandfather Oeneus long ago
Entertained Bellerophon in his halls
For twenty days, and they gave each other
Gifts of friendship. Oeneus gave
A belt bright with scarlet, and Bellerophon
A golden cup, which I left at home.
I don't remember my father Tydeus,
Since I was very small when he left for Thebes
In the war that killed so many Achaeans.
But that makes me your friend and you my guest
If ever you come to Argos, as you are my friend
And I your guest whenever I travel to Lycia.
So we can't cross spears with each other
Even in the thick of battle. There are enough
Trojans and allies for me to kill, whomever
A god gives me and I can run down myself.
And enough Greeks for you to kill as you can.
And let's exchange armor, so everyone will know
That we are friends from our fathers' days."

With this said, they vaulted from their chariots,
Clasped hands, and pledged their friendship.
But Zeus took away Glaucus' good sense,

For he exchanged his golden armor for bronze,
The worth of one hundred oxen for nine.

When Hector reached the oak tree by the Western Gate,
Trojan wives and daughters ran up to him,
Asking about their children, their brothers,
Their kinsmen, their husbands. He told them all,
Each woman in turn, to pray to the gods.
Sorrow clung to their heads like mist.

Then he came to Priam's palace, a beautiful
Building made of polished stone with a central courtyard
Flanked by porticoes, upon which opened fifty
Adjoining rooms, where Priam's sons
Slept with their wives. Across the court
A suite of twelve more bedrooms housed
His modest daughters and their husbands.
It was here that Hector's mother met him,
A gracious woman, with Laodice,
Her most beautiful daughter, in tow.
Hecuba took his hand in hers and said:

"Hector, my son, why have you left the war
And come here? Are those abominable Greeks
Wearing you down in the fighting outside,
And does your heart lead you to our acropolis
To stretch your hands upward to Zeus?
But stay here while I get you
Some honey-sweet wine, so you can pour a libation
To Father Zeus first and the other immortals,
Then enjoy some yourself, if you will drink.
Wine greatly bolsters a weary man's spirits,
And you are weary from defending your kinsmen."

Sunlight shimmered on great Hector's helmet.

"Mother, don't offer me any wine.
It would drain the power out of my limbs.
I have too much reverence to pour a libation
With unwashed hands to Zeus almighty,

Or to pray to Cronion in the black cloudbanks
Spattered with blood and the filth of battle.
But you must go to the War Goddess's temple
To make sacrifice with a band of old women.
Choose the largest and loveliest robe in the house,
The one that is dearest of all to you,
And place it on the knees of braided Athena.
And promise twelve heifers to her in her temple,
Unblemished yearlings, if she will pity
The town of Troy, its wives, and its children,
And if she will keep from holy Ilion
Wild Diomedes, who's raging with his spear.
Go then to the temple of Athena the War Goddess,
And I will go over to summon Paris,
If he will listen to what I have to say.
I wish the earth would gape open beneath him.
Olympian Zeus has bred him as a curse
To Troy, to Priam, and all Priam's children.
If I could see him dead and gone to Hades,
I think my heart might be eased of its sorrow."

Thus Hector. Hecuba went to the great hall
And called to her handmaidens, and they
Gathered together the city's old women.
She went herself to a fragrant storeroom
Which held her robes, the exquisite work
Of Sidonian women whom godlike Paris
Brought from Phoenicia when he sailed the sea
On the voyage he made for high-born Helen.
Hecuba chose the robe that lay at the bottom,
The most beautiful of all, woven of starlight,
And bore it away as a gift for Athena.
A stream of old women followed behind.

They came to the temple of Pallas Athena
On the city's high rock, and the doors were opened
By fair-cheeked Theano, daughter of Cisseus
And wife of Antenor, breaker of horses.

The Trojans had made her Athena's priestess.
With ritual cries they all lifted their hands
To Pallas Athena. Theano took the robe
And laid it on the knees of the rich-haired goddess,
Then prayed in supplication to Zeus' daughter:

"Lady Athena who defends our city,
Brightest of goddesses, hear our prayer.
Break now the spear of Diomedes
And grant that he fall before the Western Gate,
That we may now offer twelve heifers in this temple,
Unblemished yearlings. Only do thou pity
The town of Troy, its wives and its children."

But Pallas Athena denied her prayer.

While they prayed to great Zeus' daughter,
Hector came to Paris' beautiful house,
Which he had built himself with the aid
Of the best craftsmen in all wide Troy:
Sleeping quarters, a hall, and a central courtyard
Near to Priam's and Hector's on the city's high rock.
Hector entered, Zeus' light upon him,
A spear sixteen feet long cradled in his hand,
The bronze point gleaming, and the ferrule gold.
He found Paris in the bedroom, busy with his weapons,
Fondling his curved bow, his fine shield, and breastplate.
Helen of Argos sat with her household women
Directing their exquisite handicraft.

Hector meant to shame Paris and provoke him:

"This is a fine time to be nursing your anger,
You idiot! We're dying out there defending the walls.
It's because of you the city is in this hellish war.
If you saw someone else holding back from combat
You'd pick a fight with him yourself. Now get up
Before the whole city goes up in flames!"

And Paris, handsome as a god:

"That's no more than just, Hector,
But listen now to what I have to say.
It's not out of anger or spite toward the Trojans
I've been here in my room. I only wanted
To recover from my pain. My wife was just now
Encouraging me to get up and fight,
And that seems the better thing to do.
Victory takes turns with men. Wait for me
While I put on my armor, or go on ahead—
I'm pretty sure I'll catch up with you."

To which Hector said nothing.

But Helen said to him softly:

"Brother-in-law
Of a scheming, cold-blooded bitch,
I wish that on the day my mother bore me
A windstorm had swept me away to a mountain
Or into the waves of the restless sea,
Swept me away before all this could happen.
But since the gods have ordained these evils,
Why couldn't I be the wife of a better man,
One sensitive at least to repeated reproaches?
Paris has never had an ounce of good sense
And never will. He'll pay for it someday.
But come inside and sit down on this chair,
Dear brother-in-law. You bear such a burden
For my wanton ways and Paris' witlessness.
Zeus has placed this evil fate on us so that
In time to come poets will sing of us."

And Hector, in his burnished helmet:

"Don't ask me to sit, Helen, even though
You love me. You will never persuade me.
My heart is out there with our fighting men.
They already feel my absence from battle.

Just get Paris moving, and have him hurry
So he can catch up with me while I'm still
Inside the city. I'm going to my house now
To see my family, my wife and my boy. I don't know
Whether I'll ever be back to see them again, or if
The gods will destroy me at the hands of the Greeks."

And Hector turned and left. He came to his house
But did not find white-armed Andromache there.
She had taken the child and a robed attendant
And stood on the tower, lamenting and weeping—
His blameless wife. When Hector didn't find her inside,
He paused on his way out and called to the servants:

"Can any of you women tell me exactly
Where Andromache went when she left the house?
To one of my sisters or one of my brothers' wives?
Or to the temple of Athena along with the other
Trojan women to beseech the dread goddess?"

The spry old housekeeper answered him:

"Hector, if you want the exact truth, she didn't go
To any of your sisters, or any of your brothers' wives,
Or to the temple of Athena along with the other
Trojan women to beseech the dread goddess.
She went to Ilion's great tower, because she heard
The Trojans were pressed and the Greeks were strong.
She ran off to the wall like a madwoman,
And the nurse went with her, carrying the child."

Thus the housekeeper, but Hector was gone,
Retracing his steps through the stone and tile streets
Of the great city, until he came to the Western Gate.
He was passing through it out onto the plain
When his wife came running up to meet him,
His beautiful wife, Andromache,
A gracious woman, daughter of great Eëtion,
Eëtion, who lived in the forests of Plakos
And ruled the Cilicians from Thebes-under-Plakos—

His daughter was wed to bronze-helmeted Hector.
She came up to him now, and the nurse with her
Held to her bosom their baby boy,
Hector's beloved son, beautiful as starlight,
Whom Hector had named Scamandrius
But everyone else called Astyanax, Lord of the City,
For Hector alone could save Ilion now.
He looked at his son and smiled in silence.
Andromache stood close to him, shedding tears,
Clinging to his arm as she spoke these words:

"Possessed is what you are, Hector. Your courage
Is going to kill you, and you have no feeling left
For your little boy or for me, the luckless woman
Who will soon be your widow. It won't be long
Before the whole Greek army swarms and kills you.
And when they do, it will be better for me
To sink into the earth. When I lose you, Hector,
There will be nothing left, no one to turn to,
Only pain. My father and mother are dead.
Achilles killed my father when he destroyed
Our city, Thebes with its high gates,
But had too much respect to despoil his body.
He burned it instead with all his armor
And heaped up a barrow. And the spirit women
Came down from the mountain, daughters
Of the storm god, and planted elm trees around it.
I had seven brothers once in that great house.
All seven went down to Hades on a single day,
Cut down by Achilles in one blinding sprint
Through their shambling cattle and silver sheep.
Mother, who was queen in the forests of Plakos,
He took back as prisoner, with all her possessions,
Then released her for a fortune in ransom.
She died in our house, shot by Artemis' arrows.
Hector, you are my father, you are my mother,
You are my brother and my blossoming husband.
But show some pity and stay here by the tower,
Don't make your child an orphan, your wife a widow.
Station your men here by the fig tree, where the city

Is weakest because the wall can be scaled.
Three times their elite have tried an attack here
Rallying around Ajax or glorious Idomeneus
Or Atreus' sons or mighty Diomedes,
Whether someone in on the prophecy told them
Or they are driven here by something in their heart."

And great Hector, helmet shining, answered her:

"Yes, Andromache, I worry about all this myself,
But my shame before the Trojans and their wives,
With their long robes trailing, would be too terrible
If I hung back from battle like a coward.
And my heart won't let me. I have learned to be
One of the best, to fight in Troy's first ranks,
Defending my father's honor and my own.
Deep in my heart I know too well
There will come a day when holy Ilion will perish,
And Priam and the people under Priam's ash spear.
But the pain I will feel for the Trojans then,
For Hecuba herself and for Priam king,
For my many fine brothers who will have by then
Fallen in the dust behind enemy lines—
All that pain is nothing to what I will feel
For you, when some bronze-armored Greek
Leads you away in tears, on your first day of slavery.
And you will work some other woman's loom
In Argos or carry water from a Spartan spring,
All against your will, under great duress.
And someone, seeing you crying, will say,
'That is the wife of Hector, the best of all
The Trojans when they fought around Ilion.'
Someday someone will say that, renewing your pain
At having lost such a man to fight off the day
Of your enslavement. But may I be dead
And the earth heaped up above me
Before I hear your cry as you are dragged away."

With these words, resplendent Hector
Reached for his child, who shrank back screaming

Into his nurse's bosom, terrified of his father's
Bronze-encased face and the horsehair plume
He saw nodding down from the helmet's crest.
This forced a laugh from his father and mother,
And Hector removed the helmet from his head
And set it on the ground all shimmering with light.
Then he kissed his dear son and swung him up gently
And said a prayer to Zeus and the other immortals:

"Zeus and all gods: grant that this my son
Become, as I am, foremost among Trojans,
Brave and strong, and ruling Ilion with might.
And may men say he is far better than his father
When he returns from war, bearing bloody spoils,
Having killed his man. And may his mother rejoice."

And he put his son in the arms of his wife,
And she enfolded him in her fragrant bosom
Laughing through her tears. Hector pitied her
And stroked her with his hand and said to her:

"You worry too much about me, Andromache.
No one is going to send me to Hades before my time,
And no man has ever escaped his fate, rich or poor,
Coward or hero, once born into this world.
Go back to the house now and take care of your work,
The loom and the shuttle, and tell the servants
To get on with their jobs. War is the work of men,
Of all the Trojan men, and mine especially."

With these words, Hector picked up
His plumed helmet, and his wife went back home,
Turning around often, her cheeks flowered with tears.
When she came to the house of man-slaying Hector,
She found a throng of servants inside,
And raised among these women the ritual lament.
And so they mourned for Hector in his house
Although he was still alive, for they did not think
He would ever again come back from the war,
Or escape the murderous hands of the Greeks.

Paris meanwhile
Did not dally long in his high halls.
He put on his magnificent bronze-inlaid gear
And sprinted with assurance out through the city.

Picture a horse that has fed on barley in his stall
Breaking his halter and galloping across the plain,
Making for his accustomed swim in the river,
A glorious animal, head held high, mane streaming
Like wind on his shoulders. Sure of his splendor
He prances by the horse-runs and the mares in pasture.

That was how Paris, son of Priam, came down
From the high rock of Pergamum,
Gleaming like amber and laughing in his armor,
And his feet were fast.
He caught up quickly
With Hector just as he turned from the spot
Where he'd talked with his wife, and called out:

"Well, dear brother, have I delayed you too much?
Am I not here in time, just as you asked?"

Hector turned, his helmet flashing light:

"I don't understand you, Paris.
No one could slight your work in battle.
You're a strong fighter, but you slack off—
You don't have the will. It breaks my heart
To hear what the Trojans say about you.
It's on your account they have all this trouble.
Come on, let's go. We can settle this later,
If Zeus ever allows us to offer in our halls
The wine bowl of freedom to the gods above,
After we drive these bronze-kneed Greeks from Troy."

ILIAD 9

So the Trojans kept watch. But Panic,
Fear's sister, had wrapped her icy fingers
Around the Greeks, and all their best
Were stricken with unendurable grief.

When two winds rise on the swarming deep,
Boreas and Zephyr, blowing from Thrace
In a sudden squall, the startled black waves
Will crest and tangle the surf with seaweed.

The Greeks felt like that, pummeled and torn.

Agamemnon's heart was bruised with pain
As he went around to the clear-toned criers
Ordering them to call each man to assembly,
But not to shout. He pitched in himself.
It was a dispirited assembly. Agamemnon
Stood up, weeping, his face like a sheer cliff
With dark springwater washing down the stone.
Groaning heavily he addressed the troops:

"Friends, Argive commanders and counsellors:
Great Zeus, son of Cronus,
Is a hard god, friends. He's kept me in the dark
After all his promises, all his nods my way
That I'd raze Ilion's walls before sailing home.

It was all a lie, and I see now that his orders
Are for me to return to Argos in disgrace,
And this after all the armies I've destroyed.
I have no doubt that this is the high will
Of the god who has toppled so many cities
And will in the future, all glory to his power.
So this is my command for the entire army:
Clear out with our ships and head for home.
There's no hope we will take Troy's tall town."

He spoke, and they were all stunned to silence,
The silence of an army too grieved to speak,
Until at last Diomedes' voice boomed out:

"I'm going to oppose you if you talk foolishness—
As is my right in assembly, lord. Keep your temper.
First of all, you insulted me, saying in public
I was unwarlike and weak. Every Greek here,
Young and old alike, knows all about this.
The son of crooked Cronus split the difference
When he gave you gifts. He gave you a scepter
And honor with it, but he didn't give you
Strength to stand in battle, which is real power.
Are you out of your mind? Do you really think
The sons of the Achaeans are unwarlike and weak?
If you yourself are anxious to go home,
Then go. You know the way. Your ships are here
Right by the sea, and a whole fleet will follow you
Back to Mycenae. But many a long-haired Achaean
Will stay, too, until we conquer Troy. And if they won't—
Well, let them all sail back to their own native land.
The two of us, Sthenelus and I, will fight on
Until we take Ilion. We came here with Zeus."

He spoke, and all the Greeks cheered
The speech of Diomedes, breaker of horses.
Then up stood Nestor, the old charioteer:

"Son of Tydeus, you are our mainstay in battle
And the best of your age in council as well.

No Greek will find fault with your speech
Or contradict it. But it is not the whole story.
You are still young. You might be my son,
My youngest. Yet you have given prudent advice
To the Argive kings, since you have spoken aright.
But I, who am privileged to be your senior,
Will speak to all points. Nor will anyone
Scorn my words, not even King Agamemnon.
Only outlaws and exiles favor civil strife.
For the present, however, let us yield to night
And have our dinner. Guards should be posted
Outside the wall along the trench. I leave
This assignment to the younger men. But you,
Son of Atreus, take charge. You are King.
Serve the elders a feast. It is not unseemly.
Your huts are filled with wine which our ships
Transport daily over the sea from Thrace.
You have the means to entertain us and the men.
Then choose the best counsel your assembled guests
Can offer. The Achaeans are in great need
Of good counsel. The enemies' campfires
Are close to our ships. Can this gladden any heart?
This night will either destroy the army or save it."

They all heard him out and did as he said.
The guard details got their gear and filed out
On the double under their commanders:
Thrasymedes, Nestor's son; Ascalaphus
And Ialmenus, sons of Ares; Meriones,
Aphareus, and Diphyrus; and Creion,
The son of Lycomedes. Each of these seven
Had a hundred men under his command.
Spears in hand, they took up their positions
In a long line between the wall and the trench,
Where they lit fires and prepared their supper.

Agamemnon meanwhile gathered the elders
Into his hut and served them a hearty meal.
They helped themselves to the dishes before them,
And when they had enough of food and drink,

The first to spin out his plan for them was Nestor,
Whose advice had always seemed best before,
And who spoke with their best interests at heart:

"Son of Atreus, most glorious lord,
I begin and end with you, since you are
King of a great people, with authority
To rule and right of judgment from Zeus.
It is yours to speak as well as to listen,
And to stand behind others whenever they speak
To our good. The final word is yours.
But I will speak as seems best to me.
No one will have a better idea
Than I have now, nor has anyone ever,
From the time, divine prince, you wrested away
The girl Briseis from Achilles' shelter,
Defying his anger and my opposition.
I tried to dissuade you, but you gave in
To your pride and dishonored a great man
Whom the immortals esteem. You took his prize
And keep it still. But it is not too late. Even now
We must think of how to win him back
With appeasing gifts and soothing words."

And the warlord Agamemnon responded:

"Yes, old man, you were right on the mark
When you said I was mad. I will not deny it.
Zeus' favor multiplies a man's worth,
As it has here, and the army has suffered for it.
But since I did succumb to a fit of madness,
I want to make substantial amends.
I hereby announce my reparations:
Seven unfired tripods, ten gold bars,
Twenty burnished cauldrons, a dozen horses—
Solid, prizewinning racehorses
Who have won me a small fortune—
And seven women who do impeccable work,
Surpassingly beautiful women from Lesbos
I chose for myself when Achilles captured the town.

And with them will be the woman I took,
Briseus' daughter, and I will solemnly swear
I never went to her bed and lay with her
Or did what is natural between women and men.
All this he may have at once. And if it happens
That the gods allow us to sack Priam's city,
He may when the Greeks are dividing the spoils
Load a ship to the brim with gold and bronze,
And choose for himself the twenty Trojan women
Who are next in beauty to Argive Helen.
And if we return to the rich land of Argos,
He will marry my daughter, and I will honor him
As I do Orestes, who is being reared in luxury.
I have three daughters in my fortress palace,
Chrysothemis, Laodice, and Iphianassa.
He may lead whichever he likes as his bride
Back to Peleus' house, without paying anything,
And I will give her a dowry richer than any
A father has ever given his daughter.
And I will give him seven populous cities,
Cardamyle, Enope, grassy Hire,
Sacred Pherae, Antheia with its meadowlands,
Beautiful Aepeia, and Pedasus, wine country.
They are all near the sea, on sandy Pylos' frontier,
And cattlemen live there, rich in herds and flocks,
Who will pay him tribute as if he were a god
And fulfill the shining decrees of his scepter.
I will do all this if he will give up his grudge.
And he should. Only Hades cannot be appeased,
Which is why of all gods mortals hate him most.
And he should submit to me, inasmuch as I
Am more of a king and can claim to be elder."

And then spoke Nestor, the Gerenian rider:

"Son of Atreus, most glorious Agamemnon,
Your gifts for Achilles are beyond reproach.
But come, we must dispatch envoys
As soon as possible to Achilles' tent,

And I see before me who should volunteer.
Phoenix, dear to Zeus, should lead the way,
Followed by Ajax and brilliant Odysseus.
Odius and Eurybates can attend them as heralds.
Now bring water for our hands and observe silence,
That we may beseech Zeus to have mercy on us."

Nestor spoke, and his speech pleased them all.
Heralds poured water over their hands,
And then youths filled bowls to the brim with drink
And served it all around, first tipping the cups.
Having made their libations and drunk their fill,
They went out in a body from Agamemnon's hut.
Gerenian Nestor filled their ears with advice,
Glancing at each, but especially at Odysseus,
On how to persuade Peleus' peerless son.

They went in tandem along the seething shore,
Praying over and over to the god in the surf
For an easy time in convincing Achilles.
They came to the Myrmidons' ships and huts
And found him plucking clear notes on a lyre—
A beautiful instrument with a silver bridge
He had taken when he ransacked Eëtion's town—
Accompanying himself as he sang the glories
Of heroes in war. He was alone with Patroclus,
Who sat in silence waiting for him to finish.
His visitors came forward, Odysseus first,
And stood before him. Surprised, Achilles
Rose from his chair still holding his lyre.
Patroclus, when he saw them, also rose,
And Achilles, swift and sure, received them:

"Welcome. Things must be bad to bring you here,
The Greeks I love best, even in my rage."

With these words Achilles led them in
And had them sit on couches and rugs
Dyed purple, and he called to Patroclus:

"A larger bowl, son of Menoetius,
And stronger wine, and cups all around.
My dearest friends are beneath my roof."

Patroclus obliged his beloved companion.
Then he cast a carving block down in the firelight
And set on it a sheep's back and a goat's,
And a hog chine too, marbled with fat.
Automedon held the meat while Achilles
Carved it carefully and spitted the pieces.
Patroclus, godlike in the fire's glare,
Fed the blaze. When the flames died down
He laid the spits over the scattered embers,
Resting them on stones, and sprinkled the morsels
With holy salt. When the meat was roasted
He laid it on platters and set out bread
In exquisite baskets. Achilles served the meat,
Then sat down by the wall opposite Odysseus
And asked Patroclus to offer sacrifice.
After he threw the offerings in the fire,
They helped themselves to the meal before them,
And when they had enough of food and drink,
Ajax nodded to Phoenix. Odysseus saw this,
And filling a cup he lifted it to Achilles:

"To your health, Achilles, for a generous feast.
There is no shortage in Agamemnon's hut,
Or now here in yours, of satisfying food.
But the pleasures of the table are not on our minds.
We fear the worst. It is doubtful
That we can save the ships without your strength.
The Trojans and their allies are encamped
Close to the wall that surrounds our black ships
And are betting that we can't keep them
From breaking through. They may be right.
Zeus has been encouraging them with signs,
Lightning on the right. Hector trusts this—
And his own strength—and has been raging
Recklessly, like a man possessed.
He is praying for dawn to come early

So he can fulfill his threat to lop the horns
From the ships' sterns, burn the hulls to ash,
And slaughter the Achaeans dazed in the smoke.
This is my great fear, that the gods make good
Hector's threats, dooming us to die in Troy
Far from the fields of home. Up with you, then,
If you intend at all, even at this late hour,
To save our army from these howling Trojans.
Think of yourself, of the regret you will feel
For harm that will prove irreparable.
This is the last chance to save your countrymen.
Is it not true, my friend, that your father Peleus
Told you as he sent you off with Agamemnon:
'My son, as for strength, Hera and Athena
Will bless you if they wish, but it is up to you
To control your proud spirit. A friendly heart
Is far better. Steer clear of scheming strife,
So that Greeks young and old will honor you.'
You have forgotten what the old man said,
But you can still let go of your anger, right now.
Agamemnon is offering you worthy gifts
If you will give up your grudge. Hear me
While I list the gifts he proposed in his hut:
Seven unfired tripods, ten gold bars,
Twenty burnished cauldrons, a dozen horses—
Solid, prizewinning racehorses
Who have won him a small fortune—
And seven women who do impeccable work,
Surpassingly beautiful women from Lesbos
He chose for himself when you captured the town.
And with them will be the woman he took from you,
Briseus' daughter, and he will solemnly swear
He never went to her bed and lay with her
Or did what is natural between women and men.
All this you may have at once. And if it happens
That the gods allow us to sack Priam's city,
You may when the Greeks are dividing the spoils
Load a ship to the brim with gold and bronze,
And choose for yourself the twenty Trojan women
Who are next in beauty to Argive Helen.

And if we return to the rich land of Argos,
You would marry his daughter, and he would honor you
As he does Orestes, who is being reared in luxury.
He has three daughters in his fortress palace,
Chrysothemis, Laodice, and Iphianassa.
You may lead whichever you like as your bride
Back to Peleus' house, without paying anything,
And he would give her a dowry richer than any
A father has ever given his daughter.
And he will give you seven populous cities,
Cardamyle, Enope, grassy Hire,
Sacred Pherae, Antheia with its meadowlands,
Beautiful Aepeia, and Pedasus, wine country.
They are all near the sea, on sandy Pylos' frontier,
And cattlemen live there, rich in herds and flocks,
Who will pay you tribute as if you were a god
And fulfill the shining decrees of your scepter.
All this he will do if you give up your grudge.
But if Agamemnon is too hateful to you,
Himself and his gifts, think of all the others
Suffering up and down the line, and of the glory
You will win from them. They will honor you
Like a god.
                        And don't forget Hector.
You just might get him now. He's coming in close,
Deluded into thinking that he has no match
In the Greek army that has landed on his beach."

And Achilles, strong, swift, and godlike:

"Son of Laertes in the line of Zeus,
Odysseus the strategist—I can see
That I have no choice but to speak my mind
And tell you exactly how things are going to be.
Either that or sit through endless sessions
Of people whining at me. I hate it like I hate hell
The man who says one thing and thinks another.
So this is how I see it.
I cannot imagine Agamemnon,
Or any other Greek, persuading me,

Not after the thanks I got for fighting this war,
Going up against the enemy day after day.
It doesn't matter if you stay in camp or fight—
In the end, everybody comes out the same.
Coward and hero get the same reward:
You die whether you slack off or work.
And what do I have for all my suffering,
Constantly putting my life on the line?
Like a bird who feeds her chicks
Whatever she finds, and goes without herself,
That's what I've been like, lying awake
Through sleepless nights, in battle for days
Soaked in blood, fighting men for their wives.
I've raided twelve cities with our ships
And eleven on foot in the fertile Troad,
Looted them all, brought back heirlooms
By the ton, and handed it all over
To Atreus' son, who hung back in camp
Raking it in and distributing damn little.
What the others did get they at least got to keep.
They all have their prizes, everyone but me—
I'm the only Greek from whom he took something back.
He should be happy with the woman he has.
Why do the Greeks have to fight the Trojans?
Why did Agamemnon lead the army to Troy
If not for the sake of fair-haired Helen?
Do you have to be descended from Atreus
To love your mate? Every decent, sane man
Loves his woman and cares for her, as I did,
Loved her from my heart. It doesn't matter
That I won her with my spear. He took her,
Took her right out of my hands, cheated me,
And now he thinks he's going to win me back?
He can forget it. I know how things stand.
It's up to you, Odysseus, and the other kings
To find a way to keep the fire from the ships.
He's been pretty busy without me, hasn't he,
Building a wall, digging a moat around it,
Pounding in stakes for a palisade.
None of that stuff will hold Hector back.

When I used to fight for the Greeks,
Hector wouldn't come out farther from his wall
Than the oak tree by the Western Gate.
He waited for me there once, and barely escaped.
Now that I don't want to fight him anymore,
I will sacrifice to Zeus and all gods tomorrow,
Load my ships, and launch them on the sea.
Take a look if you want, if you give a damn,
And you'll see my fleet on the Hellespont
In the early light, my men rowing hard.
With good weather from the sea god,
I'll reach Phthia after a three-day sail.
I left a lot behind when I hauled myself here,
And I'll bring back more, gold and bronze,
Silken-waisted women, grey iron—
Everything except the prize of honor
The warlord Agamemnon gave me
And in his insulting arrogance took back.
So report back to him everything I say,
And report it publicly—get the Greeks angry,
In case the shameless bastard still thinks
He can steal us blind. He doesn't dare
Show his dogface here. Fine. I don't want
To have anything to do with him either.
He cheated me, wronged me. Never again.
He's had it. He can go to hell in peace,
The half-wit that Zeus has made him.
His gifts? His gifts mean nothing to me.
Not even if he offered me ten or twenty times
His present gross worth and added to it
All the trade Orchomenus does in a year,
All the wealth laid up in Egyptian Thebes,
The wealthiest city in all the world,
Where they drive two hundred teams of horses
Out through each of its hundred gates.
Not even if Agamemnon gave me gifts
As numberless as grains of sand or dust,
Would he persuade me or touch my heart—
Not until he's paid in full for all my grief.
His daughter? I would not marry

The daughter of Agamemnon son of Atreus
If she were as lovely as golden Aphrodite
Or could weave like owl-eyed Athena.
Let him choose some other Achaean
More to his lordly taste. If the gods
Preserve me and I get home safe
Peleus will find me a wife himself.
There are many Greek girls in Hellas and Phthia,
Daughters of chieftains who rule the cities.
I can have my pick of any of them.
I've always wanted to take a wife there,
A woman to have and to hold, someone with whom
I can enjoy all the goods old Peleus has won.
Nothing is worth my life, not all the riches
They say Troy held before the Greeks came,
Not all the wealth in Phoebus Apollo's
Marble shrine up in craggy Pytho.
Cattle and flocks are there for the taking;
You can always get tripods and chestnut horses.
But a man's life cannot be won back
Once his breath has passed beyond his clenched teeth.
My mother Thetis, a moving silver grace,
Tells me two fates sweep me on to my death.
If I stay here and fight, I'll never return home,
But my glory will be undying forever.
If I return home to my dear fatherland
My glory is lost but my life will be long,
And death that ends all will not catch me soon.
As for the rest of you, I would advise you too
To sail back home, since there's no chance now
Of storming Ilion's height. Zeus has stretched
His hand above her, making her people bold.
What's left for you now is to go back to the council
And announce my message. It's up to them
To come up with another plan to save the ships
And the army with them, since this one,
Based on appeasing my anger, won't work.
Phoenix can spend the night here. Tomorrow
He sails with me on our voyage home,
If he wants to, that is. I won't force him to come."

He spoke, and they were hushed in silence,
Shocked by his speech and his stark refusal.
Finally the old horseman Phoenix spoke,
Bursting into tears. He felt the ships were lost.

"If you have set your mind on going home,
Achilles, and will do nothing to save the ships
From being burnt, if your heart is that angry,
How could I stay here without you, my boy,
All by myself? Peleus sent me with you
On that day you left Phthia to go to Agamemnon,
A child still, knowing nothing of warfare
Or assemblies where men distinguish themselves.
He sent me to you to teach you this—
To be a speaker of words and a doer of deeds.
I could not bear to be left behind now
Apart from you, child, not even if a god
Promised to smooth my wrinkles and make me
As young and strong as I was when I first left
The land of Hellas and its beautiful women.
I was running away from a quarrel with Amyntor,
My father, who was angry with me
Over his concubine, a fair-haired woman
Whom he loved as much as he scorned his wife,
My mother. She implored me constantly
To make love to his concubine so that this woman
Would learn to hate the old man. I did as she asked.
My father found out and cursed me roundly,
Calling on the Furies to ensure that never
Would a child of mine sit on his knees.
The gods answered his prayers, Underworld Zeus
And dread Persephone. I decided to kill him
With a sharp sword, but some god calmed me down—
Putting in my mind what people would say,
The names they would call me—so that in fact
I would not be known as a parricide.
From then on I could not bear to linger
In my father's house, although my friends
And my family tried to get me to stay,
Entreating me, slaughtering sheep and cattle,

Roasting whole pigs on spits, and drinking
Jar after jar of the old man's wine.
For nine solid days they kept watch on me,
Working in shifts, staying up all night.
The fires stayed lit, one under the portico
Of the main courtyard, one on the porch
In front of my bedroom door. On the tenth night,
When it got dark, I broke through the latches
And vaulted over the courtyard fence,
Eluding the watchmen and servant women.
I was on the run through wide Hellas
And made it to Phthia's black soil, her flocks,
And to Lord Peleus. He welcomed me kindly
And loved me as a father loves his only son,
A grown son who will inherit great wealth.
He made me rich and settled me on the border,
Where I lived as king of the Dolopians.
I made you what you are, my godlike Achilles,
And loved you from my heart. You wouldn't eat,
Whether it was at a feast or a meal in the house,
Unless I set you on my lap and cut your food up
And fed it to you and held the wine to your lips.
Many a time you wet the tunic on my chest,
Burping up wine when you were colicky.
I went through a lot for you, because I knew
The gods would never let me have a child
Of my own. No, I tried to make you my child,
Achilles, so you would save me from ruin.
But you have to master your proud spirit.
It's not right for you to have a pitiless heart.
Even the gods can bend. Superior as they are
In honor, power, and every excellence,
They can be turned aside from wrath
When humans who have transgressed
Supplicate them with incense and prayers,
With libations and savor of sacrifice.
Yes, for Prayers are daughters of great Zeus.
Lame and wrinkled and with eyes averted,
They are careful to follow in Folly's footsteps,
But Folly is strong and fleet, and outruns them all,

Beating them everywhere and plaguing humans,
Who are cured by the Prayers when they come behind.
Revere the daughters of Zeus when they come,
And they will bless you and hear your cry.
Reject them and refuse them stubbornly,
And they will ask Zeus, Cronus' son, to have
Folly plague you, so you will pay in pain.
No, Achilles, grant these daughters of Zeus
The respect that bends all upright men's minds.
If the son of Atreus were not offering gifts
And promising more, if he were still raging mad,
I would not ask you to shrug off your grudge
And help the Greeks, no matter how sore their need.
But he is offering gifts and promising more,
And he has sent to you a delegation
Of the best men in the army, your dearest friends.
Don't scorn their words or their mission here.
No one could blame you for being angry before.
We all know stories about heroes of old,
How they were furiously angry, but later on
Were won over with gifts or appeased with words.
I remember a very old story like this, and since
We are all friends here, I will tell it to you now.
The Curetes were fighting the Aetolians
In a bloody war around Calydon town.
The Aetolians were defending their city
And the Curetes meant to burn it down.
This was all because gold-throned Artemis
Had cursed the Curetes, angry that Oeneus
Had not offered her his orchard's first fruits.
The other gods feasted on bulls by the hundred,
But Oeneus forgot somehow or other
Only the sacrifice to great Zeus' daughter.
So the Archer Goddess, angry at heart,
Roused a savage boar, with gleaming white tusks,
And sent him to destroy Oeneus' orchard.
The boar did a good job, uprooting trees
And littering the ground with apples and blossoms.
But Oeneus' son, Meleager, killed it
After getting up a party of hunters and hounds

28

From many towns: it took more than a few men
To kill this huge boar, and not before
It set many a hunter on the funeral pyre.
But the goddess caused a bitter argument
About the boar's head and shaggy hide
Between the Curetes and Aetolians.
They went to war. While Meleager still fought
The Curetes had the worst of it
And could not remain outside Calydon's wall.
But when wrath swelled Meleager's heart,
As it swells even the hearts of the wise,
And his anger rose against Althaea his mother,
He lay in bed with his wife, Cleopatra,
Child of Marpessa and the warrior Idas.
Idas once took up his bow against Apollo
To win lissome Marpessa. Her parents
Called the girl Halcyone back then
Because her mother wept like a halcyon,
The bird of sorrows, because the Archer God,
Phoebus Apollo, had stolen her daughter.
Meleager nursed his anger at Cleopatra's side,
Furious because his mother had cursed him,
Cursed him to the gods for murdering his uncle,
Her brother, that is, and she beat the earth,
The nurturing earth, with her hands, and called
Upon Hades and Persephone the dread,
As she knelt and wet her bosom with tears,
To bring death to her son. And the Fury
Who walks in darkness heard her
From the pit of Erebus, and her heart was iron.
Soon the enemy was heard at the walls again,
Battering the gates. The Aetolian elders
Sent the city's high priests to pray to Meleager
To come out and defend them, offering him
Fifty acres of Calydon's richest land
Wherever he chose, half in vineyard,
Half in clear plowland, to be cut from the plain.
And the old horseman Oeneus shook his doors,
Standing on the threshold of his gabled room,
And recited a litany of prayers to his son,

As did his sisters and his queenly mother.
He refused them all, and refused his friends,
His very best friends and boon companions.
No one could move his heart or persuade him
Until the Curetes, having scaled the walls
Were burning the city and beating down
His bedroom door. Then his wife wailed
And listed for him all the woes that befall
A captured people—the men killed,
The town itself burnt, the women and children
Led into slavery. This roused his spirit.
He clapped on armor and went out to fight.
And so he saved the Aetolians from doom
Of his own accord, and they paid him none
Of those lovely gifts, savior or not.
Don't be like that. Don't think that way,
And don't let your spirit turn that way.
The ships will be harder to save when they're burning.
Come while there are gifts, while the Achaeans
Will still honor you as if you were a god.
But if you go into battle without any gifts,
Your honor will be less, save us or not."

And strong, swift-footed Achilles answered:

"I don't need that kind of honor, Phoenix.
My honor comes from Zeus, and I will have it
Among these beaked ships as long as my breath
Still remains and my knees still move.
Now listen to this. You're listening? Good.
Don't try to confuse me with your pleading
On Agamemnon's behalf. If you're his friend
You're no longer mine, although I love you.
Hate him because I hate him. It's as simple as that.
You're like a second father to me. Stay here,
Be king with me and share half the honor.
These others can take my message. Lie down
And spend the night on a soft couch. At daybreak
We will decide whether to set sail or stay."

And he made a silent nod to Patroclus
To spread a thick bed for Phoenix. It was time
For the others to think about leaving. Big Ajax,
Telamon's godlike son, said as much:

"Son of Laertes in the line of Zeus,
Resourceful Odysseus—it's time we go.
I do not think we will accomplish
What we were sent here to do. Our job now
Is to report this news quickly, bad as it is.
They will be waiting to hear. Achilles
Has made his great heart savage.
He is a cruel man, and has no regard
For the love that his friends honored him with,
Beyond anyone else who camps with the ships.
Pitiless. A man accepts compensation
For a murdered brother, a dead son.
The killer goes on living in the same town
After paying blood money, and the bereaved
Restrains his proud spirit and broken heart
Because he has received payment. But you,
The gods have replaced your heart
With flint and malice, because of one girl,
One single girl, while we are offering you
Seven of the finest women to be found
And many other gifts. Show some generosity
And some respect. We have come under your roof,
We few out of the entire army, trying hard
To be the friends you care for most of all."

And Achilles, the great runner, answered him:

"Ajax, son of Telamon in the line of Zeus,
Everything you say is after my own heart.
But I swell with rage when I think of how
The son of Atreus treated me like dirt
In public, as if I were some worthless tramp.
Now go, and take back this message:
I won't lift a finger in this bloody war

Until Priam's illustrious son Hector
Comes to the Myrmidons' ships and huts
Killing Greeks as he goes and torching the fleet.
But when he comes to my hut and my black ship
I think Hector will stop, for all his battle lust."

He spoke. They poured their libations
And headed for the ships, Odysseus leading.
Patroclus ordered a bed made ready
For Phoenix, and the old man lay down
On fleeces and rugs covered with linen
And waited for bright dawn. Achilles slept
In an inner alcove, and by his side
Lay a woman he had brought from Lesbos
With high, lovely cheekbones, Diomede her name,
Phorbas' daughter. Patroclus lay down
In the opposite corner, and with him lay Iphis,
A silken girl Achilles had given him
When he took steep Scyrus, Enyeus' city.

By now Odysseus and Ajax
Were in Agamemnon's quarters,
Surrounded by officers drinking their health
From gold cups and shouting questions.
Agamemnon, the warlord, had priority:

"Odysseus, pride of the Achaeans, tell me,
Is he willing to repel the enemy fire
And save the ships, or does he refuse,
His great heart still in the grip of wrath?"

Odysseus, who endured all, answered:

"Son of Atreus, most glorious Agamemnon,
Far from quenching his wrath, Achilles
Is filled with even more. He spurns you
And your gifts, and suggests that you
Think of a way to save the ships and the army.
He himself threatens, at dawn's first light,
To get his own ships onto the water,

30

And he said he would advise the others as well
To sail for home, since there is no chance now
You will storm Ilion's height. Zeus has stretched
His hand above her, making her people bold.
This is what he said, as these men here
Who came with me will tell you, Ajax
And the two heralds, prudent men both.
Phoenix will spend the night there. Tomorrow
He sails with Achilles on his voyage home,
If he wants to. He will not be forced to go."

They were stunned by the force of his words
And fell silent for a long time, hushed in grief,
Until at last Diomedes said in his booming voice:

"Son of Atreus, glorious Agamemnon,
You should never have pleaded with him
Or offered all those gifts. Achilles
Was arrogant enough without your help.
Let him do what he wants, stay here
Or get the hell out. He'll fight later, all right,
When he is ready or a god tells him to.
Now I want everyone to do as I say.
Enjoy some food and wine to keep up
Your strength, and then get some sleep.
When the rosy light first streaks the sky
Get your troops and horses into formation
Before the ships. Fight in the front yourselves."

The warlords assented, taken aback
By the authority of Diomedes' speech.
Each man poured libation and went to his hut,
Where he lay down and took the gift of sleep.

ILIAD 16

While they fought for this ship, Patroclus
Came to Achilles and stood by him weeping,
His face like a sheer rock where the goat trails end
And dark springwater washes down the stone.
Achilles pitied him and spoke these feathered words:

"What are all these tears about, Patroclus?
You're like a little girl, pestering her mother
To pick her up, pulling at her hem
As she tries to hurry off and looking up at her
With tears in her eyes until she gets her way.
That's just what you look like, you know.
You have something to tell the Myrmidons?
Or myself? Bad news from back home?
Last I heard, Menoetius, your father,
And Peleus, mine, were still alive and well.
Their deaths would indeed give us cause to grieve.
Or are you broken-hearted because some Greeks
Are being beaten dead beside our ships?
They had it coming. Out with it, Patroclus—
Don't try to hide it. I have a right to know."

And with a deep groan you said to him,
Patroclus:
"Achilles, great as you are,
Don't be vengeful. They are dying out there,

All of our best—or who used to be our best—
They've all been hit and are lying
Wounded in camp. Diomedes is out,
And Odysseus, a good man with a spear,
Even Agamemnon has taken a hit.
Eurypylus, too, an arrow in his thigh.
The medics are working on them right now,
Stitching up their wounds. But you are incurable,
Achilles. God forbid I ever feel the spite
You nurse in your heart. You and your damned
Honor! What good will it do future generations
If you let us go down to this defeat
In cold blood? Peleus was never your father
Or Thetis your mother. No, the grey sea spat you out
Onto crags in the surf, with an icy scab for a soul.
  What is it? If some secret your mother
Has learned from Zeus is holding you back,
At least send *me* out, let *me* lead a troop
Of Myrmidons and light the way for our army.
And let me wear your armor. If the Trojans think
I am you, they'll back off and give the Greeks
Some breathing space, what little there is in war.
Our rested men will turn them with a shout
And push them back from our ships to Troy."

  That was how Patroclus, like a child
Begging for a toy, begged for death.

And Achilles, angry and deeply troubled:

"Ah, my noble friend, what a thing to say.
No, I'm not in on any divine secret,
Nor has my mother told me anything from Zeus.
But I take it hard when someone in power
Uses his authority to rob his equal
And strip him of his honor. I take it hard.
The girl the Greeks chose to be my prize—
After I demolished a walled city to get her—
Lord Agamemnon, son of Atreus, just took
From my hands, as if I were some tramp.

  But we'll let that be. I never meant
To hold my grudge forever. But I did say
I would not relent from my anger until
The noise of battle lapped at my own ships' hulls.
So it's on your shoulders now. Wear my armor
And lead our Myrmidons into battle,
If it is true that a dark cloud of Trojans
Has settled in over the ships and the Greeks
Are hemmed in on a narrow strip of beach.
The Trojans have become cocky, the whole city,
Because they do not see my helmeted face
Flaring close by. They would retreat so fast
They would clog the ditches with their dead—
If Lord Agamemnon knew how to respect me.
As it is they have brought the war to our camp.
So Diomedes is out, eh? It was his inspired
Spear work that kept the Trojans at arm's length.
And I haven't been hearing Agamemnon's battle cry,
As much as I hate the throat it comes from—only
Hector's murderous shout breaking like the sea
Over the Trojans, urging them on. The whole plain
Is filled with their whooping as they rout the Greeks.
  Hit them hard, Patroclus, before they burn the ships
And leave us stranded here. But before you go,
Listen carefully to every word I say.
Win me my honor, my glory and my honor
From all the Greeks, and, as their restitution,
The girl Briseis, and many other gifts.
But once you've driven the Trojans from the ships,
You come back, no matter how much
Hera's thundering husband lets you win.
Any success you have against the Trojans
Will be at the expense of my honor.
And if you get so carried away
With killing the Trojans that you press on to Troy,
One of the immortals may intervene.
Apollo, for one, loves them dearly.
So once you have made some daylight for the ships,
You come back where you belong.
The others can fight it out on the plain.

O Patroclus, I wish to Father Zeus
And to Athena and Apollo
That all of them, Greeks and Trojans alike,
Every last man on Troy's dusty plain,
Were dead, and only you and I were left
To rip Ilion down, stone by sacred stone."

And while they talked, Ajax retreated.

Zeus saw to it that everything the Trojans threw
At Ajax hit him, and his helmet tickered and rang
From all the metal points its bronze deflected
From his temples and cheeks. His left arm was sore
From holding up his shield, but the Trojans could not,
For all their pressure, force it aside.
Gulping in air, sweat pouring down his limbs,
He could scarcely breathe and had nowhere to turn.

Tell me now, Muses, who dwell on Olympus,
How fire first fell on the Achaean ships.

It was Hector who forced his way
To Ajax's side, and with his heavy sword
Lopped through the ash-wood shaft of his spear
At the socket's base, sending the bronze point
Clanging onto the ground far behind him
And leaving in Ajax's hands a blunted stick.
Ajax knew that this was the work of the gods,
That Zeus had cancelled Ajax's battle plans
And planned instead a Trojan victory.
No one could blame him for getting out of range,
And when he did, the Trojans threw their firebrands
Onto the ship, and she went up in flames.

Achilles slapped his thighs and said:

"Hurry, Patroclus! I see fire from the ships.
Don't let them take the fleet and cut off our escape.
Put on the armor while I gather the troops."

And so Patroclus armed, putting on
The bronze metalwork tailored to the body
Of Aeacus' swift grandson: the greaves
Trimmed with silver at the ankles, the corselet
Spangled with stars, the silver-studded sword,
The massive shield, and the crested helmet
That made every nod a threat.
He took two spears of the proper heft,
But left behind the massive battle pike
Of Aeacus' incomparable grandson.
No one but Achilles could handle this spear,
Made of ash, which the centaur Chiron
Had brought down from Mount Pelion and given
To Achilles' father to be the death of heroes.
Patroclus left the horses to Automedon,
The warrior he trusted most, after Achilles,
To be at his side in the crush of battle.
Automedon led beneath the yoke
The windswift horses Xanthus and Balius,
Immortal horses the gods gave to Peleus
When he married silver Thetis.
The Harpy Podarge had conceived them
When the West Wind blew through her
As she grazed in a meadow near Ocean's stream.
As trace horse Automedon brought up Pedasus,
Whom Achilles had acquired in the raid
On Eëtion's city. This faultless animal,
Though mortal, kept pace with immortal horses.

Achilles toured the rows of huts
That composed the Myrmidons' camp
And saw to it the men got armed.

Think of wolves
Ravenous for meat. It is impossible
To describe their savage strength in the hunt,
But after they have killed an antlered stag
Up in the hills and torn it apart, they come down
With gore on their jowls, and in a pack

Go to lap the black surface water in a pool
Fed by a dark spring, and as they drink,
Crimson curls float off from their slender tongues.
But their hearts are still, and their bellies gorged.

So too the Myrmidon commanders
Flanking Achilles' splendid surrogate,
And in their midst stood Achilles himself,
Urging on the horses and the men.

Achilles had brought fifty ships to Troy.
Each ship held fifty men, and the entire force
Was divided into five battalions
Whose five commanders answered to Achilles.
  Menesthius led the first battalion.
His mother, Polydore, a daughter of Peleus,
Had lain with the river god Spercheius,
Whose sky-swollen waters engendered the child.
His nominal father was a man called Boros,
Who gave many gifts to marry Polydore.
  The second battalion was led by Eudorus,
Polymele's bastard son. This woman
Once caught Hermes' eye as she danced
In Artemis' choir, and the god later
Went up to her bedroom and slept with her.
The son she bore shone like silver in battle.
After childbirth Actor's son Echecles
Led her to his house in marriage,
And her father, Phylas, kept the boy
And brought him up as if he were his own.
  Peisander led the third contingent.
He was, next to Patroclus, the best
Of all the Myrmidons with a spear.
  Old Phoenix led the fourth contingent,
And Alcimedon, Laerces' son, the fifth.

  When Achilles had the troops assembled
By battalions, he spoke to them bluntly:

"Myrmidons! I would not have a man among you forget

The threats you have been issuing against the Trojans—
From the safety of our camp—while I was in my rage.
All this time you have been calling me
The hard-boiled son of Peleus and saying to my face
That my mother must have weaned me on gall
Or I wouldn't keep my friends from battle.
That, together with hints you'd sail back home
If all I was going to do was sit and sulk. Now, however,
That there *is* a major battle to hold your interest,
I hope that each of you remembers what it means to fight."

The speech steeled their spirit. The Myrmidons
Closed ranks until there was no more space between them
Than between the stones a mason sets in the wall
Of a high house when he wants to seal it from the wind.
Helmet on helmet, shield overlapping shield, man on man,
So close the horsehair plumes on their bright crests
Rubbed each other as their heads bobbed up and down.
And in front of them all, two men with one heart,
Patroclus and Automedon made their final preparations
To lead the Myrmidons into war.
                                                  But Achilles
Went back to his hut and opened the lid
Of a beautiful, carved chest his mother Thetis
Had put aboard his ship when he sailed for Troy,
Filled with tunics and cloaks and woolen rugs.
And in it too was a chalice that no one else
Ever drank from, and that he alone used for libation
To no other god but Zeus. This chalice
He now took from the chest, purified it
With sulfur crystals, washed it with clear water,
Then cleansed his hands and filled it with bright red wine.
And then he prayed, standing in his courtyard
Pouring out the wine as he looked up to heaven.
And as he prayed, Zeus in his thunderhead listened.

"Lord Zeus, God of Dodona, Pelasgian God
Who dwells afar in the snows of Dodona
With your barefoot priests who sleep
On the ground around your sacred oak:

As you have heard my prayer before
And did honor me and smite the Achaeans,
So now too fulfill my prayer.
As I wait in the muster of the ships
And send my Patroclus into battle with my men,
Send forth glory with him.
Make bold the heart in his breast
So that Hector will see that my comrade
Knows how to fight and win without me.
And when he has driven the noise of battle
Away from our ships, may he come back to me
Unharmed, with all his weapons and men."

Zeus in his wisdom heard Achilles' prayer
And granted half of it. Yes, Patroclus
Would drive the Trojans back from the ships,
But he would not return from battle unharmed.

Achilles placed the chalice back in the chest
And stood outside his hut. He still longed to see
The grim struggle on Troy's windswept plain.

The Myrmidons under Patroclus
Filed out and swarmed up to the Trojans.

Boys will sometimes disturb a hornets' nest
By the roadside, jabbing at it and infuriating
The hive—the little fools—
Until the insects become a menace to all
And attack any traveller who happens by,
Swarming out in defense of their brood.

So too the Myrmidons.
Patroclus called to them over their shouts:

"Remember whose men you are
And for whose honor you are fighting.
And fight so that even wide-ruling Agamemnon
Will recognize his blind folly

ILIAD 18

The fight went on, like wildfire burning.
Antilochus, running hard like a herald,
Found Achilles close to his upswept hulls,
His great heart brooding with premonitions
Of what had indeed already happened.

"This looks bad,
All these Greeks with their hair in the wind
Stampeding off the plain and back to the ships.
God forbid that what my mother told me
Has now come true, that while I'm still alive
Trojan hands would steal the sunlight
From the best of all the Myrmidons.
Patroclus, Menoetius' brave son, is dead.
Damn him! I told him only to repel
The enemy fire from our ships,
And not to take on Hector in a fight."

Antilochus was in tears when he reached him
And delivered his unendurable message:

"Son of wise Peleus, this is painful news
For you to hear, and I wish it were not true.
Patroclus is down, and they are fighting
For his naked corpse. Hector has the armor."

A mist of black grief enveloped Achilles.
He scooped up fistfuls of sunburnt dust
And poured it on his head, fouling
His beautiful face. Black ash grimed
His fine-spun cloak as he stretched his huge body
Out in the dust and lay there,
Tearing out his hair with his hands.
The women, whom Achilles and Patroclus
Had taken in raids, ran shrieking out of the tent
To be with Achilles, and they beat their breasts
Until their knees gave out beneath them.
Antilochus, sobbing himself, stayed with Achilles
And held his hands—he was groaning
From the depths of his soul—for fear
He would lay open his own throat with steel.

The sound of Achilles' grief stung the air.

Down in the water his mother heard him,
Sitting in the sea depths beside her old father,
And she began to wail.
And the saltwater women
Gathered around her, all the deep-sea Nereids,
Glaucē and Thaleia and Cymodocē,
Neseia and Speio, Thoē and ox-eyed Haliē,
Cymothoē, Actaeē, and Limnoeira,
Melitē and Iaera, Amphithoē and Agauē,
Doris, Panopē, and milk-white Galateia,
Nemertes, Apseudes, and Callianassa,
Clymenē, Ianeira, Ianassa, and Maera,
Oreithyia and Amatheia, hair streaming behind her,
And all of the other deep-sea Nereids.
They filled the silver, shimmering cave,
And they all beat their breasts.

Thetis led the lament:

"Hear me, sisters, hear the pain in my heart.
I gave birth to a son, and that is my sorrow,
My perfect son, the best of heroes.

He grew like a sapling, and I nursed him
As I would a plant on the hill in my garden,
And I sent him to Ilion on a sailing ship
To fight the Trojans. And now I will never
Welcome him home again to Peleus' house.
As long as he lives and sees the sunlight
He will be in pain, and I cannot help him.
But I'll go now to see and hear my dear son,
Since he is suffering while he waits out the war."

She left the cave, and they went with her,
Weeping, and around them a wave
Broke through the sea, and they came to Troy.
They emerged on the beach where the Myrmidons' ships
Formed an encampment around Achilles.
He was groaning deeply, and his mother
Stood next to him and held her son's head.
Her lamentation hung sharp in the air,
And then she spoke in low, sorrowful tones:

"Child, why are you crying? What pain
Has come to your heart? Speak, don't hide it.
Zeus has granted your prayer. The Greeks
Have all been beaten back to their ships
And suffered horribly. They can't do without you."

Achilles answered her:

"Mother, Zeus may have done all this for me,
But how can I rejoice? My friend is dead,
Patroclus, my dearest friend of all. I loved him,
And I killed him. And the armor—
Hector cut him down and took off his body
The heavy, splendid armor, beautiful to see,
That the gods gave to Peleus as a gift
On the day they put you to bed with a mortal.
You should have stayed with the saltwater women,
And Peleus should have married a mortal.
But now—it was all so you would suffer pain
For your ravaged son. You will never again

Welcome me home, since I no longer have the will
To remain alive among men, not unless Hector
Loses his life on the point of my spear
And pays for despoiling Menoetius' son."

And Thetis, in tears, said to him:

"I won't have you with me for long, my child,
If you say such things. Hector's death means yours."

From under a great weight, Achilles answered:

"Then let me die now. I was no help
To him when he was killed out there. He died
Far from home, and he needed me to protect him.
But now, since I'm not going home, and wasn't
A light for Patroclus or any of the rest
Of my friends who have been beaten by Hector,
But just squatted by my ships, a dead weight on the earth . . .
I stand alone in the whole Greek army
When it comes to war—though some do speak better.
I wish all strife could stop, among gods
And among men, and anger too—it sends
Sensible men into fits of temper,
It drips down our throats sweeter than honey
And mushrooms up in our bellies like smoke.
Yes, the warlord Agamemnon angered me.
But we'll let that be, no matter how it hurts,
And conquer our pride, because we must.
But I'm going now to find the man who destroyed
My beloved—Hector.
As for my own fate,
I'll accept it whenever it pleases Zeus
And the other immortal gods to send it.
Not even Heracles could escape his doom.
He was dearest of all to Lord Zeus, but fate
And Hera's hard anger destroyed him.
If it is true that I have a fate like his, then I too
Will lie down in death.
But now to win glory

And make some Trojan woman or deep-breasted
Dardanian matron wipe the tears
From her soft cheeks, make her sob and groan.
Let them feel how long I've been out of the war.
Don't try, out of love, to stop me. I won't listen."

And Thetis, her feet silver on the sand:

"Yes, child. It's not wrong to save your friends
When they are beaten to the brink of death.
But your beautiful armor is in the hands of the Trojans,
The mirrored bronze. Hector himself
Has it on his shoulders. He glories in it.
Not for long, though. I see his death is near.
But you, don't dive into the red dust of war
Until with your own eyes you see me returning.
Tomorrow I will come with the rising sun
Bearing beautiful armor from Lord Hephaestus."

Thetis spoke, turned away
From her son, and said to her saltwater sisters:

"Sink now into the sea's wide lap
And go down to our old father's house
And tell him all this. I am on my way
Up to Olympus to visit Hephaestus,
The glorious smith, to see if for my sake
He will give my son glorious armor."

As she spoke they dove into the waves,
And the silver-footed goddess was gone
Off to Olympus to fetch arms for her child.

And while her feet carried her off to Olympus,
Hector yelled, a yell so bloodcurdling and loud
It stampeded the Greeks all the way back
To their ships beached on the Hellespont's shore.
They could not pull the body of Patroclus
Out of javelin range, and soon Hector,
With his horses and men, stood over it again.

Three times Priam's resplendent son
Took hold of the corpse's heels and tried
To drag it off, bawling commands to his men.
Three times the two Ajaxes put their heads down,
Charged, and beat him back. Unshaken, Hector
Sidestepped, cut ahead, or held his ground
With a shout, but never yielded an inch.

It was like shepherds against a starving lion,
Helpless to beat it back from a carcass,

The two Ajaxes unable to rout
The son of Priam from Patroclus' corpse.
And Hector would have, to his eternal glory,
Dragged the body off, had not Iris stormed
Down from Olympus with a message for Achilles,
Unbeknownst to Zeus and the other gods.
Hera had sent her, and this was her message:

"Rise, son of Peleus, most formidable of men.
Rescue Patroclus, for whom a terrible battle
Is pitched by the ships, men killing each other,
Some fighting to save the dead man's body,
The Trojans trying to drag it back
To windy Ilion. Hector's mind especially
Is bent on this. He means to impale the head
On Troy's palisade after he strips off its skin.
And you just lie there? Think of Patroclus
Becoming a ragbone for Trojan dogs. Shame
To your dying day if his corpse is defiled."

The shining sprinter Achilles answered her:

"Iris, which god sent you here?"

And Iris, whose feet are wind, responded:

"None other than Hera, Zeus' glorious wife.
But Zeus on high does not know this, nor do
Any of the immortals on snow-capped Olympus."

And Achilles, the great runner:

"How can I go to war? They have my armor.
And my mother told me not to arm myself
Until with my own eyes I see her come back
With fine weapons from Hephaestus.
I don't know any other armor that would fit,
Unless maybe the shield of Telamonian Ajax.
But he's out there in the front ranks, I hope,
Fighting with his spear over Patroclus dead."

Windfoot Iris responded:

"We know very well that they have your armor.
Just go to the trench and let the Trojans see you.
One look will be enough. The Trojans will back off
Out of fear of you, and this will give the Greeks
Some breathing space, what little there is in war."

Iris spoke and was gone. And Achilles,
Whom the gods loved, rose. Around
His mighty shoulders Athena threw
Her tasselled aegis, and the shining goddess
Haloed his head with a golden cloud
That shot flames from its incandescent glow.

Smoke is rising through the pure upper air
From a besieged city on a distant island.
Its soldiers have fought hard all day,
But at sunset they light innumerable fires
So that their neighbors in other cities
Might see the glare reflected off the sky
And sail to their help as allies in war.

So too the radiance that flared
From Achilles' head and up to the sky.
He went to the trench—away from the wall
And the other Greeks, out of respect
For his mother's tense command. Standing there,
He yelled, and behind him Pallas Athena

Amplified his voice, and shock waves
Reverberated through the Trojan ranks.

You have heard the piercing sound of horns
When squadrons come to destroy a city.

The Greek's voice was like that,
Speaking bronze that made each Trojan heart
Wince with pain.
And the combed horses
Shied from their chariots, eyes wide with fear,
And their drivers went numb when they saw
The fire above Achilles' head
Burned into the sky by the Grey-Eyed One.
Three times Achilles shouted from the trench;
Three times the Trojans and their confederates
Staggered and reeled, twelve of their best
Lost in the crush of chariots and spears.
But the Greeks were glad to pull Patroclus' body
Out of range and placed it on a litter. His comrades
Gathered around, weeping, and with them Achilles,
Shedding hot tears when he saw his loyal friend
Stretched out on the litter, cut with sharp bronze.
He had sent him off to war with horses and chariot,
But he never welcomed him back home again.

And now the ox-eyed Lady Hera
Sent the tireless, reluctant sun
Under the horizon into Ocean's streams,
Its last rays touching the departing Greeks with gold.
It had been a day of brutal warfare.

After the Trojans withdrew from battle,
They unhitched their horses from the chariots
And held an assembly before thinking of supper.
They remained on their feet, too agitated to sit,
Terrified, in fact, that Achilles,
After a long absence, was back.
Polydamas was the first to speak, prudent

Son of Panthous, the only Trojan who looked
Both ahead and behind. This man was born
The same night as Hector, and was his comrade,
As good with words as Hector was with a spear.
He had their best interests at heart when he spoke:

"Take a good look around, my friends. My advice
Is to return to the city and not wait for daylight
On the plain by the ships. We are far from our wall.
As long as this man raged against Agamemnon,
The Greeks were easier to fight against.
I too was glad when I spent the night by the ships,
Hoping we would capture their upswept hulls.
That hope has given way to a terrible fear
Of Peleus' swift son. He is a violent man
And will not be content to fight on the plain
Where Greeks and Trojans engage in combat.
It is for our city he will fight, and our wives.
We must go back. Trust me, this is how it will be:
Night is holding him back now, immortal night.
But if he finds us here tomorrow
When he comes out in his armor in daylight,
Then you will know what Achilles is,
And you will be glad to be back in sacred Ilion—
If you make it back, and are not one
Of the many Trojans the dogs and vultures
Will feast upon. I hope I'm not within earshot.
But if we trust my words, as much as it may gall,
We will camp tonight in the marketplace, where
The city is protected by its towers, walls,
And high gates closed with bolted, polished doors.
At dawn we take our positions on the wall
In full armor, and so much the worse for him
If he wants to come out from the ships and fight us
For our wall. He will go back to the ships
After he has had enough of parading
His high-necked prancers in front of the city.
He will not have the will to force his way in.
Dogs will eat him before he takes our town."

40

And Hector, glaring at him under his helmet:

"Polydamas, I don't like this talk
About a retreat and holing up in the city.
Aren't you sick of being penned inside our walls?
People everywhere used to talk about how rich
Priam's city was, all the gold, all the bronze.
Now the great houses are empty, their heirlooms
Sold away to Phrygia, to Maeonia, since Zeus
Has turned wrathful. But now—when the great god,
Son of Cronus, has vouchsafed me the glory
Of hemming the Greeks in beside the sea—
Now is no time for you to talk like a fool.
Not a Trojan here will listen. I won't let them.
  Now hear this! All troops will mess tonight
With guards posted and on general alert.
If any of you are worried about your effects,
You can hand them over for distribution!
Better our men should have them than the Greeks.
At first light we strap on our armor
And start fighting hard by the ships.
If Achilles really has risen up again
And wants to come out, he'll find it tough going,
For I will be there. I, for one,
Am not retreating. Maybe he'll win, maybe I will.
The War God doesn't care which one he kills."

Thus Hector, and the Trojans cheered,
The fools, their wits dulled by Pallas Athena.
Hector's poor counsel won all the applause,
And not a man praised Polydamas' good sense.
Then the troops started supper.

But the Greeks
Mourned Patroclus the whole night through.
Achilles began the incessant lamentation,
Laying his man-slaying hands on Patroclus' chest
And groaning over and over like a bearded lion

Whose cubs some deer hunter has smuggled out
Of the dense woods. When the lion returns,
It tracks the human from valley to valley,
Growling low the whole time. Sometimes it finds him.

Achilles' deep voice sounded among the Myrmidons:

"It was all for nothing, what I said that day
When I tried to hearten the hero Menoetius,
Telling him I would bring his glorious son
Home to Opoeis with his share of the spoils
After I had sacked Ilion. Zeus does not fulfill
A man's every thought. We two are fated
To redden the selfsame earth with our blood,
Right here in Troy. I will never return home
To be welcomed by my old father, Peleus,
Or Thetis, my mother. The earth here will hold me.
And since I will pass under the earth after you,
Patroclus, I will not bury you until
I have brought here the armor and head of Hector,
Who killed you, great soul. And I will cut
The throats of twelve Trojan princes
Before your pyre in my wrath. Until then,
You will lie here beside our upswept hulls
Just as you are, and round about you
Deep-bosomed Trojan and Dardanian women
Will lament you day and night, weeping,
Women we won with blood, sweat and tears,
Women we cut through rich cities to get."

With that, he ordered his companions
To put a great cauldron on the fire,
So they could wash the gore
From Patroclus' body without further delay.
They put a cauldron used for heating baths
Over a blazing fire and poured in the water,
Then stoked the fire with extra wood.
The flames licked the cauldron's belly
And the water grew warm. When it was boiling
In the glowing bronze, they washed the body,

Anointed it with rich olive oil,
And filled the wounds with a seasoned ointment.
Then they laid him on his bed, covered him
From head to foot with a soft linen cloth,
And spread a white mantle above it.
Then the whole night through the Myrmidons
Stood with Achilles, mourning Patroclus.

Zeus said to Hera, his wife and sister:

"So you have had your way, my ox-eyed lady.
You have roused Achilles, swift of foot. Truly,
The long-haired Greeks must be from your womb."

And the ox-eyed lady Hera replied:

"Awesome son of Cronus, what a thing to say!
Even a mortal man, without my wisdom,
Will succeed in his efforts for another man.
How then was I—the highest of goddesses
Both by my own birth and by marriage to you,
The lord and ruler of all the immortals—
Not to cobble up evil for Troy in my wrath?"

While they spoke to each other this way,
Thetis' silver feet took her to Hephaestus' house,
A mansion the lame god had built himself
Out of starlight and bronze, and beyond all time.
She found him at his bellows, glazed with sweat
As he hurried to complete his latest project,
Twenty cauldrons on tripods to line his hall,
With golden wheels at the base of each tripod
So they could move by themselves to the gods' parties
And return to his house—a wonder to see.
They were almost done. The intricate handles
Still had to be attached. He was getting these ready,
Forging the rivets with inspired artistry,
When the silver-footed goddess came up to him.
And Charis, Hephaestus' wife, lovely

In her shimmering veil, saw her, and running up,
She clasped her hand and said to her:

"My dear Thetis, so grave in your long robe,
What brings you here now? You almost never visit.
Do come inside so I can offer you something."

And the shining goddess led her along
And had her sit down in a graceful
Silver-studded chair with a footstool.
Then she called to Hephaestus, and said:

"Hephaestus, come here.
Thetis needs you for something."

And the renowned smith called back:

"Thetis? Then the dread goddess I revere
Is inside. She saved me when I lay suffering
From my long fall, after my shameless mother
Threw me out, wanting to hide my infirmity.
And I really would have suffered, had not Thetis
And Eurynome, a daughter of Ocean Stream,
Taken me into their bosom. I stayed with them
Nine years, forging all kinds of jewelry,
Brooches and bracelets and necklaces and pins,
In their hollow cave, while the Ocean's tides,
Murmuring with foam, flowed endlessly around.
No one knew I was there, neither god nor mortal,
Except my rescuers, Eurynome and Thetis.
Now the goddess has come to our house.
I owe her my life and would repay her in full.
Set out our finest for her, Charis,
While I put away my bellows and tools."

He spoke and raised his panting bulk
Up from his anvil, limping along quickly
On his spindly shanks. He set the bellows
Away from the fire, gathered up the tools

He had been using, and put them away
In a silver chest. Then he took a sponge
And wiped his face and hands, his thick neck,
And his shaggy chest. He put on a tunic,
Grabbed a stout staff, and as he went out
Limping, attendants rushed up to support him,
Attendants made of gold who looked like real girls,
With a mind within, and a voice, and strength,
And knowledge of crafts from the immortal gods.
These busily moved to support their lord,
And he came hobbling up to where Thetis was,
Sat himself down on a polished chair,
And clasping her hand in his, he said:

"My dear Thetis, so grave in your long robe,
What brings you here now? You almost never visit.
Tell me what you have in mind, and I will do it
If it is anything that is at all possible to do."

And Thetis, shedding tears as she spoke:

"Hephaestus, is there a goddess on Olympus
Who has suffered as I have? Zeus son of Cronus
Has given me suffering beyond all the others.
Of all the saltwater women he singled me out
To be subject to a man, Aeacus' son Peleus.
I endured a man's bed, much against my will.
He lies in his halls forspent with old age,
But I have other griefs now. He gave me a son
To bear and to rear, the finest of heroes.
He grew like a sapling, and I nursed him
As I would nurse a plant in my hillside garden,
And I sent him to Ilion on a sailing ship
To fight the Trojans. And now I will never
Welcome him home again to Peleus' house.
As long as he lives and sees the sunlight
He will be in pain, and I cannot help him.
The girl that the army chose as his prize
Lord Agamemnon took out of his arms.
He was wasting his heart out of grief for her,

But now the Trojans have penned the Greeks
In their beachhead camp, and the Argive elders
Have petitioned him with a long list of gifts.
He refused to beat off the enemy himself,
But he let Patroclus wear his armor,
And sent him into battle with many men.
All day long they fought by the Scaean Gates
And would have sacked the city that very day,
But after Menoetius' valiant son
Had done much harm, Apollo killed him
In the front ranks and gave Hector the glory.
So I have come to your knees, to see if you
Will give my son, doomed to die young,
A shield and helmet, a fine set of greaves,
And a corselet too. His old armor was lost
When the Trojans killed his faithful companion,
And now he lies on the ground in anguish."

And the renowned smith answered her:

"Take heart, Thetis, and do not be distressed.
I only regret I do not have the power
To hide your son from death when it comes.
But armor he will have, forged to a wonder,
And its terrible beauty will be a marvel to men."

Hephaestus left her there and went to his bellows,
Turned them toward the fire and ordered them to work.
And the bellows, all twenty, blew on the crucibles,
Blasting out waves of heat in whatever direction
Hephaestus wanted as he hustled here and there
Around his forge and the work progressed.
He cast durable bronze onto the fire, and tin,
Precious gold and silver. Then he positioned
His enormous anvil up on its block
And grasped his mighty hammer
In one hand, and in the other his tongs.

He made a shield first, heavy and huge,
Every inch of it intricately designed.

He threw a triple rim around it, glittering
Like lightning, and he made the strap silver.
The shield itself was five layers thick, and he
Crafted its surface with all of his genius.

On it he made the earth, the sky, the sea,
The unwearied sun, and the moon near full,
And all the signs that garland the sky,
Pleiades, Hyades, mighty Orion,
And the Bear they also call the Wagon,
Which pivots in place and looks back at Orion
And alone is aloof from the wash of Ocean.

On it he made two cities, peopled
And beautiful. Weddings in one, festivals,
Brides led from their rooms by torchlight
Up through the town, bridal song rising,
Young men reeling in dance to the tune
Of lyres and flutes, and the women
Standing in their doorways admiring them.
There was a crowd in the market-place
And a quarrel arising between two men
Over blood money for a murder,
One claiming the right to make restitution,
The other refusing to accept any terms.
They were heading for an arbitrator
And the people were shouting, taking sides,
But heralds restrained them. The elders sat
On polished stone seats in the sacred circle
And held in their hands the staves of heralds.
The pair rushed up and pleaded their cases,
And between them lay two ingots of gold
For whoever spoke straightest in judgment.

Around the other city two armies
Of glittering soldiery were encamped.
Their leaders were at odds—should they
Move in for the kill or settle for a division

Of all the lovely wealth the citadel held fast?
The citizens wouldn't surrender, and armed
For an ambush. Their wives and little children
Were stationed on the wall, and with the old men
Held it against attack. The citizens moved out,
Led by Ares and Pallas Athena,
Both of them gold, and their clothing was gold,
Beautiful and larger than life in their armor, as befits
Gods in their glory, and all the people were smaller.
They came to a position perfect for an ambush,
A spot on the river where stock came to water,
And took their places, concealed by fiery bronze.
Farther up they had two lookouts posted
Waiting to sight shambling cattle and sheep,
Which soon came along, trailed by two herdsmen
Playing their panpipes, completely unsuspecting.
When the townsmen lying in ambush saw this
They ran up, cut off the herds of cattle and fleecy
Silver sheep, and killed the two herdsmen.
When the armies sitting in council got wind
Of the ruckus with the cattle, they mounted
Their high-stepping horses and galloped to the scene.
They took their stand and fought along the river banks,
Throwing bronze-tipped javelins against each other.
Among them were Hate and Din and the Angel of Death,
Holding a man just wounded, another unwounded,
And dragging one dead by his heels from the fray,
And the cloak on her shoulders was red with human blood.
They swayed in battle and fought like living men,
And each side salvaged the bodies of their dead.

On it he put a soft field, rich farmland
Wide and thrice-tilled, with many plowmen
Driving their teams up and down rows.
Whenever they came to the end of the field
And turned, a man would run up and hand them
A cup of sweet wine. Then they turned again
Back up the furrow pushing on through deep soil

To reach the other end. The field was black
Behind them, just as if plowed, and yet
It was gold, all gold, forged to a wonder.

On it he put land sectioned off for a king,
Where reapers with sharp sickles were working.
Cut grain lay deep where it fell in the furrow,
And binders made sheaves bound with straw bands.
Three sheaf-binders stood by, and behind them children
Gathered up armfuls and kept passing them on.
The king stood in silence near the line of reapers,
Holding his staff, and his heart was happy.
Under an oaktree nearby heralds were busy
Preparing a feast from an ox they had slaughtered
In sacrifice, and women were sprinkling it
With abundant white barley for the reapers' dinner.

On it he put a vineyard loaded with grapes,
Beautiful in gold. The clusters were dark,
And the vines were set everywhere on silver poles.
Around it he inlaid a blue enamel ditch
And a fence of tin. A solitary path led to it,
And vintagers filed along it to harvest the grapes.
Girls, all grown up, and light-hearted boys
Carried the honey-sweet fruit in wicker baskets.
Among them a boy picked out on a lyre
A beguiling tune and sang the Linos song
In a low, light voice, and the harvesters
Skipped in time and shouted the refrain.

On it he made a herd of straight-horn cattle.
The cows were wrought of gold and tin
And rushed out mooing from the farmyard dung
To a pasture by the banks of a roaring river,
Making their way through swaying reeds.
Four golden herdsmen tended the cattle,
And nine nimble dogs followed along.
Two terrifying lions at the front of the herd
Were pulling down an ox. Its long bellows alerted
The dogs and the lads, who were running on up,

But the two lions had ripped the bull's hide apart
And were gulping down the guts and black blood.
The shepherds kept trying to set on the dogs,
But they shied away from biting the lions
And stood there barking just out of harm's way.

On it the renowned lame god made a pasture
In a lovely valley, wide, with silvery sheep in it,
And stables, roofed huts, and stone animal pens.

On it the renowned lame god embellished
A dancing ground, like the one Daedalus
Made for ringleted Ariadne in wide Cnossus.
Young men and girls in the prime of their beauty
Were dancing there, hands clasped around wrists.
The girls wore delicate linens, and the men
Finespun tunics glistening softly with oil.
Flowers crowned the girls' heads, and the men
Had golden knives hung from silver straps.
They ran on feet that knew how to run
With the greatest ease, like a potter's wheel
When he stoops to cup it in the palms of his hands
And gives it a spin to see how it runs. Then they
Would run in lines that weaved in and out.
A large crowd stood round the beguiling dance,
Enjoying themselves, and two acrobats
Somersaulted among them on cue to the music.

On it he put the great strength of the River Ocean,
Lapping the outermost rim of the massive shield.

And when he had wrought the shield, huge and heavy,
He made a breastplate gleaming brighter than fire
And a durable helmet that fit close at the temples,
Lovely and intricate, and crested with gold.
And he wrought leg-armor out of pliant tin.
And when the renowned lame god had finished this gear,
He set it down before Achilles' mother,
And she took off like a hawk from snow-capped Olympus,
Carrying armor through the sky like summer lightning.

ILIAD 24

The funeral games were over.
The troops dispersed and went to their ships,
Where they turned their attention to supper
And a good night's sleep. But sleep
That masters all had no hold on Achilles.
Tears wet his face as he remembered his friend.
He tossed and turned, yearning for Patroclus,
For his manhood and his noble heart,
And all they had done together, the shared pain,
The battles fought, the hard times at sea.
Thinking on all this, he would weep softly,
Lying now on his side, now on his back,
And now face down. Then he would rise
To his feet and wander in a daze along the shore.
Dawn never escaped him. As soon as she appeared
Over the sea and the dunes, he would hitch
Horses to his chariot and drag Hector behind.
When he had hauled him three times around
Patroclus' tomb, he would rest again in his hut,
Leaving Hector stretched face down in the dust.
But Apollo kept Hector's flesh undefiled,
Pitying the man even in death. He kept him
Wrapped in his golden aegis, so that Achilles
Would not scour the skin as he dragged him.

So Achilles defiled Hector in his rage.

The gods, looking on, pitied Hector,
And urged Hermes to steal the body,
A plan that pleased all but Hera,
Poseidon, and the Grey-Eyed One,
Who were steady in their hatred
For sacred Ilion and Priam's people
Ever since Paris in his blindness
Offended these two goddesses
And honored the one who fed his fatal lust.

Twelve days went by. Dawn.
Phoebus Apollo addressed the immortals:

"How callous can you get? Has Hector
Never burned for you thighs of bulls and goats?
Of course he has. But now you cannot
Bring yourselves to save even his bare corpse
For his wife to look upon, and his mother,
And child, and Priam, and his people, who would
Burn him in fire and perform his funeral rites.
No, it's the dread Achilles that you prefer.
His twisted mind is set on what he wants,
As savage as a lion bristling with pride,
Attacking men's flocks to make himself a feast.
Achilles has lost all pity and has no shame left.
Shame sometimes hurts men, but it helps them too.
A man may lose someone dearer than Achilles has,
A brother from the same womb, or a son,
But when he has wept and mourned, he lets go.
The Fates have given men an enduring heart.
But this man? After he kills Hector,
He ties him behind his chariot
And drags him around his dear friend's tomb.
Does this make him a better or nobler man?
He should fear our wrath, good as he may be,
For he defiles the dumb earth in his rage."

This provoked an angry response from Hera:

"What you say might be true, Silverbow,
If we valued Achilles and Hector equally.
But Hector is mortal and suckled at a woman's breast,
While Achilles is born of a goddess whom I
Nourished and reared myself, and gave to a man,
Peleus, beloved of the gods, to be his wife.
All of you gods came to her wedding,
And you too were at the feast, lyre in hand,
Our forever faithless and fair-weather friend."

And Zeus, who masses the thunderheads:

"Calm down, Hera, and don't be so indignant.
Their honor will not be the same. But Hector
Was dearest to the gods of all in Ilion,
At least to me. He never failed to offer
A pleasing sacrifice. My altar never lacked
Libation or burnt savor, our worship due.
But we will not allow his body to be stolen—
Achilles would notice in any case. His mother
Visits him continually night and day.
But I would have one of you summon Thetis
So that I might have a word with her. Achilles
Must agree to let Priam ransom Hector."

Thus spoke Zeus,
And Iris stormed down to deliver his message.
Midway between Samos and rocky Imbros,
She dove into the dark sea. The water moaned
As it closed above her, and she sank into the deep

Like a lead sinker on a line
That takes a hook of sharpened horn
Down to deal death to nibbling fish.

She found Thetis in a cave's hollow, surrounded
By her saltwater women and wailing
The fate of her faultless son, who would die
On Trojan soil, far from his homeland.
Iris, whose feet are like wind, stood near her:

"Rise, Thetis. Zeus in his wisdom commands you."

And the silver-footed goddess answered her:

"Why would the great god want me? I am ashamed
To mingle with the immortals, distraught as I am.
But I will go, and he will not speak in vain."

And she veiled her brightness in a shawl
Of midnight blue and set out with Iris before her.
The sea parted around them in waves.
They stepped forth on the beach
And sped up the sky, and found themselves
Before the face of Zeus. Around him
Were seated all the gods, blessed, eternal.
Thetis sat next to him, and Athena gave place.
Hera put in her hand a fine golden cup
And said some comforting words. Thetis drank
And handed the cup back. Then Zeus,
The father of gods and men, began to speak:

"You have come to Olympus, Thetis,
For all your incurable sorrow. I know.
Even so, I will tell you why I have called you.
For nine days the gods have argued
About Hector's corpse and about Achilles.
Some want Hermes to steal the body away,
But I accord Achilles the honor in this, hoping
To retain your friendship along with your respect.
Go quickly now and tell your son our will.
The gods are indignant, and I, above all,
Am angry that in his heart's fury
He holds Hector by the beaked ships

And will not give him up. He may perhaps fear me
And so release the body. Meanwhile,
I will send Iris to great-souled Priam
To have him ransom his son, going to the ships
With gifts that will warm Achilles' heart."

Zeus had spoken, and the silver-footed goddess
Streaked down from the peaks of Olympus
And came to her son's hut. She found him there
Lost in grief. His friends were all around,
Busily preparing their morning meal,
For which a great, shaggy ram had been slaughtered.
Settling herself beside her weeping child,
She stroked him with her hand and talked to him:

"My son, how long will you let this grief
Eat at your heart, mindless of food and rest?
It would be good to make love to a woman.
It hurts me to say it, but you will not live
Much longer. Death and Doom are beside you.
Listen now, I have a message from Zeus.
The gods are indignant, and he, above all,
Is angry that in your heart's fury
You hold Hector by these beaked ships
And will not give him up. Come now,
Release the body and take ransom for the dead."

And Achilles, swift of foot, answered her:

"So be it. Let them ransom the dead,
If the god on Olympus wills it so."

So mother and son spoke many words
To each other, with the Greek ships all around.

Meanwhile, Zeus dispatched Iris to Troy:

"Up now, swift Iris, leave Olympus
For sacred Ilion and tell Priam

He must go to the Greek ships to ransom his son
With gifts that will soften Achilles' heart.
Alone he must go, with only one attendant,
An elder, to drive the mule cart and bear the man
Slain by Achilles back to the city.
He need have no fear. We will send
As his guide and escort Hermes himself,
Who will lead him all the way to Achilles.
And when he is inside Achilles' hut,
Achilles will not kill him, but will protect him
From all the rest, for he is not a fool,
Nor hardened, nor past awe for the gods.
He will in kindness spare a suppliant."

Iris stormed down to deliver this message.
She came to the house of Priam and found there
Mourning and lamentation. Priam's sons
Sat in the courtyard around their father,
Fouling their clothes with tears. The old man,
Wrapped in his mantle, sat like graven stone.
His head and neck were covered with dung
He had rolled in and scraped up with his hands.
His daughters and sons' wives were wailing
Throughout the house, remembering their men,
So many and fine, dead by Greek hands.
Zeus' messenger stood near Priam,
Who trembled all over as she whispered:

"Courage, Priam, son of Dardanus,
And have no fear. I have come to you
Not to announce evil, but good.
I am a messenger from Zeus, who
Cares for you greatly and pities you.
You must go to the Greek ships to ransom Hector
With gifts that will soften Achilles' heart.
You must go alone, with only one attendant,
An elder, to drive the mule cart and bear the man
Slain by Achilles back to the city.

You need have no fear. We will send
As your guide and escort Hermes himself,
Who will lead you all the way to Achilles.
And when you are inside Achilles' hut,
Achilles will not kill you, but will protect you
From all the rest, for he is not a fool,
Nor hardened, nor past awe for the gods.
He will in kindness spare a suppliant."

Iris spoke and was gone, a blur in the air.
Priam ordered his sons to ready the mule cart
And fasten onto it the wicker trunk.
He himself went down to a high-vaulted chamber,
Fragrant with cedar, that glittered with jewels.
And he called to Hecuba, his wife, and said:

"A messenger has come from Olympian Zeus.
I am to go to the ships to ransom our son
And bring gifts that will soften Achilles' heart.
What do you make of this, Lady? For myself,
I have a strange compulsion to go over there,
Into the wide camp of the Achaean ships."

Her first response was a shrill cry, and then:

"This is madness. Where is the wisdom
You were once respected for at home and abroad?
How can you want to go to the Greek ships alone
And look into the eyes of the man who has killed
So many of your fine sons? Your heart is iron.
If he catches you, or even sees you,
He will not pity you or respect you,
Savage and faithless as he is. No, we must mourn
From afar, sitting in our hall. This is how Fate
Spun her stern thread for him in my womb,
That he would glut lean hounds far from his parents,
With that violent man close by. I could rip
His liver bleeding from his guts and eat it whole.

That would be at least some vengeance
For my son. He was no coward, but died
Protecting the men and women of Troy
Without a thought of shelter or flight."

And the old man, godlike Priam:

"Don't hold me back when I want to go,
And don't be a bird of ill omen
In my halls. You will not persuade me!
If anyone else on earth told me to do this,
A seer, diviner, or priest, we would
Set it aside and count it false.
But I heard the goddess myself and saw her face.
I will go, and her word will not be in vain.
If I am fated to die by the Achaean ships,
It must be so. Let Achilles cut me down
As soon as I have taken my son in my arms
And have satisfied my desire for grief."

He began to lift up the lids of chests
And took out a dozen beautiful robes,
A dozen single-fold cloaks, as many rugs,
And added as many white mantles and tunics.
He weighed and brought out ten talents of gold,
Two glowing tripods and four cauldrons with them,
And an exquisite cup, a state gift from the Thracians
And a great treasure. The old man spared nothing
In his house, not even this, in his passion
To ransom his son. Once out in the portico,
He drove off the men there with bitter words:

"Get out, you sorry excuses for Trojans!
Don't you have enough grief at home that you
Have to come here and plague me? Isn't it enough
That Zeus has given me the pain and sorrow
Of losing my finest son? You'll feel it yourselves
Soon enough. With him dead you'll be much easier

For the Greeks to pick off. But may I be dead and gone
Before I see my city plundered and destroyed."

And he waded through them, scattering them
With his staff. Then he called to his sons
In a harsh voice—Helenus and Paris,
Agathon, Pammon, Antiphonus, Polites,
Deïphobus, Hippothous, and noble Dius—
These nine, and shouted at them:

"Come here, you miserable brats. I wish
All of you had been killed by the ships
Instead of Hector. I have no luck at all.
I have fathered the best sons in all wide Troy,
And not one, not one I say, is left. Not Mestor,
Godlike Mestor, not Troilus, the charioteer,
Not Hector, who was like a god among men,
Like the son of a god, not of a mortal.
Ares killed them, and now all I have left
Are these petty delinquents, pretty boys, and cheats,
These dancers, toe-tapping champions,
Renowned throughout the neighborhood for filching goats!
Now will you please get the wagon ready
And load all this on, so I can leave?"

They cringed under their father's rebuke
And brought out the smooth-rolling wagon,
A beauty, just joinered, and clamped on
The wicker trunk. They took the mule yoke
Down from its peg, a knobbed boxwood yoke
Fitted with guide rings, and the yoke-band with it,
A rope fifteen feet long. They set the yoke with care
Upon the upturned end of the polished pole,
Placing the ring on the thole-pin, and lashed it
Tight to the knob with three turns each way,
Then tied the ends to the hitch under the hook.
This done, they brought from the treasure chamber
The lavish ransom for Hector's head and heaped it

On the hand-rubbed wagon. Then they yoked the mules,
Strong-hooved animals that pull in harness,
Splendid gifts of the Mysians to Priam.
And for Priam they yoked to a chariot horses
Reared by the king's hand at their polished stall.

So Priam and his herald, their minds racing,
Were having their rigs yoked in the high palace
When Hecuba approached them sorrowfully.
She held in her right hand a golden cup
Of honeyed wine for them to pour libation
Before they went. Standing by the horses she said:

"Here, pour libation to Father Zeus, and pray
For your safe return from the enemy camp,
Since you are set on going there against my will.
Pray to Cronion, the Dark Cloud of Ida,
Who watches over the the whole land of Troy,
And ask for an omen, that swiftest of birds
That is his messenger, the king of birds,
To appear on the right before your own eyes,
Something to trust in as you go to the ships.
But if Zeus will not grant his own messenger,
I would not advise or encourage you
To go to the ships, however eager you are."

And Priam, with grave dignity:

"I will not disregard your advice, my wife.
It is good to lift hands to Zeus for mercy."

And he nodded to the handmaid to pour
Pure water over his hands, and she came up
With basin and pitcher. Hands washed,
He took the cup from his wife and prayed,
Standing in the middle of the courtyard
And pouring out wine as he looked up to heaven:

"Father Zeus, who rules from Ida,
Most glorious, most great,

Send me to Achilles welcome and pitied.
And send me an omen, that swiftest of birds
That is your messenger, the king of birds,
To appear on the right before my own eyes,
That I may trust it as I go to the ships."

Zeus heard his prayer and sent an eagle,
The surest omen in the sky, a dusky hunter
Men call the dark eagle, a bird as large
As a doorway, with a wingspan as wide
As the folding doors to a vaulted chamber
In a rich man's house. It flashed on the right
As it soared through the city, and when they saw it
Their mood brightened.

Hurrying now, the old man
Stepped into his chariot and drove off
From the gateway and echoing portico.
In front of him the mules pulled the wagon
With Idaeus at the reins. Priam
Kept urging his horses with the lash
As they drove quickly through the city.
His kinsmen trailed behind, all of them
Wailing as if he were going to his death.
When they had gone down from the city
And onto the plain, his sons and sons-in-law
Turned back to Troy. But Zeus saw them
As they entered the plain, and he pitied
The old man, and said to his son, Hermes:

"Hermes, there's nothing you like more
Than being a companion to men, and you do obey—
When you have a mind to. So go now
And lead Priam to the Achaean ships, unseen
And unnoticed, until he comes to Achilles."

Thus Zeus, and the quicksilver courier complied,
Lacing on his feet the beautiful sandals,
Immortal and golden, that carry him over
Landscape and seascape in a rush of wind.

And he took the wand he uses to charm
Mortal eyes asleep and make sleepers awake.
Holding this wand, the tough quicksilver god
Flew down to Troy on the Hellespont,
And walked off as a young prince whose beard
Was just darkening, youth at its loveliest.

Priam and Idaeus had just driven past
The barrow of Ilus and had halted
The mules and horses in the river to drink.
By now it was dusk. Idaeus looked up
And was aware of Hermes close by.
He turned to Priam and said:

"Beware, son of Dardanus, there's someone here,
And if we're not careful we'll be cut to bits.
Should we escape in the chariot
Or clasp his knees and see if he will pity us?"

But the old man's mind had melted with fear.
The hair bristled on his gnarled limbs,
And he stood frozen with fear. But the Helper came up
And took the old man's hand and said to him:

"Sir, where are you driving your horses and mules
At this hour of the night, when all else is asleep?
Don't you fear the fury of the Achaeans,
Your ruthless enemies, who are close at hand?
If one of them should see you bearing such treasure
Through the black night, what would you do?
You are not young, sir, and your companion is old,
Unable to defend you if someone starts a fight.
But I will do you no harm and will protect you
From others. You remind me of my own dear father."

And the old man, godlike Priam, answered:

"Yes, dear son, it is just as you say.
But some god has stretched out his hand
And sent an auspicious wayfarer to meet me.

You have an impressive build, good looks,
And intelligence. Blessed are your parents."

And the Guide, limned in silver light:

"A very good way to put it, old sir.
But tell me this now, and tell me the truth:
Are you taking all of this valuable treasure
For safekeeping abroad or are you
All forsaking sacred Ilion in fear?
You have lost such a great warrior, the noblest,
Your son. He never let up against the Achaeans."

And the old man, godlike Priam, answered:

"Who are you, and from what parents born,
That you speak so well about my ill-fated son?"

And Hermes, limned in silver, answered:

"Ah, a test! And a question about Hector.
I have often seen him win glory in battle
He would drive the Argives back to their ships
And carve them to pieces with his bronze blade.
And we stood there and marvelled, for Achilles,
Angry with Agamemnon, would not let us fight.
I am his comrade in arms, from the same ship,
A Myrmidon. My father is Polyctor,
A wealthy man, and about as old as you.
He has six other sons, seven, counting me.
We cast lots, and I was chosen to come here.
Now I have come out to the plain from the ships
Because at dawn the Achaeans
Will lay siege to the city. They are restless,
And their lords cannot restrain them from battle."

And the old man, godlike Priam, answered him:

"If you really are one of Achilles' men,
Tell me this, and I want the whole truth.

Is my son still by the ships, or has Achilles
Cut him up by now and thrown him to the dogs?"

And Hermes, limned in silver light:

"Not yet, old sir. The dogs and birds have not
Devoured him. He lies beside Achilles' ship
Amid the huts just as he was at first. This is now
The twelfth day he has been lying there,
But his flesh has not decayed at all, nor is it
Consumed by worms that eat the battle-slain.
Achilles does drag him around his dear friend's tomb,
And ruthlessly, every morning at dawn,
But he stays unmarred. You would marvel, if you came,
To see him lie as fresh as dew, washed clean of blood,
And uncorrupted. All the wounds he had are closed,
And there were many who drove their bronze in him.
This is how the blessed gods care for your son,
Corpse though he be, for he was dear to their hearts."

And the old man was glad, and answered:

"Yes, my boy. It is good to offer
The immortals their due. If ever
There was anyone in my house
Who never forgot the Olympian gods,
It was my son. And so now they have
Remembered him, even in death.
But come, accept from me this fine cup,
And give me safe escort with the gods
Until I come to the hut of Peleus' son."

And Hermes, glimmering in the dark:

"Ah, an old man testing a young one.
But you will not get me to take gifts from you
Without Achilles' knowledge. I respect him
And fear him too much to defraud him.
I shudder to think of the consequences.
But I would escort you all the way to Argos,

With attentive care, by ship or on foot,
And no one would fight you for scorn of your escort."

And he leapt onto the chariot,
Took the reins and whip, and breathed
Great power into the horses and mules.
When they came to the palisade and trench
Surrounding the ships, the guards were at supper.
Hermes sprinkled them with drowsiness,
Then opened the gates, pushed back the bars,
And led in Priam and the cart piled with ransom.
They came to the hut of the son of Peleus
That the Myrmidons had built for their lord.
They built it high, out of hewn fir beams,
And roofed it with thatch reaped from the meadows.
Around it they made him a great courtyard
With thick-set staves. A single bar of fir
Held the gate shut. It took three men
To drive this bar home and three to pull it back,
But Achilles could work it easily alone.
Hermes opened the gate for Priam
And brought in the gifts for Peleus' swift son.
As he stepped to the ground he said:

"I am one of the immortals, old sir—the god
Hermes. My father sent me to escort you here.
I will go back now and not come before
Achilles' eyes. It would be offensive
For a god to greet a mortal face to face.
You go in, though, and clasp the knees
Of the son of Peleus, and entreat him
By his father and rich-haired mother
And by his son, so you will stir his soul."

And with that Hermes left and returned
To high Olympus. Priam jumped down
And left Idaeus to hold the horses and mules.
The old man went straight to the house
Where Achilles, dear to Zeus, sat and waited.

He found him inside. His companions sat
Apart from him, and a solitary pair,
Automedon and Alcimus, warriors both,
Were busy at his side. He had just finished
His evening meal. The table was still set up.
Great Priam entered unnoticed. He stood
Close to Achilles, and touching his knees,
He kissed the dread and murderous hands
That had killed so many of his sons.

Passion sometimes blinds a man so completely
That he kills one of his own countrymen.
In exile, he comes into a wealthy house,
And everyone stares at him with wonder.

So Achilles stared in wonder at Priam.
Was he a god?
And the others there stared
And wondered and looked at each other.
But Priam spoke, a prayer of entreaty:

"Remember your father, godlike Achilles.
He and I both are on the doorstep
Of old age. He may well be now
Surrounded by enemies wearing him down
And have no one to protect him from harm.
But then he hears that you are still alive
And his heart rejoices, and he hopes all his days
To see his dear son come back from Troy.
But what is left for me? I had the finest sons
In all wide Troy, and not one of them is left.
Fifty I had when the Greeks came over,
Nineteen out of one belly, and the rest
The women in my house bore to me.
It doesn't matter how many they were,
The god of war has cut them down at the knees.
And the only one who could save the city
You've just now killed as he fought for his country,
My Hector. It is for him I have come to the Greek ships,
To get him back from you. I've brought

A fortune in ransom. Respect the gods, Achilles.
Think of your own father, and pity me.
I am more pitiable. I have borne what no man
Who has walked this earth has ever yet borne.
I have kissed the hand of the man who killed my son."

He spoke, and sorrow for his own father
Welled up in Achilles. He took Priam's hand
And gently pushed the old man away.
The two of them remembered. Priam,
Huddled in grief at Achilles' feet, cried
And moaned softly for his man-slaying Hector.
And Achilles cried for his father and
For Patroclus. The sound filled the room.

When Achilles had his fill of grief
And the aching sorrow left his heart,
He rose from his chair and lifted the old man
By his hand, pitying his white hair and beard.
And his words enfolded him like wings:

"Ah, the suffering you've had, and the courage.
To come here alone to the Greek ships
And meet my eye, the man who slaughtered
Your many fine sons! You have a heart of iron.
But come, sit on this chair. Let our pain
Lie at rest a while, no matter how much we hurt.
There's nothing to be gained from cold grief.
Yes, the gods have woven pain into mortal lives,
While they are free from care.
Two jars
Sit at the doorstep of Zeus, filled with gifts
That he gives, one full of good things,
The other of evil. If Zeus gives a man
A mixture from both jars, sometimes
Life is good for him, sometimes not.
But if all he gives you is from the jar of woe,
You become a pariah, and hunger drives you
Over the bright earth, dishonored by gods and men.
Now take Peleus. The gods gave him splendid gifts

From the day he was born. He was the happiest
And richest man on earth, king of the Myrmidons,
And although he was a mortal, the gods gave him
An immortal goddess to be his wife.
But even to Peleus the god gave some evil:
He would not leave offspring to succeed him in power,
Just one child, all out of season. I can't be with him
To take care of him now that he's old, since I'm far
From my fatherland, squatting here in Troy,
Tormenting you and your children. And you, old sir,
We hear that you were prosperous once.
From Lesbos down south clear over to Phrygia
And up to the Hellespont's boundary,
No one could match you in wealth or in sons.
But then the gods have brought you trouble,
This constant fighting and killing around your town.
You must endure this grief and not constantly grieve.
You will not gain anything by torturing yourself
Over the good son you lost, not bring him back.
Sooner you will suffer some other sorrow."

And Priam, old and godlike, answered him:

"Don't sit me in a chair, prince, while Hector
Lies uncared for in your hut. Deliver him now
So I can see him with my own eyes, and you—
Take all this ransom we bring, take pleasure in it,
And go back home to your own fatherland,
Since you've taken this first step and allowed me
To live and see the light of day."

Achilles glowered at him and said:

"Don't provoke me, old man. It's my own decision
To release Hector to you. A messenger came to me
From Zeus—my own natural mother,
Daughter of the old sea god. And I know you,
Priam, inside out. You don't fool me one bit.
Some god escorted you to the Greek ships.
No mortal would have dared come into our camp,

Not even your best young hero. He couldn't have
Gotten past the guards or muscled open the gate.
So just stop stirring up grief in my heart,
Or I might not let you out of here alive, old man—
Suppliant though you are—and sin against Zeus."

The old man was afraid and did as he was told.

The son of Peleus leapt out the door like a lion,
Followed by Automedon and Alcimus, whom Achilles
Honored most now that Patroclus was dead.
They unyoked the horses and mules, and led
The old man's herald inside and seated him on a chair.
Then they unloaded from the strong-wheeled cart
The endless ransom that was Hector's blood price,
Leaving behind two robes and a fine-spun tunic
For the body to be wrapped in and brought inside.
Achilles called the women and ordered them
To wash the body well and anoint it with oil,
Removing it first for fear that Priam might see his son
And in his grief be unable to control his anger
At the sight of his child, and that this would arouse
Achilles' passion and he would kill the old man
And so sin against the commandments of Zeus.

After the female slaves had bathed Hector's body
And anointed it with olive, they wrapped it 'round
With a beautiful robe and tunic, and Achilles himself
Lifted him up and placed him on a pallet
And with his friends raised it onto the polished cart.
Then he groaned and called out to Patroclus:

"Don't be angry with me, dear friend, if somehow
You find out, even in Hades, that I have released
Hector to his father. He paid a handsome price,
And I will share it with you, as much as is right."

Achilles reentered his hut and sat down again
In his ornately decorated chair
Across the room from Priam, and said to him:

"Your son is released, sir, as you ordered.
He is lying on a pallet. At dawn's first light
You will go see him yourself.
  Now let's think about supper.
Even Niobe remembered to eat
Although her twelve children were dead in her house,
Six daughters and six sturdy sons.
Apollo killed them with his silver bow,
And Artemis, showering arrows, angry with Niobe
Because she compared herself to beautiful Leto.
Leto, she said, had borne only two, while she
Had borne many. Well, these two killed them all.
Nine days they lay in their gore, with no one
To bury them, because Zeus had turned
The people to stone. On the tenth day
The gods buried them. But Niobe remembered
She had to eat, exhausted from weeping.
Now she is one of the rocks in the lonely hills
Somewhere in Sipylos, a place they say is haunted
By nymphs who dance on the Achelous' banks,
And although she is stone she broods on the sorrows
The gods gave her.
                Well, so should we, old sir,
Remember to eat. You can mourn your son later
When you bring him to Troy. You owe him many tears."

A moment later Achilles was up and had slain
A silvery sheep. His companions flayed it
And prepared it for a meal, sliced it, spitted it,
Roasted the morsels and drew them off the spits.
Automedon set out bread in exquisite baskets
While Achilles served the meat. They helped themselves
And satisfied their desire for food and drink.
Then Priam, son of Dardanus, gazed for a while
At Achilles, so big, so much like one of the gods,
And Achilles returned his gaze, admiring
Priam's face, his words echoing in his mind.

When they had their fill of gazing at each other,
Priam, old and godlike, broke the silence:

"Show me to my bed now, prince, and quickly,
So that at long last I can have the pleasure of sleep.
My eyes have not closed since my son lost his life
Under your hands. I have done nothing but groan
And brood over my countless sorrows,
Rolling in the dung of my courtyard stables.
Finally I have tasted food and let flaming wine
Pass down my throat. I had eaten nothing till now."

Achilles ordered his companions and women
To set bedsteads on the porch and pad them
With fine, dyed rugs, spread blankets on top,
And cover them over with fleecy cloaks.
The women went out with torches in their hands
And quickly made up two beds. And Achilles,
The great sprinter, said in a bitter tone:

"You will have to sleep outside, dear Priam.
One of the Achaean counselors may come in,
As they always do, to sit and talk with me,
As well they should. If one of them saw you here
In the dead of night, he would tell Agamemnon,
And that would delay releasing the body.
But tell me this, as precisely as you can.
How many days do you need for the funeral?
I will wait that long and hold back the army."

And the old man, godlike Priam, answered:

"If you really want me to bury my Hector,
Then you could do this for me, Achilles.
You know how we are penned in the city,
Far from any timber, and the Trojans are afraid.
We would mourn him for nine days in our halls,
And bury him on the tenth, and feast the people.

On the eleventh we would heap a barrow over him,
And on the twelfth day fight, if fight we must."

And Achilles, strong, swift, and godlike:

"You will have your armistice."

And he clasped the old man's wrist
So he would not be afraid.
And so they slept,
Priam and his herald, in the covered courtyard,
Each with a wealth of thoughts in his breast.
But Achilles slept inside his well-built hut,
And by his side lay lovely Briseis.

Gods and heroes slept the night through,
Wrapped in soft slumber. Only Hermes
Lay awake in the dark, pondering how
To spirit King Priam away from the ships
And elude the strong watchmen at the camp's gates.
He hovered above Priam's head and spoke:

"Well, old man, you seem to think it's safe
To sleep on and on in the enemy camp
Since Achilles spared you. Think what it cost you
To ransom your son. Your own life will cost
Three times that much to the sons you have left
If Agamemnon and the Greeks know you are here."

Suddenly the old man was afraid. He woke up the herald.
Hermes harnessed the horses and mules
And drove them through the camp. No one noticed.
And when they reached the ford of the Xanthus,
The beautiful, swirling river that Zeus begot,
Hermes left for the long peaks of Olympus.

Dawn spread her saffron light over earth,
And they drove the horses into the city
With great lamentation. The mules pulled the corpse.

No one in Troy, man or woman, saw them before
Cassandra, who stood like golden Aphrodite
On Pergamum's height. Looking out she saw
Her dear father standing in the chariot
With the herald, and then she saw Hector
Lying on the stretcher in the mule cart.
And her cry went out through all the city:

"Come look upon Hector, Trojan men and women,
If ever you rejoiced when he came home alive
From battle, a joy to the city and all its people."

She spoke. And there was not a man or woman
Left in the city, for an unbearable sorrow
Had come upon them. They met Priam by the gates
As he brought the body through, and in the front
Hector's dear wife and queenly mother threw themselves
On the rolling cart and pulled out their hair
As they clasped his head amid the grieving crowd.
They would have mourned Hector outside the gates
All the long day until the sun went down,
Had not the old man spoken from his chariot:

"Let the mules come through. Later you will have
Your fill of grieving, after I have brought him home."

He spoke, and the crowd made way for the cart.
And they brought him home and laid him
On a corded bed, and set around him singers
To lead the dirge and chant the death song.
They chanted the dirge, and the women with them.
White-armed Andromache led the lamentation
As she cradled the head of her man-slaying Hector:

"You have died young, husband, and left me
A widow in the halls. Our son is still an infant,
Doomed when we bore him. I do not think
He will ever reach manhood. No, this city
Will topple and fall first. You were its savior,

And now you are lost. All the solemn wives
And children you guarded will go off soon
In the hollow ships, and I will go with them.
And you, my son, you will either come with me
And do menial labor for a cruel master,
Or some Greek will lead you by the hand
And throw you from the tower, a hideous death,
Angry because Hector killed his brother,
Or his father, or son. Many, many Greeks
Fell in battle under Hector's hands.
Your father was never gentle in combat.
And so all the townspeople mourn for him,
And you have caused your parents unspeakable
Sorrow, Hector, and left me endless pain.
You did not stretch your hand out to me
As you lay dying in bed, nor did you whisper
A final word I could remember as I weep
All the days and nights of my life."

The women's moans washed over her lament,
And from the sobbing came Hecuba's voice:

"Hector, my heart, dearest of all my children,
The gods loved you when you were alive for me,
And they have cared for you also in death.
My other children Achilles sold as slaves
When he captured them, shipped them overseas
To Samos, Imbros, and barren Lemnos.
After he took your life with tapered bronze
He dragged you around Patroclus' tomb, his friend
Whom you killed, but still could not bring him back.
And now you lie here for me as fresh as dew,
Although you have been slain, like one whom Apollo
Has killed softly with his silver arrows."

The third woman to lament was Helen.

"Oh, Hector, you were the dearest to me by far
Of all my husband's brothers. Yes, Paris

Is my husband, the godlike prince
Who led me to Troy. I should have died first.
This is now the twentieth year
Since I went away and left my home,
And I have never had an unkind word from you.
If anyone in the house ever taunted me,
Any of my husband's brothers or sisters,
Or his mother—my father-in-law was kind always—
You would draw them aside and calm them
With your gentle heart and gentle words.
And so I weep for you and for myself,
And my heart is heavy, because there is no one left
In all wide Troy who will pity me
Or be my friend. Everyone shudders at me."

And the people's moan came in over her voice.

Then the old man, Priam, spoke to his people:

"Men of Troy, start bringing wood to the city,
And have no fear of an Argive ambush.
When Achilles sent me from the black ships,
He gave his word he would not trouble us
Until the twelfth day should dawn."

He spoke, and they yoked oxen and mules
To wagons, and gathered outside the city.
For nine days they hauled in loads of timber.
When the tenth dawn showed her mortal light,
They brought out their brave Hector
And all in tears lifted the body high
Onto the bier, and threw on the fire.

Light blossomed like roses in the eastern sky.

The people gathered around Hector's pyre,
And when all of Troy was assembled there
They drowned the last flames with glinting wine.
Hector's brothers and friends collected

His white bones, their cheeks flowered with tears.
They wrapped the bones in soft purple robes
And placed them in a golden casket, and laid it
In the hollow of the grave, and heaped above it
A mantle of stones. They built the tomb
Quickly, with lookouts posted all around
In case the Greeks should attack early.
When the tomb was built, they all returned
To the city and assembled for a glorious feast
In the house of Priam, Zeus' cherished king.

That was the funeral of Hector, breaker of horses.

W.H. Auden, The Shield of Achilles (1953), From *The Shield of Achilles* by W. H. Auden, published by Random House.

She looked over his shoulder
For vines and olive trees,
Marble well-governed cities
And ships upon untamed seas,
But there on the shining metal
His hands had put instead
An artificial wilderness
And a sky like lead.

A plain without a feature, bare and brown,
No blade of grass, no sign of neighborhood,
Nothing to eat and nowhere to sit down,
Yet, congregated on its blankness, stood
An unintelligible multitude,
A million eyes, a million boots in line,
Without expression, waiting for a sign.

Out of the air a voice without a face
Proved by statistics that some cause was just
In tones as dry and level as the place:
No one was cheered and nothing was discussed;
Column by column in a cloud of dust
They marched away enduring a belief
Whose logic brought them, somewhere else, to grief.

She looked over his shoulder
For ritual pieties,
White flower-garlanded heifers,
Libation and sacrifice,
But there on the shining metal
Where the altar should have been,
She saw by his flickering forge-light
Quite another scene.

Barbed wire enclosed an arbitrary spot
Where bored officials lounged (one cracked a joke)
And sentries sweated for the day was hot:
A crowd of ordinary decent folk
Watched from without and neither moved nor spoke
As three pale figures were led forth and bound
To three posts driven upright in the ground.

The mass and majesty of this world, all
That carries weight and always weighs the same
Lay in the hands of others; they were small
And could not hope for help and no help came:

W.H. Auden, The Shield of Achilles (1953), From *The Shield of Achilles* by W. H. Auden, published by Random House.

What their foes like to do was done, their shame
Was all the worst could wish; they lost their pride
And died as men before their bodies died.

She looked over his shoulder
For athletes at their games,
Men and women in a dance
Moving their sweet limbs
Quick, quick, to music,
But there on the shining shield
His hands had set no dancing-floor
But a weed-choked field.

A ragged urchin, aimless and alone,
Loitered about that vacancy; a bird
Flew up to safety from his well-aimed stone:
That girls are raped, that two boys knife a third,
Were axioms to him, who'd never heard
Of any world where promises were kept,
Or one could weep because another wept.

The thin-lipped armorer,
Hephaestos, hobbled away,
Thetis of the shining breasts
Cried out in dismay
At what the god had wrought
To please her son, the strong
Iron-hearted man-slaying Achilles
Who would not live long.

Homer

ODYSSEY

Translated by
Stanley Lombardo

Introduction by
Sheila Murnaghan

Hackett Publishing Company, Inc.
Indianapolis/Cambridge

Printed in the United States of America

09 08 07 5 6 7 8

For further information, please address
Hackett Publishing Company, Inc.
P. O. Box 44937
Indianapolis, Indiana 46244–0937

www.hackettpublishing.com

Cover design by Brian Rak and John Pershing

Interior design by Meera Dash

The Palace of Odysseus illustration on page xi adapted from *Homer's Odyssey: A Companion to the Translation of Richmond Lattimore* by P. V. Jones (Bristol: Bristol Classical Press, 1988) and reprinted by permission of Duckworth.

An audiobook edition of this title narrated by Stanley Lombardo is available from Parmenides Publishing. For more information, please go to: http://www.parmenides.com.

Library of Congress Cataloging-in-Publication Data
Homer.
[Odyssey. English]
Odyssey / Homer ; translated by Stanley Lombardo ; introduction by Sheila Murnaghan.
p. cm.
Includes bibliographical references and index.
ISBN 0-87220-485-5 — ISBN 0-87220-484-7 (pbk.)
1. Epic poetry, Greek—Translations into English. 2. Odysseus (Greek mythology)—Poetry. I. Lombardo, Stanley, 1943– . II. Title.

PA4025.A5 L66 2000
883'.01—dc21 99-054175

ISBN-13: 978-0-87220-485-0 (cloth)
ISBN-13: 978-0-87220-484-3 (pbk.)

Contents

ODYSSEY 1

SPEAK, MEMORY—

Of the cunning hero,
The wanderer, blown off course time and again
After he plundered Troy's sacred heights.

Speak
Of all the cities he saw, the minds he grasped,
The suffering deep in his heart at sea
As he struggled to survive and bring his men home
But could not save them, hard as he tried—
The fools—destroyed by their own recklessness
When they ate the oxen of Hyperion the Sun,
And that god snuffed out their day of return.

Of these things,
Speak, Immortal One,
And tell the tale once more in our time.

By now, all the others who had fought at Troy—
At least those who had survived the war and the sea—
Were safely back home. Only Odysseus
Still longed to return to his home and his wife.
The nymph Calypso, a powerful goddess—
And beautiful—was clinging to him
In her caverns and yearned to possess him.
The seasons rolled by, and the year came
In which the gods spun the thread

For Odysseus to return home to Ithaca,
Though not even there did his troubles end,
Even with his dear ones around him.
All the gods pitied him, except Poseidon,
Who stormed against the godlike hero
Until he finally reached his own native land.

But Poseidon was away now, among the Ethiopians,
Those burnished people at the ends of the earth—
Some near the sunset, some near the sunrise—
To receive a grand sacrifice of rams and bulls.
There he sat, enjoying the feast.
The other gods
Were assembled in the halls of Olympian Zeus,
And the Father of Gods and Men was speaking.
He couldn't stop thinking about Aegisthus,
Whom Agamemnon's son, Orestes, had killed:

"Mortals! They are always blaming the gods
For their troubles, when their own witlessness
Causes them more than they were destined for!
Take Aegisthus now. He marries Agamemnon's
Lawful wife and murders the man on his return
Knowing it meant disaster—because we did warn him,
Sent our messenger, quicksilver Hermes,
To tell him not to kill the man and marry his wife,
Or Agamemnon's son, Orestes, would pay him back
When he came of age and wanted his inheritance.
Hermes told him all that, but his good advice
Meant nothing to Aegisthus. Now he's paid in full."

Athena glared at him with her owl-grey eyes:

"Yes, O our Father who art most high—
That man got the death he richly deserved,
And so perish all who would do the same.
But it's Odysseus I'm worried about,
That discerning, ill-fated man. He's suffered
So long, separated from his dear ones,
On an island that lies in the center of the sea,

A wooded isle that is home to a goddess,
The daughter of Atlas, whose dread mind knows
All the depths of the sea and who supports
The tall pillars that keep earth and heaven apart.
His daughter detains the poor man in his grief,
Sweet-talking him constantly, trying to charm him
Into forgetting Ithaca. But Odysseus,
Longing to see even the smoke curling up
From his land, simply wants to die. And yet you
Never think of him, Olympian. Didn't Odysseus
Please you with sacrifices beside the Greek ships
At Troy? Why is Odysseus so odious, Zeus?"

Zeus in his thunderhead had an answer for her:

"Quite a little speech you've let slip through your teeth,
Daughter. How could I forget godlike Odysseus?
No other mortal has a mind like his, or offers
Sacrifice like him to the deathless gods in heaven.
But Poseidon is stiff and cold with anger
Because Odysseus blinded his son, the Cyclops
Polyphemus, the strongest of all the Cyclopes,
Nearly a god. The nymph Thoösa bore him,
Daughter of Phorcys, lord of the barren brine,
After mating with Poseidon in a scalloped sea-cave.
The Earthshaker has been after Odysseus
Ever since, not killing him, but keeping him away
From his native land. But come now,
Let's all put our heads together and find a way
To bring Odysseus home. Poseidon will have to
Put aside his anger. He can't hold out alone
Against the will of all the immortals."

And Athena, the owl-eyed goddess, replied:

"Father Zeus, whose power is supreme,
If the blessed gods really do want
Odysseus to return to his home,
We should send Hermes, our quicksilver herald,
To the island of Ogygia without delay

To tell that nymph of our firm resolve
That long-suffering Odysseus gets to go home.
I myself will go to Ithaca
To put some spirit into his son—
Have him call an assembly of the long-haired Greeks
And rebuke the whole lot of his mother's suitors.
They have been butchering his flocks and herds.
I'll escort him to Sparta and the sands of Pylos
So he can make inquiries about his father's return
And win for himself a name among men."

Athena spoke, and she bound on her feet
The beautiful sandals, golden, immortal,
That carry her over landscape and seascape
On a puff of wind. And she took the spear,
Bronze-tipped and massive, that the Daughter uses
To level battalions of heroes in her wrath.
She shot down from the peaks of Olympus
To Ithaca, where she stood on the threshold
Of Odysseus' outer porch. Holding her spear,
She looked like Mentes, the Taphian captain,
And her eyes rested on the arrogant suitors.

They were playing dice in the courtyard,
Enjoying themselves, seated on the hides of oxen
They themselves had slaughtered. They were attended
By heralds and servants, some of whom were busy
Blending water and wine in large mixing bowls,
Others wiping down the tables with sponges
And dishing out enormous servings of meat.

Telemachus spotted her first.
He was sitting with the suitors, nursing
His heart's sorrow, picturing in his mind
His noble father, imagining he had returned
And scattered the suitors, and that he himself,
Telemachus, was respected at last.
Such were his reveries as he sat with the suitors.
And then he saw Athena.
                He went straight to the porch,

Indignant that a guest had been made to wait so long.
Going up to her he grasped her right hand in his
And took her spear, and his words had wings:

"Greetings, stranger. You are welcome here.
After you've had dinner, you can tell us what you need."

Telemachus spoke, and Pallas Athena
Followed him into the high-roofed hall.
When they were inside he placed her spear
In a polished rack beside a great column
Where the spears of Odysseus stood in a row.
Then he covered a beautifully wrought chair
With a linen cloth and had her sit on it
With a stool under her feet. He drew up
An intricately painted bench for himself
And arranged their seats apart from the suitors
So that his guest would not lose his appetite
In their noisy and uncouth company—
And so he could inquire about his absent father.
A maid poured water from a silver pitcher
Into a golden basin for them to wash their hands
And then set up a polished table nearby.
Another serving woman, grave and dignified,
Set out bread and generous helpings
From the other dishes she had. A carver set down
Cuts of meat by the platter and golden cups.
Then a herald came by and poured them wine.

Now the suitors swaggered in. They sat down
In rows on benches and chairs. Heralds
Poured water over their hands, maidservants
Brought around bread in baskets, and young men
Filled mixing bowls to the brim with wine.
The suitors helped themselves to all this plenty,
And when they had their fill of food and drink,
They turned their attention to the other delights,
Dancing and song, that round out a feast.
A herald handed a beautiful zither
To Phemius, who sang for the suitors,

Though against his will. Sweeping the strings
He struck up a song. And Telemachus,
Putting his head close to Pallas Athena's
So the others wouldn't hear, said this to her:

"Please don't take offense if I speak my mind.
It's easy for them to enjoy the harper's song,
Since they are eating another man's stores
Without paying anything—the stores of a man
Whose white bones lie rotting in the rain
On some distant shore, or still churn in the waves.
If they ever saw him make landing on Ithaca
They would pray for more foot speed
Instead of more gold or fancy clothes.
But he's met a bad end, and it's no comfort to us
When some traveler tells us he's on his way home.
The day has long passed when he's coming home.
But tell me this, and tell me the truth:
Who are you, and where do you come from?
Who are your parents? What kind of ship
Brought you here? How did your sailors
Guide you to Ithaca, and how large is your crew?
I don't imagine you came here on foot.
And tell me this, too. I'd like to know,
Is this your first visit here, or are you
An old friend of my father's, one of the many
Who have come to our house over the years?"

Athena's seagrey eyes glinted as she said:

"I'll tell you nothing but the unvarnished truth.
I am Mentes, son of Anchialus, and proud of it.
I am also captain of the seafaring Taphians.
I just pulled in with my ship and my crew,
Sailing the deep purple to foreign ports.
We're on our way to Cyprus with a cargo of iron
To trade for copper. My ship is standing
Offshore of wild country away from the city,
In Rheithron harbor under Neion's woods.
You and I have ties of hospitality,

Just as our fathers did, from a long way back.
Go and ask old Laertes. They say he never
Comes to town any more, lives out in the country,
A hard life with just an old woman to help him.
She gets him his food and drink when he comes in
From the fields, all worn out from trudging across
The ridge of his vineyard plot.
I have come
Because they say your father has returned,
But now I see the gods have knocked him off course.
He's not dead, though, not godlike Odysseus,
No way in the world. No, he's alive all right.
It's the sea keeps him back, detained on some island
In the middle of the sea, held captive by savages.
And now I will prophesy for you, as the gods
Put it in my heart and as I think it will be,
Though I am no soothsayer or reader of birds.
Odysseus will not be gone much longer
From his native land, not even if iron chains
Hold him. He knows every trick there is
And will think of some way to come home.
But now tell me this, and I want the truth:
Tall as you are, are you Odysseus' son?
You bear a striking resemblance to him,
Especially in the head and those beautiful eyes.
We used to spend quite a bit of time together
Before he sailed for Troy with the Argive fleet.
Since then, we haven't seen each other at all."

Telemachus took a deep breath and said:

"You want the truth, and I will give it to you.
My mother says that Odysseus is my father.
I don't know this myself. No one witnesses
His own begetting. If I had my way, I'd be the son
Of a man fortunate enough to grow old at home.
But it's the man with the most dismal fate of all
They say I was born from—since you want to know."

Athena's seagrey eyes glinted as she said:

"Well, the gods have made sure your family name
Will go on, since Penelope has borne a son like you.
But there is one other thing I want you to tell me.
What kind of a party is this? What's the occasion?
Some kind of banquet? A wedding feast?
It's no neighborly potluck, that's for sure,
The way this rowdy crowd is carrying on
All through the house. Any decent man
Would be outraged if he saw this behavior."

Telemachus breathed in the salt air and said:

"Since you ask me these questions as my guest—
This, no doubt, was once a perfect house,
Wealthy and fine, when its master was still home.
But the gods frowned and changed all that
When they whisked him off the face of the earth.
I wouldn't grieve for him so much if he were dead,
Gone down with his comrades in the town of Troy,
Or died in his friends' arms after winding up the war.
The entire Greek army would have buried him then,
And great honor would have passed on to his son.
But now the whirlwinds have snatched him away
Without a trace. He's vanished, gone, and left me
Pain and sorrow. And he's not the only cause
I have to grieve. The gods have given me other trials.
All of the nobles who rule the islands—
Doulichium, Samê, wooded Zacynthus—
And all those with power on rocky Ithaca
Are courting my mother and ruining our house.
She refuses to make a marriage she hates
But can't stop it either. They are eating us
Out of house and home, and will kill me someday."

And Pallas Athena, with a flash of anger:

"Damn them! You really do need Odysseus back.
Just let him lay his hands on these mangy dogs!
If only he would come through that door now
With a helmet and shield and a pair of spears,

Just as he was when I saw him first,
Drinking and enjoying himself in our house
On his way back from Ephyre. Odysseus
Had sailed there to ask Mermerus' son, Ilus,
For some deadly poison for his arrowheads.
Ilus, out of fear of the gods' anger,
Would not give him any, but my father
Gave him some, because he loved him dearly.
That's the Odysseus I want the suitors to meet.
They wouldn't live long enough to get married!
But it's on the knees of the gods now
Whether he comes home and pays them back
Right here in his halls, or doesn't.
So it's up to you
To find a way to drive them out of your house.
Now pay attention and listen to what I'm saying.
Tomorrow you call an assembly and make a speech
To these heroes, with the gods as witnesses.
The suitors you order to scatter, each to his own.
Your mother—if in her heart she wants to marry—
Goes back to her powerful father's house.
Her kinfolk and he can arrange the marriage,
And the large dowry that should go with his daughter.
And my advice for you, if you will take it,
Is to launch your best ship, with twenty oarsmen,
And go make inquiries about your long-absent father.
Someone may tell you something, or you may hear
A rumor from Zeus, which is how news travels best.
Sail to Pylos first and ask godly Nestor,
Then go over to Sparta and red-haired Menelaus.
He was the last home of all the bronzeclad Greeks.
If you hear your father's alive and on his way home,
You can grit your teeth and hold out one more year.
If you hear he's dead, among the living no more,
Then come home yourself to your ancestral land,
Build him a barrow and celebrate the funeral
Your father deserves. Then marry off your mother.
After you've done all that, think up some way
To kill the suitors in your house either openly
Or by setting a trap. You've got to stop

Acting like a child. You've outgrown that now.
Haven't you heard how Orestes won glory
Throughout the world when he killed Aegisthus,
The shrewd traitor who murdered his father?
You have to be aggressive, strong—look at how big
And well-built you are—so you will leave a good name.
Well, I'm off to my ship and my men,
Who are no doubt wondering what's taking me so long.
You've got a job to do. Remember what I said."

And Telemachus, in his clear-headed way:

"My dear guest, you speak to me as kindly
As a father to his son. I will not forget your words.
I know you're anxious to leave, but please stay
So you can bathe and relax before returning
To your ship, taking with you a costly gift,
Something quite fine, a keepsake from me,
The sort of thing a host gives to his guest."

And Athena, her eyes grey as saltwater:

"No, I really do want to get on with my journey.
Whatever gift you feel moved to make,
Give it to me on my way back home,
Yes, something quite fine. It will get you as good."

With these words the Grey-eyed One was gone,
Flown up and away like a seabird. And as she went
She put courage in Telemachus' heart
And made him think of his father even more than before.
Telemachus' mind soared. He knew it had been a god,
And like a god himself he rejoined the suitors.

They were sitting hushed in silence, listening
To the great harper as he sang the tale
Of the hard journeys home that Pallas Athena
Ordained for the Greeks on their way back from Troy.

His song drifted upstairs, and Penelope,

Wise daughter of Icarius, took it all in.
She came down the steep stairs of her house—
Not alone, two maids trailed behind—
And when she had come among the suitors
She stood shawled in light by a column
That supported the roof of the great house,
Hiding her cheeks behind her silky veils,
Grave handmaidens standing on either side.
And she wept as she addressed the brilliant harper:

"Phemius, you know many other songs
To soothe human sorrows, songs of the exploits
Of gods and men. Sing one of those
To your enraptured audience as they sit
Sipping their wine. But stop singing this one,
This painful song that always tears at my heart.
I am already sorrowful, constantly grieving
For my husband, remembering him, a man
Renowned in Argos and throughout all Hellas."

And Telemachus said to her coolly:

"Mother, why begrudge our singer
Entertaining us as he thinks best?
Singers are not responsible; Zeus is,
Who gives what he wants to every man on earth.
No one can blame Phemius for singing the doom
Of the Danaans: it's always the newest song
An audience praises most. For yourself,
You'll just have to endure it and listen.
Odysseus was not the only man at Troy
Who didn't come home. Many others perished.
You should go back upstairs and take care of your work,
Spinning and weaving, and have the maids do theirs.
Speaking is for men, for all men, but for me
Especially, since I am the master of this house."

Penelope was stunned and turned to go,
Her son's masterful words pressed to her heart.
She went up the stairs to her room with her women

And wept for Odysseus, her beloved husband,
Until grey-eyed Athena cast sleep on her eyelids.

All through the shadowy halls the suitors
Broke into an uproar, each of them praying
To lie in bed with her. Telemachus cut them short:

"Suitors of my mother—you arrogant pigs—
For now, we're at a feast. No shouting, please!
There's nothing finer than hearing
A singer like this, with a voice like a god's.
But in the morning we will sit in the meeting ground,
So that I can tell all of you in broad daylight
To get out of my house. Fix yourselves feasts
In each others' houses, use up your own stockpiles.
But if it seems better and more profitable
For one man to be eaten out of house and home
Without compensation—then eat away!
For my part, I will pray to the gods eternal
That Zeus grant me requital: Death for you
Here in my house. With no compensation."

Thus Telemachus. And they all bit their lips
And marveled at how boldly he had spoken to them.
Then Antinous, son of Eupeithes, replied:

"Well, Telemachus, it seems the gods, no less,
Are teaching you how to be a bold public speaker.
May the son of Cronus never make you king
Here on Ithaca, even if it is your birthright."

And Telemachus, taking in a breath:

"It may make you angry, Antinous,
But I'll tell you something. I wouldn't mind a bit
If Zeus granted me this—if he made me king.
You think this is the worst fate a man can have?
It's not so bad to be king. Your house grows rich,
And you're held in great honor yourself. But,
There are many other lords on seawashed Ithaca,

Young and old, and any one of them
Could get to be king, now that Odysseus is dead.
But I will be master of my own house
And of the servants that Odysseus left me."

Then Eurymachus, Polybus' son, responded:

"It's on the knees of the gods, Telemachus,
Which man of Greece will rule this island.
But you keep your property and rule your house,
And may no man ever come to wrest them away
From you by force, not while men live in Ithaca.
But I want to ask you, sir, about your visitor.
Where did he come from, what port
Does he call home, where are his ancestral fields?
Did he bring news of your father's coming
Or was he here on business of his own?
He sure up and left in a hurry, wouldn't stay
To be known. Yet by his looks he was no tramp."

And Telemachus, with a sharp response:

"Eurymachus, my father is not coming home.
I no longer trust any news that may come,
Or any prophecy my mother may have gotten
From a seer she has summoned up to the house.
My guest was a friend of my father's from Taphos.
He says he is Mentes, son of Anchialus
And captain of the seafaring Taphians."

Thus Telemachus. But in his heart he knew
It was an immortal goddess.

And now
The young men plunged into their entertainment,
Singing and dancing until the twilight hour.
They were still at it when the evening grew dark,
Then one by one went to their own houses to rest.

Telemachus' room was off the beautiful courtyard,

Built high and with a surrounding view.
There he went to his bed, his mind teeming,
And with him, bearing blazing torches,
Went true-hearted Eurycleia, daughter of Ops
And Peisenor's granddaughter. Long ago,
Laertes had bought her for a small fortune
When she was still a girl. He paid twenty oxen
And honored her in his house as he honored
His wedded wife, but he never slept with her
Because he would rather avoid his wife's wrath.
Of all the women, she loved Telemachus the most
And had nursed him as a baby. Now she bore
The blazing torches as Telemachus opened
The doors to his room and sat on his bed.
He pulled off his soft tunic and laid it
In the hands of the wise old woman, and she
Folded it and smoothed it and hung it on a peg
Beside the corded bed. Then she left the room,
Pulled the door shut by its silver handle,
And drew the bolt home with the strap.

There Telemachus
Lay wrapped in a fleece all the night through,
Pondering the journey Athena had shown him.

ODYSSEY 2

Dawn's pale rose fingers brushed across the sky,
And Odysseus' son got out of bed and dressed.
He slung his sharp sword around his shoulder,
Then tied oiled leather sandals onto his feet,
And walked out of the bedroom like a god.
Wasting no time, he ordered the heralds
To call an assembly. The heralds' cries
Rang out through the town, and the men
Gathered quickly, their long hair streaming.
Telemachus strode along carrying a spear
And accompanied by two lean hounds.
Athena shed a silver grace upon him,
And everyone marveled at him as he entered.
The elders made way as he took his father's seat.

First to speak was the hero Aegyptius,
A man bowed with age and wise beyond telling.
His son, Antiphus, had gone off to Troy
In the ships with Odysseus (and was killed
In the cave of the Cyclops, who made of him
His last savage meal). Of three remaining sons,
One, Eurynomus, ran with the suitors,
And the other two kept their father's farm.
But Aegyptius couldn't stop mourning the one that was lost
And was weeping for him as he spoke out now:

"Hear me now, men of Ithaca.
We have never once held assembly or sat
In council since Odysseus left.

Who has called us together today?
Which of the young men, or of the elders,
Has such urgent business as this?
Has he had news of the army's return,
Some early report he wants to tell us about?
Or is there some other public matter
He wants to address? He's a fine man
In my eyes, and may Zeus bless him."

Telemachus was glad to hear these words,
And he rose from his seat, eager to speak.
There he stood, in the midst of the assembly,
And the herald Peisenor, a wise counselor,
Placed the staff in the hands of Odysseus' son.
In his speech he addressed old Aegyptius first:

"You won't have to look very far to find out
Who called this assembly. I called it myself.
No, I have not had news of the army's return,
Any early report I could tell you about.
Nor is there any other public matter
I want to address. It's a private matter,
My own need. Trouble has come to my house
In two forms. First, I have lost my noble father.
He was your king once, and like a father
To all of you, gentle and kind. And now,
There is even greater trouble, far greater,
Which will destroy my house and home.
Suitors have latched on to my mother,
Against her will, and they are the sons
Of the noblest men here. They shrink
From going to her father Icarius' house
So that he could arrange his daughter's dowry
And give her away to the man he likes best.
Instead, they gather at our house day after day,
Slaughtering our oxen and sheep and fat goats,
Living high and drinking wine recklessly.
We've lost almost everything, because
We don't have Odysseus to protect our house.
We can't defend ourselves. If it came to a fight

We would only show how pathetic we are.
Not that I wouldn't defend myself
If I had the power. Things have gone too far.
The ruin of my house has become a public disgrace.
You should all be indignant, and feel shame
Before your neighbors, and fear the wrath
Of the gods, who may yet turn against you.
I beg you by Olympian Zeus and by Themis,
Who calls and dismisses assemblies of men,
Stop this, my friends, and let me be alone
In my grief—unless my father, Odysseus,
Was your enemy and did you some harm
And now you are paying me back in malice
By urging these suitors on. Better for me
If you yourselves, Ithacans all,
Were to eat up my treasures and flocks.
Then I might get restitution someday.
I'd go through the town and bend people's ears
And ask for our goods until they were all given back.
But there is nothing I can do now. There's no cure
For what you are making me suffer now."

He spoke in anger, bursting into tears
As he threw the scepter onto the ground.
The crowd was motionless with pity. No one
Had the heart to respond to him harshly,
Except Antinous, who now said:

"Well, the big speaker, the mighty orator.
You've got some nerve, Telemachus,
Laying the blame on us. It's not the suitors
Who are at fault, but your own mother,
Who knows more tricks than any woman alive.
It's been three years now, almost four,
Since she's been toying with our affections.
She encourages each man, leading us on,
Sending messages. But her mind is set elsewhere.
Here's just one of the tricks she devised:
She set up a great loom in the main hall
And started weaving a sizeable fabric

With a very fine thread, and she said to us:

'Young men—my suitors, since Odysseus is dead—
Eager as you are to marry me, you must wait
Until I finish this robe—it would be a shame
To waste my spinning—a shroud for the hero
Laertes, when death's doom lays him low.
I fear the Achaean women would reproach me
If he should lie in death shroudless for all his wealth.'

"We were persuaded by this appeal to our honor.
Every day she would weave at the great loom,
And every night she would unweave by torchlight.
She fooled us for three years with her craft.
But in the fourth year, as the seasons rolled by,
And the moons waned, and the days dragged on,
One of her women who knew all about it
Told us, and we caught her unweaving
The gloried shroud. Then we forced her to finish it.
Now here is the suitors' answer to you,
And let every Achaean hear it as well:
Send your mother away with orders to marry
Whichever man her father likes best.
But if she goes on like this much longer,
Torturing us with all she knows and has,
All the gifts Athena has given her,
Her talent for handiwork, her good sense,
Her cleverness—all of which go far beyond
That of any of the heroines of old,
Tyro or Alcmene or garlanded Mycene,
Not one of whom had a mind like Penelope's,
Even though now she is not thinking straight—
We will continue to eat you out of house and home
For as long as she holds to this way of thinking
Which the immortal gods have put in her breast.
She is building quite a reputation for herself,
But at your expense. As for us, we're staying put
Until she chooses one of the Achaeans to marry."

Telemachus, drawing a deep breath, responded:

"Antinous, I cannot throw out of my house
The mother who bore me and raised me.
As for my father, he may be alive or dead
But he is not here. It would not be fair
If I had to pay a great price to Icarius,
As I would if I sent my mother back to him
On my own initiative. And the spirits would send me
Other evils, for my mother would curse me
As she left the house, and call on the Furies.
And men all over would hold me at fault.
So I will never tell my mother to leave.
As for you, if you don't like it,
If this offends your sense of fairness,
Get out of my house! Fix yourselves feasts
In each others' houses, use up your own stockpiles.
But if it seems better and more profitable
For one man to be eaten out of house and home
Without compensation—then eat away!
But I will pray to the gods eternal
That Zeus grant me requital: Death for you
Here in my house. With no compensation."

Telemachus spoke, and Zeus in answer
Sent forth two eagles from a mountain peak.
They drifted lazily for a while on the wind,
Side by side, with wings outstretched.
But when they were directly above the assembly
With its hub-bub of voices, they wheeled about
And beat their wings hard, looking down
On the heads of all with death in their eyes.
Then they savaged each others' craws
With their talons and veered off to the east
Across the city and over the houses
Of the men below. Everyone was amazed,
And they all wondered what these birds portended.
Then the old hero Halitherses stepped forth,
Mastor's son, the best man of his time
In reading bird flight and uttering oracles.
He was full of good will in the speech that he made.

"Hear me men of Ithaca, and I mean
The suitors especially, since a great tide of woe
Is rising to engulf them. Odysseus
Shall not be away from his home much longer.
Even now he is near, sowing death for the suitors,
One and all, grim for them and grim for many others
Who dwell on Ithaca. But let us take thought now
Of how to make an end of this. Or better,
Let the suitors themselves make an end.
I am no inexperienced prophet,
But one who knows well, and I declare
That everything is coming true for that man,
Just as I told him when he left for Troy:
That after bitter pain and loss of all comrades
He would finally reach home after twenty years
Unknown to anyone. Now it is all coming true."

Eurymachus, Polybus' son, answered him:

"Get out of here, old man. Go home and prophesy
For your own children—you don't want them to get hurt.
I'm a better prophet than you when it comes to this.
There are lots of birds under the sun, flying
All over the place, and not all of them are omens.
As for Odysseus, he died a long way from here,
And you should have died with him.
Then you wouldn't spout so many prophecies,
Or be egging Telemachus on in his anger,
Hoping he'll give you a gift to take home.
I'll tell you this, and I guarantee it'll be done:
If you, with all your experience and lore,
Talk a younger man into getting angry,
First, we'll go harder on him, and second,
We'll slap you with a fine so big
It'll make you choke when you have to pay it.
And this is my advice to Telemachus:
Send your mother back to her father's house
And have them prepare a wedding feast
And all the gifts that go with a beloved daughter.
Until then, the sons of the Achaeans will not stop

Their bitter courtship. One thing's for sure,
We fear no man, no, not even Telemachus
With all his big talk. We don't give a damn
For your prophecies, old man, and when they don't
Come true, you'll be more despised than ever.
And you, Telemachus, your inheritance
Is going down the drain and will never be restored
As long as your mother puts off this marriage.
After all, we wait here patiently day after day
Competing for her, and do not go after
Other women who might make us good wives."

And Telemachus, keeping his wits about him:

"I'm done pleading with you, Eurymachus,
And all the rest of you suitors. I've had my say.
Now the gods know all this, and so do the Achaeans.
All I want now is a fast ship and twenty men
Who will crew for me as I sail here and there.
I'm going to Sparta and to sandy Pylos
For news of my father, who has been long gone.
Someone may tell me something, or I may hear
A rumor from Zeus, which is how news travels best.
If I hear my father's alive and on his way home,
I can grit my teeth and hold out one more year.
If I hear he's dead, among the living no more,
I'll come home myself to my ancestral land,
Build him a barrow and celebrate the funeral
My father deserves. Then I'll marry off my mother."

He spoke and sat down. Then up rose Mentor,
An old friend of Odysseus. It was him,
Old Mentor, that Odysseus had put in charge
Of all his house when he left with the ships.
He spoke out now with good will to all:

"Hear me now, men of Ithaca.
Kings might as well no longer be gentle and kind
Or understand the correct order of things.
They might as well be tyrannical butchers

For all that any of Odysseus' people
Remember him, a godly king as kind as a father.
I have no quarrel with the suitors. True,
They are violent and malicious men,
But at least they are risking their own lives
In devouring the house of Odysseus,
Who, they say, will never return.
It is the rest of the people I am angry with.
You all sit here in silence and say nothing,
Not a word of rebuke to make the suitors quit,
Although you easily outnumber them."

Leocritus, Evenor's son, answered him:

"What kind of thing is that to say, Mentor,
You stubborn old fool, telling us to stop?
And do you think that even with superior numbers
People are going to fight us over a dinner?
Even if Odysseus, your Ithacan hero himself
Showed up, all hot to throw the suitors
Out of his house—well, let's just say
His wife wouldn't be too happy to see him,
No matter how much she missed him, that's how ugly
His death would be. No, you're way off the mark.
Now let's everybody scatter and go home.
Mentor and Halitherses can outfit Telemachus.
They're old friends of his father. But I think
He'll be getting his news sitting here in Ithaca
For a long time to come. He's not going anywhere."

With those words the brief assembly was over.
Everyone returned to their homes, but the suitors
Went off to the house of godlike Odysseus.

Telemachus, though, went down to the shore,
Washed his hands in the surf, and prayed to Athena:

"Hear me, god of yesterday. You came to our house
And commanded me to sail the misty sea
In search of news of my long-absent father.

Now the townspeople are blocking all that,
Especially the suitors, those arrogant bastards."

He prayed, and Athena was with him,
Looking just like Mentor and with Mentor's voice.
Her words flew to Telemachus on wings:

"You won't turn out to be a fool or a coward,
Telemachus, not if any of Odysseus' spirit
Has been instilled in you. Now there was a man
Who made sure of his words and deeds! Don't worry,
You'll make this journey, and it won't be in vain.
If you're really Odysseus' and Penelope's son,
You'll finish whatever you set your mind to.
You know, few sons turn out to be like their fathers;
Most turn out worse, a few better.
No, you don't have it in you to be a fool or a coward,
And you've got something of Odysseus' brains,
So there's reason to think you'll finish this job.
Never mind, then, about the suitors' schemes.
They're mad, not an ounce of sense or justice in them,
And they have no idea of the dark death
Closing in on them, doomed all to die on a single day.
As for you, the journey you have your heart set on
Won't be delayed. I myself, your father's old comrade,
Will equip a fast ship and sail along with you.
You get the provisions and stow them aboard,
Wine in jars and barley meal in tight skins,
Food that will stick to men's ribs. I'll go through town
And round up a volunteer crew. There are plenty of ships
In Ithaca, old and new. I'll scout out the best one,
Get her rigged, and launch her onto the open sea."

Thus Athena, daughter of Zeus.

And Telemachus, the voice of the goddess
Ringing in his ears, went on to his house
With a troubled heart. There he found
The haughty suitors, flaying goats
And singeing swine in the courtyard.

Antinous came up to him with a laugh
And clasped his hand and said to him:

"Ah, Telemachus, the dauntless orator,
That's the spirit! No hard feelings now!
Let's just eat and drink as we always have.
The townspeople will provide you with everything—
A ship, a crew—to speed you on to sacred Pylos
In your search for news of your noble father."

And Telemachus, drawing in his breath:

"Antinous, there is no way I can relax
Or enjoy myself with you arrogant bastards.
Isn't it bad enough that you have eaten through
Much of my wealth while I was still a child?
Now that I'm grown, and hear things from others,
And get angrier and angrier at what I see and hear,
I'm going to do my best to nail you to the wall,
Either by going to Pylos or staying here in this land.
But I am going, and I'll make the journey count,
Even though I have to sail in another man's ship
And can't captain my own, which I'm sure suits you fine."

And he withdrew his hand from Antinous'.
The suitors, busy with preparing the feast,
Jeered at him as they swaggered through the hall:

"Hey, everybody! Telemachus is planning to murder us!
He'll bring reinforcements from sandy Pylos,
Or even from Sparta. He's really serious.
Or he'll go to Ephyre and get deadly poisons
To put in our wine-bowl and kill us all."

And another would sneer:

"Who knows?
If he goes off wandering in a hollow ship,
He may die as Odysseus did, far from his friends.
That would mean more work for us, dividing

All his possessions and giving his house
Over to his mother—and the man she marries."

That's how their talk went. But Telemachus
Went down to his father's treasure chamber,
A large room where there lay gold and bronze
Piled to the ceiling. And there were clothes in chests,
Fragrant olive oil, and great jars of wine,
Old and sweet, an undiluted, heavenly drink,
Ranged in rows along the wall, ready for Odysseus
Should he ever return after all his suffering.
The close-fitting, double doors were locked,
And the room was watched day and night
By a wise old stewardess, Eurycleia,
Daughter of Ops, son of Peisenor. Telemachus
Had summoned her and now spoke to her there:

"Nurse, siphon me off some wine in jars,
The sweetest, mellowest wine we have
After what you are holding in reserve
For Odysseus, that unlucky man,
Should he ever return from the jaws of death.
Fill twelve jars and fit them with lids,
And pour some barley meal into well-sewn skins.
I'll need twenty quarts of ground barley meal.
But don't let anyone know. Just have all this
Ready to go. I'll pick it up this evening
After my mother has gone to bed upstairs.
I'm off to Sparta and to sandy Pylos
To see if I can get some news of my father."

He spoke, and Eurycleia gave a shrill cry.
She sobbed as her words went out to him:

"Ah, where did you get this idea, child?
Why would you want to travel abroad, you,
A beloved only son? Zeus-born Odysseus
Perished far from home, in a strange land.
These men, as soon as you are gone, will plot
To have you killed by treachery, and then divide

All these things among themselves. No, stay here
With what is yours. There is no need for you
To wander and suffer on the barren sea."

And Telemachus, in his cool-headed way:

"Don't worry, nurse. There is a god
Behind all this. But swear you won't say
Anything to my mother for a dozen days or so,
Or until she misses me herself or has heard
That I am gone. I don't want her crying."

And the old woman swore to the gods
That she would say nothing. That done,
She drew the wine for him in jars
And poured the barley meal into skins,
While Telemachus went back to join the suitors.

Owl-eyed Athena saw what to do next.
Assuming the form of Telemachus,
She went through the town recruiting sailors,
Telling them to gather by the ship at dusk.
Then she asked Noemon, Phronius' son,
For a fast ship, and he cheerfully agreed.

When the sun set and shadows hung everywhere,
She drew the swift ship down to the sea,
Put in all the gear a benched sailing ship needs,
And then moored it at the harbor's mouth. The crew
Gathered around, and the goddess encouraged each man.

Then she moved on, making her way
To the house of godlike Odysseus. There
She shed sweet sleep on the suitors
And made their minds wander in their wine
And knocked the cups from their hands. Eyelids heavy,
They stumbled to their feet and one by one
Staggered through the city home and to bed.

Athena's eyes flashed in the dark.

She looked like Mentor now, and in his voice
She called Telemachus out from the hall:

"Telemachus, your crew is ready with the oars
And waiting for you. It's time to set forth."

Pallas Athena led the way quickly,
And the man followed in the deity's footsteps.
They came down to the ship and the sea
And found the crew standing on the beach,
Their hair blowing in the offshore breeze.
And Telemachus, feeling his father's blood:

"This way, men! We have provisions to haul.
Everything's ready at my house. My mother
Knows nothing of all this, nor do any
Of the women, except for one I told."

He led the way, and they brought the provisions
Down to the ship and stowed them below.
Athena went aboard, followed by Telemachus,
And they sat side by side on the stern of the ship
As the men untied the cables and then came aboard
To sit at their benches. The Grey-eyed One
Put the wind at their backs, a strong gust from the West
That came in chanting over the wine-dark water.
Telemachus called to the crew to rig the sail.
Falling to, they raised the fir mast,
Set it in its socket, braced it with forestays
And hauled up the white sail. The wind
Bellied the canvas, and an indigo wave
Hissed off the bow as the ship sped on.
When they had made all the tackle secure
In their swift black ship, they set out bowls
Brimming with wine, and poured libations
To the immortal gods, most of all
To the daughter of Zeus with seagrey eyes.

The ship bore through the night and into the dawn.

ODYSSEY 5

Dawn reluctantly
Left Tithonus in her rose-shadowed bed,
Then shook the morning into flakes of fire.

Light flooded the halls of Olympus
Where Zeus, high Lord of Thunder,
Sat with the other gods, listening to Athena
Reel off the tale of Odysseus' woes.
It galled her that he was still in Calypso's cave:

"Zeus, my father—and all you blessed immortals—
Kings might as well no longer be gentle and kind
Or understand the correct order of things.
They might as well be tryannical butchers
For all that any of Odysseus' people
Remember him, a godly king as kind as a father.
No, he's still languishing on that island, detained
Against his will by that nymph Calypso,
No way in the world for him to get back to his land.
His ships are all lost, he has no crew left
To row him across the sea's crawling back.
And now the islanders are plotting to kill his son
As he heads back home. He went for news of his father
To sandy Pylos and white-bricked Sparta."

Storm Cloud Zeus had an answer for her:

"Quite a little speech you've let slip through your teeth,
Daughter. But wasn't this exactly your plan

So that Odysseus would make them pay for it later?
You know how to get Telemachus
Back to Ithaca and out of harm's way
With his mother's suitors sailing in a step behind."

Zeus turned then to his son Hermes and said:

"Hermes, you've been our messenger before.
Go tell that ringleted nymph it is my will
To let that patient man Odysseus go home.
Not with an escort, mind you, human or divine,
But on a rickety raft—tribulation at sea—
Until on the twentieth day he comes to Schería
In the land of the Phaeacians, our distant relatives,
Who will treat Odysseus as if he were a god
And take him on a ship to his own native land
With gifts of bronze and clothing and gold,
More than he ever would have taken back from Troy
Had he come home safely with his share of the loot.
That's how he's destined to see his dear ones again
And return to his high-gabled Ithacan home."

Thus Zeus, and the quicksilver messenger
Laced on his feet the beautiful sandals,
Golden, immortal, that carry him over
Landscape and seascape on a puff of wind.
And he picked up the wand he uses to charm
Mortal eyes to sleep and make sleepers awake.

Holding this wand the tough quicksilver god
Took off, bounded onto Pieria
And dove through the ether down to the sea,

Skimming the waves like a cormorant,
The bird that patrols the saltwater billows
Hunting for fish, seaspume on its plumage,

Hermes flying low and planing the whitecaps.

When he finally arrived at the distant island

He stepped from the violet-tinctured sea
On to dry land and proceeded to the cavern
Where Calypso lived. She was at home.
A fire blazed on the hearth, and the smell
Of split cedar and arbor vitae burning
Spread like incense across the whole island.
She was seated inside, singing in a lovely voice
As she wove at her loom with a golden shuttle.
Around her cave the woodland was in bloom,
Alder and poplar and fragrant cypress.
Long-winged birds nested in the leaves,
Horned owls and larks and slender-throated shorebirds
That screech like crows over the bright saltwater.
Tendrils of ivy curled around the cave's mouth,
The glossy green vine clustered with berries.
Four separate springs flowed with clear water, criss-
Crossing channels as they meandered through meadows
Lush with parsley and blossoming violets.
It was enough to make even a visiting god
Enraptured at the sight. Quicksilver Hermes
Took it all in, then turned and entered
The vast cave.
Calypso knew him at sight.
The immortals have ways of recognizing each other,
Even those whose homes are in outlying districts.
But Hermes didn't find the great hero inside.
Odysseus was sitting on the shore,
As ever those days, honing his heart's sorrow,
Staring out to sea with hollow, salt-rimmed eyes.

Calypso, sleek and haloed, questioned Hermes
Politely, as she seated him on a lacquered chair:

"My dear Hermes, to what do I owe
The honor of this unexpected visit? Tell me
What you want, and I'll oblige you if I can."

The goddess spoke, and then set a table
With ambrosia and mixed a bowl of rosy nectar.
The quicksilver messenger ate and drank his fill,

Then settled back from dinner with heart content
And made the speech she was waiting for:

"You ask me, goddess to god, why I have come.
Well, I'll tell you exactly why. Remember, you asked.
Zeus ordered me to come here; I didn't want to.
Who would want to cross this endless stretch
Of deserted sea? Not a single city in sight
Where you can get a decent sacrifice from men.
But you know how it is: Zeus has the aegis,
And none of us gods can oppose his will.
He says you have here the most woebegone hero
Of the whole lot who fought around Priam's city
For nine years, sacked it in the tenth, and started home.
But on the way back they offended Athena,
And she swamped them with hurricane winds and waves.
His entire crew was wiped out, and he
Drifted along until he was washed up here.
Anyway, Zeus wants you to send him back home. Now.
The man's not fated to rot here far from his friends.
It's his destiny to see his dear ones again
And return to his high-gabled Ithacan home."

He finished, and the nymph's aura stiffened.
Words flew from her mouth like screaming hawks:

"You gods are the most jealous bastards in the universe—
Persecuting any goddess who ever openly takes
A mortal lover to her bed and sleeps with him.
When Dawn caressed Orion with her rosy fingers,
You celestial layabouts gave her nothing but trouble
Until Artemis finally shot him on Ortygia—
Gold-throned, holy, gentle-shafted assault goddess!
When Demeter followed her heart and unbound
Her hair for Iasion and made love to him
In a late-summer field, Zeus was there taking notes
And executed the man with a cobalt lightning blast.
And now you gods are after me for having a man.
Well, I was the one who saved his life, unprying him
From the spar he came floating here on, sole survivor

Of the wreck Zeus made of his streamlined ship,
Slivering it with lightning on the wine-dark sea.
I loved him, I took care of him, I even told him
I'd make him immortal and ageless all of his days.
But you said it, Hermes: Zeus has the aegis
And none of us gods can oppose his will.
So all right, he can go, if it's an order from above,
Off on the sterile sea. How I don't know.
I don't have any oared ships or crewmen
To row him across the sea's broad back.
But I'll help him. I'll do everything I can
To get him back safely to his own native land."

The quicksilver messenger had one last thing to say:

"Well send him off now and watch out for Zeus' temper.
Cross him and he'll really be rough on you later."

With that the tough quicksilver god made his exit.

Calypso composed herself and went to Odysseus,
Zeus' message still ringing in her ears.
She found him sitting where the breakers rolled in.
His eyes were perpetually wet with tears now,
His life draining away in homesickness.
The nymph had long since ceased to please.
He still slept with her at night in her cavern,
An unwilling lover mated to her eager embrace.
Days he spent sitting on the rocks by the breakers,
Staring out to sea with hollow, salt-rimmed eyes.
She stood close to him and started to speak:

"You poor man. You can stop grieving now
And pining away. I'm sending you home.
Look, here's a bronze axe. Cut some long timbers
And make yourself a raft fitted with topdecks,
Something that will get you across the sea's misty spaces.
I'll stock it with fresh water, food and red wine—
Hearty provisions that will stave off hunger—and
I'll clothe you well and send you a following wind

To bring you home safely to your own native land,
If such is the will of the gods of high heaven,
Whose minds and powers are stronger than mine."

Odysseus' eyes shone with weariness. He stiffened,
And shot back at her words fletched like arrows:

"I don't know what kind of send-off you have in mind,
Goddess, telling me to cross all that open sea on a raft,
Painful, hard sailing. Some well-rigged vessels
Never make it across with a stiff wind from Zeus.
You're not going to catch me setting foot on any raft
Unless you agree to swear a solemn oath
That you're not planning some new trouble for me."

Calypso's smile was like a shower of light.
She touched him gently, and teased him a little:

"Blasphemous, that's what you are—but nobody's fool!
How do you manage to say things like that?
All right. I swear by Earth and Heaven above
And the subterranean water of Styx—the greatest
Oath and the most awesome a god can swear—
That I'm not planning more trouble for you, Odysseus.
I'll put my mind to work for you as hard as I would
For myself, if ever I were in such a fix.
My heart is in the right place, Odysseus,
Nor is it a cold lump of iron in my breast."

With that the haloed goddess walked briskly away
And the man followed in the deity's footsteps.
The two forms, human and divine, came to the cave
And he sat down in the chair which moments before
Hermes had vacated, and the nymph set out for him
Food and drink such as mortal men eat.
She took a seat opposite godlike Odysseus
And her maids served her ambrosia and nectar.
They helped themselves to as much as they wanted,
And when they had their fill of food and drink
Calypso spoke, an immortal radiance upon her:

"Son of Laertes in the line of Zeus, my wily Odysseus,
Do you really want to go home to your beloved country
Right away? Now? Well, you still have my blessings.
But if you had any idea of all the pain
You're destined to suffer before getting home,
You'd stay here with me, deathless—
Think of it, Odysseus!—no matter how much
You missed your wife and wanted to see her again.
You spend all your daylight hours yearning for her.
I don't mind saying she's not my equal
In beauty, no matter how you measure it.
Mortal beauty cannot compare with immortal."

Odysseus, always thinking, answered her this way:

"Goddess and mistress, don't be angry with me.
I know very well that Penelope,
For all her virtues, would pale beside you.
She's only human, and you are a goddess,
Eternally young. Still, I want to go back.
My heart aches for the day I return to my home.
If some god hits me hard as I sail the deep purple,
I'll weather it like the sea-bitten veteran I am.
God knows I've suffered and had my share of sorrows
In war and at sea. I can take more if I have to."

The sun set on his words, and the shadows darkened.
They went to a room deep in the cave, where they made
Sweet love and lay side by side through the night.

We sailed on in shock, glad to get out alive
But grieving for the comrades we'd lost.
And we came to Aeaea, the island that is home
To Circe, a dread goddess with richly coiled hair
And a human voice. She is the sister
Of dark-hearted Aeetes, and they are both sprung
From Helios and Perse, daughter of Ocean.
Some god guided us into a harbor
And we put in to shore without a sound.
We disembarked and lay there for two days and two nights,
Eating our hearts out with weariness and grief.
But when Dawn combed her hair in the third day's light,
I took my sword and spear and went up
From the ship to open ground, hoping to see
Plowed fields, and to hear human voices.
So I climbed to a rugged lookout point
And surveyed the scene. What I saw was smoke
Rising up from Circe's house. It curled up high
Through the thick brush and woods, and I wondered
Whether I should go and have a closer look.
I decided it was better to go back to the ship
And give my crew their meal, and then
Send out a party to reconnoiter.
I was on my way back and close to the ship
When some god took pity on me,
Walking there alone, and sent a great antlered stag
Right into my path. He was on his way
Down to the river from his pasture in the woods,
Thirsty and hot from the sun beating down,

And as he came out I got him right on the spine
In the middle of his back. The bronze spear bored
All the way through, and he fell in the dust
With a groan, and his spirit flew away.
Planting my foot on him, I drew the bronze spear
Out of the wound and laid it down on the ground.
Then I pulled up a bunch of willow shoots
And twisted them together to make a rope
About a fathom long. I used this to tie
The stag's feet together so I could carry him
Across my back, leaning on my spear
As I went back to the ship. There was no way
An animal that large could be held on one shoulder.
I flung him down by the ship and roused my men,
Going up to each in turn and saying to them:

'We're not going down to Hades, my friends,
Before our time. As long as there is still
Food and drink in our ship, at least
We don't have to starve to death.'

When they heard this, they drew their cloaks
From their faces, and marveled at the size
Of the stag lying on the barren seashore.
When they had seen enough, they washed their hands
And prepared a glorious feast. So all day long
Until the sun went down we sat there feasting
On all that meat, washing it down with wine.
When the sun set and darkness came on,
We lay down to sleep on the shore of the sea.

When Dawn brushed the eastern sky with rose,
I called my men together and spoke to them:

'Listen to me, men. It's been hard going.
We don't know east from west right now,
But we have to see if we have any good ideas left.
We may not. I climbed up to a lookout point.
We're on an island, ringed by the endless sea.
The land lies low, and I was able to see

Smoke rising up through the brushy woods.'

This was too much for them. They remembered
What Antiphates, the Laestrygonian, had done,
And how the Cyclops had eaten their comrades.
They wailed and cried, but it did them no good.
I counted off the crew into two companies
And appointed a leader for each. Eurylochus
Headed up one group and I took the other,
And then we shook lots in a bronze helmet.
Out jumped the lot of Eurylochus, brave heart,
And so off he went, with twenty-two men,
All in tears, leaving us behind in no better mood.

They went through the woods and found Circe's house
In an upland clearing. It was built of polished stone
And surrounded by mountain lions and wolves,
Creatures Circe had drugged and bewitched.
These beasts did not attack my men, but stood
On their hind legs and wagged their long tails,
Like dogs fawning on their master who always brings
Treats for them when he comes home from a feast.
So these clawed beasts were fawning around my men,
Who were terrified all the same by the huge animals.
While they stood like this in the gateway
They could hear Circe inside, singing in a lovely voice
As she moved about weaving a great tapestry,
The unfading handiwork of an immortal goddess,
Finely woven, shimmering with grace and light.
Polites, a natural leader, and of all the crew
The one I loved and trusted most, spoke up then:

'Someone inside is weaving a great web,
And singing so beautifully the floor thrums with the sound.
Whether it's a goddess or a woman, let's call her out now.'

And so they called to her, and she came out
And flung open the bright doors and invited them in.
They all filed in naively behind her,
Except Eurylochus, who suspected a trap.

When she had led them in and seated them
She brewed up a potion of Pramnian wine
With cheese, barley, and pale honey stirred in,
And she laced this potion with insidious drugs
That would make them forget their own native land.
When they had eaten and drunk, she struck them
With her wand and herded them into the sties outside.
Grunting, their bodies covered with bristles,
They looked just like pigs, but their minds were intact.
Once in the pens, they squealed with dismay,
And Circe threw them acorns and berries—
The usual fare for wallowing swine.

Eurylochus at once came back to the ship
To tell us of our comrades' unseemly fate,
But, hard as he tried, he could not speak a word.
The man was in shock. His eyes welled with tears,
And his mind was filled with images of horror.
Finally, under our impatient questioning,
He told us how his men had been undone:

'We went through the woods, as you told us to,
Glorious Odysseus, and found a beautiful house
In an upland clearing, built of polished stone.
Someone inside was working a great loom
And singing in a high, clear voice, some goddess
Or a woman, and they called out to her,
And she came out and opened the bright doors
And invited them in, and they naively
Filed in behind her. But I stayed outside,
Suspecting a trap. And they all disappeared,
Not one came back. I sat and watched
For a long, long time, and not one came back.'

He spoke, and I threw my silver-studded sword
Around my shoulders, slung on my bow,
And ordered Eurylochus to retrace his steps
And lead me back there. But he grabbed me by the knees
And pleaded with me, wailing miserably:

'Don't force me to go back there. Leave me here,
Because I know that you will never come back yourself
Or bring back the others. Let's just get out of here
With those that are left. We might still make it.'

Those were his words, and I answered him:

'All right, Eurylochus, you stay here by the ship.
Get yourself something to eat and drink.
I'm going, though. We're in a really tight spot.'

And so I went up from the ship and the sea
Into the sacred woods. I was closing in
On Circe's house, with all its bewitchment,
When I was met by Hermes. He had a golden wand
And looked like a young man, a hint of a moustache
Above his lip—youth at its most charming.
He clasped my hand and said to me:

'Where are you off to now, unlucky man,
Alone, and in rough, uncharted terrain?
Those men of yours are up in Circe's house,
Penned like pigs into crowded little sties.
And you've come to free them? I don't think so.
You'll never return; you'll have to stay there, too.
Oh well, I will keep you out of harm's way.
Take this herb with you when you go to Circe,
And it will protect you from her deadly tricks.
She'll mix a potion and spike it with drugs,
But she won't be able to cast her spell
Because you'll have a charm that works just as well—
The one I'll give you—and you'll be forewarned.
When Circe strikes you with her magic wand,
Draw your sharp sword from beside your thigh
And rush at her with murder in your eye.
She'll be afraid and invite you to bed.
Don't turn her down—that's how you'll get
Your comrades freed and yourself well loved.
But first make her swear by the gods above
She will not unsex you when you are nude,

Or drain you of your manly fortitude.'

So saying, Hermes gave me the herb,
Pulling it out of the ground, and showed it to me.
It was black at the root, with a milk-white flower.
Moly, the gods call it, hard for mortal men to dig up,
But the gods can do anything. Hermes rose
Through the wooded island and up to Olympus,
And I went on to Circe's house, brooding darkly
On many things. I stood at the gates
Of the beautiful goddess' house and gave a shout.
She heard me call and came out at once,
Opening the bright doors and inviting me in.
I followed her inside, my heart pounding.
She seated me on a beautiful chair
Of finely wrought silver, and prepared me a drink
In a golden cup, and with evil in her heart
She laced it with drugs. She gave me the cup
And I drank it off, but it did not bewitch me.
So she struck me with her wand and said:

'Off to the sty, with the rest of your friends.'

At this, I drew the sharp sword that hung by my thigh
And lunged at Circe as if I meant to kill her.
The goddess shrieked and, running beneath my blade,
Grabbed my knees and said to me wailing:

'Who are you, and where do you come from?
What is your city and who are your parents?
I am amazed that you drank this potion
And are not bewitched. No other man
Has ever resisted this drug once it's past his lips.
But you have a mind that cannot be beguiled.
You must be Odysseus, the man of many wiles,
Who Quicksilver Hermes always said would come here
In his swift black ship on his way home from Troy.
Well then, sheath your sword and let's
Climb into my bed and tangle in love there,
So we may come to trust each other.'

She spoke, and I answered her:

'Circe, how can you ask me to be gentle to you
After you've turned my men into swine?
And now you have me here and want to trick me
Into going to bed with you, so that you can
Unman me when I am naked. No, Goddess,
I'm not getting into any bed with you
Unless you agree first to swear a solemn oath
That you're not planning some new trouble for me.'

Those were my words, and she swore an oath at once
Not to do me any harm, and when she finished
I climbed into Circe's beautiful bed.

Meanwhile, her serving women were busy,
Four maidens who did all the housework,
Spirit women born of the springs and groves
And of the sacred rivers that flow to the sea.
One of them brought rugs with a purple sheen
And strewed them over chairs lined with fresh linen.
Another drew silver tables up to the chairs
And set golden baskets upon them. The third
Mixed honey-hearted wine in a silver bowl
And set out golden cups. The fourth
Filled a cauldron with water and lit a great fire
Beneath it, and when the water was boiling
In the glowing bronze, she set me in a tub
And bathed me, mixing in water from the cauldron
Until it was just how I liked it, and pouring it over
My head and shoulders until she washed from my limbs
The weariness that had consumed my soul.
When she had bathed me and rubbed me
With rich olive oil, and had thrown about me
A beautiful cloak and tunic, she led me to the hall
And had me sit on a silver-studded chair,
Richly wrought and with a matching footstool.
A maid poured water from a silver pitcher
Over a golden basin for me to wash my hands
And then set up a polished table nearby.

And the housekeeper, grave and dignified,
Set out bread and generous helpings
From all the dishes she had. She told me to eat,
But nothing appealed. I sat there with other thoughts
Occupying my mind, and my mood was dark.
When Circe noticed I was just sitting there,
Depressed, and not reaching out for food,
She came up to me and spoke winged words:

'Why are you just sitting there, Odysseus,
Eating your heart out and not touching your food?
Are you afraid of some other trick? You need not be.
I have already sworn I will do you no harm.'

So she spoke, and I answered her:

'Circe, how could anyone bring himself—
Any decent man—to taste food and drink
Before seeing his comrades free?
If you really want me to eat and drink,
Set my men free and let me see them.'

So I spoke, and Circe went outside
Holding her wand and opened the sty
And drove them out. They looked like swine
Nine or ten years old. They stood there before her
And she went through them and smeared each one
With another drug. The bristles they had grown
After Circe had given them the poisonous drug
All fell away, and they became men again,
Younger than before, taller and far handsomer.
They knew me, and they clung to my hands,
And the house rang with their passionate sobbing.
The goddess herself was moved to pity.

Then she came to my side and said:

'Son of Laertes in the line of Zeus,
My wily Odysseus, go to your ship now
Down by the sea and haul it ashore.

Then stow all the tackle and gear in caves
And come back here with the rest of your crew.'

So she spoke, and persuaded my heart.
I went to the shore and found my crew there
Wailing and crying beside our sailing ship.
When they saw me they were like farmyard calves
Around a herd of cows returning to the yard.
The calves bolt from their pens and run friskily
Around their mothers, lowing and mooing.
That's how my men thronged around me
When they saw me coming. It was as if
They had come home to their rugged Ithaca,
And wailing miserably they said so to me:

'With you back, Zeus-born, it is just as if
We had returned to our native Ithaca.
But tell us what happened to the rest of the crew.'

So they spoke, and I answered them gently:

'First let's haul our ship onto dry land
And then stow all the tackle and gear in caves.
Then I want all of you to come along with me
So you can see your shipmates in Circe's house,
Eating and drinking all they could ever want.'

They heard what I said and quickly agreed.
Eurylochus, though, tried to hold them back,
Speaking to them these winged words:

'Why do you want to do this to yourselves,
Go down to Circe's house? She will turn all of you
Into pigs, wolves, lions, and make you guard her house.
Remember what the Cyclops did when our shipmates
Went into his lair? It was this reckless Odysseus
Who led them there. It was his fault they died.'

When Eurylochus said that, I considered
Drawing my long sword from where it hung

By my thigh and lopping off his head,
Close kinsman though he was by marriage.
But my crew talked me out of it, saying things like:

'By your leave, let's station this man here
To guard the ship. As for the rest of us,
Lead us on to the sacred house of Circe.'

And so the whole crew went up from the sea,
And Eurylochus did not stay behind with the ship
But went with us, in mortal fear of my temper.

Meanwhile, back in Circe's house, the goddess
Had my men bathed, rubbed down with oil,
And clothed in tunics and fleecy cloaks.
We found them feasting well in her halls.
When they recognized each other, they wept openly
And their cries echoed throughout Circe's house.
Then the shining goddess stood near me and said:

'Lament no more. I myself know
All that you have suffered on the teeming sea
And the losses on land at your enemies' hands.
Now you must eat, drink wine, and restore the spirit
You had when you left your own native land,
Your rugged Ithaca. You are skin and bones now
And hollow inside. All you can think of
Is your hard wandering, no joy in your heart,
For you have, indeed, suffered many woes.'

She spoke, and I took her words to heart.
So we sat there day after day for a year,
Feasting on abundant meat and sweet wine.
But when a year had passed, and the seasons turned,
And the moons waned and the long days were done,
My trusty crew called me out and said:

'Good god, man, at long last remember your home,
If it is heaven's will for you to be saved
And return to your house and your own native land.'

They spoke, and I saw what they meant.
So all that long day until the sun went down
We sat feasting on meat and sweet red wine.
When the sun set and darkness came on,
My men lay down to sleep in the shadowy hall,
But I went up to Circe's beautiful bed
And touching her knees I beseeched the goddess:

'Circe, fulfill now the promise you made
To send me home. I am eager to be gone
And so are my men, who are wearing me out
Sitting around whining and complaining
Whenever you happen not to be present.'

So I spoke, and the shining goddess answered:

'Son of Laertes in the line of Zeus,
My wily Odysseus—you need not stay
Here in my house any longer than you wish.
But there is another journey you must make first—
To the house of Hades and dread Persephone,
To consult the ghost of Theban Tiresias,
The blind prophet, whose mind is still strong.
To him alone Persephone has granted
Intelligence even after his death.
The rest of the dead are flitting shadows.'

This broke my spirit. I sat on the bed
And wept. I had no will to live, nor did I care
If I ever saw the sunlight again.
But when I had my fill of weeping and writhing,
I looked at the goddess and said:

'And who will guide me on this journey, Circe?
No man has ever sailed his black ship to Hades.'

And the goddess, shining, answered at once:

'Son of Laertes in the line of Zeus,
My wily Odysseus—do not worry about

A pilot to guide your ship. Just set up the mast,
Spread the white sail, and sit yourself down.
The North Wind's breath will bear her onwards.
But when your ship crosses the stream of Ocean
You will see a shelving shore and Persephone's groves,
Tall poplars and willows that drop their fruit.
Beach your ship there by Ocean's deep eddies,
And go yourself to the dank house of Hades.
There into Acheron flow Pyriphlegethon
And Cocytus, a branch of the water of Styx.
And there is a rock where the two roaring rivers
Flow into one. At that spot, hero, gather yourself
And do as I say.
Dig an ell-square pit,
And around it pour libation to all the dead,
First with milk and honey, then with sweet wine,
And a third time with water. Then sprinkle barley
And pray to the looming, feeble death-heads,
Vowing sacrifice on Ithaca, a barren heifer,
The herd's finest, and rich gifts on the altar,
And to Tiresias alone a great black ram.
After these supplications to the spirits,
Slaughter a ram and a black ewe, turning their heads
Toward Erebus, yourself turning backward
And leaning toward the streams of the river.
Then many ghosts of the dead will come forth.
Call to your men to flay the slaughtered sheep
And burn them as a sacrifice to the gods below,
To mighty Hades and dread Persephone.
You yourself draw your sharp sword and sit there,
Keeping the feeble death-heads from the blood
Until you have questioned Tiresias.
Then, and quickly, the great seer will come.
He will tell you the route and how long it will take
For you to reach home over the teeming deep.'

Dawn rose in gold as she finished speaking.
Circe gave me a cloak and tunic to wear
And the nymph slipped on a long silver robe
Shimmering in the light, cinched it at the waist

With a golden belt and put a veil on her head.
I went through the halls and roused my men,
Going up to each with words soft and sweet:

'Time to get up! No more sleeping late.
We're on our way. Lady Circe has told me all.'

So I spoke, and persuaded their heroes' hearts.
But not even from Circe's house could I lead my men
Unscathed. One of the crew, Elpenor, the youngest,
Not much of a warrior nor all that smart,
Had gone off to sleep apart from his shipmates,
Seeking the cool air on Circe's roof
Because he was heavy with wine.
He heard the noise of his shipmates moving around
And sprang up suddenly, forgetting to go
To the long ladder that led down from the roof.
He fell headfirst, his neck snapped at the spine,
And his soul went down to the house of Hades.

As my men were heading out I spoke to them:

'You think, no doubt, that you are going home,
But Circe has plotted another course for us,
To the house of Hades and dread Persephone,
To consult the ghost of Theban Tiresias.'

This broke their hearts. They sat down
Right where they were and wept and tore their hair,
But no good came of their lamentation.

While we were on our way to our swift ship
On the shore of the sea, weeping and crying,
Circe had gone ahead and tethered a ram and a black ewe
By our tarred ship. She had passed us by
Without our ever noticing. Who could see
A god on the move against the god's will?"

ODYSSEY 11

"When we reached our black ship
We hauled her onto the bright saltwater,
Set up the mast and sail, loaded on
The sheep, and boarded her ourselves,
Heartsick and weeping openly by now.
The dark prow cut through the waves
And a following wind bellied the canvas,
A good sailing breeze sent by Circe,
The dread goddess with a human voice.
We lashed everything down and sat tight,
Leaving the ship to the wind and helmsman.
All day long she surged on with taut sail;
Then the sun set, and the sea grew dark.

The ship took us to the deep, outermost Ocean
And the land of the Cimmerians, a people
Shrouded in mist. The sun never shines there,
Never climbs the starry sky to beam down at them,
Nor bathes them in the glow of its last golden rays;
Their wretched sky is always racked with night's gloom.
We beached our ship there, unloaded the sheep,
And went along the stream of Ocean
Until we came to the place spoken of by Circe.

There Perimedes and Eurylochus held the victims
While I dug an ell-square pit with my sword,
And poured libation to all the dead,
First with milk and honey, then with sweet wine,
And a third time with water. Then I sprinkled

White barley and prayed to the looming dead,
Vowing sacrifice on Ithaca—a barren heifer,
The herd's finest, and rich gifts on the altar,
And to Tiresias alone a great black ram.
After these supplications to the spirits,
I cut the sheeps' throats over the pit,
And the dark blood pooled there.
Then out of Erebus
The souls of the dead gathered, the ghosts
Of brides and youths and worn-out old men
And soft young girls with hearts new to sorrow,
And many men wounded with bronze spears,
Killed in battle, bearing blood-stained arms.
They drifted up to the pit from all sides
With an eerie cry, and pale fear seized me.
I called to my men to flay the slaughtered sheep
And burn them as a sacrifice to the gods,
To mighty Hades and dread Persephone.
Myself, I drew my sharp sword and sat,
Keeping the feeble death-heads from the blood
Until I had questioned Tiresias.

First to come was the ghost of Elpenor,
Whose body still lay in Circe's hall,
Unmourned, unburied, since we'd been hard pressed.
I wept when I saw him, and with pity in my heart
Spoke to him these feathered words:

'Elpenor, how did you get to the undergloom
Before me, on foot, outstripping our black ship?'

I spoke, and he moaned in answer:

'Bad luck and too much wine undid me.
I fell asleep on Circe's roof. Coming down
I missed my step on the long ladder
And fell headfirst. My neck snapped
At the spine and my ghost went down to Hades.
Now I beg you—by those we left behind,
By your wife and the father who reared you,

And by Telemachus, your only son,
Whom you left alone in your halls—
When you put the gloom of Hades behind you
And beach your ship on the Isle of Aeaea,
As I know you will, remember me, my lord.
Do not leave me unburied, unmourned,
When you sail for home, or I might become
A cause of the gods' anger against you.
Burn me with my armor, such as I have,
Heap me a barrow on the grey sea's shore,
In memory of a man whose luck ran out.
Do this for me, and fix in the mound the oar
I rowed with my shipmates while I was alive.'

Thus Elpenor, and I answered him:

'Pitiful spirit, I will do this for you.'

Such were the sad words we exchanged
Sitting by the pit, I on one side holding my sword
Over the blood, my comrade's ghost on the other.

Then came the ghost of my dead mother,
Anticleia, daughter of the hero Autolycus.
She was alive when I left for sacred Ilion.
I wept when I saw her, and pitied her,
But even in my grief I would not allow her
To come near the blood until I had questioned Tiresias.

And then he came, the ghost of Theban Tiresias,
Bearing a golden staff. He knew me and said:

'Odysseus, son of Laertes, master of wiles,
Why have you come, leaving the sunlight
To see the dead and this joyless place?
Move off from the pit and take away your sword,
So I may drink the blood and speak truth to you.'

I drew back and slid my silver-studded sword
Into its sheath. After he had drunk the dark blood

The flawless seer rose and said to me:

'You seek a homecoming sweet as honey,
Shining Odysseus, but a god will make it bitter,
For I do not think you will elude the Earthshaker,
Who has laid up wrath in his heart against you,
Furious because you blinded his son. Still,
You just might get home, though not without pain,
You and your men, if you curb your own spirit,
And theirs, too, when you beach your ship
On Thrinacia. You will be marooned on that island
In the violet sea, and find there the cattle
Of Helios the Sun, and his sheep, too, grazing.
Leave these unharmed, keep your mind on your homecoming,
And you may still reach Ithaca, though not without pain.
But if you harm them, I foretell doom for you,
Your ship, and your crew. And even if you
Yourself escape, you will come home late
And badly, having lost all companions
And in another's ship. And you shall find
Trouble in your house, arrogant men
Devouring your wealth and courting your wife.
Yet vengeance will be yours, and when you have slain
The suitors in your hall, by ruse or by sword,
Then you must go off again, carrying a broad-bladed oar,
Until you come to men who know nothing of the sea,
Who eat their food unsalted, and have never seen
Red-prowed ships or oars that wing them along.
And I will tell you a sure sign that you have found them,
One you cannot miss. When you meet another traveler
Who thinks you are carrying a winnowing fan,
Then you must fix your oar in the earth
And offer sacrifice to Lord Poseidon,
A ram, a bull, and a boar in its prime.
Then return to your home and offer
Perfect sacrifice to the immortal gods
Who hold high heaven, to each in turn.
And death will come to you off the sea,
A death so gentle, and carry you off
When you are worn out in sleek old age,

Your people prosperous all around you.
All this will come true for you as I have told.'

Thus Tiresias. And I answered him:

'All that, Tiresias, is as the gods have spun it.
But tell me this: I see here the ghost
Of my dead mother, sitting in silence
Beside the blood, and she cannot bring herself
To look her son in the eye or speak to him.
How can she recognize me for who I am?'

And Tiresias, the Theban prophet:

'This is easy to tell you. Whoever of the dead
You let come to the blood will speak truly to you.
Whoever you deny will go back again.'

With that, the ghost of Lord Tiresias
Went back into Hades, his soothsaying done.
But I stayed where I was until my mother
Came up and drank the dark blood. At once
She knew me, and her words reached me on wings:

'My child, how did you come to the undergloom
While you are still alive? It is hard for the living
To reach these shores. There are many rivers to cross,
Great bodies of water, nightmarish streams,
And Ocean itself, which cannot be crossed on foot
But only in a well-built ship. Are you still wandering
On your way back from Troy, a long time at sea
With your ship and your men? Have you not yet come
To Ithaca, or seen your wife in your halls?'

So she spoke, and I answered her:

'Mother, I came here because I had to,
To consult the ghost of the prophet Tiresias.
I have not yet come to the coast of Achaea
Or set foot on my own land. I have had nothing

But hard travels from the day I set sail
With Lord Agamemnon to go to Ilion,
Famed for its horses, to fight the Trojans.
But tell me truly, how did you die?
Was it a long illness, or did Artemis
Shoot you suddenly with her gentle arrows?
And tell me about my father and my son,
Whom I left behind. Does the honor I had
Still remain with them, or has it passed
To some other man, and do they all say
I will never return? And what about my wife?
What has she decided, what does she think?
Is she still with my son, keeping things safe?
Or has someone already married her,
Whoever is now the best of the Achaeans?'

So I spoke, and my mother answered at once:

'Oh, yes indeed, she remains in your halls,
Her heart enduring the bitter days and nights.
But the honor that was yours has not passed
To any man. Telemachus holds your lands
Unchallenged, and shares in the feasts
To which all men invite him as the island's lawgiver.
Your father, though, stays out in the fields
And does not come to the city. He has no bed
Piled with bright rugs and soft coverlets
But sleeps in the house where the slaves sleep,
In the ashes by the fire, and wears poor clothes.
In summer and autumn his vineyard's slope
Is strewn with beds of leaves on the ground,
Where he lies in his sorrow, nursing his grief,
Longing for your return. His old age is hard.
I died from the same grief. The keen-eyed goddess
Did not shoot me at home with her gentle shafts,
Nor did any long illness waste my body away.
No, it was longing for you, my glorious Odysseus,
For your gentle heart and your gentle ways,
That robbed me of my honey-sweet life.'

So she spoke, and my heart yearned
To embrace the ghost of my dead mother.
Three times I rushed forward to hug her,
And three times she drifted out of my arms
Like a shadow or a dream. The pain
That pierced my heart grew ever sharper,
And my words rose to my mother on wings:

'Mother, why do you slip away when I try
To embrace you? Even though we are in Hades,
Why can't we throw our arms around each other
And console ourselves with chill lamentation?
Are you a phantom sent by Persephone
To make me groan even more in my grief?'

And my mother answered me at once:

'O my child, most ill-fated of men,
It is not that Persephone is deceiving you.
This is the way it is with mortals.
When we die, the sinews no longer hold
Flesh and bones together. The fire destroys these
As soon as the spirit leaves the white bones,
And the ghost flutters off and is gone like a dream.
Hurry now to the light, and remember these things,
So that later you may tell them all to your wife.'

That was the drift of our talk.

Then the women came,
Sent by Persephone, all those who had been
The wives and daughters of the heroes of old.
They flocked together around the dark blood,
But I wanted to question them one at a time.
The best way I could think of to question them
Was to draw the sharp sword from beside my thigh,
And keep them from drinking the blood all at once.
They came up in procession then, and one by one
They declared their birth, and I questioned them all.

The first one I saw was highborn Tyro,
Who said she was born of flawless Salmoneus
And was wed to Cretheus, a son of Aeolus.
She fell in love with a river, divine Enipeus,
The most beautiful of all the rivers on earth,
And she used to play in his lovely streams.
But the Earthshaker took Enipeus' form
And lay with her in the swirling eddies
Near the river's mouth. And an indigo wave,
Towering like a mountain, arched over them
And hid the god and the mortal woman from view.
He unbound the sash that had kept her virgin
And shed sleep upon her. And when the god
Had finished his lovemaking, he took her hand
And called her name softly and said to her:

'Be happy in this love, woman. As the year turns
You will bear glorious children, for a god's embrace
Is never barren. Raise them and care for them.
Now go to your house and say nothing of this,
But I am Poseidon, who makes the earth tremble.'

With that he plunged into the surging sea.
And Tyro conceived and bore Pelias and Neleus,
Who served great Zeus as strong heroes both,
Pelias with his flocks in Iolcus' grasslands,
And Neleus down in sandy Pylos.
She bore other children to Cretheus: Aeson,
Pheres, and the charioteer Amythaon.

Then I saw Antiope, daughter of Asopus,
Who boasted she had slept in the arms of Zeus
And bore two sons, Amphion and Zethus,
Who founded seven-gated Thebes and built its walls,
Since they could not live in the wide land of Thebes
Without walls and towers, mighty though they were.

Next I saw Alcmene, Amphitryon's wife,
Who bore Heracles, the lionhearted battler,
After lying in Zeus' almighty embrace.

And I saw Megara, too, wife of Heracles,
The hero whose strength never wore out.

I saw Oedipus' mother, beautiful Epicaste,
Who unwittingly did a monstrous deed,
Marrying her son, who had killed his father.
The gods soon brought these things to light;
Yet, for all his misery, Oedipus still ruled
In lovely Thebes, by the gods' dark designs.
But Epicaste, overcome by her grief,
Hung a deadly noose from the ceiling rafters
And went down to implacable Hades' realm,
Leaving behind for her son all of the sorrows
A mother's avenging spirits can cause.

And then I saw Chloris, the great beauty
Whom Neleus wedded after courting her
With myriad gifts. She was the youngest daughter
Of Amphion, king of Minyan Orchomenus.
As queen of Pylos, she bore glorious children,
Nestor, Chromius, and lordly Periclymenus,
And magnificent Pero, a wonder to men.
Everyone wanted to marry her, but Neleus
Would only give her to the man who could drive
The cattle of mighty Iphicles to Pylos,
Spiral-horned, broad-browed, stubborn cattle,
Difficult to drive. Only Melampus,
The flawless seer, rose to the challenge,
But he was shackled by Fate. Country herdsmen
Put him in chains, and months went by
And the seasons passed and the year turned
Before he was freed by mighty Iphicles,
After he had told him all of his oracles,
And so the will of Zeus was fulfilled.

I saw Leda also, wife of Tyndareus,
Who bore to him two stout-hearted sons,
Castor the horseman and the boxer Polydeuces.
They are under the teeming earth though alive,
And have honor from Zeus in the world below,

Living and dying on alternate days.
Such is the honor they have won from the gods.

After her I saw Iphimedeia,
Aloeus' wife. She made love to Poseidon
And bore two sons, who did not live long,
Godlike Otus and famed Ephialtes,
The tallest men ever reared upon earth
And the handsomest after gloried Orion.
At nine years old they measured nine cubits
Across the chest, and were nine fathoms tall.
They threatened to wage a furious war
Against the immortal Olympian gods,
And were bent on piling Ossa on Olympus,
And forested Pelion on top of Ossa
And so reach the sky. And they would have done it,
But the son of Zeus and fair-haired Leto
Destroyed them both before the down blossomed
Upon their cheeks and their beards had come in.

And I saw Phaedra and Procnis
And lovely Ariadne, whom Theseus once
Tried to bring from Crete to sacred Athens
But had no joy of her. Artemis first
Shot her on Dia, the seagirt island,
After Dionysus told her he saw her there.

And I saw Maera and Clymene
And hateful Eriphyle, who valued gold
More than her husband's life.
But I could not tell you
All the wives and daughters of heroes I saw.
It would take all night. And it is time
To sleep now, either aboard ship with the crew
Or here in this house. My journey home
Is up to you, and to the immortal gods."

He paused, and they sat hushed in silence,
Spellbound throughout the shadowy hall.
And then white-armed Arete began to speak:

"Well, Phaeacians, does this man impress you
With his looks, stature, and well-balanced mind?
He is my guest, moreover, though each of you
Shares in that honor. Do not send him off, then,
Too hastily, and do not stint your gifts
To one in such need. You have many treasures
Stored in your halls by grace of the gods."

Then the old hero Echeneus spoke up:

"Friends, the words of our wise queen
Are not wide of the mark. Give them heed.
But upon Alcinous depend both word and deed."

And Alcinous answered:

"Arete's word will stand, as long as I live
And rule the Phaeacians who love the oar.
But let our guest, though he longs to go home,
Endure until tomorrow, until I have time
To make our gift complete. We all have a stake
In getting him home, but mine is greatest,
For mine is the power throughout the land."

And Odysseus, who missed nothing:

"Lord Alcinous, most renowned of men,
You could ask me to stay for even a year
While you arranged a send-off with glorious gifts,
And I would assent. Better far to return
With a fuller hand to my own native land.
I would be more respected and loved by all
Who saw me come back to Ithaca."

Alcinous answered him:

"Odysseus, we do not take you
For the sort of liar and cheat the dark earth breeds
Among men everywhere, telling tall tales
No man could ever test for himself.

Your words have outward grace and wisdom within,
And you have told your tale with the skill of a bard—
All that the Greeks and you yourself have suffered.
But tell me this, as accurately as you can:
Did you see any of your godlike comrades
Who went with you to Troy and met their fate there?
The night is young—and magical. It is not yet time
To sleep in the hall. Tell me these wonders.
Sit in our hall and tell us of your woes
For as long as you can bear. I could listen until dawn."

And Odysseus, his mind teeming:

"Lord Alcinous, most glorious of men,
There is a time for words and a time for sleep.
But if you still yearn to listen, I will not refuse
To tell you of other things more pitiable still,
The woes of my comrades who died after the war,
Who escaped the Trojans and their battle-cry
But died on their return through a woman's evil.

When holy Persephone had scattered
The women's ghosts, there came the ghost
Of Agamemnon, son of Atreus,
Distraught with grief. Around him were gathered
Those who died with him in Aegisthus' house.
He knew me as soon as he drank the dark blood.
He cried out shrilly, tears welling in his eyes,
And he stretched out his hands, trying to touch me,
But he no longer had anything left of the strength
He had in the old days in those muscled limbs.
I wept when I saw him, and with pity in my heart
I spoke to him these winged words:

'Son of Atreus, king of men, most glorious
Agamemnon—what death laid you low?
Did Poseidon sink your fleet at sea,
After hitting you hard with hurricane winds?
Or were you killed by enemy forces on land,
As you raided their cattle and flocks of sheep

Or fought to capture their city and women?'

And Agamemnon answered at once:

'Son of Laertes in the line of Zeus,
My crafty Odysseus—No,
Poseidon did not sink my fleet at sea
After hitting us hard with hurricane winds,
Nor was I killed by enemy forces on land.
Aegisthus was the cause of my death.
He killed me with the help of my cursed wife
After inviting me to a feast in his house,
Slaughtered me like a bull at a manger.
So I died a most pitiable death,
And all around me my men were killed
Relentlessly, like white-tusked swine
For a wedding banquet or dinner party
In the house of a rich and powerful man.
You have seen many men cut down, both
In single combat and in the crush of battle,
But your heart would have grieved
As never before at the sight of us lying
Around the wine-bowl and the laden tables
In that great hall. The floor steamed with blood.
But the most piteous cry I ever heard
Came from Cassandra, Priam's daughter.
She had her arms around me down on the floor
When Clytemnestra ran her through from behind.
I lifted my hands and beat the ground
As I lay dying with a sword in my chest,
But that bitch, my wife, turned her back on me
And would not shut my eyes or close my lips
As I was going down to Death. Nothing
Is more grim or more shameless than a woman
Who sets her mind on such an unspeakable act
As killing her own husband. I was sure
I would be welcomed home by my children
And all my household, but she, with her mind set
On stark horror, has shamed not only herself
But all women to come, even the rare good one.'

Thus Agamemnon, and I responded:

'Ah, how broad-browed Zeus has persecuted
The house of Atreus from the beginning,
Through the will of women. Many of us died
For Helen's sake, and Clytemnestra
Set a snare for you while you were far away.'

And Agamemnon answered me at once:

'So don't go easy on your own wife either,
Or tell her everything you know.
Tell her some things, but keep some hidden.
But your wife will not bring about your death,
Odysseus. Icarius' daughter,
Your wise Penelope, is far too prudent.
She was newly wed when we went to war.
We left her with a baby boy still at the breast,
Who must by now be counted as a man,
And prosperous. His father will see him
When he comes, and he will embrace his father,
As is only right. But my wife did not let me
Even fill my eyes with the sight of my son.
She killed me before I could do even that.
But let me tell you something, Odysseus:
Beach your ship secretly when you come home.
Women just can't be trusted any more.
And one more thing. Tell me truthfully
If you've heard anything about my son
And where he is living, perhaps in Orchomenus,
Or in sandy Pylos, or with Menelaus in Sparta.
For Orestes has not yet perished from the earth.'

So he spoke, and I answered him:

'Son of Atreus, why ask me this?
I have no idea whether he is alive or dead,
And it is not good to speak words empty as wind.'

Such were the sad words we had for each other

As we stood there weeping, heavy with grief.

Then came the ghost of Achilles, son of Peleus,
And those of Patroclus and peerless Antilochus
And Ajax, who surpassed all the Danaans,
Except Achilles, in looks and build.
Aeacus' incomparable grandson, Achilles, knew me,
And when he spoke his words had wings:

'Son of Laertes in the line of Zeus,
Odysseus, you hard rover, not even you
Can ever top this, this bold foray
Into Hades, home of the witless dead
And the dim phantoms of men outworn.'

So he spoke, and I answered him:

'Achilles, by far the mightiest of the Achaeans,
I have come here to consult Tiresias,
To see if he has any advice for me
On how I might get back to rugged Ithaca.
I've had nothing but trouble, and have not yet set foot
On my native land. But no man, Achilles,
Has ever been as blessed as you, or ever will be.
While you were alive the army honored you
Like a god, and now that you are here
You rule the dead with might. You should not
Lament your death at all, Achilles.'

I spoke, and he answered me at once:

'Don't try to sell me on death, Odysseus.
I'd rather be a hired hand back up on earth,
Slaving away for some poor dirt farmer,
Than lord it over all these withered dead.
But tell me about that boy of mine.
Did he come to the war and take his place
As one of the best? Or did he stay away?
And what about Peleus? What have you heard?
Is he still respected among the Myrmidons,

Or do they dishonor him in Phthia and Hellas,
Crippled by old age in hand and foot?
And I'm not there for him up in the sunlight
With the strength I had in wide Troy once
When I killed Ilion's best and saved the army.
Just let me come with that kind of strength
To my father's house, even for an hour,
And wrap my hands around his enemies' throats.
They would learn what it means to face my temper.'

Thus Achilles, and I answered him:

'I have heard nothing of flawless Peleus,
But as for your son, Neoptolemus,
I'll tell you all I know, just as you ask.
I brought him over from Scyros myself,
In a fine vessel, to join the Greek army
At Troy, and every time we held council there,
He was always the first to speak, and his words
Were never off the mark. Godlike Nestor and I
Alone surpassed him. And every time we fought
On Troy's plain, he never held back in the ranks
But charged ahead to the front, yielding
To no one, and he killed many in combat.
I could not begin to name them all,
All the men he killed when he fought for us,
But what a hero he dismantled in Telephus' son,
Eurypylus, dispatching him and a crowd
Of his Ceteian compatriots. Eurypylus
Came to Troy because Priam bribed his mother.
After Memnon, I've never seen a handsomer man.
And then, too, when all our best climbed
Into the wooden horse Epeius made,
And I was in command and controlled the trapdoor,
All the other Danaan leaders and counselors
Were wiping away tears from their eyes
And their legs shook beneath them, but I never saw
Neoptolemus blanch or wipe away a tear.
No, he just sat there handling his sword hilt
And heavy bronze spear, and all he wanted

Was to get out of there and give the Trojans hell.
And after we had sacked Priam's steep city,
He boarded his ship with his share of the loot
And more for valor. And not a scratch on him.
He never took a hit from a spear or sword
In close combat, where wounds are common.
When Ares rages anyone can be hit.'

So I spoke, and the ghost of swift-footed Achilles
Went off with huge strides through the fields of asphodel,
Filled with joy at his son's preeminence.

The other ghosts crowded around in sorrow,
And each asked about those who were dear to him.
Only the ghost of Telamonian Ajax
Stood apart, still furious with me
Because I had defeated him in the contest at Troy
To decide who would get Achilles' armor.
His goddess mother had put it up as a prize,
And the judges were the sons of the Trojans
And Pallas Athena. I wish I had never won.
That contest buried Ajax, that brave heart,
The best of the Danaans in looks and deeds,
After the incomparable son of Peleus.
I tried to win him over with words like these:

'Ajax, son of flawless Telamon,
Are you to be angry with me even in death
Over that accursed armor? The gods
Must have meant it to be the ruin of the Greeks.
We lost a tower of strength to that armor.
We mourn your loss as we mourn the loss
Of Achilles himself. Zeus alone
Is to blame. He persecuted the Greeks
Terribly, and he brought you to your doom.
No, come back, Lord Ajax, and listen!
Control your wrath and rein in your proud spirit.'

I spoke, but he said nothing. He went his way
To Erebus, to join the other souls of the dead.

He might yet have spoken to me there, or I
Might yet have spoken to him, but my heart
Yearned to see the other ghosts of the dead.

There I saw Minos, Zeus' glorious son,
Scepter in hand, judging the dead
As he sat in the wide-gated house of Hades;
And the dead sat, too, and asked him for judgments.

And then Orion loomed up before me,
Driving over the fields of asphodel
The beasts he had slain in the lonely hills,
In his hands a bronze club, forever unbroken.

And I saw Tityos, a son of glorious Earth,
Lying on the ground, stretched over nine acres,
And two vultures sat on either side of him
And tore at his liver, plunging their beaks
Deep into his guts, and he could not beat them off.
For Tityos had raped Leto, a consort of Zeus,
As she went to Pytho through lovely Panopeus.

And I saw Tantalus there in his agony,
Standing in a pool with water up to his chin.
He was mad with thirst, but unable to drink,
For every time the old man bent over
The water would drain away and vanish,
Dried up by some god, and only black mud
Would be left at his feet. Above him dangled
Treetop fruits, pears and pomegranates,
Shiny apples, sweet figs, and luscious olives.
But whenever Tantalus reached up for them,
The wind tossed them high to the shadowy clouds.

And I saw Sisyphus there in his agony,
Pushing a monstrous stone with his hands.
Digging in hard, he would manage to shove it
To the crest of a hill, but just as he was about
To heave it over the top, the shameless stone
Would teeter back and bound down to the plain.

Then he would strain every muscle to push it back up,
Sweat pouring from his limbs and dusty head.

And then mighty Heracles loomed up before me—
His phantom that is, for Heracles himself
Feasts with the gods and has as his wife
Beautiful Hebe, daughter of great Zeus
And gold-sandaled Hera. As he moved
A clamor arose from the dead around him,
As if they were birds flying off in terror.
He looked like midnight itself. He held his bow
With an arrow on the string, and he glared around him
As if he were always about to shoot. His belt,
A baldric of gold crossing his chest,
Was stark horror, a phantasmagoria
Of Bears, and wild Boars, and green-eyed Lions,
Of Battles, and Bloodshed, Murder and Mayhem.
May this be its maker's only masterpiece,
And may there never again be another like it.
Heracles recognized me at once,
And his words beat down on me like dark wings:

'Son of Laertes in the line of Zeus,
Crafty Odysseus—poor man, do you too
Drag out a wretched destiny
Such as I once bore under the rays of the sun?
I was a son of Zeus and grandson of Cronus,
But I had immeasurable suffering,
Enslaved to a man who was far less than I
And who laid upon me difficult labors.
Once he even sent me here, to fetch
The Hound of Hell, for he could devise
No harder task for me than this. That hound
I carried out of the house of Hades,
With Hermes and grey-eyed Athena as guides.'

And Heracles went back into the house of Hades.
But I stayed where I was, in case any more
Of the heroes of yesteryear might yet come forth.
And I would have seen some of them—

Heroes I longed to meet, Theseus and Peirithous,
Glorious sons of the gods—but before I could,
The nations of the dead came thronging up
With an eerie cry, and I turned pale with fear
That Persephone would send from Hades' depths
The pale head of that monster, the Gorgon.

I went to the ship at once and called to my men
To get aboard and untie the stern cables.
They boarded quickly and sat at their benches.
The current bore the ship down the River Ocean.
We rowed at first, and then caught a good tailwind."

ODYSSEY 21

Owl-eyed Athena now prompted Penelope
To set before the suitors Odysseus' bow
And the grey iron, implements of the contest
And of their death.
Penelope climbed
The steep stairs to her bedroom and picked up
A beautiful bronze key with an ivory handle
And went with her maids to a remote storeroom
Where her husband's treasures lay—bronze, gold,
And wrought iron. And there lay the curved bow
And the quiver, still loaded with arrows,
Gifts which a friend of Odysseus had given him
When they met in Lacedaemon long ago.
This was Iphitus, Eurytus' son, a godlike man.
They had met in Messene, in the house of Ortilochus.
Odysseus had come to collect a debt
The Messenians owed him: three hundred sheep
They had taken from Ithaca in a sea raid,
And the shepherds with them. Odysseus
Had come to get them back, a long journey
For a young man, sent by his father and elders.
Iphitus had come to search for twelve mares
He had lost, along with the mules they were nursing.
These mares turned out to be the death of Iphitus
When he came to the house of Heracles,
Zeus' tough-hearted son, who killed him,
Guest though he was, without any regard
For the gods' wrath or the table they had shared—
Killed the man and kept the strong-hoofed mares.

It was while looking for these mares that Iphitus
Met Odysseus and gave him the bow
Which old Eurytus had carried and left to his son.
Odysseus gave him a sword and spear
To mark the beginning of their friendship
But before they had a chance to entertain each other
Zeus' son killed Iphitus, son of Eurytus,
A man like the gods. Odysseus did not take
The bow with him on his black ship to Troy.
It lay at home as a memento of his friend,
And Odysseus carried it only on Ithaca.

Penelope came to the storeroom
And stepped onto the oak threshold
Which a carpenter in the old days had planed,
Leveled, and then fitted with doorposts
And polished doors. Lovely in the half-light,
She quickly loosened the thong from the hook,
Drove home the key and shot back the bolts.
The doors bellowed like a bull in a meadow
And flew open before her. Stepping through,
She climbed onto a high platform that held chests
Filled with fragrant clothes. She reached up
And took the bow, case and all, from its peg,
Then sat down and laid the gleaming case on her knees
Her eyes welling with tears. Then she opened the case
And took out her husband's bow. When she had her fill
Of weeping, she went back to the hall
And the lordly suitors, bearing in her hands
The curved bow and the quiver loaded
With whining arrows. Two maidservants
Walked beside her, carrying a wicker chest
Filled with the bronze and iron gear her husband
Once used for this contest. When the beautiful woman
Reached the crowded hall, she stood
In the doorway flanked by her maidservants.
Then, covering her face with her shining veil,
Penelope spoke to her suitors:

"Hear me, proud suitors. You have used this house

For an eternity now—to eat and drink
In its master's absence, nor could you offer
Any excuse except your lust to marry me.
Well, your prize is here, and this is the contest.
I set before you the great bow of godlike Odysseus.
Whoever bends this bow and slips the string on its notch
And shoots an arrow through all twelve axes,
With him will I go, leaving behind this house
I was married in, this beautiful, prosperous house,
Which I will remember always, even in my dreams."

Penelope said this, and then ordered Eumaeus
To set out for the suitors the bow and grey iron.
All in tears, Eumaeus took them and laid them down,
And the cowherd wept, too, when he saw
His master's bow. Antinous scoffed at them both:

"You stupid yokels! You can't see farther than your own noses.
What a pair! Disturbing the lady with your bawling.
She's sad enough already because she's lost her husband.
Either sit here in silence or go outside to weep,
And leave the bow behind for us suitors. This contest
Will separate the men from the boys. It won't be easy
To string that polished bow. There is no man here
Such as Odysseus was. I know. I saw him myself
And remember him well, though I was still a child."

So Antinous said, hoping in his heart
That he would string the bow first and shoot an arrow
Through the iron. But the only arrow
He would touch first would be the one shot
Into his throat from the hands of Odysseus,
The man he himself was dishonoring
While inciting his comrades to do the same.

And then Telemachus, with a sigh of disgust:

"Look at me! Zeus must have robbed me of my wits.
My dear mother declares, for all her good sense,
That she will marry another and abandon this house,

And all I do is laugh and think it is funny.
Well, come on, you suitors, here's your prize,
A woman the likes of whom does not exist
In all Achaea, or in sacred Pylos,
Nowhere in Argos or in Mycenae,
Or on Ithaca itself or on the dark mainland.
You all know this. Why should I praise my mother?
Let's get going. Don't start making excuses
To put off stringing the bow. We'll see what happens.
And I might give that bow a try myself.
If I string it and shoot an arrow through the axeheads,
It won't bother me so much that my honored mother
Is leaving this house and going off with another,
Because I would at least be left here as someone
Capable of matching his father's prowess."

With that he took off his scarlet cloak, stood up,
And unstrapped his sword from his shoulders.
Then he went to work setting up the axeheads,
First digging a long trench true to the line
To hold them in a row, and then tamping the earth
Around each one. Everyone was amazed
That he made such a neat job of it
When he had never seen it done before.
Then he went and took his stance on the threshold
And began to try the bow. Three times
He made it quiver as he strained to string it,
And three times he eased off, although in his heart
He yearned to draw that bow and shoot an arrow
Through the iron axeheads. And on his fourth try
He would have succeeded in muscling the string
Onto its notch, but Odysseus reined him in,
Signaling him to stop with an upward nod.
So Telemachus said for all to hear:

"I guess I'm going to be a weakling forever!
Or else I'm still too young and don't have the strength
To defend myself against an enemy.
But come on, all of you who are stronger than me—
Give the bow a try and let's settle this contest."

And he set the bow aside, propping it against
The polished, jointed door, and leaning the arrow
Against the beautiful latch. Then Telemachus
Sat down on the chair from which he had risen.

Antinous, Eupeithes' son, then said:

"All right. We go in order from left to right,
Starting from where the wine gets poured."

Everyone agreed with Antinous' idea.
First up was their soothsayer, Leodes,
Oenops' son. He always sat in the corner
By the wine-bowl, and he was the only one
Who loathed the way the suitors behaved.
He now carried the bow and the arrow
Onto the threshold, took his stance,
And tried to bend the bow and string it,
But his tender, unworn hands gave out,
And he said for all the suitors to hear:

"Friends, I'm not the man to string this bow.
Someone else can take it. I foresee it will rob
Many a young hero of the breath of life.
And that will be just as well, since it is far better
To die than live on and fall short of the goal
We gather here for, with high hopes day after day.
You might hope in your heart—you might yearn—
To marry Penelope, the wife of Odysseus,
But after you've tried this bow and seen what it's like,
Go woo some other Achaean woman
And try to win her with your gifts. And Penelope
Should just marry the highest bidder,
The man who is fated to be her husband."

And he set the bow aside, propping it against
The polished, jointed door, and leaning the arrow
Against the beautiful latch. Then
He sat down on the chair from which he had risen.
And Antinous heaped contempt upon him:

"What kind of thing is that to say, Leodes?
I'm not going to stand here and listen to this.
You think this bow is going rob some young heroes
Of life, just because you can't string it?
The truth is your mother didn't bear a son
Strong enough to shoot arrows from bows.
But there are others who will string it soon enough."

Then Antinous called to Melanthius, the goatherd:

"Get over here and start a fire, Melanthius,
And set by it a bench with a fleece over it,
And bring out a tub of lard from the pantry,
So we can grease the bow, and warm it up.
Then maybe we can finish this contest."

He spoke, and Melanthius quickly rekindled the fire
And placed by it a bench covered with a fleece
And brought out from the pantry a tub of lard
With which the young men limbered up the bow—
But they still didn't have the strength to string it.

Only Antinous and godlike Eurymachus,
The suitors' ringleaders—and their strongest—
Were still left in the contest.

Meanwhile,
Two other men had risen and left the hall—
The cowherd and swineherd—and Odysseus himself
Went out, too. When the three of them
Were outside the gates, Odysseus said softly:

"Cowherd and swineherd, I've been wondering
If I should tell you what I'm about to tell you now.
Let me ask you this. What would you do
If Odysseus suddenly showed up here
Out of the blue, just like that?
Would you side with the suitors or Odysseus?
Tell me how you stand."

And the cattle herder answered him:

"Father Zeus, if only this would come true!
Let him come back. Let some god guide him.
Then you would see what these hands could do."

And Eumaeus prayed likewise to all the gods
That Odysseus would return.

When Odysseus
Was sure of both these men, he spoke to them again:

"I am back, right here in front of you.
After twenty hard years I have returned to my home.
I know that only you two of all my slaves
Truly want me back. I have heard
None of the others pray for my return.
So this is my promise to you. If a god
Beats these proud suitors down for me,
I will give you each a wife, property,
And a house built near mine. You two shall be
Friends to me and brothers to Telemachus.
And look, so you can be sure of who I am,
Here's a clear sign, that scar from the wound
I got from a boar's tusk when I went long ago
To Parnassus with the sons of Autolycus."

And he pulled his rags aside from the scar.
When the two men had examined it carefully,
They threw their arms around Odysseus and wept,
And kept kissing his head and shoulders in welcome.
Odysseus kissed their heads and hands,
And the sun would have gone down on their weeping,
Had not Odysseus stopped them, saying:

"No more weeping and wailing now. Someone might come
Out of the hall and see us and tell those inside.
We'll go back in now—not together, one at a time.
I'll go first, and then you. And here's what to watch for.
None of the suitors will allow the bow and quiver

To be given to me. It'll be up to you, Eumaeus,
To bring the bow over and place it in my hands.
Then tell the women to lock the doors to their hall,
And if they hear the sound of men groaning
Or being struck, tell them not to rush out
But to sit still and do their work in silence.
Philoetius, I want you to bar the courtyard gate
And secure it quickly with a piece of rope."

With this, Odysseus entered his great hall
And sat down on the chair from which he had risen.
Then the two herdsmen entered separately.

Eurymachus was turning the bow
Over and over in his hands, warming it
On this side and that by the fire, but even so
He was unable to string it. His pride hurt,
Shoulders sagging, he groaned and then swore:

"Damn it! It's not just myself I'm sorry for,
But for all of us—and not for the marriage either.
That hurts, but there are plenty of other women,
Some here in Ithaca, some in other cities.
No, it's that we fall so short of Odysseus'
Godlike strength. We can't even string his bow!
We'll be laughed at for generations to come!"

Antinous, son of Eupeithes, answered him:

"That'll never happen, Eurymachus,
And you know it. Now look, today is a holiday
Throughout the land, a sacred feast
In honor of Apollo, the Archer God.
This is no time to be bending bows.
So just set it quietly aside for now.
As for the axes, why don't we leave them
Just as they are? No one is going to come
Into Odysseus' hall and steal those axes.
Now let's have the cupbearer start us off
So we can forget about the bow

And pour libations. Come morning,
We'll have Melanthius bring along
The best she-goats in all the herds,
So we can lay prime thigh-pieces
On the altar of Apollo, the Archer God,
And then finish this business with the bow."

Antinous' proposal carried the day.
The heralds poured water over everyone's hands,
And boys filled the mixing bowls up to the brim
And served out the wine, first pouring
A few drops into each cup for libation.
When they had poured out their libations
And drunk as much as they wanted, Odysseus
Spoke among them, his heart full of cunning:

"Hear me, suitors of the glorious queen—
And I address Eurymachus most of all,
And godlike Antinous, since his speech
Was right on the mark when he said that for now
You should stop the contest and leave everything
Up to the gods. Tomorrow the Archer God
Will give the victory to whomever he chooses.
But come, let me have the polished bow.
I want to see, here in this hall with you,
If my grip is still strong, and if I still have
Any power left in these gnarled arms of mine,
Or if my hard traveling has sapped all my strength."

They seethed with anger when they heard this,
Afraid that he would string the polished bow,
And Antinous addressed him contemptuously:

"You don't have an ounce of sense in you,
You miserable tramp. Isn't it enough
That we let you hang around with us,
Undisturbed, with a full share of the feast?
You even get to listen to what we say,
Which no other stranger, much less beggar, can do.
It's wine that's screwing you up, as it does

104

Anyone who guzzles it down. It was wine
That deluded the great centaur, Eurytion,
In the hall of Peirithous, the Lapith hero.
Eurytion got blind-drunk and in his madness
Did a terrible thing in Peirithous' house.
The enraged Lapiths sliced off his nose and ears
And dragged him outside, and Eurytion
Went off in a stupor, mutilated and muddled.
Men and centaurs have been at odds ever since.
Eurytion hurt himself because he got drunk.
And you're going to get hurt, too, I predict,
Hurt badly, if you string the bow. No one
In all the land will show you any kindness.
We'll send you off in a black ship to Echetus,
Who maims them all. You'll never get out alive.
So just be quiet and keep on drinking,
And don't challenge men who are younger than you."

It was Penelope who answered Antinous:

"It is not good, or just, Antinous,
To cheat any of Telemachus' guests
Who come to this house. Do you think
That if this stranger proves strong enough
To string Odysseus' bow, he will then
Lead me to his home and make me his wife?
I can't imagine that he harbors this hope.
So do not ruin your feast on that account.
The very idea is preposterous."

Eurymachus responded to this:

"Daughter of Icarius, wise Penelope,
Of course it's preposterous that this man
Would marry you. That's not what we're worried about.
But we are embarrassed at what men—and women—will say:
'A bunch of weaklings were wooing the wife
Of a man they couldn't touch—they couldn't even string
His polished bow. Then along came a vagrant
Who strung it easily and shot through the iron.'

That's what they'll say, to our lasting shame."

And Penelope, her eyes narrowing:

"Eurymachus, men who gobble up
The house of a prince cannot expect
To have a good reputation anywhere.
So there isn't any point in bringing up honor.
This stranger is a very well-built man
And says he is the son of a noble father.
So give him the bow and let us see what happens.
And here is my promise to all of you.
If Apollo gives this man the glory
And he strings the bow, I will clothe him
In a fine cloak and tunic, and give him
A javelin to ward off dogs and men,
And a double-edged sword, and sandals
For his feet, and I will give him passage
To wherever his heart desires."

This time it was Telemachus who answered:

"As for the bow, Mother, no man alive
Has a stronger claim than I do to give it
To whomever I want, or to deny it—
No, none of the lords on rocky Ithaca
Nor on the islands over toward Elis,
None of them could force his will upon me,
Not even if I wanted to give this bow
Outright, case and arrows and all,
As a gift to the stranger.
Go to your rooms,
Mother, and take care of your work,
Spinning and weaving, and have the maids do theirs.
This bow is men's business, and my business
Especially, since I am the master of this house."

Penelope was stunned and turned to go,
Her son's masterful words pressed to her heart.
She went up the stairs to her room with her women

And wept for Odysseus, her beloved husband,
Until grey-eyed Athena cast sleep on her eyelids.

Downstairs, the noble swineherd was carrying
The curved bow across the hall. The suitors
Were in an uproar, and one of them called out:

"Where do you think you're going with that bow,
You miserable swineherd? You're out of line.
Go back to your pigsties, where your own dogs
Will wolf you down—a nice, lonely death—
If Apollo and the other gods smile upon us."

Afraid, the swineherd stopped in his tracks
And set the bow down. Men were yelling at him
All through the hall, and now Telemachus weighed in:

"Keep going with the bow. You'll regret it
If you try to obey everyone. I may be
Younger than you, but I'll chase you back
Into the country with a shower of stones.
I am stronger than you. I wish I were as strong
When it came to the suitors. I'd throw more than one
Out of here in a sorry state. They're all up to no good."

This got the suitors laughing hilariously
At Telemachus. The tension in the room eased,
And the swineherd carried the bow
Across to Odysseus and put it in his hands.
Then he called Eurycleia aside and said:

"Telemachus says you should lock the doors to the hall,
And if the women hear the sound of men groaning
Or being struck, tell them not to rush out
But to sit still and do their work in silence."

Eumaeus' words sank in, and Eurycleia
Locked the doors to the crowded hall.

Meanwhile, Philoetius left without a word
And barred the gates to the fenced courtyard.

Beside the portico there lay a ship's hawser
Made of papyrus. Philoetius used this
To secure the gates, and then he went back in,
Sat down on the chair from which he had risen,
And kept his eyes on Odysseus.

He was handling the bow, turning it over and over
And testing its flex to make sure that worms
Had not eaten the horn in its master's absence.
The suitors glanced at each other
And started to make sarcastic remarks:

"Ha! A real connoisseur, an expert in bows!"

"He must have one just like it in a case at home."

"Or plans to make one just like it, to judge by the way
The masterful tramp keeps turning it in his hands."

"May he have as much success in life
As he'll have in trying to string that bow."

Thus the suitors, while Odysseus, deep in thought,
Was looking over his bow. And then, effortlessly,

Like a musician stretching a string
Over a new peg on his lyre, and making
The twisted sheep-gut fast at either end,

Odysseus strung the great bow. Lifting it up,
He plucked the string, and it sang beautifully
Under his touch, with a note like a swallow's.
The suitors were aghast. The color drained
From their faces, and Zeus thundered loud,
Showing his portents and cheering the heart
Of the long-enduring, godlike Odysseus.
One arrow lay bare on the table. The rest,
Which the suitors were about to taste,
Were still in the quiver. Odysseus picked up
The arrow from the table and laid it upon

The bridge of the bow, and, still in his chair,
Drew the bowstring and the notched arrow back.
He took aim and let fly, and the bronze-tipped arrow
Passed clean through the holes of all twelve axeheads
From first to last. And he said to Telemachus:

"Well, Telemachus, the guest in your hall
Has not disgraced you. I did not miss my target,
Nor did I take all day in stringing the bow.
I still have my strength, and I'm not as the suitors
Make me out to be in their taunts and jeers.
But now it is time to cook these men's supper,
While it is still light outside, and after that,
We'll need some entertainment—music and song—
The finishing touches for a perfect banquet."

He spoke, and lowered his brows. Telemachus,
The true son of godlike Odysseus, slung on
His sharp sword, seized his spear, and gleaming in bronze
Took his place by his father's side.

ODYSSEY 23

The old woman laughed as she went upstairs
To tell her mistress that her husband was home.
She ran up the steps, lifting her knees high,
And, bending over Penelope, she said:

"Wake up, dear child, so you can see for yourself
What you have yearned for day in and day out.
Odysseus has come home, after all this time,
And has killed those men who tried to marry you
And who ravaged your house and bullied your son."

And Penelope, alert now and wary:

"Dear nurse, the gods have driven you crazy.
The gods can make even the wise mad,
Just as they often make the foolish wise.
Now they have wrecked your usually sound mind.
Why do you mock me and my sorrowful heart,
Waking me from sleep to tell me this nonsense—
And such a sweet sleep. It sealed my eyelids.
I haven't slept like that since the day Odysseus
Left for Ilion—that accursed city.
Now go back down to the hall.
If any of the others had told me this
And wakened me from sleep, I would have
Sent her back with something to be sorry about!
You can thank your old age for this at least."

And Eurycleia, the loyal nurse:

"I am not mocking you, child. Odysseus
Really is here. He's come home, just as I say.
He's the stranger they all insulted in the great hall.
Telemachus has known all along, but had
The self-control to hide his father's plans
Until he could pay the arrogant bastards back."

Penelope felt a sudden pang of joy. She leapt
From her bed and flung her arms around the old woman,
And with tears in her eyes she said to her:

"Dear nurse, if it is true, if he really has
Come back to his house, tell me how
He laid his hands on the shameless suitors,
One man alone against all of that mob."

Eurycleia answered her:

"I didn't see and didn't ask. I only heard the groaning
Of men being killed. We women sat
In the far corner of our quarters, trembling,
With the good solid doors bolted shut
Until your son came from the hall to call me,
Telemachus. His father had sent him to call me.
And there he was, Odysseus, standing
In a sea of dead bodies, all piled
On top of each other on the hard-packed floor.
It would have warmed your heart to see him,
Spattered with blood and filth like a lion.
And now the bodies are all gathered together
At the gates, and he is purifying the house
With sulfur, and has built a great fire,
And has sent me to call you. Come with me now
So that both your hearts can be happy again.
You have suffered so much, but now
Your long desire has been fulfilled.
He has come himself, alive, to his own hearth,
And has found you and his son in the hall.
As for the suitors, who did him wrong,
He's taken his revenge on every last man."

And Penelope, ever cautious:

"Dear nurse, don't gloat over them yet.
You know how welcome the sight of him
Would be to us all, and especially to me
And the son he and I bore. But this story
Can't be true, not the way you tell it.
One of the immortals must have killed the suitors,
Angry at their arrogance and evil deeds.
They respected no man, good or bad,
So their blind folly has killed them. But Odysseus
Is lost, lost to us here, and gone forever."

And Eurycleia, the faithful nurse:

"Child, how can you say this? Your husband
Is here at his own fireside, and yet you are sure
He will never come home! Always on guard!
But here's something else, clear proof:
The scar he got from the tusk of that boar.
I noticed it when I was washing his feet
And wanted to tell you, but he shrewdly clamped
His hand on my mouth and wouldn't let me speak.
Just come with me, and I will stake my life on it.
If I am lying you can torture me to death."

Still wary, Penelope replied:

"Dear nurse, it is hard for you to comprehend
The ways of the eternal gods, wise as you are.
Still, let us go to my son, so that I may see
The suitors dead and the man who killed them."

And Penelope descended the stairs, her heart
In turmoil. Should she hold back and question
Her husband? Or should she go up to him,
Embrace him, and kiss his hands and head?
She entered the hall, crossing the stone threshold,
And sat opposite Odysseus, in the firelight
Beside the farther wall. He sat by a column,

Looking down, waiting to see if his incomparable wife
Would say anything to him when she saw him.
She sat a long time in silence, wondering.
She would look at his face and see her husband,
But then fail to know him in his dirty rags.
Telemachus couldn't take it any more:

"Mother, how can you be so hard,
Holding back like that? Why don't you sit
Next to father and talk to him, ask him things?
No other woman would have the heart
To stand off from her husband who has come back
After twenty hard years to his country and home.
But your heart is always colder than stone."

And Penelope, cautious as ever:

"My child, I am lost in wonder
And unable to speak or ask a question
Or look him in the eyes. If he really is
Odysseus come home, the two of us
Will be sure of each other, very sure.
There are secrets between us no one else knows."

Odysseus, who had borne much, smiled,
And his words flew to his son on wings:

"Telemachus, let your mother test me
In our hall. She will soon see more clearly.
Now, because I am dirty and wearing rags,
She is not ready to acknowledge who I am.
But you and I have to devise a plan.
When someone kills just one man,
Even a man who has few to avenge him,
He goes into exile, leaving country and kin.
Well, we have killed a city of young men,
The flower of Ithaca. Think about that."

And Telemachus, in his clear-headed way:

"You should think about it, Father. They say
No man alive can match you for cunning.
We'll follow you for all we are worth,
And I don't think we'll fail for lack of courage."

And Odysseus, the master strategist:

"Well, this is what I think we should do.
First, bathe yourselves and put on clean tunics
And tell the women to choose their clothes well.
Then have the singer pick up his lyre
And lead everyone in a lively dance tune,
Loud and clear. Anyone who hears the sound,
A passerby or neighbor, will think it's a wedding,
And so word of the suitors' killing won't spread
Down through the town before we can reach
Our woodland farm. Once there we'll see
What kind of luck the Olympian gives us."

They did as he said. The men bathed
And put on tunics, and the women dressed up.
The godlike singer, sweeping his hollow lyre,
Put a song in their hearts and made their feet move,
And the great hall resounded under the tread
Of men and silken-waisted women dancing.
And people outside would hear it and say:

"Well, someone has finally married the queen,
Fickle woman. Couldn't bear to keep the house
For her true husband until he came back."

But they had no idea how things actually stood.

Odysseus, meanwhile, was being bathed
By the housekeeper, Eurynome. She
Rubbed him with olive oil and threw about him
A beautiful cloak and tunic. And Athena
Shed beauty upon him, and made him look
Taller and more muscled, and made his hair
Tumble down his head like hyacinth flowers.

Imagine a craftsman overlaying silver
With pure gold. He has learned his art
From Pallas Athena and Lord Hephaestus,
And creates works of breathtaking beauty.

So Athena herself made his head and shoulders
Shimmer with grace. He came from the bath
Like a god, and sat down on the chair again
Opposite his wife, and spoke to her and said:

"You're a mysterious woman.
The gods
Have given to you, more than to any
Other woman, an unyielding heart.
No other woman would be able to endure
Standing off from her husband, come back
After twenty hard years to his country and home.
Nurse, make up a bed for me so I can lie down
Alone, since her heart is a cold lump of iron."

And Penelope, cautious and wary:

"You're a mysterious man.
I am not being proud
Or scornful, nor am I bewildered—not at all.
I know very well what you looked like
When you left Ithaca on your long-oared ship.
Nurse, bring the bed out from the master bedroom,
The bedstead he made himself, and spread it for him
With fleeces and blankets and silky coverlets."

She was testing her husband.
Odysseus
Could bear no more, and he cried out to his wife:

"By God, woman, now you've cut deep.
Who moved my bed? It would be hard
For anyone, no matter how skilled, to move it.
A god could come down and move it easily,
But not a man alive, however young and strong,

Could ever pry it up. There's something telling
About how that bed's built, and no one else
Built it but me.
There was an olive tree
Growing on the site, long-leaved and full,
Its trunk thick as a post. I built my bedroom
Around that tree, and when I had finished
The masonry walls and done the roofing
And set in the jointed, close-fitting doors,
I lopped off all of the olive's branches,
Trimmed the trunk from the root on up,
And rounded it and trued it with an adze until
I had myself a bedpost. I bored it with an auger,
And starting from this I framed up the whole bed,
Inlaying it with gold and silver and ivory
And stretching across it oxhide thongs dyed purple.
So there's our secret. But I do not know, woman,
Whether my bed is still firmly in place, or if
Some other man has cut through the olive's trunk."

At this, Penelope finally let go.
Odysseus had shown he knew their old secret.
In tears, she ran straight to him, threw her arms
Around him, kissed his face, and said:

"Don't be angry with me, Odysseus. You,
Of all men, know how the world goes.
It is the gods who gave us sorrow, the gods
Who begrudged us a life together, enjoying
Our youth and arriving side by side
To the threshold of old age. Don't hold it against me
That when I first saw you I didn't welcome you
As I do now. My heart has been cold with fear
That an imposter would come and deceive me.
There are many who scheme for ill-gotten gains.
Not even Helen, daughter of Zeus,
Would have slept with a foreigner had she known
The Greeks would go to war to bring her back home.
It was a god who drove her to that dreadful act,
Or she never would have thought of doing what she did,

The horror that brought suffering to us as well.
But now, since you have confirmed the secret
Of our marriage bed, which no one has ever seen—
Only you and I and a single servant, Actor's daughter,
Whom my father gave me before I ever came here
And who kept the doors of our bridal chamber—
You have persuaded even my stubborn heart."

This brought tears from deep within him,
And as he wept he clung to his beloved wife.

Land is a welcome sight to men swimming
For their lives, after Poseidon has smashed their ship
In heavy seas. Only a few of them escape
And make it to shore. They come out
Of the grey water crusted with brine, glad
To be alive and set foot on dry land.

So welcome a sight was her husband to her.
She would not loosen her white arms from his neck,
And rose-fingered Dawn would have risen
On their weeping, had not Athena stepped in
And held back the long night at the end of its course
And stopped gold-stitched Dawn at Ocean's shores
From yoking the horses that bring light to men,
Lampus and Phaethon, the colts of Dawn.

Then Odysseus said to his wife:

"We have not yet come to the end of our trials.
There is still a long, hard task for me to complete,
As the spirit of Tiresias foretold to me
On the day I went down to the house of Hades
To ask him about my companions' return
And my own. But come to bed now,
And we'll close our eyes in the pleasure of sleep."

And Penelope calmly answered him:

"Your bed is ready for you whenever

ODYSSEY 24

Hermes, meanwhile, was calling forth
The ghosts of the suitors. He held the wand
He uses to charm mortal eyes to sleep
And make sleepers awake; and with this beautiful,
Golden wand he marshaled the ghosts,
Who followed along squeaking and gibbering.

Bats deep inside an eerie cave
Flit and gibber when one of them falls
From the cluster clinging to the rock overhead.

So too these ghosts, as Hermes led them
Down the cold, dank ways, past
The streams of Ocean, past the White Rock,
Past the Gates of the Sun and the Land of Dreams,
Until they came to the Meadow of Asphodel,
Where the spirits of the dead dwell, phantoms
Of men outworn.

Here was the ghost of Achilles,
And those of Patroclus, of flawless Antilochus,
And of Ajax, the best of the Achaeans
After Achilles, Peleus' incomparable son.
These ghosts gathered around Achilles
And were joined by the ghost of Agamemnon,
Son of Atreus, grieving, he himself surrounded
By the ghosts of those who had died with him
And met their fate in the house of Aegisthus.
The son of Peleus was the first to greet him:

"Son of Atreus, we believed that you of all heroes
Were dear to thundering Zeus your whole life through,
For you were the lord of the great army at Troy,
Where we Greeks endured a bitter campaign.
But you too had an early rendezvous with death,
Which no man can escape once he is born.
How much better to have died at Troy
With all the honor you commanded there!
The entire Greek army would have raised you a tomb,
And you would have won glory for your son as well.
As it was, you were doomed to a most pitiable death."

And the ghost of Agamemnon answered:

"Godlike Achilles, you did have the good fortune
To die in Troy, far from Argos. Around you fell
Some of the best Greeks and Trojans of their time,
Fighting for your body, as you lay there
In the howling dust of war, one of the great,
Your horsemanship forgotten. We fought all day
And would never have stopped, had not Zeus
Halted us with a great storm. Then we bore your body
Back to the ships and laid it on a bier, and cleansed
Your beautiful flesh with warm water and ointments,
And the men shed many hot tears and cut their hair.
Then your mother heard, and she came from the sea
With her saltwater women, and an eerie cry
Rose over the deep. The troops panicked,
And they would have run for the ships, had not
A man who was wise in the old ways stopped them,
Nestor, whose counsel had prevailed before.
Full of concern, he called out to the troops:

'Argives and Achaeans, halt! This is no time to flee.
It is his mother, with her immortal nymphs,
Come from the sea to mourn her dead son.'

"When he said that the troops settled down.
Then the daughters of the Old Man of the Sea
Stood all around you and wailed piteously,

And they dressed you in immortal clothing.
And the Muses, all nine, chanted the dirge,
Singing responsively in beautiful voices.
You couldn't have seen a dry eye in the army,
So poignant was the song of the Muses.
For seventeen days we mourned you like that,
Men and gods together. On the eighteenth day
We gave you to the fire, slaughtering sheep
And horned cattle around you. You were burned
In the clothing of the gods, with rich unguents
And sweet honey, and many Greek heroes
Paraded in arms around your burning pyre,
Both infantry and charioteers,
And the sound of their marching rose to heaven.
When the fire had consumed you,
We gathered your white bones at dawn, Achilles,
And laid them in unmixed wine and unguents.
Your mother had given us a golden urn,
A gift of Dionysus, she said, made by Hephaestus.
In this urn lie your white bones, Achilles,
Mingled with those of the dead Patroclus.
Just apart lie the bones of Antilochus
Whom you honored most after Patroclus died.
Over them all we spearmen of the great army
Heaped an immense and perfect barrow
On a headland beside the broad Hellespont
So that it might be seen from far out at sea
By men now and men to come.
Your mother, Thetis,
Had collected beautiful prizes from the gods
And now set them down in the middle of the field
To honor the best of the Achaean athletes.
You have been to many heroes' funeral games
Where young men contend for prizes,
But you would have marveled at the sight
Of the beautiful prizes silver-footed Thetis
Set out for you. You were very dear to the gods.
Not even in death have you lost your name,
Achilles, nor your honor among men.
But what did I get for winding up the war?

Zeus worked out for me a ghastly death
At the hands of Aegisthus and my murderous wife."

As these two heroes talked with each other,
Quicksilver Hermes was leading down
The ghosts of the suitors killed by Odysseus.
When Hermes and these ghosts drew near,
The two heroes were amazed and went up to see
Who they were. The ghost of Agamemnon
Recognized one of them, Amphimedon,
Who had been his host in Ithaca, and called out:

"Amphimedon! Why have you come down
Beneath the dark earth, you and your company,
All men of rank, all the same age? It's as if
Someone had hand-picked the city's best men.
Did Poseidon sink your ships and drown you
In the wind-whipped waves? Was it that, or
Did an enemy destroy you on land
As you cut off their cattle and flocks of sheep—
Or as they fought for their city and women?
Tell me. Remember who is asking—
An old friend of your house. I came there
With godlike Menelaus to urge Odysseus
To sail with the fleet to Ilion. A full month
That journey to Ithaca took us—hard work
Persuading Odysseus, destroyer of cities."

The ghost of Amphimedon responded:

"Son of Atreus, most glorious Agamemnon,
I remember all that, just as you tell it,
And I will tell you exactly what happened to us,
And how it ended in our bitter death.
We were courting the wife of Odysseus,
Long gone by then. She loathed the thought
Of remarrying, but she wouldn't give us a yes or no.
Her mind was bent on death and darkness for us.
Here is one of the tricks she dreamed up:
She set up a loom in the hall and started weaving—

114

A huge, fine-threaded piece—and then came out and said:

'Young men—my suitors, since Odysseus is dead—
Eager as you are to marry me, you must wait
Until I finish this robe—it would be a shame
To waste my spinning—a shroud for the hero
Laertes, when death's doom lays him low.
I fear the Achaean women would reproach me
If he should lie shroudless for all his wealth.'

"We went along with this appeal to our honor.
Every day she would weave at the great loom,
And every night she would unweave by torchlight.
She fooled us for three years with her craft.
But in the fourth year, as the seasons rolled by,
And the moons waned, and the days dragged on,
One of her women who knew all about it
Told us, and we caught her unweaving
The gloried shroud. Then we forced her to finish it.
When it was done she washed it and showed it to us,
And it shone like the sun or the moon.
It was then
That some evil spirit brought Odysseus
From who knows where to the border of his land,
Where the swineherd lived. Odysseus' son
Put in from Pylos in his black ship and joined him.
These two, after they had plotted an ugly death
For the suitors, came up to the town, first Telemachus
And then later Odysseus, led by the swineherd,
Who brought his master wearing tattered clothes,
Looking for all the world like a miserable old beggar,
Leaning on a staff, his rags hanging off him.
None of us could know who he was, not even
The older men, when he showed up like that.
We threw things at him and gave him a hard time.
He just took it, pelted and taunted in his own house,
Until, prompted by Zeus, he and Telemachus
Removed all the weapons from the hall
And locked them away in a storeroom.
Then he showed all his cunning. He told his wife

To set before the suitors his bow and grey iron—
Implements for a contest, and for our ill-fated death.
None of us were able to string that bow.
We couldn't even come close. When it came
Around to Odysseus, we cried out and objected,
'Don't give the bow to that beggar,
No matter what he says!' Telemachus alone
Urged him on and encouraged him to take it.
And he did. The great Odysseus
Took the bow, strung it easily, and shot an arrow
Straight through the iron. Then he stood on the threshold,
Poured the arrows out, and glaring around him
He shot Lord Antinous. And then he shot others,
With perfect aim, and we fell thick and fast.
You could see that some god was helping them,
The way they raged through the hall, cutting us down
Right and left; and you could hear
The hideous groans of men as their heads
Were bashed in. The floor smoked with blood.
        That's how we died, Agamemnon. Our bodies
Still lie uncared for in Odysseus' halls.
Word has not yet reached our friends and family,
Who could wash the black blood from our wounds
And lay us out with wailing, as is due the dead."

And the ghost of Agamemnon responded:

"Well done, Odysseus, Laertes' wily son!
You won a wife of great character
In Icarius' daughter. What a mind she has,
A woman beyond reproach! How well Penelope
Kept in her heart her husband, Odysseus.
And so her virtue's fame will never perish,
And the gods will make among men on earth
A song of praise for steadfast Penelope.
But Tyndareus' daughter was evil to the core,
Killing her own husband, and her song will be
A song of scorn, bringing ill-repute
To all women, even the virtuous."

PRINCETON MODERN GREEK STUDIES

This series is sponsored by the Princeton University Program
in Hellenic Studies under the auspices of the
Stanley J. Seeger Hellenic Fund

Firewalking and Religious Healing: The Anastenaria of Greece and the American Firewalking Movement by Loring M. Danforth

Kazantzakis: Politics of the Spirit by Peter Bien

Dance and the Body Politic in Northern Greece by Jane K. Cowan

Contested Identities: Gender and Kinship in Modern Greece edited by Peter Loizos and Evthymios Papataxiarchis

Yannis Ritsos: Repetitions, Testimonies, Parentheses translated and edited by Edmund Keeley

Demons and the Devil: Moral Imagination in Modern Greek Culture by Charles Stewart

A Place in History: Social and Monumental Time in a Cretan Town by Michael Herzfeld

The Enlightenment as Social Criticism: Iosipos Moisiodax and Greek Culture in the Eighteenth Century by Paschalis M. Kitromilides

C. P. Cavafy: Collected Poems translated by Edmund Keeley & Philip Sherrard: edited by George Savidis

C.P. CAVAFY

COLLECTED POEMS

translated by

Edmund Keeley and Philip Sherrard

edited by

George Savidis

REVISED EDITION

PRINCETON UNIVERSITY PRESS

PRINCETON, NEW JERSEY

Published by Princeton University Press, 41 William Street, Princeton, New Jersey 08540

Library of Congress Cataloging-in-Publication Data

Cavafy, Constantine, 1863–1933.
[Poems. English]
Collected poems / C. P. Cavafy; translated by Edmund Keeley and Philip Sherrard; edited by George Savidis.—Rev. ed.
p. cm.—(Princeton modern Greek studies)
(Lockert library of poetry in translation)
Includes index.
ISBN 0-691-06984-0 (Cl)—ISBN 0-691-01537-6 (Pb)
I. Cavafy, Constantine, 1863–1933—Translations into English. I. Keeley, Edmund. II. Sherrard, Philip. III. Savvidēs, Geōrgios P. IV. Title. V. Series. VI. Series: Lockert library of poetry in translation
PA5610.K2A24 1992 889'.132—dc20 92-1198

The Lockert Library of Poetry in Translation is supported by a bequest from Charles Lacy Lockert (1888–1974)

This book has been composed in Linotron Times Roman

Eleventh printing, for the revised edition, 1992

Princeton University Press books are printed on acid-free paper and meet the guidelines for permanence and durability of the Committee on Production Guidelines for Book Longevity of the Council on Library Resources

Printed in the United States of America

13 15 17 19 20 18 16 14 12

(Pbk.)

Translations included in this volume have appeared, either in earlier or current versions, in The New Yorker, The New York Review of Books, Quarterly Review of Literature, The Nation, Evergreen Review, Antaeus, The Dutton Review, University, New Letters, Shenandoah, Boundary 2, The Malahat Review, The Nassau Lit, Arion's Dolphin, Granite *and* Poetry *("The Footsteps," "The Ides of March," "Theodotos"),*

Edmund Keeley is indebted to the John Simon Guggenheim Memorial Foundation for a fellowship that assisted his work on this volume

In memory of our friend

George Seferis

who also loved Cavafy's poems

ITHAKA

As you set out for Ithaka
hope the voyage is a long one,
full of adventure, full of discovery.
Laistrygonians and Cyclops,
angry Poseidon—don't be afraid of them:
you'll never find things like that on your way
as long as you keep your thoughts raised high,
as long as a rare excitement
stirs your spirit and your body.
Laistrygonians and Cyclops,
wild Poseidon—you won't encounter them
unless you bring them along inside your soul,
unless your soul sets them up in front of you.

Hope the voyage is a long one.
May there be many a summer morning when,
with what pleasure, what joy,
you come into harbors seen for the first time;
may you stop at Phoenician trading stations
to buy fine things,
mother of pearl and coral, amber and ebony,
sensual perfume of every kind—
as many sensual perfumes as you can;
and may you visit many Egyptian cities
to gather stores of knowledge from their scholars.

Keep Ithaka always in your mind.
Arriving there is what you are destined for.
But do not hurry the journey at all.
Better if it lasts for years,
so you are old by the time you reach the island,
wealthy with all you have gained on the way,
not expecting Ithaka to make you rich.

Ithaka gave you the marvelous journey.
Without her you would not have set out.
She has nothing left to give you now.

And if you find her poor, Ithaka won't have fooled you.
Wise as you will have become, so full of experience,
you will have understood by then what these Ithakas mean.

BY JOSEPH BRODSKY

Elegy for John Donne and Other Poems
Selected Poems
A Part of Speech
Less Than One
To Urania
Marbles
Watermark
On Grief and Reason

A PART OF SPEECH

JOSEPH BRODSKY

The Noonday Press
Farrar, Straus and Giroux
New York

122

*Published in Canada by HarperCollins*CanadaLtd
*Printed in the United States of America
First edition, 1980
Eighth printing, 1996*

*Library of Congress Cataloging in Publication Data
Brodskiĭ, Iosif / A part of speech.
Translation of Chast' rechi.
Includes bibliographical references.
I. Title.
PG3479.4.R64C4513 1980 891.71'44 80-613*

Some of these poems first appeared, in somewhat different form, in *The New Yorker*, *The New York Review of Books*, *Bananas*, *Confrontation*, *The Iowa Review*, *The Kenyon Review*, *The Los Angeles Times*, *Paintbrush*, and *Vogue*.
Grateful acknowledgment is made for permission to reprint from: *Kontinent* edited by Vladimir Maximov, Doubleday & Co., Inc., translation © 1976 by André Deutsch Limited and Doubleday & Co., Inc.; *Joseph Brodsky: Selected Poems*, translated by George L. Kline, Harper & Row, Publishers, Inc., translation and introduction © 1973 by George L. Kline; *The Mind-Reader* by Richard Wilbur, Harcourt Brace Jovanovich, Inc., translation © 1975 by Richard Wilbur

*The text of this book was developed with
the editorial counsel of Barry Rubin*

To my mother and father

Odysseus to Telemachus

My dear Telemachus,
                                        The Trojan War
is over now; I don't recall who won it.
The Greeks, no doubt, for only they would leave
so many dead so far from their own homeland.
But still, my homeward way has proved too long.
While we were wasting time there, old Poseidon,
it almost seems, stretched and extended space.

I don't know where I am or what this place
can be. It would appear some filthy island,
with bushes, buildings, and great grunting pigs.
A garden choked with weeds; some queen or other.
Grass and huge stones . . . Telemachus, my son!
To a wanderer the faces of all islands
resemble one another. And the mind
trips, numbering waves; eyes, sore from sea horizons,
run; and the flesh of water stuffs the ears.
I can't remember how the war came out;
even how old you are—I can't remember.

Grow up, then, my Telemachus, grow strong.
Only the gods know if we'll see each other
again. You've long since ceased to be that babe
before whom I reined in the plowing bullocks.
Had it not been for Palamedes' trick
we two would still be living in one household.
But maybe he was right; away from me
you are quite safe from all Oedipal passions,
and your dreams, my Telemachus, are blameless.

1972 / Translated by George L. Kline

THE COMPLETE GREEK TRAGEDIES

Edited by David Grene and Richmond Lattimore

EURIPIDES · III

HECUBA

Translated by William Arrowsmith

ANDROMACHE

Translated by John Frederick Nims

THE TROJAN WOMEN

Translated by Richmond Lattimore

ION

Translated by Ronald Frederick Willetts

THE UNIVERSITY OF CHICAGO PRESS

CHICAGO & LONDON

The University of Chicago Press, Chicago 60637
The University of Chicago Press, Ltd., London

Printed in the United States of America

International Standard Book Number: 0-226-30782-4
Library of Congress Catalog Card Number: 55-5787

00 99 98 97 96 95 94 93 92 91 90 16 17 18 19 20 21 22 23

TABLE OF CONTENTS

THE TROJAN WOMEN

CHARACTERS

Poseidon

Athene

Hecuba

Talthybius

Cassandra

Andromache

Astyanax

Menelaus

Helen

Chorus of Trojan women

THE TROJAN WOMEN

SCENE: *The action takes place shortly after the capture of Troy. All Trojan men have been killed, or have fled; all women and children are captives. The scene is an open space before the city, which is visible in the background, partly demolished and smoldering. Against the walls are tents, or huts, which temporarily house the captive women. The entrance of the Chorus is made, in two separate groups which subsequently unite, from these buildings, as are those of Cassandra and Helen. The entrances of Talthybius, Andromache, and Menelaus are made from the wings. It is imaginable that the gods are made to appear high up, above the level of the other actors, as if near their own temples on the Citadel. As the play opens, Hecuba is prostrate on the ground (it is understood that she hears nothing of what the gods say).*

(*Enter Poseidon.*)

Poseidon

I am Poseidon. I come from the Aegean depths
of the sea beneath whose waters Nereid choirs evolve
the intricate bright circle of their dancing feet.
For since that day when Phoebus Apollo and I laid down
on Trojan soil the close of these stone walls, drawn true
and straight, there has always been affection in my heart
unfading, for these Phrygians and for their city;
which smolders now, fallen before the Argive spears,
ruined, sacked, gutted. Such is Athene's work, and his,
the Parnassian, Epeius of Phocis, architect
and builder of the horse that swarmed with inward steel,
that fatal bulk which passed within the battlements,
whose fame hereafter shall be loud among men unborn,
the Wooden Horse, which hid the secret spears within.
Now the gods' groves are desolate, their thrones of power
blood-spattered where beside the lift of the altar steps
of Zeus Defender, Priam was cut down and died.

The ships of the Achaeans load with spoils of Troy
now, the piled gold of Phrygia. And the men of Greece
who made this expedition and took the city, stay
only for the favoring stern-wind now to greet their wives
and children after ten years' harvests wasted here.

The will of Argive Hera and Athene won
its way against my will. Between them they broke Troy.
So I must leave my altars and great Ilium,
since once a city sinks into sad desolation
the gods' state sickens also, and their worship fades.
Scamander's valley echoes to the wail of slaves,
the captive women given to their masters now,
some to Arcadia or the men of Thessaly
assigned, or to the lords of Athens, Theseus' strain;
while all the women of Troy yet unassigned are here
beneath the shelter of these walls, chosen to wait
the will of princes, and among them Tyndareus' child
Helen of Sparta, named—with right—a captive slave.

Nearby, beside the gates, for any to look upon
who has the heart, she lies face upward, Hecuba
weeping for multitudes her multitude of tears.
Polyxena, one daughter, even now was killed
in secrecy and pain beside Achilles' tomb.
Priam is gone, their children dead; one girl is left,
Cassandra, reeling crazed at King Apollo's stroke,
whom Agamemnon, in despite of the gods' will
and all religion, will lead by force to his secret bed.

O city, long ago a happy place, good-bye;
good-bye, hewn bastions. Pallas, child of Zeus, did this.
But for her hatred, you might stand strong-founded still.

(*Athene enters.*)

Athene

August among the gods, O vast divinity,
closest in kinship to the father of all, may one
who quarreled with you in the past make peace, and speak?

Poseidon

You may, lady Athene; for the strands of kinship
close drawn work no weak magic to enchant the mind.

Athene

I thank you for your gentleness, and bring you now
questions whose issue touches you and me, my lord.

Poseidon

Is this the annunciation of some new word spoken
by Zeus, or any other of the divinities?

Athene

No; but for Troy's sake, on whose ground we stand, I come
to win the favor of your power, and an ally.

Poseidon

You hated Troy once; did you throw your hate away
and change to pity now its walls are black with fire?

Athene

Come back to the question. Will you take counsel with me
and help me gladly in all that I would bring to pass?

Poseidon

I will indeed; but tell me what you wish to do.
Are you here for the Achaeans' or the Phrygians' sake?

Athene

For the Trojans, whom I hated this short time since,
to make the Achaeans' homecoming a thing of sorrow.

Poseidon

This is a springing change of sympathy. Why must
you hate too hard, and love too hard, your loves and hates?

Athene

Did you not know they outraged my temple, and shamed me?

Poseidon

I know that Ajax dragged Cassandra there by force.

Athene

And the Achaeans did nothing. They did not even speak.

Poseidon
Yet Ilium was taken by your strength alone.

Athene
True; therefore help me. I would do some evil to them.

Poseidon
I am ready for anything you ask. What will you do?

Athene
Make the home voyage a most unhappy coming home.

Poseidon
While they stay here ashore, or out on the deep sea?

Athene
When they take ship from Ilium and set sail for home
Zeus will shower down his rainstorms and the weariless beat
of hail, to make black the bright air with roaring winds.
He has promised my hand the gift of the blazing thunderbolt
to dash and overwhelm with fire the Achaean ships.
Yours is your own domain, the Aegaean crossing. Make
the sea thunder to the tripled wave and spinning surf,
cram thick the hollow Euboean fold with floating dead;
so after this Greeks may learn how to use with fear
my sacred places, and respect all gods beside.

Poseidon
This shall be done, and joyfully. It needs no long
discourse to tell you. I will shake the Aegaean Sea.
Myconos' nesses and the swine-back reefs of Delos,
the Capherean promontories, Scyros, Lemnos
shall take the washed up bodies of men drowned at sea.
Back to Olympus now, gather the thunderbolts
from your father's hands, then take your watcher's post, to wait
the chance, when the Achaean fleet puts out to sea.

That mortal who sacks fallen cities is a fool,
who gives the temples and the tombs, the hallowed places
of the dead to desolation. His own turn must come.

(The gods leave the stage. Hecuba seems to waken, and gets slowly to her feet as she speaks.)

Hecuba
Rise, stricken head, from the dust;
lift up the throat. This is Troy, but Troy
and we, Troy's kings, are perished.
Stoop to the changing fortune.
Steer for the crossing and the death-god,
hold not life's prow on the course against
wave beat and accident.
Ah me,
what need I further for tears' occasion,
state perished, my sons, and my husband?
O massive pride that my fathers heaped
to magnificence, you meant nothing.
Must I be hushed? Were it better thus?
Should I cry a lament?
Unhappy, accursed,
limbs cramped, I lie
backed on earth's stiff bed.
O head, O temples
and sides; sweet, to shift,
let the tired spine rest
weight eased by the sides alternate,
against the strain of the tears' song
where the stricken people find music yet
in the song undanced of their wretchedness.

You ships' prows, that the fugitive
oars swept back to blessed Ilium
over the sea's blue water
by the placid harbors of Hellas
to the flute's grim beat
and the swing of the shrill boat whistles;
you made the crossing, made fast ashore
the Egyptians' skill, the sea cables,
alas, by the coasts of Troy;

it was you, ships, that carried the fatal bride
of Menelaus, Castor her brother's shame,
the stain on the Eurotas.
Now she has killed
the sire of the fifty sons,
Priam; me, unhappy Hecuba,
she drove on this reef of ruin.

Such state I keep
to sit by the tents of Agamemnon.
I am led captive
from my house, an old, unhappy woman,
like my city ruined and pitiful.
Come then, sad wives of the Trojans
whose spears were bronze,
their daughters, brides of disaster,
let us mourn the smoke of Ilium.
And I, as among winged birds
the mother, lead out
the clashing cry, the song; not that song
wherein once long ago,
when I held the scepter of Priam,
my feet were queens of the choir and led
the proud dance to the gods of Phrygia.

(The First Half-chorus comes out of the shelter at the back.)

First Half-chorus

Hecuba, what are these cries?
What news now? For through the walls
I heard your pitiful weeping.
and fear shivered in the breasts
of the Trojan women, who within
sob out the day of their slavery.

Hecuba

My children, the ships of the Argives
will move today. The hand is at the oar.

First Half-chorus

They will? Why? Must I take ship
so soon from the land of my fathers?

Hecuba

I know nothing. I look for disaster.

First Half-chorus

Alas!
Poor women of Troy, torn from your homes,
bent to forced hard work.
The Argives push for home.

Hecuba

Oh,
let her not come forth,
not now, my child
Cassandra, driven delirious
to shame us before the Argives;
not the mad one, to bring fresh pain to my pain.
Ah no.
Troy, ill-starred Troy, this is the end;
your last sad people leave you now,
still alive, and broken.

(The Second Half-chorus comes out of the shelter at the back.)

Second Half-chorus

Ah me. Shivering, I left the tents
of Agamemnon to listen.
Tell us, our queen. Did the Argive council
decree our death?
Or are the seamen manning the ships now,
oars ready for action?

Hecuba

My child, do not fear so. Lighten your heart.
But I go stunned with terror.

Second Half-chorus

Has a herald come from the Danaans yet?
Whose wretched slave shall I be ordained?

Hecuba

You are near the lot now.

Second Half-chorus

Alas!
Who will lead me away? An Argive?
To an island home? To Phthiotis?
Unhappy, surely, and far from Troy.

Hecuba

And I,
whose wretched slave
shall I be? Where, in my gray age,
a faint drone,
poor image of a corpse,
weak shining among dead men? Shall
I stand and keep guard at their doors,
shall I nurse their children, I who in Troy
held state as a princess?

(The two half-choruses now unite to form a single Chorus.)

Chorus

So pitiful, so pitiful
your shame and your lamentation.
No longer shall I move the shifting pace
of the shuttle at the looms of Ida.
I shall look no more on the bodies of my sons.
No more. Shall I be a drudge besides
or be forced to the bed of Greek masters?
Night is a queen, but I curse her.
Must I draw the water of Pirene,
a servant at sacred springs?
Might I only be taken to Athens, domain
of Theseus, the bright, the blessed!

Never to the whirl of Eurotas, not Sparta
detested, who gave us Helen,
not look with slave's eyes on the scourge
of Troy, Menelaus.

I have heard the rumor
of the hallowed ground by Peneus,
bright doorstone of Olympus,
deep burdened in beauty of flower and harvest.
There would I be next after the blessed,
the sacrosanct hold of Theseus.
And they say that the land of Aetna,
the Fire God's keep against Punic men,
mother of Sicilian mountains, sounds
in the herald's cry for games' garlands;
and the land washed
by the streaming Ionian Sea,
that land watered by the loveliest
of rivers, Crathis, with the red-gold tresses
who draws from the depths of enchanted wells
blessings on a strong people.

See now, from the host of the Danaans
the herald, charged with new orders, takes
the speed of his way toward us.
What message? What command? Since we count as slaves
even now in the Dorian kingdom.

(Talthybius enters, followed by a detail of armed soldiers.)

Talthybius

Hecuba, incessantly my ways have led me to Troy
as the messenger of all the Achaean armament.
You know me from the old days, my lady; I am sent,
Talthybius, with new messages for you to hear.

Hecuba

It comes, beloved daughters of Troy; the thing I feared.

Talthybius
You are all given your masters now. Was this your dread?

Hecuba
Ah, yes. Is it Phthia, then? A city of Thessaly?
Tell me. The land of Cadmus?

Talthybius
All are allotted separately, each to a man.

Hecuba
Who is given to whom? Oh, is there any hope
left for the women of Troy?

Talthybius
I understand. Yet ask not for all, but for each apart.

Hecuba
Who was given my child? Tell me, who shall be lord
of my poor abused Cassandra?

Talthybius
King Agamemnon chose her. She was given to him.

Hecuba
Slave woman to that Lacedaemonian wife?
My unhappy child!

Talthybius
No. Rather to be joined with him in the dark bed of love.

Hecuba
She, Apollo's virgin, blessed in the privilege
the gold-haired god gave her, a life forever unwed?

Talthybius
Love's archery and the prophetic maiden struck him hard.

Hecuba
Dash down, my daughter,
the keys of your consecration,
break the god's garlands to your throat gathered.

Talthybius
Is it not high favor to be brought to a king's bed?

Hecuba
My poor youngest, why did you take her away from me?

Talthybius
You spoke now of Polyxena. Is it not so?

Hecuba
To whose arms did the lot force her?

Talthybius
She is given a guardianship, to keep Achilles' tomb.

Hecuba
To watch, my child? Over a tomb?
Tell me, is this their way,
some law, friend, established among the Greeks?

Talthybius
Speak of your child in words of blessing. She feels no pain.

Hecuba
What did that mean? Does she live in the sunlight still?

Talthybius
She lives her destiny, and her cares are over now.

Hecuba
The wife of bronze-embattled Hector: tell me of her,
Andromache the forlorn. What shall she suffer now?

Talthybius
The son of Achilles chose her. She was given to him.

Hecuba
And I, my aged strength crutched for support on staves,
whom shall I serve?

Talthybius
You shall be slave to Odysseus, lord of Ithaca.

Hecuba
Oh no, no!
Tear the shorn head,
rip nails through the folded cheeks.

Must I?
To be given as slave to serve that vile, that slippery man,
right's enemy, brute, murderous beast,
that mouth of lies and treachery, that makes void
faith in things promised
and that which was beloved turns to hate. Oh, mourn,
daughters of Ilium, weep as one for me.
I am gone, doomed, undone,
O wretched, given
the worst lot of all.

Chorus

I know your destiny now, Queen Hecuba. But mine?
What Hellene, what Achaean is my master now?

Talthybius

Men-at-arms, do your duty. Bring Cassandra forth
without delay. Our orders are to deliver her
to the general at once. And afterwards we can bring
to the rest of the princes their allotted captive women.
But see! What is that burst of a torch flame inside?
What can it mean? Are the Trojan women setting fire
to their chambers, at point of being torn from their land
to sail for Argos? Have they set themselves aflame
in longing for death? I know it is the way of freedom
in times like these to stiffen the neck against disaster.
Open, there, open; let not the fate desired by these,
dreaded by the Achaeans, hurl their wrath on me.

Hecuba

You are wrong, there is no fire there. It is my Cassandra
whirled out on running feet in the passion of her frenzy.

(Cassandra, carrying a flaming torch, bursts from the shelter.)

Cassandra

Lift up, heave up; carry the flame; I bring fire of worship,
torches to the temple.
Io, Hymen, my lord. Hymenaeus.

Blessed the bridegroom.
Blessed am I indeed to lie at a king's side,
blessed the bride of Argos.
Hymen, my lord, Hymenaeus.
Yours were the tears, my mother,
yours was the lamentation for my father fallen,
for your city so dear beloved,
but mine this marriage, my marriage,
and I shake out the torch-flare,
brightness, dazzle,
light for you, Hymenaeus,
Hecate, light for you,
for the bed of virginity as man's custom ordains.

Let your feet dance, rippling the air; let go the chorus,
as when my father's
fate went in blessedness.
O sacred circle of dance.
Lead now, Phoebos Apollo; I wear your laurel,
I tend your temple,
Hymen, O Hymenaeus.
Dance, Mother, dance, laugh; lead; let your feet
wind in the shifting pattern and follow mine,
keep the sweet step with me,
cry out the name Hymenaeus
and the bride's name in the shrill
and the blessed incantation.
O you daughters of Phrygia robed in splendor,
dance for my wedding,
for the lord fate appointed to lie beside me.

Chorus

Can you not, Queen Hecuba, stop this bacchanal before
her light feet whirl her away into the Argive camp?

Hecuba

Fire God, in mortal marriages you lift up your torch,
but here you throw a melancholy light, not seen

through my hopes that went so high in days gone past. O child,
there was a time I dreamed you would not wed like this,
not at the spear's edge, not under force of Argive arms.
Let me take the light; crazed, passionate, you cannot carry
it straight enough, poor child. Your fate is intemperate
as you are, always. There is no relief for you.

(Attendants come from the shelter. Hecuba gently takes the torch from Cassandra and gives it to them to carry away.)

You Trojan women, take the torch inside, and change
to songs of tears this poor girl's marriage melodies.

Cassandra

O Mother, star my hair with flowers of victory.
I know you would not have it happen thus; and yet
this is a king I marry; then be glad; escort
the bride. Oh, thrust her strongly on. If Loxias
is Loxias still, the Achaeans' pride, great Agamemnon
has won a wife more fatal than ever Helen was.
Since I will kill him; and avenge my brothers' blood
and my father's in the desolation of his house.
But I leave this in silence and sing not now the ax
to drop against my throat and other throats than mine,
the agony of the mother murdered, brought to pass
from our marriage rites, and Atreus' house made desolate.
I am ridden by God's curse still, yet I will step so far
out of my frenzy as to show this city's fate
is blessed beside the Achaeans'. For one woman's sake,
one act of love, these hunted Helen down and threw
thousands of lives away. Their general—clever man—
in the name of a vile woman cut his darling down,
gave up for a brother the sweetness of children in his house,
all to bring back that brother's wife, a woman who went
of her free will, not caught in constraint of violence.
The Achaeans came beside Scamander's banks, and died

day after day, though none sought to wrench their land from them
nor their own towering cities. Those the War God caught
never saw their sons again, nor were they laid to rest
decently in winding sheets by their wives' hands, but lie
buried in alien ground; while all went wrong at home
as the widows perished, and barren couples raised and nursed
the children of others, no survivor left to tend
the tombs, and what is left there, with blood sacrificed.
For such success as this congratulate the Greeks.
No, but the shame is better left in silence, for fear
my singing voice become the voice of wretchedness.
The Trojans have that glory which is loveliest:
they died for their own country. So the bodies of all
who took the spears were carried home in loving hands,
brought, in the land of their fathers, to the embrace of earth
and buried becomingly as the rite fell due. The rest,
those Phrygians who escaped death in battle, day by day
came home to happiness the Achaeans could not know;
their wives, their children. Then was Hector's fate so sad?
You think so. Listen to the truth. He is dead and gone
surely, but with reputation, as a valiant man.
How could this be, except for the Achaeans' coming?
Had they held back, none might have known how great he was.
The bride of Paris was the daughter of Zeus. Had he
not married her, fame in our house would sleep in silence still.
Though surely the wise man will forever shrink from war,
yet if war come, the hero's death will lay a wreath
not lustreless on the city. The coward alone brings shame.
Let no more tears fall, Mother, for our land, nor for
this marriage I make; it is by marriage that I bring
to destruction those whom you and I have hated most.

Chorus

You smile on your disasters. Can it be that you
some day will illuminate the darkness of this song?

Talthybius

Were it not Apollo who has driven wild your wits
I would make you sorry for sending the princes of our host
on their way home in augury of foul speech like this.
Now pride of majesty and wisdom's outward show
have fallen to stature less than what was nothing worth
since he, almighty prince of the assembled Hellenes,
Atreus' son beloved, has stooped—by his own will—
to find his love in a crazed girl. I, a plain man,
would not marry this woman or keep her as my slave.
You then, with your wits unhinged by idiocy,
your scolding of Argos and your Trojans glorified
I throw to the winds to scatter them. Come now with me
to the ships, a bride—and such a bride—for Agamemnon.

Hecuba, when Laertes' son calls you, be sure
you follow; if what all say who came to Ilium
is true, at the worst you will be a good woman's slave.

Cassandra

That servant is a vile thing. Oh, how can heralds keep
their name of honor? Lackeys for despots be they, or
lackeys to the people, all men must despise them still.
You tell me that my mother must be slave in the house
of Odysseus? Where are all Apollo's promises
uttered to me, to my own ears, that Hecuba
should die in Troy? Odysseus I will curse no more,
poor wretch, who little dreams of what he must go through
when he will think Troy's pain and mine were golden grace
beside his own luck. Ten years he spent here, and ten
more years will follow before he at last comes home, forlorn
after the terror of the rock and the thin strait,
Charybdis; and the mountain striding Cyclops, who eats
men's flesh; the Ligyan witch who changes men to swine,
Circe; the wreck of all his ships on the salt sea,
the lotus passion, the sacred oxen of the Sun

slaughtered, and dead flesh moaning into speech, to make
Odysseus listening shiver. Cut the story short:
he will go down to the water of death, and return alive
to reach home and the thousand sorrows waiting there.

Why must I transfix each of Odysseus' labors one by one?
Lead the way quick to the house of death where I shall
take my mate.
Lord of all the sons of Danaus, haughty in your mind of pride,
not by day, but evil in the evil night you shall find your grave
when I lie corpse-cold and naked next my husband's sepulcher,
piled in the ditch for animals to rip and feed on, beaten by
streaming storms of winter, I who wore Apollo's sacraments.
Garlands of the god I loved so well, the spirit's dress of pride,
leave me, as I leave those festivals where once I was so gay.
See, I tear your adornments from my skin not yet defiled by
touch,
throw them to the running winds to scatter, O lord of prophecy,
Where is this general's ship, then? Lead me where I must set my
feet on board.
Wait the wind of favor in the sails; yet when the ship goes out
from this shore, she carries one of the three Furies in my shape.
Land of my ancestors, good-bye; O Mother, weep no more for
me.
You beneath the ground, my brothers, Priam, father of us all,
I will be with you soon and come triumphant to the dead below,
leaving behind me, wrecked, the house of Atreus, which destroyed our house.

(Cassandra is taken away by Talthybius and his soldiers. Hecuba collapses.)

Chorus

Handmaids of aged Hecuba, can you not see
how your mistress, powerless to cry out, lies prone? Oh, take
her hand and help her to her feet, you wretched maids.
Will you let an aged helpless woman lie so long?

Hecuba

No. Let me lie where I have fallen. Kind acts, my maids,
must be unkind, unwanted. All that I endure
and have endured and shall, deserves to strike me down.
O gods! What wretched things to call on—gods!—for help
although the decorous action is to invoke their aid
when all our hands lay hold on is unhappiness.
No. It is my pleasure first to tell good fortune's tale,
to cast its count more sadly against disasters now.
I was a princess, who was once a prince's bride,
mother by him of sons pre-eminent, beyond
the mere numbers of them, lords of the Phrygian domain,
such sons for pride to point to as no woman of Troy,
no Hellene, none in the outlander's wide world might match.
And then I saw them fall before the spears of Greece,
and cut this hair for them, and laid it on their graves.
I mourned their father, Priam. None told me the tale
of his death. I saw it, with these eyes. I stood to watch
his throat cut, next the altar of the protecting god.
I saw my city taken. And the girls I nursed,
choice flowers to wear the pride of any husband's eyes,
matured to be dragged by hands of strangers from my arms.
There is no hope left that they will ever see me more,
no hope that I shall ever look on them again.
There is one more stone to key this arch of wretchedness:
I must be carried away to Hellas now, an old
slave woman, where all those tasks that wrack old age shall be
given me by my masters. I must work the bolt
that bars their doorway, I whose son was Hector once;
or bake their bread; lay down these withered limbs to sleep
on the bare ground, whose bed was royal once; abuse
this skin once delicate the slattern's way, exposed
through robes whose rags will mock my luxury of long since.
Unhappy, O unhappy. And all this came to pass
and shall be, for the way one woman chose a man.
Cassandra, O Daughter, whose excitements were the god's,

you have paid for your consecration now; at what a price!
And you, my poor Polyxena, where are you now?
Not here, nor any boy or girl of mine, who were
so many once, is near me in my unhappiness.
And you would lift me from the ground? What hope? What use?
Guide these feet long ago so delicate in Troy,
a slave's feet now, to the straw sacks laid on the ground
and the piled stones; let me lay down my head and die
in an exhaustion of tears. Of all who walk in bliss
call not one happy yet, until the man is dead.

(*Hecuba, after being led to the back of the stage, flings herself to the ground once more.*)

Chorus

Voice of singing, stay
with me now, for Ilium's sake;
take up the burden of tears,
the song of sorrow;
the dirge for Troy's death
must be chanted;
the tale of my captivity
by the wheeled stride of the four-foot beast of the Argives,
the horse they left in the gates,
thin gold at its brows,
inward, the spears' high thunder.
Our people thronging
the rock of Troy let go the great cry:
"The war is over! Go down,
bring back the idol's enchanted wood
to the Maiden of Ilium, Zeus' daughter."
Who stayed then? Not one girl, not one
old man, in their houses,
but singing for happiness
let the lurking death in.

And the generation of Troy
swept solid to the gates

to give the goddess
her pleasure: the colt immortal, unbroken,
the nest of Argive spears,
death for the children of Dardanus
sealed in the sleek hill pine chamber.
In the sling of the flax twist shipwise
they berthed the black hull
in the house of Pallas Athene
stone paved, washed now in the blood of our people.
Strong, gay work
deep into black night
to the stroke of the Libyan lute
and all Troy singing, and girls'
light feet pulsing the air
in the kind dance measures;
indoors, lights everywhere,
torchflares on black
to forbid sleep's onset.

I was there also: in the great room
I danced the maiden of the mountains,
Artemis, Zeus' daughter.
When the cry went up, sudden,
bloodshot, up and down the city, to stun
the keep of the citadel. Children
reached shivering hands to clutch
at the mother's dress.
War stalked from his hiding place.
Pallas did this.
Beside their altars the Trojans
died in their blood. Desolate now,
men murdered, our sleeping rooms gave up
their brides' beauty
to breed sons for Greek men,
sorrow for our own country.

(A wagon comes on the stage. It is heaped with a number of spoils of war, in the midst of which sits Andromache holding Astyanax. While the chorus continues speaking, Hecuba rises once more.)

Hecuba look, I see her, rapt
to the alien wagon, Andromache,
close to whose beating breast clings
the boy Astyanax, Hector's sweet child.
O carried away—to what land?—unhappy woman,
on the wagon floor, with the brazen arms
of Hector, of Troy
captive and heaped beside you,
torn now from Troy, for Achilles' son
to hang in the shrines of Phthia.

Andromache

I am in the hands of Greek masters.

Hecuba

Alas!

Andromache

Must the incantation

Hecuba

(ah me!)

Andromache

of my own grief win tears from you?

Hecuba

It must—O Zeus!

Andromache

My own distress?

Hecuba

O my children

Andromache

once. No longer.

Hecuba

Lost, lost, Troy our dominion

Andromache
unhappy

Hecuba
and my lordly children.

Andromache
Gone, alas!

Hecuba
They were mine.

Andromache
Sorrows only.

Hecuba
Sad destiny

Andromache
of our city

Hecuba
a wreck, and burning.

Andromache
Come back, O my husband.

Hecuba
Poor child, you invoke
a dead man; my son once

Andromache
my defender.

Hecuba
And you, whose death shamed the Achaeans,

Andromache
lord of us all once,
O patriarch, Priam,

Hecuba
take me to my death now.

Andromache
Longing for death drives deep;

Hecuba
O sorrowful, such is our fortune;

Andromache
lost our city

Hecuba
and our pain lies deep under pain piled over.

Andromache
We are the hated of God, since once your youngest escaping
death, brought down Troy's towers in the arms of a worthless
woman,
piling at the feet of Pallas the bleeding bodies of our young men
sprawled, kites' food, while Troy takes up the yoke of captivity.

Hecuba
O my city, my city forlorn

Andromache
abandoned, I weep this

Hecuba
miserable last hour

Andromache
of the house where I bore my children.

Hecuba
O my sons, this city and your mother are desolate of you.
Sound of lamentation and sorrow,
tears on tears shed. Home, farewell, since the dead have forgotten
all sorrows, and weep no longer.

Chorus
They who are sad find somehow sweetness in tears, the song
of lamentation and the melancholy Muse.

Andromache
Hecuba, mother of the man whose spear was death
to the Argives, Hector: do you see what they have done to us?

Hecuba
I see the work of gods who pile tower-high the pride
of those who were nothing, and dash present grandeur down.

Andromache

We are carried away, sad spoils, my boy and I; our life
transformed, as the aristocrat becomes the serf.

Hecuba

Such is the terror of necessity. I lost
Cassandra, roughly torn from my arms before you came.

Andromache

Another Ajax to haunt your daughter? Some such thing
it must be. Yet you have lost still more than you yet know.

Hecuba

There is no numbering my losses. Infinitely
misfortune comes to outrace misfortune known before.

Andromache

Polyxena is dead. They cut your daughter's throat
to pleasure dead Achilles' corpse, above his grave.

Hecuba

O wretched. This was what Talthybius meant, that speech
cryptic, incomprehensible, yet now so clear.

Andromache

I saw her die, and left this wagon seat to lay
a robe upon her body and sing the threnody.

Hecuba

Poor child, poor wretched, wretched darling, sacrificed,
but without pity, and in pain, to a dead man.

Andromache

She is dead, and this was death indeed; and yet to die
as she did was better than to live as I live now.

Hecuba

Child, no. No life, no light is any kind of death,
since death is nothing, and in life the hopes live still.

Andromache

O Mother, our mother, hear me while I reason through
this matter fairly—might it even hush your grief?

Death, I am sure, is like never being born, but death
is better thus by far than to live a life of pain,
since the dead with no perception of evil feel no grief,
while he who was happy once, and then unfortunate,
finds his heart driven far from the old lost happiness.
She died; it is as if she never saw the light
of day, for she knows nothing now of what she suffered.
But I, who aimed the arrows of ambition high
at honor, and made them good, see now how far I fall,
I, who in Hector's house worked out all custom that brings
discretion's name to women. Blame them or blame them not,
there is one act that swings the scandalous speech their way
beyond all else: to leave the house and walk abroad.
I longed to do it, but put the longing aside, and stayed
always within the inclosure of my own house and court.
The witty speech some women cultivate I would
not practice, but kept my honest inward thought, and made
my mind my only and sufficient teacher. I gave
my lord's presence the tribute of hushed lips, and eyes
quietly downcast. I knew when my will must have its way
over his, knew also how to give way to him in turn.
Men learned of this; I was talked of in the Achaean camp,
and reputation has destroyed me now. At the choice
of women, Achilles' son picked me from the rest, to be
his wife: a lordly house, yet I shall be a slave.
If I dash back the beloved memory of Hector
and open wide my heart to my new lord, I shall be
a traitor to the dead love, and know it; if I cling
faithful to the past, I win my master's hatred. Yet
they say one night of love suffices to dissolve
a woman's aversion to share the bed of any man.
I hate and loathe that woman who casts away the once
beloved, and takes another in her arms of love.
Even the young mare torn from her running mate and teamed
with another will not easily wear the yoke. And yet
this is a brute and speechless beast of burden, not

like us intelligent, lower far in nature's scale.
Dear Hector, when I had you I had a husband, great
in understanding, rank, wealth, courage: all my wish.
I was a virgin when you took me from the house
of my father; I gave you all my maiden love, my first,
and now you are dead, and I must cross the sea, to serve,
prisoner of war, the slave's yoke on my neck, in Greece.
No, Hecuba; can you not see my fate is worse
than hers you grieve, Polyxena's? That one thing left
always while life lasts, hope, is not for me. I keep
no secret deception in my heart—sweet though it be
to dream—that I shall ever be happy any more.

Chorus

You stand where I do in misfortune, and while you mourn
your own life, tell me what I, too, am suffering.

Hecuba

I have never been inside the hull of a ship, but know
what I know only by hearsay and from painted scenes,
yet think that seamen, while the gale blows moderately,
take pains to spare unnecessary work, and send
one man to the steering oar, another aloft, and crews
to pump the bilge from the hold. But when the tempest comes,
and seas wash over the decks they lose their nerve, and let
her go by the run at the waves' will, leaving all to chance.
So I, in this succession of disasters, swamped,
battered by this storm immortally inspired, have lost
my lips' control and let them go, say anything
they will. Yet still, beloved child, you must forget
what happened with Hector. Tears will never save you now.
Give your obedience to the new master; let your ways
entice his heart to make him love you. If you do
it will be better for all who are close to you. This boy,
my own son's child, might grow to manhood and bring back—
he alone could do it—something of our city's strength.

On some far day the children of your children might
come home, and build. There still may be another Troy.

But *we* say this, and others will speak also. See,
here is some runner of the Achaeans come again.
Who is he? What news? What counsel have they taken now?

(*Talthybius enters again with his escort.*)

Talthybius

O wife of Hector, once the bravest man in Troy,
do not hate me. This is the will of the Danaans and
the kings. I wish I did not have to give this message.

Andromache

What can this mean, this hint of hateful things to come?

Talthybius

The council has decreed for your son—how can I say this?

Andromache

That he shall serve some other master than I serve?

Talthybius

No man of Achaea shall ever make this boy his slave.

Andromache

Must he be left behind in Phrygia, all alone?

Talthybius

Worse; horrible. There is no easy way to tell it.

Andromache

I thank your courtesy—unless your news be really good.

Talthybius

They will kill your son. It is monstrous. Now you know the truth.

Andromache

Oh, this is worse than anything I heard before.

Talthybius

Odysseus. He urged it before the Greeks, and got his way.

Andromache

This is too much grief, and more than anyone could bear.

Talthybius
He said a hero's son could not be allowed to live.

Andromache
Even thus may his own sons some day find no mercy.

Talthybius
He must be hurled from the battlements of Troy.

(He goes toward Andromache, who clings fast to her child, as if to resist.)

No, wait!
Let it happen this way. It will be wiser in the end.
Do not fight it. Take your grief as you were born to take it,
give up the struggle where your strength is feebleness
with no force anywhere to help. Listen to me!
Your city is gone, your husband. You are in our power.
How can one woman hope to struggle against the arms
of Greece? Think, then. Give up the passionate contest.
This
will bring no shame. No man can laugh at your submission.
And please—I request you—hurl no curse at the Achaeans
for fear the army, savage over some reckless word,
forbid the child his burial and the dirge of honor.
Be brave, be silent; out of such patience you can hope
the child you leave behind will not lie unburied here,
and that to you the Achaeans will be less unkind.

Andromache
O darling child I loved too well for happiness,
your enemies will kill you and leave your mother forlorn.
Your own father's nobility, where others found
protection, means your murder now. The memory
of his valor comes ill-timed for you. O bridal bed,
O marriage rites that brought me home to Hector's house
a bride, you were unhappy in the end. I lived
never thinking the baby I had was born for butchery
by Greeks, but for lordship over all Asia's pride of earth.

Poor child, are you crying too? Do you know what they
will do to you? Your fingers clutch my dress. What use,
to nestle like a young bird under the mother's wing?
Hector cannot come back, not burst from underground
to save you, that spear of glory caught in the quick hand,
nor Hector's kin, nor any strength of Phrygian arms.
Yours the sick leap head downward from the height, the fall
where none have pity, and the spirit smashed out in death.
O last and loveliest embrace of all, O child's
sweet fragrant body. Vanity in the end. I nursed
for nothing the swaddled baby at this mother's breast;
in vain the wrack of the labor pains and the long sickness.
Now once again, and never after this, come close
to your mother, lean against my breast and wind your arms
around my neck, and put your lips against my lips.

(She kisses Astyanax and relinquishes him.)

Greeks! Your Greek cleverness is simple barbarity.
Why kill this child, who never did you any harm?
O flowering of the house of Tyndareus! Not his,
not God's daughter, never that, but child of many fathers
I say; the daughter of Vindictiveness, of Hate,
of Blood, Death; of all wickedness that swarms on earth.
I cry it aloud: Zeus never was your father, but you
were born a pestilence to all Greeks and the world beside.
Accursed; who from those lovely and accursed eyes
brought down to shame and ruin the bright plains of Troy.
Oh, seize him, take him, dash him to death if it must be done;
feed on his flesh if it is your will. These are the gods
who damn us to this death, and I have no strength to save
my boy from execution. Cover this wretched face
and throw me into the ship and that sweet bridal bed
I walk to now across the death of my own child.

(Talthybius gently lifts the child out of the wagon, which leaves the stage, carrying Andromache away.)

Chorus

Unhappy Troy! For the sweetness in one woman's arms'
embrace, unspeakable, you lost these thousands slain.

Talthybius

Come, boy, taken from the embrace beloved
of your mourning mother. Climb the high circle
of the walls your fathers built. There
end life. This was the order.
Take him.

(He hands Astyanax to the guards, who lead him out.)

I am not the man
to do this. Some other
without pity, not as I ashamed,
should be herald of messages like this.

(He goes out.)

Hecuba

O child of my own unhappy child,
shall your life be torn from your mother
and from me? Wicked. Can I help,
dear child, not only suffer? What help?
Tear face, beat bosom. This is all
my power now. O city,
O child, what have we left to suffer?
Are we not hurled
down the whole length of disaster?

Chorus

Telamon, O king in the land where the bees swarm,
Salamis the surf-pounded isle where you founded your city
to front that hallowed coast where Athene broke
forth the primeval pale branch of olive,
wreath of the bright air and a glory on Athens the shining:
O Telamon, you came in your pride of arms
with Alcmena's archer
to Ilium, our city, to sack and destroy it
on that age-old venture.

This was the first flower of Hellenic strength Heracles brought
in anger
for the horses promised; and by Simois' calm waters
checked the surf-wandering oars and made fast the ships' stern
cables.
From which vessels came out the deadly bow hand,
death to Laomedon, as the scarlet wind of the flames swept over
masonry straight-hewn by the hands of Apollo.
This was a desolation of Troy
twice taken; twice in the welter of blood the walls Dardanian
went down before the red spear.

In vain, then, Laomedon's child,
you walk in delicate pride
by the golden pitchers
in loveliest servitude
to fill Zeus' wine cups;
while Troy your mother is given to the flame to eat,
and the lonely beaches
mourn, as sad birds sing
for the young lost,
for the sword hand and the children
and the aged women.
Gone now the shining pools where you bathed,
the fields where you ran
all desolate. And you,
Ganymede, go in grace by the thrones of God
with your young, calm smile even now
as Priam's kingdom
falls to the Greek spear.

O Love, Love, it was you
in the high halls of Dardanus,
the sky-daughters of melody beside you,
who piled the huge strength of Troy
in towers, the gods' own hands
concerned. I speak no more

against Zeus' name.
But the light men love, who shines
through the pale wings of morning,
balestar on this earth now,
watched the collapse of tall towers:
Dawn. Her lord was of this land;
she bore his children,
Tithonus, caught away by the golden car
and the starry horses,
who made our hopes so high.
For the gods loved Troy once.
Now they have forgotten.

(Menelaus comes on the stage, attended by a detail of armed soldiers.)

Menelaus

O splendor of sunburst breaking forth this day, whereon
I lay my hands once more on Helen, my wife. And yet
it is not, so much as men think, for the woman's sake
I came to Troy, but against that guest proved treacherous,
who like a robber carried the woman from my house.
Since the gods have seen to it that *he* paid the penalty,
fallen before the Hellenic spear, his kingdom wrecked,
I come for *her* now, the wife once my own, whose name
I can no longer speak with any happiness,
to take her away. In this house of captivity
she is numbered among the other women of Troy, a slave.
And those men whose work with the spear has won her back
gave her to me, to kill, or not to kill, but lead
away to the land of Argos, if such be my pleasure.
And such it is; the death of Helen in Troy I will let
pass, have the oars take her by sea ways back to Greek
soil, and there give her over to execution;
blood penalty for friends who are dead in Ilium here.
Go to the house, my followers, and take her out;
no, drag her out; lay hands upon that hair so stained

with men's destruction. When the winds blow fair astern
we will take ship again and bring her back to Hellas.

Hecuba

O power, who mount the world, wheel where the world rides,
O mystery of man's knowledge, whosoever you be,
Zeus named, nature's necessity or mortal mind,
I call upon you; for you walk the path none hears
yet bring all human action back to right at last.

Menelaus

What can this mean? How strange a way to call on gods.

Hecuba

Kill your wife, Menelaus, and I will bless your name.
But keep your eyes away from her. Desire will win.
She looks enchantment, and where she looks homes are set fire;
she captures cities as she captures the eyes of men.
We have had experience, you and I. We know the truth.

(Men at arms bring Helen roughly out of the shelter. She makes no resistance.)

Helen

Menelaus, your first acts are argument of terror
to come. Your lackeys put their hands on me. I am dragged
out of my chambers by brute force. I know you hate
me; I am almost sure. And still there is one question
I would ask you, if I may. What have the Greeks decided
to do with me? Or shall I be allowed to live?

Menelaus

You are not strictly condemned, but all the army gave
you into my hands, to kill you for the wrong you did.

Helen

Is it permitted that I argue this, and prove
that my death, if I am put to death, will be unjust?

Menelaus

I did not come to talk with you. I came to kill.

Hecuba

No, Menelaus, listen to her. She should not die
unheard. But give me leave to take the opposite case;
the prosecution. There are things that happened in Troy
which you know nothing of, and the long-drawn argument
will mean her death. She never can escape us now.

Menelaus

This is a gift of leisure. If she wishes to speak
she may. But it is for your sake, understand, that I give
this privilege I never would have given to her.

Helen

Perhaps it will make no difference if I speak well
or badly, and your hate will not let you answer me.
All I can do is to foresee the arguments
you will use in accusation of me, and set against
the force of your charges, charges of my own.
First, then!

She mothered the beginning of all this wickedness.
For Paris was her child. And next to her the old king,
who would not destroy the infant Alexander, that dream
of the firebrand's agony, has ruined Troy, and me.
This is not all; listen to the rest I have to say.
Alexander was the judge of the goddess trinity.
Pallas Athene would have given him power, to lead
the Phrygian arms on Hellas and make it desolate.
All Asia was Hera's promise, and the uttermost zones
of Europe for his lordship, if her way prevailed.
But Aphrodite, picturing my loveliness,
promised it to him, if he would say her beauty surpassed
all others. Think what this means, and all the consequence.
Cypris prevailed, and I was won in marriage: all
for Greek advantage. Asia is not your lord; you serve
no tyrant now, nor take the spear in his defense.
Yet Hellas' fortune was my own misfortune. I,

sold once for my body's beauty stand accused, who should
for what has been done wear garlands on my head.
I know.

You will say all this is nothing to the immediate charge:
I did run away; I did go secretly from your house.
But when he came to me—call him any name you will:
Paris? or Alexander? or the spirit of blood
to haunt this woman?—he came with a goddess at his side;
no weak one. And you—it was criminal—took ship for Crete
and left me there in Sparta in the house, alone.

You see?

I wonder—and I ask this of myself, not you—
why *did* I do it? What made me run away from home
with the stranger, and betray my country and my hearth?
Challenge the goddess then, show your greater strength than
Zeus'
who has the other gods in his power, and still is slave
to Aphrodite alone. Shall I not be forgiven?
Still you might have some show of argument against me.
When Paris was gone to the deep places of death, below
ground, and the immortal practice on my love was gone,
I should have come back to the Argive ships, left Troy.
I did try to do it, and I have witnesses,
the towers' gatekeepers and the sentinels on the wall,
who caught me again and again as I let down the rope
from the battlements and tried to slip away to the ground.
For Deiphobus, my second husband: he took me away
by force and kept me his wife against the Phrygians' will.

O my husband, can you kill me now and think you kill
in righteousness? I was the bride of force. Before,
I brought their houses to the sorrow of slavery
instead of conquest. Would you be stronger than the gods?
Try, then. But even such ambition is absurd.

Chorus

O Queen of Troy, stand by your children and your country!
Break down the beguilement of this woman, since she speaks
well, and has done wickedly. This is dangerous.

Hecuba

First, to defend the honor of the gods, and show
that the woman is a scandalous liar. I will not
believe it! Hera and the virgin Pallas Athene
could never be so silly and empty-headed
that Hera would sell Argos to the barbarians,
or Pallas let Athenians be the slaves of Troy.
They went to Ida in girlish emulation, vain
of their own loveliness? Why? Tell me the reason Hera
should fall so much in love with the idea of beauty.
To win some other lord more powerful than Zeus?
Or has Athene marked some god to be her mate,
she, whose virginity is a privilege won from Zeus,
who abjures marriage? Do not trick out your own sins
by calling the gods stupid. No wise man will believe you.
You claim, and I must smile to hear it, that Aphrodite
came at my son's side to the house of Menelaus;
who could have caught up you and your city of Amyclae
and set you in Ilium, moving not from the quiet of heaven.
Nonsense. My son was handsome beyond all other men.
You looked at him, and sense went Cyprian at the sight,
since Aphrodite is nothing but the human lust,
named rightly, since the word of lust begins the god's name.
You saw him in the barbaric splendor of his robes,
gorgeous with gold. It made your senses itch. You thought,
being queen only in Argos, in little luxury,
that once you got rid of Sparta for the Phrygian city
where gold streamed everywhere, you could let extravagance
run wild. No longer were Menelaus and his house
sufficient to your spoiled luxurious appetites.

So much for that. You say my son took you away
by force. What Spartan heard you cry for help? You did
cry out? Or did you? Castor, your brother, was there, a young
man, and his twin not yet caught up among the stars.
Then when you had reached Troy, and the Argives at your heels
came, and the agony of the murderous spears began,
when the reports came in that Menelaus' side
was winning, you would praise him, simply to make my son
unhappy at the strength of his love's challenger,
forgetting your husband when the luck went back to Troy.
You worked hard: not to make yourself a better woman,
but to make sure always to be on the winning side.
You claim you tried to slip away with ropes let down
from the ramparts, and this proves you stayed against your will?
Perhaps. But when were you ever caught in the strangling noose,
caught sharpening a dagger? Which any noble wife
would do, desperate with longing for her lord's return.
Yet over and over again I gave you good advice:
"Make your escape, my daughter; there are other girls
for my sons to marry. I will help you get away
to the ships of the Achaeans. Let the Greeks, and us,
stop fighting." So I argued, but you were not pleased.
Spoiled in the luxury of Alexander's house
you liked foreigners to kiss the ground before your feet.
All that impressed you.
And now you dare to come outside,
figure fastidiously arranged, to look upon
the same air as your husband, O abominable
heart, who should walk submissively in rags of robes,
shivering with anxiety, head Scythian-cropped,
your old impudence gone and modesty gained at last
by reason of your sinful life.
O Menelaus,
mark this, the end of my argument. Be true to your
high reputation and to Hellas. Grace both, and kill

Helen. Thus make it the custom toward all womankind
hereafter, that the price of adultery is death.

Chorus

Menelaus, keep the ancestral honor of your house.
Punish your wife, and purge away from Greece the stigma
on women. You shall seem great even to your enemies.

Menelaus

All you have said falls into line with my own thought.
This woman left my household for a stranger's bed
of her own free will, and all this talk of Aphrodite
is for pure show. Away, and face the stones of the mob.
Atone for the long labors of the Achaeans in
the brief act of dying, and know your penance for my shame.

(Helen drops before him and embraces his knees.)

Helen

No, by your knees! I am not guilty of the mind's
infection, which the gods sent. Do not kill! Have pity!

Hecuba

Be true to the memory of all your friends she murdered.
It is for them and for their children that I plead.

(Menelaus pushes Helen away.)

Menelaus

Enough, Hecuba. I am not listening to her now.
I speak to my servants: see that she is taken away
to where the ships are beached. She will make the voyage home.

Hecuba

But let her not be put in the same ship with you.

Menelaus

What can you mean? That she is heavier than she was?

Hecuba

A man in love once never is out of love again.

Menelaus

Sometimes; when the beloved's heart turns false to him.
Yet it shall be as you wish. She shall not be allowed

in the same ship I sail in. This was well advised.
And once in Argos she must die the vile death earned
by her vile life, and be an example to all women
to live temperately. This is not the easier way;
and yet her execution will tincture with fear
the lust of women even more depraved than she.

(Helen is led out, Menelaus following.)

Chorus

Thus, O Zeus, you betrayed all
to the Achaeans: your temple
in Ilium, your misted altar,
the flame of the clotted sacraments,
the smoke of the skying incense,
Pergamum the hallowed,
the ivied ravines of Ida, washed
by the running snow. The utter
peaks that surprise the sun bolts,
shining and primeval place of divinity.

Gone are your sacrifices, the choirs'
glad voices singing to the gods
night long, deep into darkness;
gone the images, gold on wood
laid, the twelves of the sacred moons,
the magic Phrygian number.
Can it be, can it be, my lord, you have forgotten
from your throne high in heaven's
bright air, my city which is ruined
and the flame storm that broke it?

O my dear, my husband,
O wandering ghost
unwashed, unburied; the sea hull must carry me
in the flash of its wings' speed
to Argos, city of horses, where
the stone walls built by giants invade the sky.
The multitudes of our children stand

clinging to the gates and cry through their tears.
And one girl weeps:
"O Mother, the Achaeans take me away
lonely from your eyes
to the black ship
where the oars dip surf
toward Salamis the blessed,
or the peak between two seas
where Pelops' hold
keeps the gates at the Isthmus."

Oh that as Menelaus' ship
makes way through the mid-sea
the bright pronged spear immortal of thunder might smash it
far out in the Aegaean,
as in tears, in bondage to Hellas
I am cut from my country;
as she holds the golden mirror
in her hands, girls' grace,
she, God's daughter.
Let him never come home again, to a room in Laconia
and the hearth of his fathers;
never more to Pitana's streets
and the bronze gates of the Maiden;
since he forgave his shame
and the vile marriage, the sorrows
of great Hellas and the land
watered by Simois.

(Talthybius returns. His men carry, laid on the shield of Hector, the body of Astyanax.)

But see!
Now evils multiply in our land.
Behold, O pitiful wives
of the Trojans. This is Astyanax,
dead, dashed without pity from the walls, and borne
by the Danaans, who murdered him.

Talthybius

Hecuba, one last vessel of Achilles' son
remains, manned at the oar sweeps now, to carry back
to the shores of Phthiotis his last spoils of war.
Neoptolemus himself has put to sea. He heard
news of old Peleus in difficulty and the land
invaded by Acastus, son of Pelias.
Such news put speed above all pleasure of delay.
So he is gone, and took with him Andromache,
whose lamentations for her country and farewells
to Hector's tomb as she departed brought these tears
crowding into my eyes. And she implored that you
bury this dead child, your own Hector's son, who died
flung from the battlements of Troy. She asked as well
that the bronze-backed shield, terror of the Achaeans once,
when the boy's father slung its defense across his side,
be not taken to the hearth of Peleus, nor the room
where the slain child's Andromache must be a bride
once more, to waken memories by its sight, but used
in place of the cedar coffin and stone-chambered tomb
for the boy's burial. He shall be laid in your arms
to wrap the body about with winding sheets, and flowers,
as well as you can, out of that which is left to you.
Since she is gone. Her master's speed prevented her
from giving the rites of burial to her little child.

The rest of us, once the corpse is laid out, and earth
is piled above it, must raise the mast tree, and go.
Do therefore quickly everything that you must do.
There is one labor I myself have spared you. As
we forded on our way here Scamander's running water,
I washed the body and made clean the wounds. I go
now, to break ground and dig the grave for him, that my
work be made brief, as yours must be, and our tasks end
together, and the ships be put to sea, for home.

Hecuba

Lay down the circled shield of Hector on the ground:
a hateful thing to look at; it means no love to me.

(Talthybius and his escort leave. Two soldiers wait.)

Achaeans! All your strength is in your spears, not in
the mind. What were you afraid of, that it made you kill
this child so savagely? That Troy, which fell, might be
raised from the ground once more? Your strength meant
  nothing, then.
When Hector's spear was fortunate, and numberless
strong hands were there to help him, we were still destroyed.
Now when the city is fallen and the Phrygians slain,
this baby terrified you? I despise the fear
which is pure terror in a mind unreasoning.

O darling child, how wretched was this death. You might
have fallen fighting for your city, grown to man's
age, and married, and with the king's power like a god's,
and died happy, if there is any happiness here.
But no. You grew to where you could see and learn, my child,
yet your mind was not old enough to win advantage
of fortune. How wickedly, poor boy, your fathers' walls,
Apollo's handiwork, have crushed your pitiful head
tended and trimmed to ringlets by your mother's hand,
and the face she kissed once, where the brightness now is blood
shining through the torn bones—too horrible to say more.
O little hands, sweet likenesses of Hector's once,
now you lie broken at the wrists before my feet;
and mouth beloved whose words were once so confident,
you are dead; and all was false, when you would lean across
my bed, and say: "Mother, when you die I will cut
my long hair in your memory, and at your grave
bring companies of boys my age, to sing farewell."
It did not happen; now I, a homeless, childless, old
woman must bury your poor corpse, which is so young.
Alas for all the tendernesses, my nursing care,

and all your slumbers gone. What shall the poet say,
what words will he inscribe upon your monument?
Here lies a little child the Argives killed, because
they were afraid of him. That? The epitaph of Greek shame.
You will not win your father's heritage, except
for this, which is your coffin now: the brazen shield.

O shield, who guarded the strong shape of Hector s arm:
the bravest man of all, who wore you once, is dead.
How sweet the impression of his body on your sling,
and at the true circle of your rim the stain of sweat
where in the grind of his many combats Hector leaned
his chin against you, and the drops fell from his brow!

Take up your work now; bring from what is left some robes
to wrap the tragic dead. The gods will not allow us
to do it right. But let him have what we can give.

That mortal is a fool who, prospering, thinks his life
has any strong foundation; since our fortune's course
of action is the reeling way a madman takes,
and no one person is ever happy all the time.

(Hecuba's handmaidens bring out from the shelter a basket of robes and ornaments. During the scene which follows, the body of Astyanax is being made ready for burial.)

Chorus

Here are your women, who bring you from the Trojan spoils
such as is left, to deck the corpse for burial.

Hecuba

O child, it is not for victory in riding, won
from boys your age, not archery—in which acts our people
take pride, without driving competition to excess—
that your sire's mother lays upon you now these treasures
from what was yours before; though now the accursed of God,
Helen, has robbed you, she who has destroyed as well
the life in you, and brought to ruin all our house.

Chorus

My heart,
you touched my heart, you who were once
a great lord in my city.

Hecuba

These Phrygian robes' magnificence you should have worn
at your marriage to some princess uttermost in pride
in all the East, I lay upon your body now.
And you, once so victorious and mother of
a thousand conquests, Hector's huge beloved shield:
here is a wreath for you, who die not, yet are dead
with this body; since it is better far to honor you
than the armor of Odysseus the wicked and wise.

Chorus

Ah me.
Earth takes you, child;
our tears of sorrow.
Cry aloud, our mother.

Hecuba

Yes.

Chorus

The dirge of the dead.

Hecuba

Ah me.

Chorus

Evils never to be forgotten.

Hecuba

I will bind up your wounds with bandages, and be
your healer: a wretched one, in name alone, no use.
Among the dead your father will take care of you.

Chorus

Rip, tear your faces with hands
that beat like oars.
Alas.

Hecuba

Dear women. . . .

Chorus

Hecuba, speak to us. We are yours. What did you cry aloud?

Hecuba

The gods meant nothing except to make life hard for me,
and of all cities they chose Troy to hate. In vain
we sacrificed. And yet had not the very hand
of God gripped and crushed this city deep in the ground,
we should have disappeared in darkness, and not given
a theme for music, and the songs of men to come.
You may go now, and hide the dead in his poor tomb;
he has those flowers that are the right of the underworld.
I think it makes small difference to the dead, if they
are buried in the tokens of luxury. All this
is an empty glorification left for those who live.

(The soldiers take up and carry away the body of Astyanax.)

Chorus

Sad mother, whose hopes were so huge
for your life. They are broken now.
Born to high blessedness
and a lordly line
your death was horror.

But see, see
on the high places of Ilium
the torchflares whirling in the hands
of men. For Troy
some ultimate agony.

(Talthybius comes back, with numerous men.)

Talthybius

I call to the captains who have orders to set fire
to the city of Priam: shield no longer in the hand
the shining flame. Let loose the fire upon it. So

with the citadel of Ilium broken to the ground
we can take leave of Troy, in gladness, and go home.

I speak to you, too, for my orders include this.
Children of Troy, when the lords of the armament sound
the high echoing crash of the trumpet call, then go
to the ships of the Achaeans, to be taken away
from this land. And you, unhappiest and aged woman,
go with them. For Odysseus' men are here, to whom
enslaved the lot exiles you from your native land.

Hecuba
Ah, wretched me. So this is the unhappy end
and goal of all the sorrows I have lived. I go
forth from my country and a city lit with flames.
Come, aged feet; make one last weary struggle, that I
may hail my city in its affliction. O Troy, once
so huge over all Asia in the drawn wind of pride,
your very name of glory shall be stripped away.
They are burning you, and us they drag forth from our land
enslaved. O gods! Do I call upon those gods for help?
I cried to them before now, and they would not hear.
Come then, hurl ourselves into the pyre. Best now
to die in the flaming ruins of our fathers' house!

Talthybius
Unhappy creature, ecstatic in your sorrows! Men,
take her, spare not. She is Odysseus' property.
You have orders to deliver her into his hands.

Hecuba
O sorrow.
Cronion, Zeus, lord of Phrygia,
prince of our house, have you seen
the dishonor done to the seed of Dardanus?

Chorus
He has seen, but the great city
is a city no more, it is gone. There is no Troy.

Hecuba
O sorrow.
Ilium flares.
The chambers of Pergamum take fire,
the citadel and the wall's high places.

Chorus
Our city fallen to the spear
fades as smoke winged in the sky,
halls hot in the swept fire
and the fierce lances.

Hecuba
O soil where my children grew.

Chorus
Alas.

Hecuba
O children, hear me; it is your mother who calls.

Chorus
They are dead you cry to. This is a dirge.

Hecuba
I lean my old body against the earth
and both hands beat the ground.

Chorus
I kneel to the earth, take up
the cry to my own dead,
poor buried husband.

Hecuba
We are taken, dragged away

Chorus
a cry of pain, pain

Hecuba
under the slave's roof

Chorus
away from my country.

Hecuba

Priam, my Priam. Dead
graveless, forlorn,
you know not what they have done to me.

Chorus

Now dark, holy death
in the brutal butchery closed his eyes.

Hecuba

O gods' house, city beloved

Chorus

alas

Hecuba

you are given the red flame and the spear's iron.

Chorus

You will collapse to the dear ground and be nameless.

Hecuba

Ash as the skyward smoke wing
piled will blot from my sight the house where I lived once.

Chorus

Lost shall be the name on the land,
all gone, perished. Troy, city of sorrow,
is there no longer.

Hecuba

Did you see, did you hear?

Chorus

The crash of the citadel.

Hecuba

The earth shook, riven

Chorus

to engulf the city.

Hecuba

O
shaking, tremulous limbs,

this is the way. Forward:
into the slave's life.

Chorus

Mourn for the ruined city, then go away
to the ships of the Achaeans.

(Hecuba is led away, and all go out, leaving the stage empty.)

Virgil

AENEID

Translated by
Stanley Lombardo

Introduction by
W. R. Johnson

Hackett Publishing Company, Inc.
Indianapolis/Cambridge

Printed in the United States of America

11 10 09 08 07 2 3 4 5 6 7

For further information, please address:

Hackett Publishing Company, Inc.
P.O. Box 44937
Indianapolis, IN 46244-0937

www.hackettpublishing.com

Cover design by Brian Rak and Abigail Coyle

Composition by William Hartman

Printed at Victor Graphics, Inc.

Cover photo: Names on the Vietnam Veterans' Memorial.
Reproduced courtesy of CORBIS.

154

Library of Congress Cataloging-in-Publication Data

Virgil.
[Aeneis. English]
Aeneid / Virgil ; translated by Stanley Lombardo, introduction by W. R. Johnson.
p. cm.
Includes bibliographical references.
ISBN 0-87220-732-3 (cloth)—ISBN 0-87220-731-5 (pbk.)
1. Epic poetry, Latin—Translations into English. 2. Aeneas (Legendary character)—Poetry. 3. Legends—Rome—Poetry. I. Lombardo, Stanley, 1943– II. Title.
PA6807.A5L58 2005
873'.01—dc22
2004022685

ISBN-13: 978-0-87220-732-5 (cloth)
ISBN-13: 978-0-87220-731-8 (pbk.)

Contents

AENEID ONE

Arms I sing—and a man,
The first to come from the shores
Of Troy, exiled by Fate, to Italy
And the Lavinian coast; a man battered
On land and sea by the powers above
In the face of Juno's relentless wrath;
A man who also suffered greatly in war
Until he could found his city and bring his gods
Into Latium, from which arose
The Latin people, our Alban forefathers,
And the high walls of everlasting Rome.

Muse, tell me why the Queen of Heaven
Was so aggrieved, her godhead so offended,
That she forced a man of faultless devotion
To endure so much hardship. Can there be
Anger so great in the hearts of gods on high?

There was an ancient city, Carthage,
Colonized by Tyrians, facing Italy
And the Tiber's mouth far across the sea;
A city rich in resources, fierce in war,
And favored by Juno more than any other
Place on earth, even more than Samos. Here
Were her arms, her chariot; this was the city
The goddess cherished and strove to make
Capital of the world, if the Fates permitted.
But she had heard that a scion of Trojan blood

Would someday level Carthage's citadel;
That a Trojan people, an imperial power,
Would destroy Libya: so the Parcae
Were spinning out Fate. The Goddess
Brooded on this and on the Trojan War,
Which she herself, Saturnian Juno,
Had waged on behalf of her beloved Greeks,
Ever mindful of the Judgment of Paris—
The cause of the war—and her savage grief
Over her beauty scorned by that hateful race.
Nor could she forget the spiteful honor given
To ravaged Ganymede.
Incensed with these memories,
The Goddess kept the Trojan remnant
That had escaped the Greeks—and Achilles' rage—
Tossed all over the sea's expanse,
Far from Latium, doomed to wander
The circling waters year after year.

So massive was the labor of founding Rome.

Sicily had scarcely dropped out of sight,
And they were sailing joyfully on the open sea,
Bronze prows shearing the seaspume,
When Juno, nursing her heart's eternal wound,
Said to herself:

"Am I to admit defeat,
Unable to keep these Trojans and their king
From Italy? Forbidden by the Fates, am I?
Pallas could burn the Argives' fleet
And drown all hands for one man's offense—
Oïlean Ajax's fit of passion.
She herself hurled Jupiter's fire from heaven,
Splintered the ships, churned up the sea,
And whirled up Ajax, exhaling flames
From his pierced lungs, and impaled him on a crag.
But I, who walk among the gods as their queen,
Sister of Jupiter and Jupiter's wife—I

Have to wage war for years on end
Against this one race. Who will worship Juno
After this, or bow down before her holy altars?"

Her heart inflamed, the Goddess went
To Aeolia, a country of clouds
And raging winds. Here in a vast cave
Aeolus rules the squalls and gales,
Keeping them chained in vaulted cells.
The indignant winds roar at their prison doors,
Rumbling deep in the mountain. But Aeolus
Sits on high and with his scepter calms
Their frenzied souls. If he did not,
They would swoop over land and sea
And through the deep sky, sweeping
Everything before them. Fearing just this,
The Father Almighty hid them away
In dark caves and piled above them
A mountain massif. And he gave them a king,
One who would know by chartered agreement
When to restrain and when to unleash them.
It was to Aeolus that Juno came as a suppliant:

"Aeolus, by order of the Father of Gods and Men
You calm the waves or provoke them with wind.
A race I despise sails the Tyrrhenian Sea,
Bringing Ilium's conquered gods to Italy.
Hit them hard with a storm and sink their ships,
Or scatter the fleet and litter the sea with corpses.
I have fourteen Nymphs with lovely bodies,
The most radiant of which, Deiopeia,
I will pronounce your wife, to have and to hold,
In return for this favor. She will live with you
All her years and bear you beautiful children."

And Aeolus:

"It is yours to consider what you want,
My Queen, and mine to fulfill your commands.
To you I owe this modest realm and Jove's good will.

You grant me a seat at the table of the gods,
And you make me master of cloud and storm."

With that, he drove the butt of his spear
Against the cavernous mountainside, and the winds,
In battle formation, rushed out of all ports
And whirled over the earth. Swooping down,
They fell on the sea. Eurus and Notus
Churned up the depths, and with them Africus,
Whose dark squall line rolled huge waves shoreward.
The crews began to shout, the rigging creaked,
And then, in an instant, clouds stole the daylight
From the Trojans' eyes. Night lay black on the sea.
The sky's roof thundered and flashed with lightning,
And everywhere men saw the presence of death.

Aeneas' limbs suddenly went numb with cold.
He groaned and, lifting both palms to heaven, said:

"Three times, four times luckier were those
Who died before their parents' eyes
Under Troy's high walls! O Diomedes,
Bravest of the Greeks, if only I had been killed
By your right hand on Ilium's plain,
Where Hector went down under Achilles' spear,
Where huge Sarpedon lies, where the Simois rolls
So many shields and helmets caught in its current
And the bodies of so many brave heroes!"

As he was speaking a howling wind from the North
Struck against the sail. Waves shot to the stars.
The oars shattered. The prow swung around,
Exposing the side to the waves, and then
A mountain of water broke over the fleet.
The crews of some ships bobbed high on the crest,
While the wave's deep trough revealed to others
The deep seafloor churning with sand.
The South Wind twirled a trio of ships
Onto the Altars—the Italians' grim name
For the hulk of reef lurking under the sea.

The East Wind pushed another three ships
Into the shallows and ground them onto
The Syrtes' shoals, bedding them down
In pockets of sand. Another ship,
Which carried the Lycians and trusted Orontes,
Sank before Aeneas' own eyes. A wall of water
Crashed onto the deck, and the pilot flew headfirst
Into the sea. The ship spun around twice, three times,
Caught in a whirlpool that sucked it down quickly.
You could see men swimming here and there
In the vast gulf. Wicker shields, plaques,
And Trojan finery floated on the waves.
And now Ilioneus' strong ship, now Achates',
Now the ships that carried Abas and old Aletes
Were battered by the storm. Their joints sagged,
And they took on water through their splitting seams.

Meanwhile, the news filtered down to Neptune
Of the turmoil above. He heard the murmur
From the churning surface, and he felt
The still, bottom water rise in upheaval.
Lifting his serene face above the waves,
He peered out and saw Aeneas' fleet
Scattered, and the Trojans overwhelmed
By rough seas and the sky's downpour.
His sister's treachery was all too obvious.
Calling Eurus and Zephyrus, he said to them:

"Do you have so much confidence, Winds,
In your family connections? Do you dare
Overturn heaven and earth and raise tons of water
Up to the sky—without my divine sanction?
Why, I ought to . . . ! But settling the waves comes first.
You won't get off so lightly next time.
Now clear out of here! And tell your king this:
The sea and the trident were allotted to me,
Not to him. His domain is the outsized rock
That you and yours, Eurus, call home. Aeolus
Can puff himself up there, in his own hall,
And lord it over the prison of the winds."

Thus Neptune, and—no sooner said than done—
He calmed the sea, chased off the massed clouds,
And brought back the sun. Cymothöe and Triton,
Working together, pushed the ships off the jagged reef.
Neptune himself levered them up with his trident,
Cut channels through the shoals, and eased the swells,
His chariot's wheels skimming the whitecaps.

Riots will often break out in a crowded assembly
When the rabble are roused. Torches and stones
Are soon flying—Fury always finds weapons—
But then all eyes light upon a loyal citizen,
A man of respect. The crowd stands still
In hushed expectation. And with grave words
He masters their tempers and calms their hearts.

So too the crashing sea fell silent, as its sire,
Surveying the watery expanse, drove his chariot
Under a clear sky, giving the horses free rein.

Aeneas' men, numb with fatigue,
Made for the nearest land, the coast of Libya.

They found a deep bay, across whose mouth
An island stands and makes a good port:
The waves that roll in from the open sea
Break on its sides and ripple on to shore.
The bay is flanked by high cliffs. Twin crags
Rise like threats toward the sky, but the water below
Is sheltered and silent. Above, shimmering woods,
And, rising higher, a dark grove with sinister shadows.
Opposite the looming crags is a cave,
With sweet-water springs and stone seats inside,
A haunt of the Nymphs. Sea-weary ships
Need not be tied in this harbor, nor moored
By hooked anchors that bite the seafloor.

Aeneas puts in here with the seven ships
That are left of his fleet. Lusting for dry land,
The Trojans disembark on the welcome beach,

Laying their brine-soaked bodies on the sand.
Achates strikes a flint and catches a spark
In leaves, then feeds the flames with dry tinder.
The men bring out whatever grain they can salvage
From the spoiled stores and, weary of it all,
Parch the kernels and grind grain on stones.

Aeneas now climbed up to an isolated point
With a view of the sea spread out below,
Hoping to see where the storm might have left
The Phrygian galleys of Antheus
Or of Capys, or to glimpse Caicus' armor
Mounted high on the stern. There was no ship in sight,
But he did see three stags browsing on the shore
And behind them an entire herd, feeding
In a long line down through the valley. Aeneas
Stood still, as did faithful Achates,
Who passed over feathered arrows and bow.
He brought down the leaders, each standing tall
With a thicket of antlers, and then he shot
At the herd itself, scattering them with his arrows
Into the woods. He did not stop shooting
Until he had triumphantly brought down
Seven good-sized animals, one for each ship.
Back at the port, Aeneas divided the meat
Among all of his men and distributed wine
That the hero Acestes had stored in jars
And given to them at their departure
From Sicily's shores. And then Aeneas
Spoke to his men to ease their hearts:

"Trojans! This is not our first taste of trouble.
You have suffered worse than this, my friends,
And God will grant an end to this also.
You faced Scylla's fury in her thundering crags
And braved the Cyclops' rocks. Recall your courage
And put aside your fear and grief. Someday, perhaps,
It will help to remember these troubles as well.
Through all sorts of perils, through countless dangers,
We are headed for Latium, where the Fates promise us

A peaceful home, and where Troy will rise again.
Endure, and save yourselves for happier times."

Aeneas said this, and though he was sick
With worry, he put on a good face
And pushed his anguish deep into his heart.
They set about preparing a feast from the kill.
Some did the skinning and butchering
And skewered the still quivering flesh on spits.
Others set cauldrons on the shore and tended fires.
The meal revived their strength. Spread out
Along the grass, they took their fill of old wine
And fat venison. When the feast was finished,
They talked long about their lost companions,
Hoping they were still alive, but fearing
They had met their end and would hear no more
When their names were called.
Loyal Aeneas grieved especially
For bold Orontes, and lamented in silence
The bitter loss of Amycus and Lycus,
Of brave Gyas and brave Cloanthus.

The day was at an end, and Jupiter
Was looking down from heaven's zenith
At the sail-winged sea and at the shores
Of all the peopled lands spread far and wide,
And as he looked he paused at the sky's pinnacle
And turned his luminous eyes toward Libya,
Pondering the world's woes. And Venus, sad,
Her eyes shining with tears, said to him:

"Lord of Lightning, eternal Ruler of Gods and Men,
What has my Aeneas done to offend you?
What have my Trojans done? They have suffered
One disaster after another, and still the whole world
Is barred to them to keep them out of Italy.
Surely someday, in the turning of time,
The Romans are to arise from this race.
They will continue Teucer's bloodline
And give birth to rulers who will hold
Earth and sea under their dominion.
You promised. What has changed your mind,
Father? That promise was what consoled me
At Troy's heartrending downfall. I balanced one fate
Against another. But the fortunes of these men,
After all their mishaps, have still not changed.
What end, O Lord, will you grant to their toils?
Antenor was able to escape the Greeks,
Cross safely over the Illyrian gulfs,
Pass the Liburnians' inmost realms,
And skirt the springs of the Timavus
Where it bursts through nine roaring mouths
And floods the fields under a sounding sea.
There he founded the town of Padua,
Settled his Teucrians, named his race,
And fixed the arms of Troy on a temple wall.
Now he is at rest and enjoys peaceful ease.
But we, your own flesh and blood,
To whom you have opened the heights of heaven,
Have lost our ships—O the infamy!—
And because of one deity's anger are betrayed
And disbarred from the shores of Italy.
Is this the reward for devotion? Is this
How you restore our ancestral power?"

Smiling at her with the look that calms storms
And clears the sky, the Father of Gods and Men
Kissed his daughter lightly and said:

"Spare your fears, Cytherean. Your people's destiny
Remains unmoved. You will see Lavinium
And its promised walls, and you will raise
Great-souled Aeneas to the stars on high.
I have not changed my mind. Your son—
I will speak at length, since you are so worried,
Unrolling Fate's scroll and revealing its secrets—
Your son will wage a great war in Italy,
Crush barbarous nations, and set up laws
And city walls for his own people, reigning

In Latium until three summers have passed
And three winters since the Rutulians' defeat.
But the boy Ascanius, surnamed Iülus—
His name was Ilus while Ilium still stood—
Will be in power for thirty great cycles
Of the rolling months, will move his throne
From Lavinium, and build the mighty walls
Of Alba Longa. This kingdom will endure
For three hundred years under Hector's race,
Until Ilia, Vesta's royal priestess,
Pregnant by Mars, shall give birth to twins.
Then Romulus, proud in the tawny hide
Of the wolf who nursed him, will continue
The lineage, build the walls of Mars,
And call the people, after his own name,
Romans. For these I set no limits
In time or space, and have given to them
Eternal empire, world without end.
Even Juno, who in her spite and fear
Now vexes earth, sea, and sky, shall adopt
A better view, and with me cherish the Romans,
Lords of the world, the people of the toga.
That is my pleasure. And there will come a time
As the years glide on, when the descendants
Of Trojan Assaracus shall subdue
Glorious Mycenae, Phthia, and Argos.
From this resplendent line shall be born
Trojan Caesar, who will extend his Empire
To the Ocean and his glory to the stars,
A Julian in the lineage of great Ilus.
And you, Venus, free at last from care,
Will someday welcome him into heaven,
Laden with Oriental spoils of war,
And his name too will be invoked in vows.
Then war shall be no more, and the ages
Will grow mild. Grey-haired Faith, and Vesta,
And Quirinus with his brother Remus
Will make laws. The Gates of War,
Iron upon bolted iron, shall be closed,
And inside, impious Fury will squat enthroned

On the savage weapons of war, hands bound tight
Behind his back with a hundred brazed knots,
Howling horrible curses from his blood-filled mouth."

Thus Jupiter, and from heaven he dispatched
Mercury, Maia's winged son, so that Carthage,
With its newly built towers, would lie open
To welcome the Trojans, and that Dido,
In her ignorance of Fate, would not ban them
From her land. The god wings his way
Through the vast sky, quickly touches down
On Libya's shore, and just as quickly
Accomplishes his mission. At the god's will
The Phoenicians put aside their fighting spirit,
And, above all, the Queen conceived
A great benevolence toward the Trojans.

Aeneas, meanwhile, aware of his duty,
Was up thinking the whole night through.
When Dawn kissed his face with light, he resolved
To set forth and explore the strange coastline
To see which way the wind had blown him
And to see who lived there, man or beast,
In the untilled land that lay before him.
Then, he would report back to his men.
He hid the fleet under a rocky overhang
Steeped in a forest's shimmering shade.
Then he strode forth, with Achates
His only companion, gripping in his hand
A pair of javelins tipped with flared iron.

And there, in the middle of the forest,
Was his mother, coming toward him.
She looked and dressed like a young woman
And bore a huntress's weapons. She could have been
A Spartan girl, or Harpalyce of Thrace,
Who outruns horses and the Hebrus' rapids.
A supple bow was slung over her shoulders
In the style of a huntress, and she let her hair

Fly loose in the wind. Her flowing robe was cinched up
In a knot, offering a glimpse of her knees.
She spoke first:

"Have either of you seen
Any of my sisters? They're sporting quivers
And lynx hides. They may have wandered here,
Or are hot on the trail of a frothing boar."

Thus Venus, and the son of Venus responded:

"I've neither heard nor seen any of your sisters.
But how should I address you, Maiden? Your face
Is hardly mortal, and your voice does not sound human.
Surely you are a goddess. Apollo's sister?
One of the Nymphs? Whoever you are, Goddess,
Be gracious to us, lighten our burden,
And tell us, under what sky are we now?
Into what part of the world have we been tossed?
We are strangers in a strange land, lost,
Driven here by the wind and immense seas.
Many victims will fall by my hand at your altars."

And Venus:

"I am hardly worthy of such honor.
It is customary among Tyrian girls
To carry quivers and lace on high scarlet boots.
What you see around you is Tyrian country
And a Punic city from Agenor's bloodline,
But it borders on Libya, a warlike nation.
Dido rules here, having left her city, Tyre,
To escape from her brother. It's a long story,
Full of intrigue, but I will sum it up for you.
Dido's husband, Sychaeus, was the richest man
In Phoenicia, and loved dearly
By ill-starred Dido. Her father, with good omens,
Had given her to him untouched and virgin.
But her brother, Pygmalion, who ruled the land,
Was a most wicked man. A feud rose up
Between the two men, and impious Pygmalion,
Blind with gold-lust and contemptuous
Of his sister's love, secretly cut down Sychaeus
Before the altars, alone and off guard.
The villain hid his crime for a long time
And with many pretenses cruelly kept alive
Poor Dido's vain hopes. But the actual ghost
Of her unburied husband visited her dreams,
Lifting his pale face in wondrous ways.
He showed her the bloodstained altars,
Bared his pierced chest, and revealed the crime
At the dark heart of the noble house.
Then he urged her to flee the country,
And, to aid her journey, he showed her where
An ancient, secret treasure was buried,
Untold tons of silver and gold. Roused by all this,
Dido prepared for flight, joined by others
Who either feared or hated the cruel tyrant.
They commandeered ships, loaded them with gold,
And all the wealth of avaricious Pygmalion
Was shipped out to sea. A woman did this.
They arrived at the place where now you see
The soaring walls of a new city—Carthage.
They bought as much land as they could surround
With the hide of an ox, and so its name Byrsa.
But who are you? From what shores did you sail,
And where are you going?"

Faced with such questions,
Aeneas sighed and drew his voice from deep within:

"Goddess, if I were to start from the beginning
And tell you the whole tale of our suffering,
Dusk would gather over the dying day.
We are from Troy. Perhaps the name
Of that ancient city means something to you.
We have wandered the seas, and a storm
Has driven us to the coast of Libya.
I am Aeneas, devoted to my city's gods,
Refugees I rescued from enemy hands,

And my ship's most precious cargo. My fame
Has reached the heavens above. My quest
Is for Italy to be our fatherland, and to found
A race descended from Jove most high.
I embarked on the Phrygian sea with twenty ships,
My mother charting my course
As I pursued my destiny. Scarcely seven
Have survived the winds and the waves.
Lost, destitute, I wander the Libyan desert,
A man expelled from both Europe and Asia."

Venus would not endure any further self-pity
And interrupted him in mid-complaint:

"Whoever you are, I can hardly believe
You draw your breath cursed by the gods.
After all, here you are at our Tyrian town.
Just get yourself to the Queen's doorstep.
I foretell that your ships and comrades are safe,
Driven to shore by winds from the North—
Unless I've learned nothing about reading birds.
Observe the serenity of those twelve gliding swans.
An eagle, Jove's bird, swooped down from above
And disturbed their flight in the open sky,
But now they are flying in a long line again.
Some have landed, and you can see the others
Looking down for a good place to alight.
Just as those birds, in formation again,
Sport with wings whirring, rimming the sky
And issuing their song, so too your ships,
With their hearty crews, are either in port
Or entering the harbor under full sail.
Well, go on. Just let your feet follow the road."

She spoke, and as she turned, her neck
Shone with roselight. An immortal fragrance
From her ambrosial locks perfumed the air,
Her robes flowed down to cover her feet,
And every step revealed her divinity.

Aeneas knew his own mother, and his voice
Fell away from her as she disappeared:

"You! Do you have to cheat your son
With empty appearances? Why can't we
At least embrace and talk to each other
In our own true voices?"

With this rebuke,
Aeneas turned toward the city.
Venus, for her part, enclosed both her son
And his companion in a dark cloud,
Cloaking them in mist so that none would see them
As they walked along and so detain them
With questions about their reasons for coming.
And then she was gone, aloft to Paphus,
Happy to see her temple again, where Arabian
Incense curls up from one hundred altars
And fresh wreaths of flowers sweeten the air.

The two heroes, meanwhile, followed the path
And ascended a hill high above the city.
Looking down, Aeneas was amazed
At the sheer size of the place—once a few hovels—
The city gates, the bustle on the paved streets.
The Tyrians were hard at work, building walls,
Fortifying the citadel, rolling boulders by hand,
Marking out sites for houses with trenches.
As Aeneas watched, they made laws, chose officials,
Installed a senate. Some were dredging
The harbor, others laying the foundation
For a theater, carving huge columns out of a cliff
To grace the stage that was yet to be built—

Like bees under an early summer sun
Leading a new swarm out to the wildflowers,
Or stuffing honey into the comb,
Swelling the cells with nectar, or unloading
The pollen other bees bring to the stall,
Or warding off the worthless brood of drones:

The busy hive seethes with all their activity
And the fragrant honey is redolent of thyme.

"Happy are they whose walls are rising."

Thus Aeneas, as he surveyed the city's heights.
And then, hidden in the miraculous cloud
He mingled with the citizens, invisible to all.

At the city's center there was a shady grove.
It was here the Phoenicians when they made land,
Refugees from the surge and storms of the sea,
Had dug up the token foretold by Juno,
The head of a spirited horse, an augury
Of success in war and a prosperous people.
Here Sidonian Dido had dedicated
A huge temple to Juno, rich with offerings
And the goddess's presence. A bronze threshold
Surmounted the steps; the joints and beams glowed
With bronze, and bronze doors slowly groaned open
On heavy hinges. It was in this grove that Aeneas
Could finally relax; here he first dared
To hope for safe harbor and have confidence,
After all his trials, in a turn for the better.
For while he was waiting for the Queen,
Touring the temple, marveling at the city's
Great good fortune and at the work
Of various artisans blended together,
He saw pictured on the walls the whole Trojan War,
Whose fame had already spread through the world.
There were the sons of Atreus, there Priam,
And there Achilles, raging at each of them.
Aeneas stopped and said with tears in his eyes:

"Is there any place on earth, Achates,
Not filled with our sorrows? Look,
There is Priam! Here, too, honor matters;
Here are the tears of the ages, and minds touched
By human suffering. Breathe easy, my friend.
Troy's renown will yet be your salvation."

Thus Aeneas,
And he fed his soul on empty pictures,
Sighing, weeping, his face a flood of tears
As he scanned the murals of the Trojan War.

On one panel the Greeks are in full retreat,
With the Trojan youth hard on their heels.
In the other direction crested Achilles
Bears down on the Trojans with his chariot.

A little farther on he sees through his tears
The snowy canvas of Rhesus' tents,
His camp betrayed in their first night at Troy
And savaged by the blood-soaked son of Tydeus,
Who then drove the fiery steeds of Rhesus
To the Greek camp, before they ever tasted
Trojan fodder or drank from the Xanthus.

On another panel Troilus, just a boy
And no match for Achilles in combat,
Has lost his armor and is being dragged
By his stampeding horses. Fallen backward
From his empty chariot, he still holds the reins
While his neck and hair trail in the dust
And the plain is scored by the tip of his spear.

Meanwhile, Trojan women, their hair streaming,
Are going to the temple of implacable Pallas,
Bearing a robe and beating their breasts
In supplication. The goddess's head is turned away,
And she keeps her eyes fixed on the ground.

And now Achilles has dragged Hector
Three times around the walls of Troy
And is selling the lifeless body for gold.
Aeneas is choked with grief when he sees the spoils,
The chariot, the corpse of his friend,
And Priam stretching out weaponless hands.

And now Aeneas recognizes himself
In close combat with the foremost Achaeans

And sees the eastern ranks, dark Memnon's armor,
And Penthesilea among her thousands of Amazons
With their crescent shields. Burning with fury,
She binds a golden belt below one naked breast,
A warrior queen daring to do battle with men.

While Aeneas' gaze was fixed on these marvels,
The Queen was making her way to the temple,
The most beautiful Dido, and as she walked
A throng of youths crowded around her.

On the Eurotas' banks or the ridges of Cynthus
Diana leads the dances, and a thousand Oreads
Circle around her this way and that. A quiver
Hangs from her shoulder, and as she treads
She towers above the other goddesses,
And Latona's heart beats with secret joy.

So too Dido, moving through their midst,
Urged on the work of building a kingdom.
Then, under the temple's vaulted entrance
And flanked by guards, she ascended her throne.
She was making laws for her people,
Distributing duties or assigning them by lot,
When suddenly Aeneas saw, coming toward him
In a crowd, Antheus, Sergestus, and brave Cloanthus
Along with other Trojans whom the black storm
Had scattered and driven to distant shores.
Aeneas was stunned, Achates too, with joy and fear.
They burned with desire to clasp hands with them
But were confused and uncertain of the situation.
They kept themselves hidden inside the cloud
And watched. What has happened to their comrades?
On what shore did they leave their ships?
Why have they come here? These are chosen men
From all the ships, making for the temple
With loud cries and prayers for indulgence.

When they had entered and were allowed to speak,
The eldest, Ilioneus, calmly began:

"Queen, whom Jupiter has permitted
To found a new city and to curb with justice
The arrogance of the surrounding tribes,
We are Trojans, blown by winds over the sea.
In our misery we pray you to prohibit
The burning of our ships. Spare a pious race,
And look with grace upon our fortunes.
We have not come to pillage your homes
And carry the booty down to the shore.
There is no such violence in our hearts
And no such arrogance in a conquered race.
There is a place the Greeks call Hesperia,
An ancient land, strong in war and rich in soil.
Oenotrians once lived there. Now, it is said,
A younger race has named it Italy
After their leader. We were on course
For that land, when a sudden squall
Rose up—Orion behind it—and drove us
Onto blind shoals, scattering our ships
Amid trackless rocks and overwhelming waves.
We few drifted along and came to your shores.
But what race of men is this? What land
Is so barbarous that it allows this conduct?
We are denied access to the very shore!
These warmongers forbid us to set foot
On the border of their land. You may scorn
Our common humanity and mortal arms,
But the gods will remember good and evil.
We had a king, Aeneas, no one more just
Or devoted, no one greater in battle.
If Fate still preserves him, if he still breathes
The sky's pure air and does not yet lie with the shades,
We have no fear, nor would you regret
Being first to contend with him in courtesy.
There are cities in Sicily too, and arms,
And a hero of Trojan blood, Acestes.
Allow us to beach our storm-battered fleet,
To mill planks and trim oars from your woods,
So that if we find our comrades and leader,
And we are destined to go to Italy, to Italy

And to Latium we may gladly set forth.
But if all is lost, and you, noble father
Of the Trojan people, have gone down
In the Libyan sea, and Iülus
Is our hope no more, then at least we can seek
The straits of Sicily—whence we came here—
And our homes there, with Acestes as our king."

Thus Ilioneus, and all the Trojans
Murmured in approval.

Dido, eyes lowered, responded briefly:

"Fear no more, Teucrians, ease your hearts.
Stern necessity and my kingdom's newness
Force me to such measures to protect our frontier.
Who does not know of Aeneas and Troy,
Of that city's warriors and its exploits,
Of the conflagrations of that great war?
Punic hearts are not so dull and unfeeling,
Nor is Tyre so far from the course of the sun.
Whether you choose great Hesperia, land of Saturn,
Or Sicily, the realm of Acestes,
I will speed you safely on your journey.
Or would you like to settle here, share my kingdom?
The city I am founding is yours. Draw up your ships.
Trojan and Tyrian I will treat the same.
I only wish that Aeneas himself were here,
Driven in by the same South Wind. Be sure
I will dispatch our best men to scour the coast
And search every corner of Libya.
He may have been cast ashore and
May be wandering now in some wood or town."

Aeneas and Achates, alert to every word,
Had long been burning to burst from the cloud,
And now Achates turned to Aeneas and said:

"What do you think, Goddess-born? You see
That all is safe, our ships and men restored.

Only one is missing, and he went down in the gulf
Before our own eyes. Everything else agrees
With your mother's words."

He had scarcely finished
When the enveloping cloud parted
And dissolved into thin air. There stood Aeneas,
Gleaming in the clear light, his face and shoulders
Like a god's. His mother breathed upon him
The radiance of youth, breathed glory on his hair,
And she gave his eyes an exultant luster
Like the sheen of hand-rubbed ivory,
Or Parian marble, or silver set in gold.
Unforeseen, unexpected, he addressed the Queen:

"The man you seek is before you. I am
Aeneas, of Troy, saved from Libyan seas.
Dido, you alone have pitied Ilium's
Unutterable woes, and now you offer us—
The remnant left by the Greeks, outworn
By every misfortune on land and sea,
A destitute band—you offer us
A share of your city and your home.
We do not have the means to render worthy thanks,
Nor do any Trojan survivors anywhere
In the wide world. May the gods—
If any powers above look down on the pious,
If there is any justice anywhere—may the gods
And your good conscience reward you
As you deserve. What happy age bore you?
What noble parents gave birth to such a child?
While rivers run to the sea, while shadows
Move over mountainsides, while the sky
Pastures the stars, ever shall your honor,
Your name, and your praises endure,
Whatever the lands that summon me."

Aeneas spoke, and he reached out
For dear Ilioneus with his right hand,

Serestus with his left, and then the others,
His brave Gyas and brave Cloanthus.

Dido, stunned by his sudden appearance
And his great ill fortune, responded:

"Goddess-born, what misfortune has plagued you,
What force has driven you onto savage coasts?
You, then, are Aeneas, whom Venus bore to Anchises
Near the waters of the Simois river in Troy?
I remember well when Teucer came to Sidon,
Exiled by his father and seeking new realms
With the aid of Belus, my own father,
Who was waging war in Cyprus then,
Establishing his power in that rich land.
Since that time I have known about Troy,
Known you by name, and the Pelasgian leaders.
The Trojans' enemy sang Troy's praises
And wanted it known that he was of Trojan stock.
And so, young men, come under my roof.
My fortune too has long been adverse
But at last has allowed me to rest in this land.
My own acquaintance with suffering
Has taught me to aid others in need."

Thus Dido, and as she led Aeneas into her palace
She proclaimed sacrifices in his honor
In all the temples. Meanwhile, she sent
To his comrades on the shore twenty bulls,
A hundred boars with great, bristling backs,
And as many fat lambs with their dams,
The day's joyful gifts.
The palace gleamed
With luxurious furnishings as the great hall
Was being prepared for a banquet:
Coverlets embroidered with royal purple,
Heavy silver on the tables, gold cups engraved
With the heroic deeds of a long lineage
Stretching back to the origin of the race.

But Aeneas' love for his son, Ascanius,
Would not allow his mind to rest. He sent
Achates, on the run, to the ships
To report the news and to bring the boy
Back to the city. Ascanius was all Aeneas' care.
He also told Achates to bring presents
Snatched from ruined Ilium: a mantle
Stiff with gold-stitched figures, and a veil
Fringed with saffron acanthus, both worn
By Helen, who brought them from Mycenae—
Wondrous gifts from her mother, Leda—
When she sailed for Troy and her illicit wedding;
The scepter, too, of Priam's eldest daughter,
Ilione; and a pearl necklace; and a coronet
With a double band of jewels and gold.
And so Achates hurried off to the ships.

Venus, meanwhile, was busily concocting
Another scheme. She would send Cupid—
Transformed to look just like Ascanius—
To come in the place of that sweet boy
And with his gifts enflame the Queen's heart
And infiltrate her bones with fire.
The Cytherean feared this dubious union,
Tyrians speaking two tongues. She chafed
Under Juno's arrogance, and at nightfall
Her anxiety mounted. She turned, therefore,
To the winged God of Love and spoke to him:

"My son, my strength and my power, you alone
Scorn your father's Typhoean lightning blasts,
And so to your godhead I come on bended knee.
You know how your brother, Aeneas,
Is beaten about the sea by Juno's wrath,
And you have often grieved at my grief for him.
Phoenician Dido now has him, and detains him
With soft words. I dread the outcome
Of Juno's hospitality. She will not be idle
During this great turn of events. And so,
I plan to catch the Queen off guard and by guile

Encircle her with passion, so that no power
Can change her, and she will be bound to me,
By her great love for my Aeneas.
Now here is how I think you can do this.
The young prince, my pride and joy and all my care,
Is preparing to go, at his father's summons,
To the Sidonian city, bearing such gifts
As have survived the sea and the flames of Troy.
I will wrap him in slumber and tuck him away
In my sacred shrine, either high on Cythera
Or on Idalium, so that he will never know
Of my trickery or get in the way.
For a single night, no more, feign his looks.
Boy that you are, wear the boy's familiar face.
And when amid the royal feast and flowing wine
Dido, her joy knowing no bounds, takes you
Onto her lap, embraces you and plants
Sweet kisses on your mouth, breathe into her
Your secret fire and poison her unobserved."

Love obeyed his dear mother, donned his wings,
And walked off joyously with Iülus' gait.
Iülus himself Venus bathed in the waters
Of calm repose and, holding him to her breast,
Lifted him up to Idalia's high groves,
Where soft marjoram breathed upon him,
Nestled in blossoms sweet in the shade.

And so Cupid, obedient to his mother's word,
And delighting in the company of Achates,
Carried the royal gifts to the palace.
When he arrived, the Queen had already
Taken her place amid gorgeous tapestries,
Reclining on a golden couch in the great hall.
Father Aeneas and the Trojan youth gathered
And were made to recline on purple coverlets.
Servants poured water on their hands, served bread
From baskets, and brought them soft napkins.
There were fifty maids working in the kitchen
To prepare all the banquet's dishes in order

And to keep the hearth-fire for the Penates.
Another hundred, and as many male servants,
All the same age, laid the food on the table
And set out the cups.
The Tyrians too
Crowded the festive hall and were told to recline
On embroidered couches. They marveled
At Aeneas' gifts, and they marveled at Iülus,
At the god's glowing complexion, at the words
He feigned, and at the robe and the veil
Elaborately stitched with saffron acanthus.
Dido especially, doomed to a wretched end,
Could not satisfy her soul. The ill-fated Phoenician
Burned with desire when she gazed at the boy
And was equally moved at the sight of the gifts.
The boy, when he had hung on Aeneas' neck
And satisfied the deluded father's love,
Went to the Queen. And she clung to him
With all her heart, her eyes were riveted on him,
And she cuddled him on her lap. Poor Dido.
She had no idea how great a god had settled there.
Mindful of his Acidalian mother,
Little by little he began to blot out Sychaeus
And tried to captivate with a living passion
Her slumbering soul and her heart long unused.

At the first lull in the feast the tables were cleared.
Great bowls were set out and crowned with wine.
The palace grew loud, and the guests' voices
Echoed through the halls. Glowing lamps
Hung down from the fretted gold ceiling,
And flaming torches vanquished the night.
Dido called for a heavy gold drinking bowl
Crusted with jewels and filled it with wine—
A bowl used by Belus and Belus' descendants.
Then silence reigned in the great hall again.

"Jupiter, Lord of Hospitality,
Grant that this day be a happy one
For Tyrians and Trojan travelers alike,

And may our children remember it!
May Bacchus, giver of joy, be near,
May Juno bless us, and may all Tyrians
Favor our gathering with grace and good cheer."

Dido prayed and then poured a drop
Onto the table. After this libation,
Her lips were the first to touch the bowl's rim.
Then she passed it to Bitias with a challenge,
And he promptly drained the foaming bowl,
Soaking himself in the brimming gold.
Then the other lords drank.
Long-haired Iopas,
A bard taught by mighty Atlas,
Now sounded his golden lyre.
He sang
Of the wandering moon and the sun's toils,
Of the origin of human and animal kind,
Of how rain falls and why lightning flashes,
Of Arcturus, the Bears, and the misty Hyades,
Of why the winter sun rushes down to Ocean,
And why long winter nights are so slow to end.

The Tyrians applauded again and again,
And the Trojans joined in. And Dido,
Unhappy woman, prolonged the night
With varied conversation
And drank deeply the long draught of love.
She asked about Priam over and over,
Asked much about Hector, wanted to know
What armor Memnon wore when he arrived,
What the horses of Diomedes were like,
And how great was Achilles.

"Still better,"
She cries, "Tell us, my dear guest,
The whole story from the beginning—
The treachery of the Greeks, the downfall
Of your people, and your own wanderings.
Seven summers have now seen you roving
Through every land and over all the seas."

AENEID THREE

"After the gods saw fit to overthrow
The power of Asia and Priam's guiltless race,
After proud Ilium fell, and Neptune's Troy
Lay smoking on the ground, we were driven
By signs from heaven to seek another home
On far, desolate shores. We built a fleet
Close to Antandros and the mountains
Of Phrygian Ida. There, with no idea
Of our destiny, we mustered our men,
And when summer came my father, Anchises,
Ordered us to spread our sails to Fate.
With tears in my eyes, I left my native shores
And harbors and the plains where once was Troy.
An exile, I took to sea with my men, my son,
And the great gods of my country and home.

There lies at a distance a land dear to Mars.
Its wide fields, once ruled by Lycurgus,
Are tilled by Thracians, old allies of Troy
While Fortune still smiled. There I sailed
And on its curving shore began to build,
Under adverse auspices, my first city,
And named it after myself, Aeneadae.

I was bringing offerings to Venus
And the gods who bless new beginnings,
And I was preparing to slaughter a sleek bull
To the Lord of Heaven there on the shore.
Nearby was a mound, its summit crowned
With cornel shrubs and bristling myrtle.
I went over to it and bent down to pull
Some greenery from the soil to deck the altars,
When I witnessed an awful portent:
The first bush that I uprooted oozed drops
Of black blood that clotted on the ground.
A cold horror numbed my limbs, and icy fear
Coursed through my veins. Still, I pulled up
Another sapling, trying to understand
The mystery within. This one bled too.
Greatly troubled, I prayed to the Nymphs
And Father Mars, lord of Thracian fields,
To lighten this omen and turn it to good.
But when I pulled, with greater effort,
Upon a third branch, struggling on my knees
In the sand (should I speak or be silent?)
I heard a groan from deep within the mound,
A piteous voice that sighed on the air:

'Why are you rending my flesh, Aeneas?
Spare a buried man, do not commit
This sacrilege. I am no stranger to you,
But Trojan born, nor is it wood and bark
That wells with blood. Flee this savage land,
This avaricious coast. For I am Polydorus,
Transfixed by spears and overgrown
With an iron crop of sprouted blades.'

Fear now pushed me to the breaking point.
My hair stood on end, my voice choked.
This Polydorus had been sent by Priam,
With a fortune in gold, to be reared
By the king of Thrace. This was when Priam
Had lost all hope that his besieged city
Could be saved by arms. But the Thracian,
Seeing that Troy's power was broken,
Joined forces with victorious Agamemnon
And broke all faith. He cut down Polydorus
And seized the treasure. O cursed lust for gold,

To what do you not drive the human heart!
When the fear had ebbed from my bones
I reported these portents to the elders,
My father especially, and sought their judgment.
They were of one mind: to quit this accursed land
Where hospitality had been desecrated
And sail with the wind. We held a funeral
For Polydorus, heaping the mound high with earth
And erecting to his shade somber altars
Dark with cypress and deep purple ribbons.
The Trojan women stood around them,
Hair unbound in ceremony, while we offered cups
Foaming with warm milk and bowls brimming
With sacrificial blood. So we interred his spirit
And called his name for the very last time.

As soon as we had good sailing weather
And a whispering southerly called us to sea,
The crews launched the ships. Out from shore
We watched cities and lands fade in the distance.

In the middle of the sea lies a hallowed island,
Dear to the Nereids and Aegean Neptune.
The Archer God, loyal to the isle of his birth,
Stopped its wandering and moored it in place
Close to Myconos and Gyaros—the island
Delos, secure at last from the winds.
I pulled in there, and the island welcomed
Our weary men in its peaceful haven.
Onshore we paid homage to Apollo's city.
Anius, both king and priest of Phoebus,
Ran up to meet us, his brows bound with fillets
And sacred laurel. He recognized Anchises
As an old friend and, clasping our hands
In welcome, led us under his roof.

I began to pray in the god's ancient stone temple:

'Grant us, God of Thymbra, a home of our own,
Grant our weary band walls, a nation,

A city that will endure. Preserve a second Troy
For the remnant left alive by the Greeks
And merciless Achilles. Whom shall we follow?
Where shall we go? Where settle down?
Give us an omen, Father, slip into our hearts.'

These words were barely out when it seemed
Everything trembled. The door, the god's laurel,
The whole mountain shook, and the holy tripod
Bellowed loud as the shrine was laid open.
We fell to the ground, and a voice filled our ears:

'Enduring sons of Dardanus,
The land that bore you from paternal stock
Will welcome you back to her fruitful bosom.
Seek your ancient mother. From that land
The house of Aeneas will rule the world,
His son's sons and their sons thereafter.'

Thus Apollo, and amid tumultuous joy
Everyone asked, 'To what land, what city,
Does Phoebus mean we should finally return?'
Then my father, searching old memories, said:

'Listen, my lords, and learn what to hope for.
Crete, the island of great Jupiter, lies
In the middle of the sea. Mount Ida is there,
And there too is the cradle of our race.
Men live in a hundred cities there,
The realm most rich from which Teucer came,
Our earliest ancestor. If I remember rightly,
He sailed from Crete to our Rhoetian shores
And chose a site for his kingdom. Ilium
And high Pergamum had not yet been built.
Men lived in the lowlands. And from Crete came
The Great Mother Cybele, the Corybants' cymbals,
Our own wooded Mount Ida, the Mysteries' silence,
And the lions yoked to Cybele's chariot.
We must follow where the god leads,
Appease the winds, and sail for Cnossus.

It is not a far run. If Jupiter is with us,
The third dawn will anchor us off Cretan shores.'

Anchises spoke, and offered due sacrifice:
A bull to Neptune and to you, Apollo;
A black sheep to the Storms, a white to the Zephyrs.

A rumor reached us that Idomeneus,
The Cretan hero, had gone into exile,
That the island was deserted, our enemy gone
And the houses abandoned and empty.
We left Ortygia and flew over the sea,
Past Naxos ridged with Bacchic revels,
Past green Donysa and Olearos,
Past gleaming Paros and the Cyclades,
Threading the straits between the islands.
The seamen outdid each other chanting,
'On to Crete, the land of our fathers!'
And a following wind pushed us along
Until we glided up to the ancient shores
The Curetes once haunted. And so I began
To build my city. I called it Pergamum
And urged my people, who loved the old name,
To cherish their homes and raise the citadel
High with buildings.
                                        Our ships were just dry,
Drawn up on the beach, our youth beginning
Their families and farms, and I was busy
Making laws and parceling land, when suddenly
Heaven's air turned foul and pestilential,
And we were afflicted with a wretched plague,
A season of death that spread even to our crops.
Our people lost their sweet lives, or dragged
Their bodies around like corpses. Then Sirius
Scorched our sterile fields. The grass withered,
And the sickly crops denied us sustenance.
My father urged us to recross the sea
And ask Delian Apollo what end he might put
To our weary fate, where we might seek aid
In our distress, where to bend our course.

It was night, and all living things slept,
When the sacred images of the gods,
The Phrygian Penates I took with me
Out of burning Troy, seemed to stand
Before my sleeping eyes, clear in the moonlight
That flooded through the latticed windows,
And with these words they dispelled my cares:

'What Apollo would tell you on Ortygia
He tells you now, sending us unbidden
To your very door. We followed you,
Followed your arms when Ilium was burned;
Under you we traversed the swelling sea;
And we will exalt your coming descendants
To heaven's stars and give to their city
Empire over all. Prepare great walls
For the great, and do not shirk exile's long toil.
You must change your home. These are not the shores
Delian Apollo counseled; not on Crete
Did he bid you settle. There is a place
The Greeks call Hesperia, an ancient land,
Strong in arms and rich of soil. Oenotrians
Once lived there. Their descendants now
Have named it after their leader—Italy.
This is our true home. Here Dardanus was born,
The father of our race, and his brother Iasius.
Arise, then, be glad, and bring these tidings,
True beyond doubt, to your aged father:
Seek Corythus and the land of Ausonia.
Jupiter denies you the Dictaean fields.'

Awed by this vision and the voice of the gods—
It was not just a dream; I saw them clearly,
Their veiled heads and living faces,
And a cold sweat poured down my body—
I leapt out of bed, lifted both palms to heaven,
And with a prayer to the gods made pure offerings
Upon my hearth. This rite completed,
I rose with joy and told my father
All that had happened. He acknowledged

Our twofold lineage and his confusion
About our ancestry in two ancient lands.
Then he said:

'My son, steeled by Ilium's fate,
It was Cassandra, Cassandra alone
Who foretold to me our race's destiny,
Often naming Hesperia, naming Italy.
But who would believe that Teucrians would come
To Hesperia's shores? Who would be moved
By Cassandra's prophecies? Let us yield
To Apollo, and pursue the better course.'

My father finished, and we all cheered.
We abandoned this home too,
And, leaving a few behind, we spread our sails
And raced our hollow keels over the barren sea.

When our ships were sailing out on deep water
With no land in sight, but only sea and sky,
A brooding thunderhead settled in above us,
Bringing dark squalls to the shuddering waves.
Huge seas rolled under the winds, heaving us
All over the swirling abyss. Dark clouds
Shrouded the day, and foggy night
Blotted out the sky while jagged lightning
Split the air again and again. We were thrown
Far off course, wandering the blind waves.
Even Palinurus could not tell day from night
Or remember our heading. Three sunless days
We drifted the misty sea, three starless nights.
On the fourth day we raised land at last and saw
Mountains in the distance and curling smoke.
Down came the sails, and we manned the oars,
Churning the blue seawater into foam.

Delivered from the sea, I first made shore
In the Strophades, the Greek name given
To the islands set in the Ionian Sea,
Which dark Celaeno and the other Harpies

Made their home after they fled in fear
From the tables they kept in Phineas' palace.
No monster, no curse, no plague more grim
Ever raised itself from the water of Styx.
These birds have maiden faces, they drop
Foulest excrement, their hands are claws,
And their faces are pale with hunger.
When we entered the harbor we saw sleek cattle
Scattered over the plains and flocks of goats
Untended in the meadows. Swords drawn,
We rushed upon them, calling the gods
And Jove himself to share the bounty.
Then we built couches on the curved shore
And began to feast. But suddenly the Harpies
Swooped down from the mountains, beating
Their clanging wings, and plundered our feast,
Fouling every dish with their filthy touch,
And from the loathsome stench came hideous screams.
We set up the tables again, this time under
An overhanging rock deep in a hollow,
And relit the altar fires—and again they came
From their hidden lair, a clamorous flock
Circling above their prey with taloned feet,
And then they polluted the feast with their maws.
I ordered my men to take up arms and wage war
Against these dread creatures. We hid our swords
In the long grass and concealed our shields.
When they swooped down screeching along the shore,
Misenus gave the signal from his high lookout,
Sounding his brass horn, and my men charged
Into strange combat, determined to despoil
Those filthy birds of the sea. But their feathers
Felt nothing, they could not be wounded,
And they soared to the sky leaving their prey
Half-eaten and foul. One only, Celaeno,
A bird of ill omen, perched high on a cliff
And broke into prophetic speech:

'Sons of treacherous Laomedon,
Is this how you pay us for killing our cattle,

By waging war on the innocent Harpies
And driving us from our ancestral land?
Mark my words well. What the Father Almighty
Told to Apollo, and Phoebus Apollo to me,
I, first of the Furies, reveal now to you.
You are sailing the seas to reach Italy,
And so you shall, and enter her harbors.
But you shall not surround your city with walls
Until terrible hunger—and the way you wronged us—
Drives you to chew and swallow your tables.'

Celaeno spoke and then winged her way
Back to the forest. My men felt their blood
Turn icy with fear. Their spirits fell,
And they pleaded with me to sue for peace,
Resort to vows and prayers rather than arms,
Whether these were goddesses or hellish birds.
Father Anchises, with hands outstretched,
Called from the beach upon the great gods,
With proclamations of due sacrifice:

'Gods, stop their threats. Gods, avert harm.
Save the pious, O Gracious Ones.'

And he ordered
The stern cables torn from the shore
And the rigging uncoiled. A strong southerly
Stretched the sails and we escaped on sea-surge,
Where wind and pilot called our course.
Wooded Zacynthus appeared in mid-sea,
Then Dulichium, Samê, and craggy Neritus.
We passed Ithaca's cliffs, the realm of Laertes,
And cursed the island that nursed Ulysses.
Leucate's storm-whipped peaks soon came into view,
And Apollo's temple, dreaded by sailors.
Weary, we sailed up to the little town
And cast anchor. Our sterns fringed the shore.

Safe on land we never hoped to gain,
We purified ourselves with rites of Jove

And made the altars blaze with sacrifices.
Then we thronged the shore for Trojan Games.
My men, stripped and oiled, competed
In their age-old wrestling matches,
Glad to have slipped past so many Greek towns
And still be on their journey.
Time went by.
The sun rolled through the year's great circle,
And winter roughened the sea with icy winds.
I affixed a bronze shield, once borne by Abas,
To the doorposts and inscribed this verse:

THESE ARMS AENEAS DEDICATES
FROM VICTORIOUS GREEKS

Then I gave the order to man the benches
And pull out from the harbor. The crews
Outdid each other, sweeping the sea with oars.
In no time we dropped the peaks of Phaeacia,
Grazed the shores of Epirus, and entered
The Chaonian port of towering Buthrotum.

There we heard the incredible report
That Priam's son Helenus ruled
Over Greek cities, having won the bride
And kingdom of Pyrrhus, son of Achilles,
And that Andromache again had passed
To a Trojan husband. I was amazed
And burned with desire to question him
About this strange turn of events.
I was making my way up from the harbor
Just when, as it happened, Andromache
Was offering a ritual feast for the dead
In a grove outside the city, beside the waters
Of a pretend Simois, pouring libations
To the ashes of Hector and calling his ghost
To the empty mound of green turf
Hallowed with twin altars and with her tears.
She saw me coming, saw the Trojan arms,

And could not believe her eyes. She stiffened,
The warmth left her body, and she fainted.
After a long time she gasped out these words:

'Is the face I see real? Are you a true messenger,
Goddess-born? Are you alive? Or if the light
Has left you, where is Hector?'

She spoke
And poured forth her tears, filling the place
With her cries, so frantic I was scarcely able
To reach her with my few stammered words:

'Yes, I am alive, through all my trials.
You can believe what you see is true.
O, what has happened to you since you lost
Your noble husband? What fortune could be
Worthy of you—Hector's Andromache?
Are you still married to Pyrrhus?'

Eyes downcast,
Andromache lowered her voice and said:

'Priam's virgin daughter, Polyxena,
Was most fortunate of all, condemned to die
At an enemy's tomb beneath Troy's walls,
And never a slave in a conqueror's bed.
We, our city burnt, were taken overseas
And bore the disdainful pride of Achilles' son,
Giving birth in slavery. Later, he courted
Leda's Hermione and a Spartan marriage
And transferred me to Helenus,
A slave to a slave. Orestes, inflamed
With jealousy over his stolen bride
And hounded by the Furies, caught Pyrrhus
Off guard and killed him at his father's altar.
Helenus inherited part of Pyrrhus' realm
And called it Chaonia after Chaon of Troy
And built upon its hill a Pergamum,
This Iliadic citadel.

But you, what winds
Drove you on your fated course? What god
Has pushed you to our shores all unaware?
And what about your boy, Ascanius?
Is he alive and breathing heaven's air?
Even in Troy he . . .
Still, does he miss his lost mother?
Do his father, Aeneas, and his uncle Hector
Inspire him to ancestral valor?'

These words poured out of her as she wept,
And she was raising a futile lament
When the hero Helenus, Priam's son,
Came from the city with a great company.
He recognized us as kin and led us
Joyfully to the city's gates, yet weeping
Profusely at every word. As I advanced
I recognized a little Troy, a Pergamum
Modeled on the great one, a dry creek
Named after the Xanthus, and I embraced
Another Scaean gate. My fellow Teucrians
Enjoyed the friendly city as much as I did.
The king welcomed them in a broad colonnade,
And they poured libations in the center
Of a great hall, holding their wine-bowls
As the feast was served on platters of gold.

Day followed day, the breeze called the sails,
And a strong southerly bellied the canvas.
I approached the seer and made this request:

'Helenus, son of Troy, you speak for the gods.
You know the will of Clarian Apollo,
His tripod and laurel, and you know the stars,
The sounds of birds and birds on the wing.
All the omens concerning my journey
Have been favorable. All the oracles
Have counseled me to make for Italy
And distant lands. Only the Harpy,
Celaeno, has prophesied a portent

Horrible to speak of and threatened
Wrath and famine. Tell me now yourself,
What are the main perils I must shun,
And how may I overcome my trials?'

At this, Helenus first offered sacrifice,
Prayed for grace, and unbound his sacred brow.
Then he led me by the hand to the gates
Of your temple, Apollo, my mind soaring
With your presence, and prophesied:

'Goddess-born, it is clear that your journey
Over the deep is sanctioned on high, for so
The Lord of the Gods has ordained,
And so the wheel of destiny turns. I will,
Therefore, unfold for you a few things
Out of many, so you may more safely
Traverse the welcoming oceans and find
Haven in Ausonia. The Fates forbid
Helenus to know more, and Saturnian Juno
Censors my speech.
First, the Italy
That you, unknowing, think is near,
And whose ports you are preparing to enter
As if they were close, can only be reached
Along long coastlines and a long, pathless path.
You must first bend your oar in Sicily's waves
And sail your ships in the Ausonian sea
Past the netherworld lakes and Circe's isle
Before founding your city in a land secure.
I will now list signs for you to remember:
In great distress you will find a huge sow
Lying under oaks near a hidden stream
With a litter of thirty, a white sow
Lying on the ground nursing white young.
That shall be the site of your city,
And a sure rest from all of your labors.
Have no fear of gnawing your tables;
The Fates will find a way, Apollo will come.
Avoid the near coast of Italy
Washed by our sea. All of the towns are held
By evil Greeks. The Narycian Locri
Have built a city there. Cretan Idomeneus
Has occupied the Sallentine plains.
The famous town of Philoctetes is there,
Little Petelia, defended by her walls.
But when your ships have crossed the high seas
And stand moored, and you have built altars
And fulfill vows on the shore, veil your hair
With a purple robe, so that no hostile face
May appear in the fires and spoil the omens.
Both you yourself and your men should hold
To this manner of sacrifice. Let your children,
And theirs after, remain pure in religion.
When you leave, and the wind has borne you
To the coast of Sicily, and the straits of Pelorus
Begin to widen, make for land on the left
And seas on the left in a long circuit round.
Shun the shore and water on the right.
These lands, they say, broke apart from each other
Long ago, in a catastrophic
Upheaval (the ages can bring titanic changes),
When the two countries were a continuous whole.
The sea surged between, cutting off Sicily
From Hesperia, and in a seething channel
Washed fields and cities on separate coasts.
Scylla lurks on the right shore, and on the left
Insatiable Charybdis. At the bottom
Of her swirling abyss she sucks down
Tons of saltwater in three gulps, then spews
All of it up again, spraying the stars.
Scylla, though, lies in her cave's dark gloom,
Extruding neck and jaws, and dragging ships
Onto her rocks. She looks human above,
A beautiful woman down to her loins.
Below, she is a scaly monster, joining
A belly of wolves to dolphins' flukes.
Better to round Pachynus slowly,
Make the turn at this promontory,
And double back to complete the long lap,

Than even to glimpse Scylla's hideous form
In her vast cavern, or to come within sight
Of the rocks that echo with her cyan hounds.
    And this above all: If Helenus possesses
Any foresight, if I have as a seer
Any claim to belief, if Phoebus Apollo
Fills my soul with his truth—this one thing,
Goddess-born, this one thing before all,
I will foretell and repeat again and again:
Worship Juno. Pray to her first. Joyfully
Chant vows to Juno. Shower her majesty
With suppliant gifts and win her grace.
    At last you will leave Sicily behind
And be sent to the shores of Italy.
When you come to Cumae, its mystic lakes,
And the woods of Avernus, you will meet
A prophetess who in her frenzy
Chants the future and commits it to leaves
With marks and signs. Whatever verses
The virgin priestess scratches on leaves
She arranges in order and stores in her cave.
There they remain in their numbered ranks.
But if the door is opened and a light breeze
Disturbs the soft leaves and scatters them,
She does not bother to gather them up
As they fly through the cave, does not care
To arrange them again and order the verse,
And so those who inquired receive no advice
And learn to hate the Sibyl and her shrine.
Here you must spare no expense of time.
Though your men complain and your journey calls
And you have the chance to fill your sails with wind,
You must visit the prophetess. And plead with her
To open her lips and prophesy in person.
She will unfold for you Italy's nations,
The wars to come, how to flee some toils
And how to face others. Venerated,
She will also grant you a favorable voyage.
This counsel you are allowed to hear from my lips.
Go, and by your deeds lift Troy to the stars.'

Helenus finished his kindly advice,
And then ordered that gifts of heavy gold
And sawn ivory be brought to our ships,
And he himself stowed in our hulls
Massive silver and cauldrons from Dodona,
A coat of golden mail, and a superb helmet
Crested with plumes, arms of Pyrrhus himself.
There were gifts, too, for my father, and horses,
And pilots to guide us. . . .
Extra oarsmen, and gear for my crews.

Meanwhile, Anchises ordered the ships
Rigged with sails, so we could catch the wind,
And Helenus addressed him with deep respect:

'Anchises, worthy of wedlock with Venus,
Cherished by the gods, twice rescued from Troy,
Before you lies Ausonia. Sail to seize it!
Yet you must drift past this shore. Far is that part
Of Italy promised by Phoebus Apollo.
Go forth, blessed by the love of a pious son.
My long speech delays the rising wind.'

Andromache, too, sad at this last parting,
Brought robes embroidered with woven gold
And for Ascanius a Phrygian cloak,
And paid him more honor, loading him
With gifts from her loom, saying:

'Take these also, the work of my hands, child,
And let them remind you of the enduring love
Of Andromache, the wife of Hector.
Take these last gifts of your people, you,
The sole surviving image of my Astyanax!
He was just like you in his eyes, his hands,
The expression on his face. He would be
The same age as you are now, a growing boy.'

Tears welled up as I said my good-byes:

'Live happily. Your destiny is complete,
We are still called from one fate to another.
Your rest is won. You have no seas to plow,
No quest for ever-receding Ausonian fields.
Before your eyes is an image of the Xanthus
And a Troy that your own hands have built,
Under better auspices, I hope and pray,
And less vulnerable to the Greeks.
If I ever enter the Tiber and its valley
And look upon walls granted to my race,
We will have sister cities and be allies,
Hesperia allied to Epirus
With the same Dardanus as ancestor
And the same tragic past. We will make them
One Troy in spirit, and may it pass
Into the care of our children's children.'

We sailed past the near Ceraunian cliffs
Along the shortest sea-lanes to Italy.
Evening fell, and the hills grew dark.
We allotted the next day's rowers
And spread out on the dry sand
For refreshment and rest.
                    Sleep flowed
Through our bodies like a river. Night,
Driven by the Hours, was just half through,
When Palinurus woke. He rose
And tested the winds, listening.
His eyes scanned all the stars
Gliding in the sky, Arcturus,
The rainy Hyades, the two Bears,
And Orion armored in gold.
He saw their steady light in the clear air
And gave a piercing signal from his ship.
We broke camp quickly and headed out,
Spreading our sails. Soon the stars faded
In the roselight of Dawn, and we saw
Dim on the horizon the hills of Italy.
'Italy!' Achates was the first to call,

The golden sandals whose wings carry him over
Landscape and seascape in a blur of wind.
Then he took the wand he uses to summon
Pale ghosts from Orcus or send them down
To Tartarus' gloom—the same wand he uses
To charm mortals to sleep and make sleepers awake
And unseal the dead's eyelids. Holding this wand
He now rides the wind, sailing through thunderheads.
As he flies along, he makes out the summit
And steep slopes of Atlas, who shoulders the sky.
His pine-clad head is forever dark with clouds
And beaten by storms. Snow mantles his shoulders,
And icy streams drip from his frozen grey beard.
Mercury glided to a halt here, poised in the air,
And then gathered himself for a dive to the sea,
Where he skimmed the waves

like a cormorant
That patrols a broken shoreline hunting for fish.

And so the god flew from the mountain giant, Atlas,
(Whose daughter, Maia, was Mercury's mother)
And came at last to the beaches of Libya.

The wing-footed messenger stepped ashore,
And when he reached the huts he saw Aeneas
At work, towers and houses rising around him.
His sword was enstarred with yellow jasper,
And from his shoulders hung a mantle blazing
With Tyrian purple, a splendid gift from Dido,
Who had stitched the fabric with threads of gold.

Mercury weighed in at once:

"Are you, of all people,
Laying the foundations of lofty Carthage
And building a beautiful city—for a woman?
What about your own realm, your own affairs?
The ruler of the gods—and of all the universe—
Has sent me down to you from bright Olympus,

Bearing his message through the rushing winds.
What are you thinking of, wasting your time in Libya?
If your own glory means nothing to you,
Think of the inheritance you owe to Ascanius—
A kingdom in Italy and the soil of Rome."

With these words on his lips, Mercury vanished
Into thin air, visible no more to human eyes.

Aeneas stood there amazed, choking with fear.
He bristled all over, speechless, astounded,
And he burned with desire to leave that sweet land,
In awe of the commandment from the gods above.
But what should he do? What can he say
To the Queen in her passion? How will he choose
His opening words? His mind ranges all over,
Darting this way and that, and as he weighs
His options, this seems the best choice:
He calls his captains, Mnestheus, Sergestus,
And brave Serestus, and he orders them
To prepare the fleet for silent running, get the men
To the shore and the gear in order, but conceal
The reason for this change of plans. Meanwhile,
He explains that—since good Dido knows nothing
And would never dream that a love so strong
Could ever be destroyed—he himself will find
A way to approach her, the proper occasion
To break the news to her gently.
The captains
Were more than happy to fulfill his commands.

But the Queen (are lovers ever really fooled?)
Had a presentiment of treachery. Fearing all
Even when all seemed safe, she was the first
To detect a shift in the wind. It was evil Rumor
Who whispered that the fleet was preparing
To set out to sea.
She went out of her mind,
Raging through the city

as wild and furious
As a maenad when the holy mysteries have begun,
Her blood shaking when she hears the cry "Bacchus!"
In the nocturnal frenzy on Mount Cithaeron,
And the mountain echoes the sacred call.

Finally she corners Aeneas and says:

"Traitor! Did you actually hope to conceal
This crime and sneak away without telling me?
Does our love mean nothing to you? Does it matter
That we pledged ourselves to each other?
Do you care that Dido will die a cruel death?
Preparing to set sail in the dead of winter,
Launching your ships into the teeth of this wind!
How can you be so cruel? If Troy still stood,
And you weren't searching for lands unknown,
You wouldn't even sail for Troy in this weather!
Is it me? Is it me you are fleeing?
By these tears, I beg you, by your right hand,
Which is all I have left, by our wedding vows,
Still so fresh—if I have ever done anything
To deserve your thanks, if there is anything in me
That you found sweet, pity a house destined to fall,
And if there is still room for prayers, I beg you,
Please change your mind. It is because of you
The Libyan warlords hate me and my own Tyrians
Abhor me. Because of you that my honor
Has been snuffed out, the good name I once had,
My only hope to ascend to the stars.
To what death do you leave me, dear guest
(The only name I can call the man
I once called husband)? For what should I wait?
For my brother Pygmalion to destroy my city,
For Gaetulian Iarbas to lead me off to captivity?
If you had at least left me with child
Before deserting me, if only a baby Aeneas
Were playing in my hall to help me remember you,
I wouldn't feel so completely used and abandoned."

Dido finished. Aeneas, Jupiter's message
Still ringing in his ears, held his eyes steady
And struggled to suppress the love in his heart.
He finally made this brief reply:

"My Queen,
I will never deny that you have earned my gratitude,
In more ways than can be said; nor will I ever regret
Having known Elissa, as long as memory endures
And the spirit still rules these limbs of mine.
I do have a few things to say on my own behalf.
I never hoped to steal away from your land
In secret, and you should never imagine I did.
Nor have I ever proposed marriage to you
Or entered into any nuptial agreement.
If the Fates would allow me to lead my own life
And to order my priorities as I see fit,
The welfare of Troy would be my first concern,
And the remnants of my own beloved people.
Priam's palace would still be standing
And Pergamum rising from the ashes of defeat.
But now the oracles of Gryneian Apollo,
Of Lycian Apollo, have commanded with one voice
That the great land of Italy is my journey's end.
There is my love, my country. If the walls
Of Carthage, vistas of a Libyan city,
Have a hold on you, a Phoenician woman,
Why do you begrudge the Trojans
A settlement in Ausonia? We too have the right
To seek a kingdom abroad.
The troubled ghost
Of my father, Anchises, admonishes me
Every night in my dreams, when darkness
Covers the earth, and the fiery stars rise.
And my dear son, Ascanius—am I to wrong him
By cheating him of his inheritance,
A kingdom in Hesperia, his destined land?
And now the gods' herald, sent by Jove himself,
(I swear by your head and mine) has come down
Through the rushing winds, ordering me to leave.

I saw the god myself, in broad daylight,
Entering the walls, and heard his very words.
So stop wounding both of us with your pleas.
It is not my own will—this quest for Italy."

While he is speaking she looks him up and down
With icy, sidelong glances, stares at him blankly,
And then erupts into volcanic fury:

"Your mother was no goddess, you faithless bastard,
And you aren't descended from Dardanus, either.
No, you were born out of flint in the Caucasus,
And suckled by tigers in the wilds of Scythia.
Ah, why should I hold back? Did he sigh as I wept?
Did he even look at me? Did he give in to tears
Or show any pity for the woman who loved him?
What shall I say first? What next? It has come to this—
Neither great Juno nor the Saturnian Father
Looks on these things with impartial eyes.
Good faith is found nowhere. I took him in,
Shipwrecked and destitute on my shore,
And insanely shared my throne with him.
I recovered his fleet and rescued his men.
Oh, I am whirled by the Furies on burning winds!
And now prophetic Apollo, now the Lycian oracles,
Now the gods' herald, sent by Jupiter himself,
Has come down through the rushing winds
With dread commands! As if the gods lose sleep
Over business like this! Go on, leave! I'm not
Arguing with you any more. Sail to Italy,
Find your kingdom overseas. But I hope,
If there is any power in heaven, you will suck down
Your punishment on rocks in mid-ocean,
Calling Dido's name over and over. Gone
I may be, but I'll pursue you with black fire,
And when cold death has cloven body from soul,
My ghost will be everywhere. You will pay,
You despicable liar, and I will hear the news;
Word will reach me in the deeps of hell."

With these words she breaks off their talk
And in her anguish flees from the daylight
And out of his sight, leaving him there
Hesitant with fear, and with so much more to say.
Her maids support her as she collapses, take her
To her marble room, and lay her on her bed.

Aeneas, loyal and true, yearns to comfort her,
Soothe her grief, and say the words that will
Turn aside her sorrow. He sighs heavily,
And although great love has shaken his soul,
He obeys the gods' will and returns to the fleet.

Then the Trojans redouble their efforts
And haul their ships down all along the shore.
Keels are caulked and floated, leafy tree limbs
Are brought in for oars, and beams left rough
In the men's impatience to leave. You could see them
Streaming down from every part of the city.

Ants, preparing for winter, will busily plunder
A huge pile of seeds and store it in their nest.
The black line threads through the fields as the insects
Transport their spoils on a narrow road through the grass.
Some push the huge grains along with their shoulders,
Others patrol the line and keep it moving,
And the whole trail is seething with their work.

What was it like, Dido, to see all this? What sighs
Escaped your lips, when from your high tower
You saw the shoreline crawling with Trojans,
And the sea roiled with the shouts of sailors?

Cruel Love, what do you not force human hearts to bear?
Again Dido collapses into tears, again feels compelled
To beg Aeneas and to bow down to Love,
Lest she leave something untried and so die in vain:

"Look at them, Anna, scuttling across the shore,
Streaming down from every direction. The canvas

Can hardly wait for the breeze, and the sailors
Are laughing as they hang the sterns with garlands.
I had the strength to foresee this sorrow,
And I will have the strength to endure it, Sister.
There is one more thing I will ask of you.
You are the only one that traitor befriended,
Confiding in you even his deepest feelings.
Only you will know the best way to approach him.
Go, my dear, bend your knee before our archenemy.
Tell him I never joined the Greek alliance at Aulis
To burn down Troy, never sent my warships
To Pergamum, nor defiled his father's ashes
Or disturbed his ghost. Why, then, does he refuse
To admit my words into his obstinate ears?
What is his hurry? Is he too rushed to grant
The final request of his wretched lover:
To wait for favorable winds for his flight?
I am no longer asking for our marriage back—
The marriage he betrayed—nor that he do without
His precious Latium or relinquish his realm.
All I want is time, some breathing room for my passion,
Until Fate has taught me how the vanquished should grieve.
Beg from him this last favor, Sister. If he grants it,
I will pay it back with interest—by my death."

Thus Dido's prayer, and her sister sadly
Bore it to Aeneas, then bore it again. Unmoved
By her tears, he made no response to her words.
Fate stood in the way, and a god sealed the man's ears.

Alpine winds swoop down from the North
And struggle to uproot an ancient oak.
They blow upon it from every side until its leaves
Strew the ground and the strong trunk-wood creaks.
But the tree clings to the crag, and as high as its crown
Reaches to heaven, so deep do its roots sink into the earth.

So too the hero, battered with appeals
On this side and that. His great heart feels

Unendurable pain, but his mind does not move,
And the tears that fall to the ground change nothing.

And now Dido, in awe of her doom,
Prays for death. She is weary of looking upon
The dome of heaven, and, furthering her resolve
To leave the light, she saw as she placed offerings
On the incense-fumed altar a fearful omen:
The holy water turned black, and the wine,
When she poured it, congealed into gore.
She told no one of this, not even her sister.
There was more. Dido had in the palace
A marble shrine to her deceased husband,
A shrine she honored by keeping it wreathed
With snow-white wool and festal fronds.
Now she heard, or seemed to hear, her husband's voice,
When dusk had melted the edges of the world,
Calling her. And the owl, alone on the rooftop,
Would draw out its song into an eerie wail.
And the sayings of seers from days gone by
Would fill her with terror. And then in her sleep
A fierce Aeneas would pursue her as she raved.
And then she would be alone, abandoned forever,
Forever traveling a long, lonesome road
Through a desert landscape, searching for her Tyrians—

Like mad Pentheus when he sees the maenads,
And sees a double sun and a duplicate Thebes;
Or like Orestes stalked by Furies on an empty stage,
Pursued by his mother with torches and snakes
While the avenging Fiends lurk in the doorway.

And so Dido, worn down by grief, went mad.
Determined to die, she worked out by herself
The time and the means, and only then
Did she address her sister, hiding her plan
Behind a face radiant with serenity and hope:

"O Sister, I have found a way—be glad for me—
Either to get him back or free myself from love.

On the shore of Ocean, near the setting sun,
Lies farthest Ethiopia, where gigantic Atlas
Turns on his shoulders the star-studded heavens.
A priestess from there, of the Massylian tribe,
Has been presented to me. She guarded the sanctuary
Of the Hesperides, protected the golden apples
On their tree, and feasted the dragon
On honey and the poppy's drowsy opium.
She claims her incantations can set hearts free
Or plunge them into the depths of despair,
All as she chooses. She can stop rivers cold,
Make the stars turn backward, and conjure up
The spirits of night. You will hear the ground bellow
Under your feet, see elms stroll down mountains.
I swear by the gods, Anna, and by your dear head,
I am reluctant to resort to black magic. Still,
Build a pyre secretly in the central courtyard
Under the open sky and pile upon it
The weapons our impious hero left
On our bedroom walls, and all his forgotten clothes,
And the marriage bed that was my undoing.
It will do me good to destroy every reminder
Of that evil man—as the priestess told me."

She fell silent, and the color drained from her face.

In spite of everything, her sister Anna
Did not believe that Dido was inventing
These strange rites to disguise her own funeral.
She could not conceive of passion so great
And feared no worse for Dido now
Than at the death of Sychaeus.
                    And so,
Anna prepared the pyre.

But the Queen, out in the open courtyard—
Where the pyre now reared heavenward,
Vast with billets of pine and sawn oak—
Hangs the place with garlands and funeral fronds.

Upon the bed she arranges his clothes, the sword
That he left, and his picture, knowing well
What was to come.
There were altars
Around the courtyard, and the priestess
Shook her hair out free and chanted thunderous prayers
To three hundred gods, to Erebus and Chaos,
To three-bodied Hecate and Diana's three faces,
Virgin huntress, Moon, and pale Proserpina.
She sprinkled water as being from Avernus
And with a bronze knife harvested by moonlight
Herbs selected for their milky, black poison.
She calls for the love charm of a newborn foal
Torn from his forehead before his mother can eat it.
Dido herself, sacred cakes of barley in her pious hand,
Stands close to the altars, one foot unsandaled,
Her dress unbound. Then she calls to witness,
As one about to die, first Gods and then Stars
Who share Destiny's secrets. And then she prays
To whatever Power makes a final reckoning
For lovers who love on unequal terms.

It was night, and all over earth weary bodies
Lay peacefully asleep. Woods and wild seas
Had fallen still, and the stars were midway
In their gliding orbits. Ox and meadow were quiet,
And all the brilliant birds who haunt
The lapping lakes and tangled hedgerows
Were nestled in sleep under the dark, silent sky.

But not Dido, unhappy heart. She never drifted off
Into sleep, nor let night settle on her eyes or breast.
Her anxiety mounts, and her love surges back
And seethes, wave after wave on a furious sea.
At last she breaks into speech, debating in her heart:

"What am I doing? Should I entertain once more
My former suitors—and hear them laugh at me?
Go begging for a marriage among the Nomads,
After scorning their proposals time and again?
Shall I follow the Trojans' fleet and be subject
To their every command? After all, aren't they
So grateful for the help I gave them
That they could never forget my past kindnesses?
Even if I wanted to, who would let me on board,
Welcome someone so hated onto their ships?
Poor Dido, do you not yet appreciate
The treachery bred into Laomedon's race?
What then? Shall I crew with the Trojans
Cruising cheerfully away, all on my own?
Or should I, at the head of my own Tyrian fleet,
Give them pursuit, order my people to hoist sail
Into the wind again, a people I could scarcely persuade
To abandon their city back in Phoenicia?
No, Dido, die as you deserve, end your sorrow
With a sword.
You, my dear sister, caving in to my tears,
First loaded my frenzied soul with these sorrows
And put me in the enemy's path. It was not my lot
To live a blameless life as a widow, as free
As a wild thing, untouched by these cares.
I have not kept my vow to Sychaeus' ashes."

As these cries erupted from Dido's heart,
Aeneas, bent on leaving, with everything in order,
Was catching some sleep on his ship's high stern,
And in his sleep he had a vision of Mercury,
Returning to him in the same form as before,
The same voice and face, the same golden hair
And graceful body—and, as before, with a warning:

"Goddess-born, how can you sleep in a crisis like this?
Are you blind to the perils surrounding you,
Madman? Don't you hear a sailing breeze blowing?
Dido's heart revolves around evil. Determined
To die, she seethes with tides of raw passion.
Will you not flee now, while flight is still possible?
You will soon see this sea awash with timbers
And the shore in flames—if Dawn finds you

183

Lingering here. Push off, then, without delay.
A woman is a fickle and worrisome thing."

And with these words he melted into the dark.

Aeneas was deeply shaken by this apparition.
He tore himself from sleep and woke his crew:

"On the double, men, unfurl those sails
And get to the benches! A god has come down
From heaven again, urging us to cut the cables
And get out of here as fast as we can.
We will follow you, Holy One, whoever you are,
And gladly obey your commands again.
Be with us once more, grant us your grace,
And set propitious stars in the sky before us."

He spoke, drew his sword
Flashing from its sheath, and severed
The stern cable. Aeneas' fervor
Spread through the fleet. They ran to their posts
And shoved off from the shore, blanketing the sea
With their hulls. Leaning into the oars,
They swept the blue water and churned it to foam.

Dawn left Tithonus' saffron bed
And sprinkled the world with early light.
The Queen, in her tower, watched the day whiten
And saw the fleet moving on under level sails.
She knew the shores and harbors were empty,
The oarage gone. She beat her lovely breast
Three times, four times, and tore her golden hair.

"O God!" she said. "Will he get away,
Will this interloper make a mockery of us?
To arms, the whole city, after him!
Launch the fleet! Bring fire, man the oars!
What am I saying? Where am I?
What has come over me? Oh, Dido, only now

Do you feel your guilt? Better to have felt it
When you gave away your crown. Behold
The pledge, the loyalty, of the man they say
Bears his ancestral gods, bore on his shoulders
His age-worn father! Could I have not torn him
Limb from limb and fed him to the fishes?
Murdered his friends? Minced Ascanius himself
And served him up as a meal to his father?
The battle could have gone either way: What of it?
Doomed to die, whom did I have to fear?
I should have torched his camp with my own hands,
Annihilated father and son and the whole race,
And thrown myself on top of the conflagration.
O Sun, fiery witness to all earthly deeds,
And Juno, complicit in my unhappy love,
Hecate, worshiped with howls at midnight crossroads,
Avenging Furies, and gods of dying Elissa—
Attend to this, turn the force of your wrath
Upon sins that deserve it—O hear my prayer!
If this criminal is destined to make harbor again,
If this is what the Fates and Jupiter demand,
May he still have to fight a warlike nation,
Be driven from his land and torn from Iülus.
May he plead for aid and see his people slaughtered.
And when he has accepted an unjust peace,
May he not enjoy his reign or the light of day
But die before his time and lie unburied
On a desolate shore. This is what I pray for.
These last words I pour out with my blood.
And you, my Tyrians, must persecute his line
Throughout the generations—this your tribute
To Dido's ashes. May treaties never unite
These nations, may no love ever be lost between them.
And from my bones may some avenger rise up
To harry the Trojans with fire and sword,
Now and whenever we have the power.
May coast oppose coast, waves batter waves,
Arms clash with arms, may they be ever at war,
They themselves and their children forever."

Dido said these things and then set her mind
On a quick escape from the hated light. She exchanged
A few words with Barce, Sychaeus' nurse; her own
Was black ashes back in the old country.

"Dear Nurse, bring my sister Anna here.
Have her sprinkle her body with river water
And bring along the victims for expiation. You
Come with her, and wreathe your brows with wool.
I intend to complete the rites to Stygian Jove
That I have begun, and so end my troubles,
And to send the Trojan's pyre up in flames."

She spoke. The old woman quickened her step.
Dido trembled, panicked at the enormity
Of what she had begun. Eyes bloodshot,
Blotched cheeks quivering, pale with looming death,
She burst into the innermost part of the house,
Climbed the pyre like a madwoman, and unsheathed
The Trojan sword—a gift not sought for such a use.
The sight of the familiar bed and the clothes he wore
Made her stop in tears. Struggling to collect herself,
She lay upon the couch and spoke her final words:

"Love's spoils, sweet while heaven permitted,
Receive this soul, and free me from these cares.
I have lived, and I have completed the course
Assigned by Fortune. Now my mighty ghost
Goes beneath the earth. I built an illustrious city.
I saw my walls. I avenged my husband
And made my evil brother pay. Happy,
All too happy, if Dardanian ships
Had never touched our shores!"

Dido spoke,
And pressing her face into the couch:

"We will die unavenged, but we will die.
This is how I want to pass into the dark below.
The cruel Trojan will watch the fire from the sea
And carry with him the omens of my death."

With these words on her lips her companions saw her
Collapse onto the sword, saw the blade
Foaming with blood and her hands spattered.
A cry rises to the roof, and Rumor
Dances wildly through the shaken town.
The houses ring with lamentation
And the wails of women. Great dirges
Hang in the air. It was as if Carthage itself
Or ancient Tyre had fallen to the enemy,
And flames rolled through the houses of men
And over the temples of the gods.

Anna, in great distress, heard the cries.
She rushed through the crowd, clawing her face
With her nails, and beating her breasts
With her fists, and then spoke to her dying sister:

"So this is what it was all about, Sister.
You cheated me, didn't you? This is what
Your pyre was for, your altars, your fire—
To deceive me. What should I lament first,
Deserted like this? Did you scorn my company
In death? You should have called on me
To share your fate, to die by the sword
With the same agony, at the same moment!
Did I build this pyre with my own hands
Calling upon the gods of our fathers,
So that when you were lying upon it like this
I would not be here? Cruel! You have destroyed
Yourself, me, the Sidonian elders, and your city.
Ah, let me bathe her wounds, and if any last breath
Still lingers on her lips, let me catch it on mine."

She had reached the top of the pyre by now
And was holding her sister close to her bosom,
Sobbing as she used her dress to stanch
The blood's dark flow. Dido, trying to lift
Her heavy eyes, grew faint again. The wound hissed
Deep in her chest. Three times she struggled
To prop herself upon her elbow,

Three times she rolled back on the bed.
With wandering eyes she sought the light
In heaven's dome and moaned when she found it.

Then Almighty Juno, pitying Dido's long agony
And hard death, sent Iris down from Olympus
To free her struggling soul from its mortal coils.
Her death was neither fated nor deserved
But before her day and in the heat of passion.
Proserpina had not yet plucked from her head
A golden lock, nor allotted her a place
In the Stygian gloom. And so Iris flew down
Through the sky on sparkling, saffron wings,
Trailing in the sunlight a thousand changing hues,
And then stood above Dido's head.

"This offering
I consecrate to Dis and release you from your body."

As soon as she had cut the lock, all the body's warmth
Ebbed away, and Dido's life withdrew into the winds.

AENEID SIX

Aeneas wept as he spoke, and let the fleet
Glide along until it reached Cumae. Keels
Backed into the long arc of Euboean beach,
Prows seaward, as the anchors bit
Into the sea's shelving floor. Crews flashed ashore
Onto the banks of Italy. Some kindled fire
From veins of flint, some foraged timber
From the wilderness, others located streams.
But Aeneas, on a mission of his own,
Sought the high, holy places of Apollo
And the Sibyl's deeps, the immense caverns
Where the prophetic god from Delos breathes
Into her mind and soul and opens the future.
Aeneas and his men were soon within
The groves of Trivia and under golden eaves.

Daedalus once, fleeing Minoan Crete
On beating wings, trusted himself
To the open sky, an unused path,
North toward the Bears and a light landing
On this Chalcidian height,
And dedicated here his airy oarage
To you, Phoebus, and founded this temple.

On the doors, the murder of Androgeus
And the annual penalty for the Athenians,
Seven of their sons offered for sacrifice.
The urn stands ready, the lots are drawn. Opposite,

Rising from the sea, the island of Crete,
Raw passion for a bull, and Pasiphaë
In her furtive position, raising her knees.
And there too the mixed breed, the Minotaur,
Hybrid monument to unspeakable desire.
Here the Labyrinth winds its inextricable course,
And here is Daedalus himself, pitying
Princess Ariadne's great love, unraveling
The twisted skein of the maze, guiding Theseus'
Blind footsteps with a thread. And you also,
Icarus, would have played a great part
In this masterpiece, if grief had allowed:
Twice the artist attempted your fate in gold,
Twice the father's hands fell.

Aeneas' eyes
Would have scanned every last detail.
But Achates, sent ahead, was back,
And with him was Deïphobe, Glaucus' daughter,
Priestess of Phoebus and Trivia. A figure
Of divine awe, she had this to say to Aeneas:

"This is no time for looking at pictures.
You should be sacrificing seven bulls
From a sacred herd, and seven chosen sheep."

She spoke, and when Aeneas' men
Had seen to the sacrifice the priestess
Called the Trojans under the looming temple.

The flank of that Euboean cliff was carved
Into a hundred cavernous mouths, gaping orifices
That roar the Sibyl's oracular responses.
The virgin priestess greeted them at the threshold:

"It is time to demand your destiny. The god! Behold,
The god!"

And as she spoke there before the gates
Her color changed, her hair spread out

Into fiery points, she panted for air,
And her breast heaved with feral madness.
She was larger than life now, and her voice
Was no longer human, as the god's power
Took possession of her:

"You hesitate
To pray, hesitate, Aeneas of Troy?
The great mouths of this thunderstruck hall
Will not open until you pray."

And she was silent.
Fear seeped like icy water through the Trojans' bones,
And their lord poured forth his heart in prayer:

"Phoebus, who has always pitied Troy
In its darkest times, who guided the arrow
From Paris' hand into the body of Achilles,
And who guided me through so many seas
Pounding so many distant shores,
The remote Massylian tribes, the lands
Fringed by the shoals of the Syrtes—
Now at last we have in our grasp
The ever-receding shore of Italy.
May Troy's fortune follow us no farther.
You also, gods and goddesses
Whom Ilium's great glory offended,
May now justly spare the Dardan race.
And you, most holy prophetess, who hold
The future in your mind, grant the realm
That has been pledged to me by Fate,
Grant that the Teucrians settle in Italy
With the wandering, harried gods of Troy.
Then to Phoebus and Trivia I will dedicate
A temple of solid marble and holy days
In Phoebus' name. And a great shrine
Awaits you in our realm, gracious priestess,
An inner sanctum where I will deposit
Your prophecies and the mystic sayings

Told to my people and ordain your priests.
Only do not entrust your verses to leaves,
Playthings swirling when the wind gusts,
But chant them out loud."

Aeneas finished.
But the priestess had not yet taken Apollo's
Bit in her mouth, and she convulsed like a maenad
Monstrous in the cave, desperate to shake
The great god from her breast. All the more,
Though, he tired her rabid mouth, tamed
Her wild heart, and molded her to his will.
And now the cave's hundred mouths
Opened of their own accord and transmitted
The oracle's response through the empty air:

"You have escaped the perils of the sea,
But perils more grave await you on land.
The Dardanians will enter Lavinium—
Be sure of that—but will wish they had never come.
War, I see horrible war, and the Tiber
Foaming with blood. You will have another
Simois and Xanthus, another Doric camp.
A second Achilles has been born in Latium
To a goddess mother, and Juno will
Continue to afflict the Teucrians,
While you, a suppliant, shall beg for help
Throughout Italy. And the cause
Of all this suffering for the Trojans
Shall be once more a foreign bride,
An alien marriage.
Do not yield, but oppose your troubles
All the more boldly, as far as your fate
And fortune allow. Salvation will come first
From where you least expect it—
A Greek city will open wide its gates."

In words such as these the Sibyl of Cumae
Chanted eerie riddles from her shrine
In the echoing cave, shrounding truth

In darkness, as Apollo shook the reins
And twisted the goad in her raving heart.
As soon as her frenzy ceased, and her lips
Were hushed, the Trojan hero began:

"Virgin priestess, trouble of any kind,
However strange, no longer surprises me.
I expect it, and I have thought this through.
I ask for one thing. It is said that here
Are the dark lord's gate and the murky swamp
Of Acheron's backwater. Let me pass.
Open the sacred doors and show me the way,
So that I might see my father face to face.
I saved him, I carried him on my shoulders
Through fire and a thousand enemy spears.
He was at my side through the long journey,
Sharing the perils of sea and sky, crippled
As he was, beyond what his age allowed.
It was his pleas that convinced me to come
As suppliant to you. Pity father and son,
Gracious one, for you have the power.
Not in vain did Hecate appoint you
Mistress of the groves of Avernus.
If Orpheus could call forth his wife's ghost,
Enchanting the shades with his Thracian lyre,
If Pollux could ransom his brother, taking turns
With death, traveling the way so many times—
Not to mention Theseus and Hercules.
I too am descended from Jove most high."

So Aeneas prayed, clutching the altars.
And the Sibyl answered:

"Goddess-born son
Of Trojan Anchises, the road down
To Avernus is easy. Day and night
The door to black Dis stands open.
But to retrace your steps and come out
To the upper air, this is the task,
The labor. A few, whom Jupiter
Has favored, or whom bright virtue
Has lifted to heaven, sons of the gods,
Have succeeded. All the central regions
Are swathed in forest, and Cocytus
Enfolds it with its winding, dark water.
But if you have such longing, such dread desire
To cross the Styx twice, twice to see
Black Tartarus, and if it pleases you
To indulge this madness as a sacred mission,
Listen to what you must do first.
Hidden in a darkling tree there lies
A golden bough, blossoming gold
In leaf and pliant branch, held sacred
To the goddess below. A grove conceals
This bough on every side, and umber shadows
Veil it from view in a valley dim.
No one may pass beneath the earth
Until he has plucked from the tree
This golden-leaved fruit. Fair Proserpina
Decrees it be brought to her as a gift.
When one bough is torn away another
Grows in its place and leafs out in gold.
Search it out with your deepest gaze
And, when you find it, pluck it with your hand.
It will come off easily, of itself,
If the Fates call you. Otherwise you will not
Wrench it off by force or cut it with steel.
Farther, there lies unburied (ah, you do not know)
The lifeless body of your friend,
Defiling the entire fleet with his death
While you seek counsel at my doorstep.
Bear him to his resting place and bury him
In the tomb. Then lead black cattle here
As first victims to expiate your sins.
Only then will you see the Stygian groves
And realms closed to the living."

She spoke,
Closed her lips, and said no more.

Aeneas
Left the cave and walked on with downcast eyes,
Pondering these mysteries. Loyal Achates
Walked with him, just as worried, and the two
Talked with each other, trying to sort out
Which comrade might be dead, whose unburied body
The seer spoke of. Then they came to the shore
And saw on the beach the body of Misenus,
Dead before his time—Misenus, son of Aeolus,
Second to none at rousing men to war
With his bugle's call. He had been the companion
Of great Hector and fought at his side,
As good with a spear as he was with his horn.
But when Achilles deprived Hector of life,
Misenus joined the ranks of Aeneas,
Unwilling to follow a lesser hero.
But today he had been sounding a conch shell,
Making it blare and sing like the sea, insanely
Challenging the gods to a contest. Triton
Was jealous and, if the tale is true, caught
The man and drowned him in the rocks and surf.
And so they gathered around and mourned,
And Aeneas led the echoing dirge,
Since this also was his duty. Then,
In tears, they hurried to carry out
The Sibyl's orders, piling up trees
For his tomb's altar and rearing it skyward.
Then into the primeval forest, the deep lairs
Of wild things—and down fell the pines,
The ilex rang with the axe, ash logs and oak
Were split with wedges, and enormous trunks
Rolled down the mountainside.

Aeneas
Led the way in this work also, wielding
The same tools and cheering on his men.
But his heart was heavy, and as he gazed
At the deep woods a prayer came to his lips:

"Let the golden bough show itself now

On a tree in this forest, since the prophetess
Was all too right about you, Misenus!"

He had scarcely spoken when twin doves
Came fluttering down from heaven
Before his very eyes and settled
On the green grass. Aeneas' mind soared
When he saw his mother's birds, and he prayed:

"Show me the way, float on the air to the heart
Of the forest, where the earth lies soft
In the shadow of the radiant bough
And you, Goddess and Mother, do not fail me
In these doubtful times."

And he stood quietly,
Watching, tracking their direction in the trees.
The doves, as they fed, flew only as far
As someone following could keep them in sight.
But when they came to the jaws of Avernus,
With its foul smell, they ascended swiftly,
And then, gliding down through the limpid air,
They sat side by side on their chosen perch,
A tree through whose branches there shone
A discordant halo, a haze of gold.

During winter's cold, deep in the woods,
Mistletoe blooms with strange leafage
On a tree not its own and entwines
The burled branches with its yellow fruit.

Such was the gold seen on the dark ilex,
And so rustled its foil in the gentle breeze.
Aeneas seized it at once, and though the bough
Hesitated, he broke it off eagerly and brought it
Safely back beneath the Sibyl's roof.

The Trojans were still lamenting Misenus
There on the shore, performing final rites
For thankless ash. First, they built a huge pyre

Out of resinous pine and split oak,
Then trimmed its sides with gloomy foliage
And set up before it funereal cypresses.
They adorned the top with glittering arms.
Others heated water in bronze cauldrons
And bathed and anointed the cold body.
A cry went up. And then they placed the corpse,
Wet with their tears, onto the couch
And draped it with his familiar purple robes.
A small group lifted the heavy bier,
A poignant service, and with eyes averted
In ancestral manner, lit the fire. Flames crackled
Around the gifts heaped on the pyre—frankincense,
Platters of food, bowls filled with olive oil.
After the embers collapsed and the flames
Died away, they doused the remnant
Of glowing ash with wine. Corynaeus
Gathered the bones and placed them in an urn.
Then he circled the company three times,
Sprinkling them with water fresh as dew
From an olive branch, and so purified the men.
Then he spoke some last words. Aeneas,
In an act of piety, heaped above Misenus
A huge burial mound—with the hero's arms,
Horn, and oar—beneath a soaring hill
That is still called Misenus
And will bear that name throughout the ages.

The funeral was finished. Aeneas turned all his attention
To the Sibyl's commands.

There was a deep cave
With a jagged, yawning mouth, sheltered
By a dusky lake and a wood's dark shade.
Over this no winged thing could fly, so putrid
And so foul were the fumes that issued
From the cave's black jaws and rose to the sky
(And so the Greeks called the place Avernus).
Here the priestess set in line four black bulls,
Poured wine upon their brows, and plucked

The topmost bristles from between their horns.
They set them on the sacred fire as first offerings,
Calling on Hecate, mistress of the moon
And of Erebus below. Others slit the bulls' throats
And caught their warm blood in bowls
While Aeneas himself sacrificed a lamb,
Black-fleeced, to Night, the Eumenides' mother,
And to Earth, her great sister. To you,
Proserpina, he offered a barren heifer.
Then began a sacrifice to the Lord of Styx,
As at night's darkest hour the hero lay
Carcasses of bulls on the altars, pouring rich oil
On their burning entrails. But, look, under
The threshold of the rising sun the ground rumbled.
The wooded ridges trembled, and dogs howled
As through the gloom the goddess drew near.

"Begone,
Begone, you uninitiated!" shrieked the seer.
"Stand off from the grove! And you, Aeneas,
Onto the road and unsheathe your sword. Now
Is the time for courage and a heart of iron."

She spoke, then plunged wildly into the cave,
And Aeneas matched her stride for stride.

Gods of the world below, silent shades,
Chaos and Phlegethon, soundless tracts of Night—
Grant me the grace to tell what I have heard,
And lay bare the mysteries in earth's abyss.

On they went, shrouded in desolate night,
Through shadow, through the empty halls
Of Dis and his ghostly domain, as dim

As a path in the woods under a faint moon
When Jupiter has buried the sky in gloom
And night has stolen color from the world.

Just before the entrance, in the very jaws
Of Orcus, Grief and avenging Cares

Have set their beds. Pale Diseases
Dwell there, sad Old Age, Fear, Hunger—
The tempter—and foul Poverty,
All fearful shapes, and Death and Toil,
And Death's brother Sleep, Guilty Joys,
And on the threshold opposite, lethal War,
The Furies in iron cells, and mad Strife,
Her snaky hair entwined with bloody bands.

In the middle a huge elm stands, spreading
Its aged branches, the abode of false Dreams
That cling to the bottom of every leaf.
At the doors are stabled the monstrous shapes
Of Centaurs, and biform Scyllas, and Briareus
With a hundred heads, the Lernaean Hydra,
Hissing horribly, the Chimaera armed with flame,
Gorgons, Harpies, and the hybrid shade of Geryon.
Suddenly panicked, Aeneas drew his sword
And turned its edge against their advance,
And if his guide had not observed
That they were hollow, bodiless forms,
Flitting images, he would have charged
And slashed vainly through empty shadows.

From here a road led to the Tartarean waters
Of Acheron, where a huge whirlpool,
Churning with mire, belched all its sand
Into Cocytus. The keeper of these waters
Was Charon, the grim ferryman, frightening
In his squalor. Unkempt hoary whiskers
Bristled on his chin, his eyes like flares
Were sunk in flame, and a filthy cloak hung
By a knot from his shoulder. He poled the boat
Himself, and trimmed the sails, hauling the dead
In his rusty barge. He was already old,
But a god's old age is green and raw.

And now a whole crowd rushed streaming
To the banks, mothers and husbands, bodies
Of high-souled heroes finished with life,

Boys and unwed girls, and young men
Placed upon the pyre before their parents' eyes.

As many as leaves that fall in the woods
At autumn's first frost, as many as birds
That teem to shore when the cold year
Drives them over the sea to sunny lands.

There they stood, begging to be the first
Ferried across, hands stretched out in love
For the farther shore. But the grim boatman
Culled through the crowd, accepting some,
But keeping the others back from the sand.

Aeneas, shocked by this mob of souls, said:

"What does this mean, priestess, the spirits
Crowding to the river? How is it decided
That some must leave the banks while others
Sweep the bruised water with oars?"

And the priestess, ancient of years:

"Son of Anchises and true son of the gods,
You are looking at the lagoons of Cocytus
And the river Styx, by whose name
Even the gods fear to swear falsely.
The crowd you see are the unburied dead;
The ferryman is Charon; his passengers
Are the dead entombed. He may not carry
Any across the raucous, dread water
Until their bones are at rest. Else,
A hundred years they must roam the shoreline
And only then may return to cross these shoals."

The son of Anchises stopped in his tracks,
Pondering all this, and pitied in his heart
Their unjust lot. He saw among them,
Sad and bereft of death's due, Leucaspis,
And Orontes, captain of the Lycian fleet,

Overwhelmed by the storm that engulfed their ships
As they sailed the windy seas out of Troy.

And now there came Palinurus, who
While reckoning their course from Libya
By the stars had fallen from the stern
Into the waves. Aeneas hardly knew him,
Forlorn in the deep gloom, but finally
Recognized him and called out:

"Palinurus,
What god tore you from us and plunged you
Into the open sea? Apollo, never before
Found false, deluded me when he foretold
You would escape the sea and reach Ausonia."

And Palinurus:

"Delphi did not mislead you,
My captain, nor did any god drown me.
The rudder I was holding to steer our course
Ripped apart, and as I fell headlong I
Dragged it down with me. I swear by the wild sea
I was not so afraid for myself as for your ship,
Afraid that stripped of its gear and its pilot overboard
It might founder and sink in the heavy weather.
Three stormy nights the South Wind drove me
Over boundless seas. As the fourth dawn broke
I rode the crest of a wave and sighted
Italy. I fought my way toward land and thought
I had safety in my grasp. I hooked my fingers
On a crag of shore, but weighed down
By my dripping clothes I was easy prey
For a band of marauders. Wind and surf
Now roll my body along the tide line.
By the sweet light and the air of heaven,
By your father, by the promise Iülus holds,
Save me from these woes, Aeneas unconquered!
Either cast earth upon me—it is in your power
If you sail back to Velia—or if your divine mother

Shows you how (surely it is not your plan
To sail the great Styx without divine power),
Give me your hand and take me with you
Across these waves, so that I may at least
Find in death my final resting place."

Thus Palinurus, and the Sibyl answered him:

"Where did you get this outrageous desire?
Are you, unburied, to look upon the Styx,
The Furies' stream, and approach these shores
Unbidden? Stop hoping that the gods' decrees
Can be bent with prayer. But hear this
And bear it in your heart as consolation.
The neighboring peoples, in cities far and wide,
Will be driven by portents to appease your bones,
Will build a tomb, and to the tomb will tender
Solemn offerings, and forever the place
Will be called Palinurus."

By these words
His anguish was relieved, his grief dispelled.
And the land rejoices in the name Palinurus.

Continuing their journey, they drew near the river.
Out on the water the boatman saw them
Heading to the bank through the silent wood,
And before they could speak he rebuked them:

"Hold it right there, whoever you are
Coming to our river in arms! Why are you here?
This is the Land of Shadows, of Sleep
And drowsy Night. Living bodies
May not be transported in this Stygian keel.
I was not happy to take Hercules
Across the lake, or Theseus and Pirithoüs,
Invincible sons of the gods though they were.
One of them wanted to drag off in chains
The Tartarean watchdog from Pluto's throne—

And dragged him off trembling. The others tried
To carry off the queen from the bedroom of Dis."

Apollo's prophetess responded briefly:

"There is no such treachery here. Calm down.
Our weapons offer no threat of violence.
The giant watchdog may howl from his cave
Eternally and frighten the bloodless shades.
Proserpina may keep her chastity intact
Within her uncle's doors. Aeneas of Troy,
Famed as a warrior and man of devotion,
Goes down to his father in lowest Erebus.
If this picture of piety in no way moves you,
Yet this bough" (she showed it under her robe)
"You must acknowledge."

Charon's engorged rage
Subsided. No more was said. Marveling
At the venerable gift, the fateful bough
So long unseen, he turned the dark-blue prow
Toward shore. There he cleared the deck,
Pushed the shades from the benches, and laid out
The gangplank. He took aboard his hollow boat
Huge Aeneas. Groaning under his weight,
The ragtag craft took on water. At last,
The swamp crossed, the ferryman disembarked
Hero and seer unharmed in the muddy sedge.

Crouching in a cavern on the farther shore
Cerberus made these regions resound,
Barking like thunder from all three of his throats.
The seer, close enough now to see the snakes
Bristling on his necks, flung a honeyed cake
Laced with drugs into his ravenous jaws.
Cerberus snatched it from the air and then
Went slack, easing his huge, limp bulk
To the ground, stretching out over all his den,
Dead to the world. Aeneas entered the cave
And left behind the water of no return.

Now came the sound of wailing, the weeping
Of the souls of infants, torn from the breast
On a black day and swept off to bitter death
On the very threshold of their sweet life.
Nearby are those falsely condemned to die.
These places are not assigned without judge
And jury. Minos presides and shakes the urn,
Calls the silent conclave, conducts the trial.

In the next region are those wretched souls
Who contrived their own deaths. Innocent
But loathing the light, they threw away their lives
And now would gladly bear any hardship
To be in the air above. But it may not be.
The unlovely water binds them to Hell,
Styx confines them in its nine circling folds.

Not far from here the Fields of Lamentation,
As they are called, stretch into the vastness.
Here those whom Love has cruelly consumed
Languish concealed in sequestered myrtle glades,
Sorrow clinging to them even as they wander
These lost paths in death. In this region of Hell
Aeneas makes out Phaedra, Procris,
And mournful Eriphyle, displaying the wounds
She received from her son. He sees Evadne
And Pasiphaë and, walking with them,
Laodamia, and Caeneus, a young man once,
Now a woman, returned to her original form.
And among them, her wound still fresh,
Phoenician Dido wandered that great wood.
The Trojan hero stood close to her there
And in the gloom recognized her dim form

As faint as the new moon a man sees,
Or thinks he sees, through the evening's haze.

He broke into tears and spoke to her
With tender love:

"Oh, Dido, so the message was true
That you were dead, that you took your own life
With steel. Was I really the cause of your death?
I swear by the stars, by the powers above,
And by whatever faith lies in the depths below,
It was not my choice to leave your land, my Queen.
The gods commanded me to go, as they force me now
With their high decrees to go through this shadowland,
This moldy stillness, the abyss of Night.
I could not believe that I would cause you
Such grief by leaving. Stop! Don't turn away!
Who are you running from? Fate will never
Let us speak with each other again."

With such words Aeneas tried to soothe
Her burning soul. Tears came to his eyes,
But Dido kept her own eyes fixed on the ground,
As unmoved by his words as if her averted face
Were made of flint or Marpesian marble.
Finally she left, a stranger to him now, and fled
Into a darkling grove, where her old husband,
Sychaeus, comforted her and returned her love.
But Aeneas, struck by the injustice
Of her fate, wept as he watched her
Disappear, and pitied her as she went.

Aeneas and the Sibyl now made their way
To the farthest fields, a place set apart
For the great war heroes. Here Diomedes
And renowned Parthenopaeus met Aeneas,
And the pale shade of Adrastus. And here,
Lamented on earth and fallen in war,
Were many Dardanians. Aeneas moaned
When he saw their long ranks:
Glaucus, Medon, and Thersilochus,
Antenor's three sons; Polyboetes,
Priest of Ceres, and Idaeus,
Still with his chariot, still bearing arms.
They crowded around him, right and left,
And it was not enough for these shades

To have seen him: they want to linger,
To walk beside him and learn why he came.
But as soon as the foremost Danaans
And the battalions of Agamemnon
Saw Aeneas' arms flashing in the gloom,
They trembled with fear. Some turned to run,
As if fleeing again to their beachhead camp.
Others tried to shout, but their voices,
Thin and faint, mocked their gaping mouths.

And here Aeneas saw Deïphobus,
Son of Priam, his whole body mangled
And his face cruelly mutilated, shredded,
And both hands gone. His ears had been torn
From the sides of his head, and his nostrils lopped
With a shameful wound. Aeneas scarcely
Recognized him as he trembled, struggling
To hide his brutal disfigurement. He paused
But then addressed him in familiar tones:

"Deïphobus, mighty warrior
Of Teucer's high blood, who took delight
In such torture? Who dared treat you like this?
Word reached me that on that last night, weary
With endless slaughter of Greeks, you fell
On a heap of tangled corpses. I set up for you
An empty tomb on the Rhoetian shore
And called three times upon your ghost.
Your name and your arms guard the place.
You, my friend, I could not see, nor bury you
In your native soil before I had to leave."

And Priam's son responded:

"My friend,
You have left nothing undone but have paid
All that is due to Deïphobus' shade.
My own fate, and that lethal Spartan woman,
Plunged me into this misery. She left
These memorials! You know how we spent

That last night in delusive joy. You know,
You remember all too well. When the Horse
Leapt to the city's high, holy place, its womb
Heavy with infantry, Helen feigned
A ritual dance and led the Trojan women
Crying in ecstasy around Pergamum's heights
While she herself held the huge, blazing torch
That signaled the Greeks from the citadel.
I was asleep in our ill-starred bedroom,
Worn out with care, wrapped in slumber
As peaceful as death, while Helen,
My incomparable wife, was busy removing
Every weapon from the house and even slipped
My trusty sword from under my head.
Then she called Menelaus inside,
Hoping this would please her lover
And wipe out the memory of her old sins.
Why draw it out? They burst into my room,
Ulysses with them, the evil counselor.
O Gods,
If my face is pious enough to pray for vengeance
Make the Greeks pay in kind!
But you,
Tell me now, what has brought you here,
Alive? Were you driven here while roaming the sea,
Or by Heaven's command? Why do you visit
The drear confusion of this sunless realm?"

While they were talking, Dawn had climbed
High up the sky in her roselight chariot,
And they might have spent all their allotted time
On these matters had not the Sibyl warned:

"Night is coming on, Aeneas, yet we
Weep away the hours. Here is the place
Where the road splits into two. To the right,
Winding under the walls of great Dis,
Is the way to Elysium. But the left road

Takes the wicked to their punishment
In Tartarus."

Deïphobus responded:

"Do not be angry, great priestess. I will go
And return to my place in the shadows. But you,
Glory of our race, go. Go to a happier fate."

And on this word he turned away.

Aeneas suddenly looked back and saw,
Under a cliff to the left, a great fortification
Surrounded by a triple wall and encircled
By a river of fire—Phlegethon—
That rolled thunderous rocks in its current.
The Gate was flanked by adamantine columns
That could not be destroyed by any force,
Human or divine. High on a tower of iron,
Tisiphone sat, draped in a bloody pall,
Sleeplessly watching the portal night and day.
Groans, the crack of the lash, iron clanking,
And dragging chains grated on the ear.
Stunned by the noise, Aeneas froze in his tracks.

"What evil is here, priestess, what forms of torture,
What lamentation rising on the air?"

And the Sibyl began:

"Teucrian hero,
No virtuous soul may ever set foot
On this accursed threshold, but when Hecate
Made me mistress of the groves of Avernus
She showed me all of the punishments
The gods inflict.
Cretan Rhadamanthus
Rules this iron realm. He queries each soul,
Hears his lies, and forces him to confess

The sins whose atonement he has postponed,
In his deluded vanity, until too late. At once,
Tisiphone pounces upon the guilty soul
With her avenging scourge, brandishing
Glaring serpents in her left fist as she calls
Her sister Furies. Then, metal grinding
Upon metal, slowly open the Gates of Hell.
Do you see the face of the Fury who guards
The vestibule? The Hydra lurking within
Is much worse—fifty gaping black throats.
Then there is the pit of Tartarus itself,
Plunging down into darkness twice as deep
As Olympus is high. Here Earth's ancient brood,
The Titans, struck down by the thunderbolt,
Writhe in the abyss. And here too I saw
The twin sons of Aloeus, the Giants who tried
To tear open the sky and pull Jupiter down.
And I saw Salmoneus suffering torment
For aping the Olympian's thunder and lightning.
Torches shaking, he drove his chariot
Through all the cities of Greece in triumph,
And he brought his show of smoke and mirrors
Home to Elis, demanding a divinity's honors
For mimicking with bronze and horses' hooves
The inimitable rumble of thunderheads.
But the Father Almighty hurled his bolt—
No smoky torch—through the thick clouds
And blasted the sinner into perdition.
And Tityos is there, another son of Earth,
His body stretched over nine full acres,
And a monstrous vulture with a hooked beak
Gnaws away at his immortal liver
And tortured entrails, pecking deep for its feasts.
The bird lives in his bowels while his flesh,
Like his pain, is renewed endlessly.
And then there are the Lapiths, Ixion
And Pirithoüs, above whom a black rock
Totters, ever about to fall. Before their eyes
A banquet fit for a king is spread,
And high festive couches gleam with gold.

Reclining there, the eldest Fury
Keeps their hands from touching the table,
Rearing up with a torch and roaring 'No!'
Here are those who hated their brothers,
Struck a parent, or betrayed a client;
Those who hoarded the wealth they had won,
Saving none for their kin (the largest group this);
Those slain for adultery; those who did not fear
To desert their masters in treasonous war—
All these await their punishment within.
Do not ask its form, or what fortune undid them.
Some roll huge stones, or hang outstretched
On the spokes of a wheel. Theseus sits
And will sit forever. Phlegyas in his agony
Lifts his voice through the gloom, admonishing all:
'Learn justice, beware, do not slight the gods.'
This one sold his country for gold and installed
A tyrant; another made and unmade laws
For a price. This one went to his daughter's bed.
All dared a great crime, and did what they dared.
Not if I had a hundred mouths, a hundred tongues,
And a voice of iron, could I recount
All the crimes or tell all their punishments."

Thus the aged priestess of Apollo.

"But come, pick up your pace, and complete
What you came for," the Sibyl continued. "Hurry!
I see the walls forged by the Cyclopes
And the gates in the archway opposite, where
We have been told to place our offering."

They went side by side down dusky paths
And drew near the doors. Aeneas
Stood on the threshold, sprinkled his body
With fresh water, and fixed the bough in place.

The offering to the goddess complete,
Aeneas and the Sibyl now came
To regions of joy, the green and pleasant fields

Of the Blissful Groves. Air and sky
Are more spacious here, and the light shines
With an amethyst glow. The land here knows
Its own sun and stars.
Some are at exercise
On the grassy wrestling ground, some contend
On the yellow sand, others tread a dance
And chant a choral song. And Orpheus,
In the long robes of a Thracian priest,
Accompanies them on his seven-toned lyre,
Plucking notes with his fingers and ivory quill.
Here too is the ancient race of Teucer,
A people most fair, high-souled heroes
Born in better times—Ilus, Assaracus,
And Dardanus, founder of Troy.

Aeneas
Wonders at their weapons and chariots,
Mere phantoms, and yet their spears
Stand fixed in the ground, and their horses
Graze unyoked over all the plain.
The pleasure they took in arms and chariots
When they were alive, in keeping sleek horses,
Is still theirs now beneath the earth.
And he sees others, to the right and left,
Scattered on the grass, feasting, or singing
Songs of joy in a fragrant grove of laurel
Where the Eridanus rolls its mighty waters
Through forests to the world above.
Here too are those
Wounded fighting in their country's defense,
Those who in life were priests and poets,
Bards whose words were worthy of Apollo;
Also, those who enriched life with inventions
Or earned remembrance for service rendered—
Their brows bound with bands as white as snow.
When they had gathered around, the Sibyl
Addressed them, Musaeus especially,
Who stood head and shoulders above the others:

"Tell me, blessed souls, and you, best of poets,
Which part of this realm harbors Anchises?
For him we have crossed the rivers of Erebus."

The great soul Musaeus answered her briefly:

"We have no fixed homes but dwell in shadowed
Groves, recline on riverbanks, and live in meadows
Freshened by streams. But if you so wish,
Over this ridge I can show you an easy path."

He led them up and pointed out to them
Shining fields below. The pair went down.

Anchises, deep in a green valley, was reviewing
As a proud father the souls of his descendants
Yet to be born into the light, contemplating
Their destinies, their great deeds to come.
When he saw his son striding toward him
Through the grass, he stretched out
His trembling hands, tears wet his cheeks,
And these words fell from his lips:

"You have come at last! I knew your devotion
Would see you through the long, hard road.
I can look upon your face, and we can hear
Each other's familiar voices again.
I have been counting the hours carefully
Until this day, and my love has not deceived me.
All the lands and seas, all the dangers
You have been through, my son! How I feared
You would come to harm in Libya."

And Aeneas:

"You, Father, your sad image,
Kept appearing to me, leading me here.
Our ships stand offshore in the Italian sea.
Let me hold your hands in mine, Father,
Do not pull away from my embrace!"

As Aeneas said this he began to weep.
Three times he tried to put his arms
Around his father's neck. Three times
His father's wraith slipped through his hands,
As light as wind, as fleeting as a dream.

While they talked in this sequestered valley
A secluded grove caught Aeneas' eye.
A stream drifted past its rustling thickets—
The river Lethe—and around it hovered
Nations of souls, innumerable

As bees on a cloudless summer day
That settle upon wildflowers in a field
And swarm so thickly around the white lilies
That the whole meadow hums and murmurs.

Aeneas was shaken at the sight
And asked, in his ignorance, the reason
For this congregation. What was the river,
And who were the men crowding its banks?
Father Anchises answered:

"These are souls owed another body by Fate.
In the ripples of Lethe they sip the waters
Of forgetfulness and timeless oblivion.
I have been longing to show them to you,
The census of my generations, so that you
May rejoice as I do at finding Italy."

"Father, can it be that souls go from here
To the world above and return again
To their gross bodies? What is this yearning
For these poor souls to taste the light?"

Aeneas asked this.

"I will tell you, my son,
And not keep you in doubt."

Anchises answered,
And he revealed the mysteries one by one.

"First, heaven and earth, the sea's expanse,
The moon's bright globe, the sun and stars
Are all sustained by a spirit within.
Every part is infused with Mind,
Which moves the Whole, the source of life
For man and beast and all winged things
And the monsters of the marmoreal deep.
A divine fire pulses within those seeds of life,
A celestial energy, but it is slowed and dulled
By mortal frames, earthly bodies doomed to die.
And so men fear and desire, sorrow and exult,
And, shut in the shade of their prison-houses,
Cannot see the sky. Nor, when the last gleam
Of life flickers out, are all the ills
That flesh is heir to completely uprooted,
But many corporeal taints remain,
Ingrained in the soul in myriad ways.
And so we are disciplined and expiate
Our bygone sins. Some souls are hung
Spread to the winds; others are cleansed
Under swirling waters or purged by fire.
We each suffer our own ghosts. Then we are sent
Through spacious Elysium, and a few enjoy
The Blessed Fields, until the fullness of time
Removes the last trace of stain, leaving only
The pure flame of ethereal spirit.
All these,
When they have rolled the wheel of time
Through a thousand years, will be called by God
In a great assembly to the river Lethe,
So that they return to the vaulted world
With no memory and may begin again
To desire rebirth in a human body."

Anchises paused, and he led his son,
Along with the Sibyl, into the heart

Of the murmuring crowd. He chose a mound
From which he could scan all their faces
As they passed by in long procession.

"Now I will set forth the glory that awaits
The Trojan race, the illustrious souls
Of the Italian heirs to our name.
I will teach you your destiny.

That youth you see leaning on an untipped spear
Is first in line to be reborn, first in the upper air
From Italian blood mingled with ours,
Silvius, an Alban name, your last child,
Born in your twilight years and reared by your wife,
Lavinia, in a sylvan home,
To be a king and father of kings.
We shall rule through him in Alba Longa.

Next comes Procas, pride of our race,
Then Capys and Numitor, and then
Your avatar, Aeneas Sylvius,
Equal to you in piety and arms,
If ever he succeeds to Alba's throne.
Look at these young men, their strength,
Their brows shaded with civic oak!
They will build for you Nomentum, Gabii,
And the town of Fidena. They will crown
Collatia's hills with towers and will found
Pometii and Inuus, Bola and Cora,
Famous names someday, now places without names.
Then a son of Mars will support his grandsire—
Romulus, born to Ilia from the line of Assaracus.
Do you see the double plumes on his head,
And how the Father of Gods honors him
As one of his own? Under his auspices,
My son, Rome will extend her renowned empire
To earth's horizons, her glory to the stars.
She will enclose seven hills within the wall
Of one city, blessed with a brood of heroes

Also by Rosemary Lloyd:

Mallarmé: The Poet and His Circle
Closer and Closer Apart: Jealousy in Literature
The Land of Lost Content: Children and Childhood in Nineteenth-Century French Literature

Baudelaire's World

ROSEMARY LLOYD

CORNELL UNIVERSITY PRESS
Ithaca & London

First published 2002 by Cornell University Press

Printed in the United States of America

Library of Congress Cataloging-in-Publication Data

Lloyd, Rosemary.
Baudelaire's world / Rosemary Lloyd.
p. cm.
Includes bibliographical references and index.
ISBN 0-8014-4026-2 (cloth : alk. paper)
1. Baudelaire, Charles, 1821–1867. I. Title.
PW2191.Z5 L59 2002
841'.8—dc21

2002007299

Cornell University Press strives to use environmentally responsible suppliers and materials to the fullest extent possible in the publishing of its books. Such materials include vegetable-based, low-VOC inks and acid-free papers that are recycled, totally chlorine-free, or partly composed of nonwood fibers. For further information, visit our website at www.cornellpress.cornell.edu.

Cloth printing 10 9 8 7 6 5 4 3 2 1

"The Swan"

For Victor Hugo

Andromache, I think of you! This meager stream,
This poor despondent glass where lately shone
The mighty majesty of a widow's grief,
Deceitful Simois swollen by your tears,

Suddenly made my fruitful memory bloom
As I was crossing the new Carrousel.
The old Paris is dead and gone (a city's shape
Changes faster, alas, than does a mortal's heart.)

It's only in my mind I see the huddled huts,
Piles of half-finished capitals and shafts,
The grass, the broad blocks puddles had stained green,
And, glinting in the windows, the jumbled bric-a-brac.

There long ago sprawled out a menagerie,
There one morning, under the sky's bright cold,
When Work yawned awake, when road crews
Sent a dark storm into the silent air, I saw

A swan broken out of its cage,
Palmate feet rasping the dry pavement,
On the ruts of the road dragging its white feathers.
Near a waterless watercourse the beast, beak agape,

Nervously bathed its wings in the dust,
And said, heart full of its lovely mother-lake:
"Rain, when will you fall? When will the thunder roar?"
I watched this poor creature, this strange fatal myth,

To the heavens occasionally, like Ovid's humanity,
To the heavens, ironic and cruelly blue,
On its shuddering neck stretching its thirsty head
As if it were sending reproaches to God!

II

Paris changes! But nothing in my misery
Has altered! New palaces, scaffolding, blocks,
Old suburbs, everything serves me as allegory,
Old memories in me lie weightier than rocks

In front of the Louvre an image oppresses me.
I think of my great swan, with its gestures of madness,
Like exiles equally ridiculous and sublime,
And gnawed by unceasing desire! and then of you,

Andromache, from the arms of a great husband fallen,
Lowly beast, under the hand of the arrogant Pyrrhus,
Over an empty tomb bowed down in ecstasy;
Hector's widow alas! and wife to Helenus.

I think of the Negress, scrawny and consumptive,
Scrabbling in the mud and seeking with wild eye
The absent coconuts of Africa the superb
Behind the immense barricade of the fog.

Of whoever has lost what is never restored,
Never, never again!! Those whose thirst is slaked with tears
Suckling on Grief as if on a good she-wolf!
Of emaciated orphans who wither like flowers!

Thus in the forest where my spirit seeks exile
An old Memory rings out likely a wildly wound horn!
I think of sailors abandoned on islands,
The captives, the vanquished! . . . and many more still. . . .

OVID

METAMORPHOSES

TRANSLATED AND WITH NOTES BY

CHARLES MARTIN

INTRODUCTION BY

BERNARD KNOX

W. W. NORTON & COMPANY NEW YORK LONDON

The Introduction by Bernard Knox previously appeared in *The New York Review of Books*, with the exception of the final paragraph. Reprinted with kind permission of *The New York Review of Books*.

Detail of Grecian vase depicting the kidnapping of Europa by Jupiter disguised as a bull, ca. 470 A.D. © Christel Gerstenberg/CORBIS.

Printed in the United States of America
First published as a Norton paperback 2005

For information about permission to reproduce selections from this book, write to Permissions, W. W. Norton & Company, Inc., 500 Fifth Avenue, New York, NY 10110

Manufacturing by The Haddon Craftsmen, Inc.
Book design by Chris Welch
Production manager: Amanda Morrison

Library of Congress Cataloging-in-Publication Data

Ovid, 43 B.C.-17 or 18 A.D.
[Metamorphoses. English]
Metamorphoses / Ovid ; translated by Charles Martin.—1st ed.
p. cm.
Includes bibliographical references.
ISBN 0-393-05810-7 (hardcover)
1. Fables, Latin—Translations into English. 2. Metamorphosis—Mythology—Poetry.
3. Mythology, Classical—Poetry. I. Martin, Charles, 1942– II. Title.
PA6522.M2M44 2004
873'.01—dc22
2003014491

ISBN 0-393-32642-X pbk.
ISBN 978-0-393-32642-0 pbk.

W. W. Norton & Company, Inc., 500 Fifth Avenue, New York, N.Y. 10110
www.wwnorton.com

W. W. Norton & Company Ltd., Castle House, 75/76 Wells Street, London W1T 3QT

1 2 3 4 5 6 7 8 9 0

TO JOHANNA

Iphigenia on Aulis

His father, Priam, mourned, quite unaware
that Aesacus still lived on borrowed wings:
and Hector and his brothers pointlessly
conducted funeral rites before a tomb
with the name AESACUS carved into the stone;
Paris had failed to show up for the service,
but afterward brought an abducted bride
and a long war back to his own country:
a thousand ships and the whole Greek nation,
bound by their oath, came after in pursuit,
and would have promptly taken their revenge,
if fierce winds had not made the sea impassable,
and if Boeotia had not held the fleet
at the fishing port of Aulis; there, as they
prepared to offer sacrifice to Jove
in the manner of their country, and the ancient
altar was glowing with fresh-kindled flame,
the Greeks observed a dark-blue serpent winding
itself around a nearby pine tree's trunk.
   Eight fledglings nested high up in that tree,
and they, together with their mother, who
flew round her little lost ones, disappeared
into the serpent's gullet as he grabbed them!
   All were astounded save the prescient
augur, Thestorides, who spoke the truth:
"Rejoice, O Greeks, for victory is ours!
Troy will be taken, though it will take time!"
   In his interpretation of events,
each of the nine birds was a year of war.
Their living predator, who coiled around
the leafy branches, was turned into stone
that had the serpent's form engraved on it.
   The north wind still blew fierce on the Aegean,

and military convoys kept to port:
some held that Neptune, having built its walls,
intended to protect the Trojan city,
but not Thestorides: not ignorant,
and not one to keep silent when he knew
that a virgin goddess's fierce wrath must be
placated by a mortal virgin's blood.
And after piety had given way
to patriotics and the common good,
and kingship triumphed over fatherhood,
Iphigenia waited at the altar,
prepared to sacrifice her spotless blood,
surrounded by her grief-stricken attendants;
the goddess suddenly was overcome,
yielded, and cast a cloud before their eyes;
and there, in the officiating throng
of bloody ritual and beseeching voices,
Diana substituted—so they say—
a deer for Iphigenia.
Therefore, when
the goddess's cruelty had been appeased
by bloodshed and her anger (and the Ocean's)
had both subsided, the thousand ships discovered
a favoring wind, and after many trials,
at last they came to the Phrygian sands.

The house of Rumor

At the world's center is a place between
the land and seas and the celestial regions
where the tripartite universe is joined;
from this point everything that's anywhere
(no matter how far off) can be observed,
and every voice goes right into its ears.
Rumor lives here; she chose this house herself,
well situated on a mountaintop,

210

and added on some features of her own;
it has innumerable entrances
and a thousand apertures—but not one door:
by day and night it lies completely open.
It is constructed of resounding brass
that murmurs constantly and carries back
all that it hears, which it reiterates;
there is no quiet anywhere within,
and not a part of it is free from noise;
no clamor here, just whispered murmurings,
as of the ocean heard from far away,
or like the rumbling of thunder when
great Jupiter has made the dark clouds speak.
Crowds fill the entryway, a fickle mob
that comes and goes; and rumors everywhere,
thousands of fabrications mixed with fact,
wander the premises, while false reports
flit all about. Some fill their idle ears
with others' words, and some go bearing tales
elsewhere, while everywhere the fictions grow,
as everyone adds on to what he's heard.
Here are Credulity and Heedless Error,
with Empty Joy and Fearful Consternation;
and here, with Unexpected Treachery,
are Whispers of Uncertain Origin;
nothing that happens, whether here on earth
or in the heavens or the seas below,
is missed by Rumor as she sweeps the world.

Cycnus

Rumor let it be known that a Greek fleet
replete with gallant soldiers was approaching;
its arrival—not unexpected—was observed
by the opposing Trojans, who defended
their shores and kept the enemy from landing;

and you were first to fall, Protesilaüs,
dispatched by Hector's spear; those early fights
cost the Greeks greatly as they came to know
what skill brave Hector had at slaughtering.
Nor were the Phrygians exempted from
discovering how capably Achaeans
butchered *their* enemies, and soon the shores
grew red with blood; now Cycnus out of Troy,
the son of Neptune, cut his thousand down,
and now Achilles in his chariot
pressed on relentlessly against his foe,
flattening ranks of Trojans with each thrust
of his great spear, fashioned out of wood
from a tree harvested on Pelion;
and as he searched for Hector or for Cycnus,
met with the latter on the battlefield
(for Hector's fate had been postponed ten years);
then urging on his horses, whose white necks
strained at the yoke, Achilles drove
his chariot straight for the enemy,
and shook his spear to threaten him, and cried,
"Young man, whoever you might be,
take consolation, dead, from knowing that
your slayer is Thessalian Achilles."
So spoke the hero, and his weighty spear
followed directly on his utterance,
but though his cast was nothing less than certain,
the sharp point struck—and merely dinged the breast
of his opponent without harming him.
"O goddess-born," the other one replied,
"for your celebrity has preceded you,
why do you marvel that we stand unscathed?"
(It was indeed a marvel to Achilles.)
"Neither the golden, horsehair-crested helmet
that you observe me wearing, nor the curved shield,
the burden that I bear on my left side,
serves any purpose other than adornment.
Mars also, for this reason, puts on armor!
Deprive me then, of my protective gear,
and I'll *still* walk away from here unhurt.
"Breeding matters: it is good to be the son—
not of a Nereid—but of the one
who rules Nereus, his daughters—*and* the sea!"
He spoke and cast his spear at the Achaean,
but it was fated just to strike his shield,
tearing through bronze and nine layers of hide,
and lodging in the tenth.
He shook it off
and hurled another back with his strong hand,
but once again did not inflict a wound
on the undamaged body of his foe,
nor did a third spear even land on Cycnus,
although he offered himself openly;
you will have seen a bull in the arena,
who, with his terrifying horns, pursues
the provocation of a scarlet cape,
only to discover that he's missed it:
Achilles, raging, was not otherwise.
He checks his spear: is the tip still on? It is.
"My arm," he said, "that once was so very strong,
has lost its power—but only in this case?
—For surely, it was strong enough when I
was first to breech the walls at Lyrnesus,
or when this arm dyed Tenedos and Thebes,
Eetion's city, with their defenders' blood,
or left the Caïcus' swift current purple
from slaughter of the tribes along its shores,
or when Telephus—twice—felt my spear's heft!

"And here as well, among so many dead,
these heaps of corpses piled up on the shore
which I have seen and made, this arm of mine
has done—and still can do—its mighty work!"
He spoke as one who lacks all confidence
in the heroic deeds of yesterday,
and cast his spear directly at Menoetes,
one of the rank and file from Lycia,
and tore right through his armor and his breast.
And as the dying foot soldier crashed down
headlong upon the heavy earth, Achilles
withdrew the spear from its hot wound, and said,
"This is the hand, and this, the very spear
with which I have just now gained victory,
and which I'll use on him in the same way,
and hope to get the same results again!"
So speaking, he found Cycnus in the fray:
unerring ash struck unevading shoulder,
the left one, with a thud—then bounded off
as from a wall or from a solid cliff:
Achilles saw that Cycnus had been bloodied
where he had struck him and rejoiced—in vain:
there was no wound—it was Menoetes' blood!
Then truly outraged, roaring like a madman,
Achilles leapt from his high chariot,
and seeking his invulnerable foe,
he drew his shining sword and closed with him;
he noticed that although the other's shield
and armor had been punctured by his blade,
it lost its edge on his unyielding body.
Achilles could endure no more of this:
with shield and sword hilt as his weapons, he
assaulted him about the face and head,
blow after blow, until, as one gives way

the other one pursues, perturbs, keeps pressing him,
gives him no time to pull himself together.
Fear seizes Cycnus, and his vision blurs;
the path he flees on is obstructed by
a boulder in the middle of the plain;
as he lies with his back pressed hard against it,
Achilles seizes him and whirls him round
and flings him heavily against the earth.
Then kneeling on his shield on Cycnus' breast,
he strips the thongs that tied his helmet on
beneath the chin, and wraps them round his throat
and strangles him.
Preparing to despoil
his conquered enemy, he notices
the armor that he seeks has been abandoned,
for Neptune took the body of his foe
and transformed Cycnus into that white bird
whose name, until quite recently, he bore.

Caeneus

This effort, this contention, earned a rest
of several days, when arms were put away,
and on both sides, the combatants stood down;
as wakeful sentries paced the Trojan walls
and Argive trenches, the warriors relaxed.
Achilles, who had triumphed over Cycnus,
was pacifying Pallas with the blood
of a slain heifer; when its entrails were
ablaze upon the altars, and the reek
of burning flesh, so cherished by the gods,
had made its way to heaven, the immortals
received their portion, and the rest of it
was set out on the tables to be eaten.
The officers all took their ease, reclining
on couches where they stuffed themselves with meat

and drove away their cares and thirst with wine.
No lyres for this lot, no poetry,
no flutes of boxwood, pierced with many holes:
what pleases them is to extend the night
by telling stories of heroic deeds;
they reenact old wars, their own and others,
and are delighted to remember all
the dangers they've endured and gotten through:
what else has great Achilles to discuss?
What else is there to speak of in his presence?
The subject of their stories was, in fact,
his latest victory: the fall of Cycnus
seemed quite a marvel to this gathering:
that any youth should have a body which
no spear could penetrate to wound,
and which, in fact, turned blunted steel away,
astounded all the Greeks—even Achilles.
But Nestor told them, "Cycnus was unique,
the only one in all your generation
who spurned the sword, impervious to wounds.
But I have seen Thessalian Caeneus—
oh, this was long ago—who could endure
a thousand blows without a single wound!
"Thessalian Caeneus, yes, indeed,
the one who used to dwell on Mount Othrys,
and once was famous for heroic deeds—
but what was most amazing about *him*,
was that he had been born . . . a *her*."
Astonished
by such a marvel, his whole audience
implored him to continue with the story.
Achilles, among others, interjected:
"Do tell! For this entire company,
O fluent elder, source of sagacity,

is equal in its eagerness to learn
who Caeneus was, how he changed his sex,
in what campaign or battle did you know him,
and how was he defeated—if he was."
Nestor replied: "Though my extreme old age
is something of an obstacle to me,
and much of what I witnessed in my youth
I have forgotten, still I remember much,
and nothing stands out more in memory,
among so many acts of war and peace,
than this does. But if great expanse of years
makes one a living witness of so much
that happened, I have lived two centuries
already, and am living in my third!
"The daughter of Elatus was a maiden
named Caenis, celebrated for her beauty,
the most attractive of Thessalian women
in all the nearby cities, and in yours,
Achilles, for she grew up in your town.
"A host of suitors hoped in vain to wed her—
your father Peleus might have been one
had he not taken Thetis as his bride
already, or had they not been betrothed.
"But Caenis had no wish for any marriage,
and one day, as the story went, while she
was traveling alone along the shore,
the sea god, Neptune, forced himself on her.
"And after he had taken his delight
by ravishing the maiden, he announced,
'Whatever you desire will be granted!
Fear no refusal; ask and it is given.'
(The story that I mentioned said this too.)
"Caenis replied: 'The injury you've done me
requires a great wish to be set right;

that I might never suffer this again,
allow that I may be no more a woman,
and you will have fulfilled me utterly.'

"The words she ended her prayer with were deeper
than those that she began it with, and seemed
as though they could be coming from a man.
And so it was: for Neptune had already
assented, and now gave much greater gifts:
that she should be impervious to wounds,
and never fall a victim to the sword.

"Caeneus went off happily with these,
and spent his days in masculine pursuits,
wandering in the fields of Peneus,
delighting in his new phallicity.

214

The death of Achilles

But the god who rules the waters with his trident
still felt paternal sorrow for his son
Cycnus, who had been changed into a swan,
as he lamented the death of Phaëthon,
and exercised his unremitting wrath
on manslaying Achilles, whom he hated.
War had been waged for almost ten years now,
and Neptune urged Apollo's intervention:
"O most obliging of my brother's sons,
with whom I built Troy's ineffectual walls,
do you not groan at sight of that citadel
so soon to fall? And do you not lament
for the many thousands slain defending it?
And of those many, whom I will not speak of,
does not the shade of Hector rise from below,
his corpse appearing just as when Achilles
shamefully dragged him round the Trojan walls?
"But he who has a greater thirst for blood
than even Mars himself, the pillager
of our handiwork—Achilles—he still lives!
Give him to me, and I will make him feel
what I can do with my three-pronged spear!
"But since I am not permitted to engage
my enemy in combat hand to hand,

the task is yours: slay him with an arrow,
unseen and unexpected."
So Apollo,
agreeing with his uncle, gave assent,
and in a cloud, came to the Trojan front,
where, in the midst of slaughter, he discerned
Paris, lackadaisically shooting
his arrows at anonymous Achaeans.
Revealing his divinity to him,
Apollo said, "Why do you waste your barbs
on nobodies? If you have any care
for your own people, take aim at Achilles,
and so avenge his slaughter of your brothers!"
And with these words, he showed him where Achilles
was devastating Trojans with his spear,
and made him turn his bow in that direction,
and with his own death-dealing hand, he guided
that certain arrow to its fated target.
Not since the death of Hector had old Priam
a cause for celebration; now he had:
that you, Achilles, conqueror of many,
are overcome by an unheroic
adulterer who snatched a Grecian's wife!
Better that you were slain in battle by
an Amazon, wielding her double axe.
Now he who was the terror of the Trojans,
the glory and protector of the Greeks,
invincible Achilles, has been burned
upon the pyre; one god and the same
armed this great hero and consumed him quite;
now he is ashes: and the little left
of great Achilles scarcely fills an urn,
although his living glory fills the world.

That glory is the measure of the man,
and it is this that is Achilles' essence,
nor does he feel the emptiness of death.

His very shield—that you should be aware
whose it once was—now instigates a battle,
and for his arms, arms are now taken up.
None of the lesser leaders, such as Ajax,
the son of Oileos, or Diomedes,
or Menelaüs dares to lay a claim,
nor any of the other leaders, more
distinguished for their age and experience;
only Ajax, the son of Telamon,
and Ulysses are bold enough to do so.

Now Agamemnon, to spare himself the thankless
burden of deciding on this issue,
ordered the Argive leaders to assemble
in the middle of the camp, and hear the case,
and come to a decision by themselves.

The leaders were seated while the common grunts
stood round them in a circle. Ajax rose,
the master of the seven-layered shield,
now barely able to contain his anger.
He looked back at the fleet along the shore,
then pointed to it, fiercely glowering:
"By Jupiter, it is appropriate
to plead my case before these ships," he said,
and fitting that I clash here with Ulysses,
who did not hesitate to yield them up
to Hector's torches—which I held at bay,
then put to flight!
"There's more security
in flinging lies than fighting hand to hand.
But I'm as slow to speak as he to act;
I am his master on the battlefield,
as he is mine—when it comes to talking.
"Nor is it necessary, fellow Greeks,
that I remind you once again of my great deeds,
for you have seen them: let Ulysses tell
his stories of events that went unwitnessed,
which none but night, it seems, was privy to.
"I realize I seek a great reward,
but having such a rival is demeaning
and cheats me of the honor I am due:
Ajax cannot be proud to win a prize,
no matter how substantial, that Ulysses
can have the expectation of receiving;
he has already gotten his reward,
for when his claim has been rejected, he
can boast that he and I were fairly matched!
"But even if my courage were in doubt,
my lineage would prove superior

to his, for I am the son of Telamon,
who, under Hercules, once captured Troy,
then sailed to Colchis for the Golden Fleece;
Telamon's father was Aeacus, the stern judge
of the silent underworld, where Sisyphus
is forced to push a huge rock up a hill.
Since Jupiter, the highest god in heaven,
acknowledges Aeacus as his son,
I am the great-great-grandson of great Jove!
"But this connection should not advance my cause
unless I am related to Achilles:
and he's my cousin! I seek a cousin's arms!
And why do you, O son of Sisyphus,
and most like him in lies and thievery,
seek to associate Aeacus' line
with the name of an unrelated family?
"Is it because I freely took up arms
that arms are now denied me? Is the better man
the one who was the last to go to war,
who sought to shirk the action by feigned madness,
till someone who was cleverer than he,
but not as self-serving, Palamedes,
exposed this coward's trickery and forced him
to take up the very weapons that he shunned?
Shall he now have the best of arms, who wished
no arms at all? Shall I go without honor,
deprived of my own cousin's worthy gifts,
because I was the first to go to battle?
"Would that Ulysses had been *truly* mad,
or that we had believed him: either way
the fellow never would have come to Troy
and driven us to crimes! You, Philoctetes,
would not have been—to our shame—abandoned
on Lemnos, where, they say, you hide yourself

in woods and caves, and move the rocks to groans
with curses you call down upon Ulysses,
well merited, and not—if there are gods—
called down in vain! And he who took the oath
to fight in our cause, a leader who
inherited the bow of Hercules,
now perishes of hunger and disease,
is clothed and nurtured by the birds brought down
with arrows fate intended for the Trojans!
"No matter: he still lives, at least—because
he chose not to accompany Ulysses,
unlike unfortunate Palamedes,
who would prefer to have been left behind,
and would be living now—or would have died
without dishonor; for Ulysses here,
reacting to the exposure of his madness,
accused him of betraying our cause,
and as his proof of this fictitious crime,
produced the gold which he himself had hidden!
And so, by means of exile or by murder,
he has reduced the strength of our forces;
that's how he fights, and why he must be feared.
"Although his eloquence surpasses Nestor's,
the man will never manage to persuade me
that abandoning old Nestor was no crime:
for when, exhausted by extreme old age
and held back by his wounded mount, he begged
Ulysses' aid, his friend deserted him;
not only I, but Diomedes too,
is well aware of this: he called to him
repeatedly and seized him as he fled,
reproaching him for his timidity!
"The gods, however, even out the scales:
behold, Ulysses is in need of aid,

who did not offer it; he who once left
another must himself be left behind;
a precedent that he himself has set.
He cries to his companions for relief;
arriving, I observe him trembling, pale,
all discomposed by his impending doom;
I plant my massive shield in front of him
and save—no praise is due—his worthless life.
"Will you keep on contesting me? If so,
let us return, then, to the battlefield,
to the enemy, your wound, your constant fear:
crouch down again behind my shield and argue!
But once I had relieved him of the danger,
he took off on those legs he couldn't stand on—
his 'wound,' remember? No laggard here!
"Hector shows up and leads the gods to battle,
and where he charges, not just you, Ulysses,
are terrified, but even brave men too,
so great a fear that warrior inspires.
And while he was rejoicing in a string
of bloody victories, I laid him low
with a great rock I hurled from quite a distance;
when he sought someone out for single combat,
I was the only one to undertake it;
you prayed the lot would fall to me, Achaeans,
and your prayers were answered. If you would learn
the fortunes of that battle, know that I
survived it undefeated by great Hector!
"Look where the Trojans rush out of their city,
carrying iron, fire, and the force of Jove
against our helpless fleet! Where's glib Ulysses?
A thousand ships, the hope of your return,
and who protected them but me, alone!
Give me the armor in exchange for them!

"In truth, if I may say so, it's the prize
that seeks association with *my* glory,
and would be honored much more than would I—
for it's the armor would be given Ajax,
not Ajax the armor.
"To my heroic deeds
Ulysses should compare the way he dealt
with Rhesus, Dolon, and Helenus,
his capture of the statue of Athena:
none of these deeds was done in the light of day,
and none without his Diomedes' help;
but if, on such weak merits, you decide
to give the armor, then divide it up
and give the larger share to Diomedes!
"What use does someone like Ulysses—who
conducts maneuvers secretly, unarmed,
relying on his cunning to deceive
a careless foe—what use has he for armor?
The rays reflecting from the golden helmet
would spoil his ambush and reveal him hiding;
nor could his head support the weight of it,
not any more than his unwarlike arm
could heft the spear shaft grown on Pelion;
nor is the shield, engraved to represent
the world in all its vastness, suitable
for his left hand—the timid, thieving one!
"Indecent man, why do you ask for gifts
that cannot but enfeeble you? Gifts which,
if ever by some error on the part
of the Achaeans, were presented to you,
would not inspire terror in our foe,
but greed to strip such prizes from your corpse!
"And flight, most timid one, your only gift,
and the one in which you *do* surpass us all,

will be impeded for you by that burden.
"To all these reasons let us add one more:
your shield, so rarely used, is still brand new,
while mine, which bears a multitude of scars,
is urgently in need of a replacement.
"And finally, what need is there for words?
Let us be seen in action: send the armor
back to our foe, then order its recapture,
and give it to the one who rescues it."
Ajax concluded: an approving murmur
broke out among the soldiers standing there.
Ulysses rose, paused briefly, and looked up
to gaze upon the leaders, then began
to speak the words they had been waiting for,
ingratiating in his eloquence.
"If our prayers had triumphed—yours and mine,
my fellow Greeks—there'd be no doubt at all
as to the winner of this important match,
and you would have your armor, now, Achilles,
and we would now have you; but since his fate
unfairly must deny him to you, to me—"
and here he made as though to wipe his eyes,
"the one who should relieve him of his armor
is the one who brought him to relieve the Greeks.
"I don't want my opponent here to profit
simply because he seems to be (and is)
just a bit slow—or that I should be harmed
for being clever, or for having used
my cleverness to your advantage always;
my eloquence now takes its master's side,
but it has often spoken up for you;
I would not have it garner any envy,
for each should do his best with his own gifts.
"My race and family, the famous deeds

of famous ancestors are not my own:
since Ajax raised this issue, though, by claiming
that Jove was *his* great-grandfather, I
have to reply that he was also *mine*,
the founding father of *my* father's line:
my father was Laertes; Arcesius,
the son of Jupiter, was his; and nowhere
in my father's line was anyone convicted
of criminal offenses, or condemned
to exile; moreover, on my mother's side,
Mercury adds his luster to our name;
my lineage, on both sides, is divine!
"But the reason why I ask you for these arms
is not because of my more noble birth
(owing to my mother) nor because
my father was innocent of fratricide:
this case must be decided on its merits:
that Telamon and Peleus were brothers
should not advantage Ajax: not origin,
but honor ought to be considered here
in seeing which of us deserves the plunder!
"For if inheritance is linear,
Achilles had a father, Peleus,
and a son, Pyrrhus: so where is there a place
for Ajax in Achilles' family?
Let the arms be sent to Phthia or Scyros!
Teucer was a cousin of Achilles,
no less than Ajax: does *he* seek the armor,
and if he did, would he be like to win?
"Plain speech is what is called for in this contest:
I have done more than words can manifest,
yet I will try to tell my deeds in order.
"Achilles' mother, an immortal nymph,
foreseeing the destruction of her son,

attempted to disguise him as a woman:
though her deception took in everyone,
including Ajax, it was I who introduced
some arms that would arouse a manly spirit
among the items in the women's quarters;
although he was still dressed up as a maiden,
at once Achilles grasped the spear and shield:
'O goddess-born,' I said, 'Troy waits for you,
a city destined for destruction—why
do you prevent yourself from sacking it?'
I seized his hand, inspired and possessed him,
then sent that brave man off to do brave things.

"So everything that *he* did was *my* doing;
my spear defeated Telephus in battle,
whom *I* restored, when he entreated *me*;
if Thebes has fallen, *I* deserve the thanks,
and you can credit *me* with Lesbos and
the cities of Apollo: Tenedos,
Chryse, and Cilla; give me Scyros too,
and grant that it was *my* right arm alone
reduced the walls of Lyrnesus to rubble,
and—not to speak of other actions—*I*,
and no one else, gave you the only man
able to destroy the warlike Hector; yes,
through *me* that famous hero met his end!
I seek these arms then, in exchange for those
by which the hidden hero was discovered;
I gave him arms while he was living; now,
after his death, I ask them back again.

"When one man's troubles spread to all of Greece,
and a thousand ships were idling at Aulis,
all waiting for a wind that wouldn't come,
or when it came, came from an adverse quarter,
our leader, Agamemnon, was commanded

by an unyielding oracle to offer
his blameless daughter as a sacrifice
to fierce Diana; this he would not do,
since, in that king, there was a father, who
in his great anger cried out against heaven;
I was the one that, with ingenious speech,
turned the kind parent into the public man
(and I confess it here and beg your pardon,
Agamemnon), although I found it hard
to plead my case before a biased judge.

"He was persuaded, for the common good,
and by his high command, and by his brother,
to temper his affection for his daughter
with a concern for doing the right thing.

"They sent me also to the mother, who
would not hear reason, but must be deceived
by cunning—and if Ajax had been sent,
those ships would still be waiting for a breeze!

"As your ambassador to Ilium,
I went into the Trojans' Senate House,
which was still full of heroes in those days,
but I, as ordered, pled the cause of Greece;
I charged Paris with abduction, and demanded
that they give Helen and the plunder back;
Priam and Antenor were moved by my speech,
but Paris, his brothers, and accomplices
were scarcely kept from laying their indecent
hands on me—Menelaüs—you know this!
That was the first day when I shared your dangers.

"It would take far too long for me to tell
of all the services that I performed
as an advisor and as engineer
during the course of that long, drawn-out war.

"After the first engagements, the enemy

for a long time stayed within their city,
and so no opportunity for combat
presented itself; at last, and not before
the tenth year, did we do battle with our foe:
and what had you been doing all this time,
who have no expertise *except* in battles?
What use were you?
"Would you know what *I* did?
I set up ambushes and dug a trench
around our fortifications; furthermore
I gave encouragement to our allies,
so that they could endure the tedium
of such a long engagement; I advised
on how to keep us armed and well provisioned,
and served on other missions as required.
"But look: deluded by a phantasm
appearing in his sleep at Jove's command,
the king gives orders to give up the war,
orders which he defends as being Jove's:
so now let Ajax put an end to this,
let Ajax now insist on Troy's destruction,
and fight, since he is such a warrior!
"Why doesn't he restrain them, and provide
a bulwark where the wavering could rally?
That wouldn't be too much for such a braggart!
But he was busy fleeing: ashamed, I saw
you turn your back and raise disgraceful sails!
"At once I cried out, 'Men, what are you doing?
What madness now incites you to run off
just when the city is within our grasp?
What will we have to show for these ten years,
what can we carry home except disgrace?'
"And I said other things like that as well,
for disappointment gave me eloquence,

which turned them from the ships and brought them back.
"Then Agamemnon called for an assembly
of the Greek alliance, still panic-stricken;
not even then was Ajax bold enough
to make a peep, although Thersites dared
to mock the kings with insubordination—
but thanks to me, he didn't get off lightly!
I got up and exhorted them once more
to take the battle to our enemy,
replacing their lost courage with my speech.
From then on, whatever acts of bravery
Ajax may claim in truth belong to me,
who dragged him back from his intended flight.
"And lastly, Ajax, who among the Greeks
has praise for you and seeks your company?
But Diomedes has joined his cause with mine
in all his actions; I have his approval,
and he can always count on his Ulysses—
and that is something, to be singled out,
chosen from all the Greeks by Diomedes!
"Nor was I picked by lottery to go:
but careless of the dangers posed by night
and by our enemy, I took out Dolon,
who was scouting us, as we were scouting him;
but not before I'd gotten him to tell me
the battle plans of the dishonest Trojans.
"I understood their strategy completely
and had no need for more discoveries:
I could return to certain commendation,
but not content with that, I made my way
to the tents of Rhesus; there, in his own camp,
I slaughtered him and his whole retinue.
"A victor now, with all I'd prayed for won,
I proceeded in a captured chariot

in imitation of a joyful triumph;
the enemy insisted on those horses
as that night's price; deny the arms to me
and let Ajax be the more generous!

"Why should I tell again of how my sword
brought devastation to the rank and file
of Sarpedon, the Lycian commander?
Or how I slew a bloody multitude:
Coeranos, the son of Iphitus,
and Alastor and Chromius I killed,
and Alcander, and Halius and Noëmon,
and Chersidamas and Thoön as well,
and Charopes and Ennomos, pursued
by Fates implacable, and others who
were not as famous, but who nonetheless
my strong right arm left broken on the ground
beneath the walls of Troy.

"O citizens,
I have my scars, and they are glorious
for where I've gotten them—but do not trust
in empty words: look on them for yourselves,"
he said, uncovering himself to them.

"My breast," he said, "has always been engaged
in this great cause of yours. But Ajax here
has paid out nothing for so many years
in blood shed for his comrades that he's earned
a body free of scars!

"So what if he brings up
how he defended the whole Grecian fleet
against the might of Troy and Jove combined?
I grant it: let him have the credit owed
his great accomplishment; but he should not
take all the glory; some belongs to you,
for Patroclus, as great Achilles, drove
the Trojans back and saved the fleet from burning.

"He even thinks himself the only one
who dared trade spears with Hector on the field,
ignoring the king, the rulers, and myself;
he was but ninth in our chain of command,
and only won the task by lottery.
What was the outcome of this fight of yours,
bravest of warriors? Hector withdrew,
unblemished even by the slightest scratch!

"It grieves me to think back to our sorrow
when Achilles, bulwark of the Greeks, was slain.
The tears that I shed then did not prevent me
from lifting him and carrying him off
upon these shoulders—yes, indeed—I bore
the body of Achilles on these shoulders,
and at the same time bore his armor off—
a deed I am now striving to repeat.

"I've shown the strength to bear so great a weight,
and have the spirit to appreciate
the honor you confer upon the bearer:
am I to think that this was the ambition
of his immortal mother for her son,
that these exquisite gifts, the consummate
masterworks of the gods' own armorer,
were meant to grace a rude and brainless soldier?

"He has no understanding of the world
depicted on the shield, its sea and lands
and stars arranged in patterns high in heaven,
the Pleiades, the Hyades, the Bear
who is exempt from setting in the ocean,
and opposite, Orion's gleaming sword:
he grasps at armor that his mind *can't* grasp.

"Does he not realize that in blaming me
for hiding from the rigors of the war,

and for arriving after it began,
he deprecates great-spirited Achilles?
If pretense is a crime, then we're both guilty,
and if delay is culpable, then my
offense is lessened: I arrived here first!
My devoted wife and his devoted mother
kept us from leaving, but after those first days
were given them, the rest were given you;
and though I were unable to refute
the crimes I'm charged with—well, I could care less,
since those are faults I share with such a man,
and by Ulysses' ingenuity
was Achilles found; but Ajax looked around
and nowhere a Ulysses could he see.
"Nor should it shock us that his stupid mouth
should so abuse me, for you also are
the targets of his indecent reproaches.
Can it be baseness for me to accuse
Palamedes unjustly, but correct
for you to find him guilty of the charges?
Palamedes could not defend himself
against so great a crime; his guilt was proven,
and you not only heard that guilt proclaimed,
but saw it in the evidence produced!
"Nor is it my fault that Philoctetes
languishes on Lemnos: you consented;
defend your action. Yes, I persuaded him
to go on leave and to absent himself
from the rigors of the journey to the war,
and try to ease his awful state with rest.
He listened to me—and he's still alive!
So my advice was not just well intended,
but in its outcome was successful too,
though only my intentions really mattered.

"And now that our augurs have decided
that Philoctetes has to be brought here
before the city can be overcome,
don't give this task to me: it would be better
if Ajax went—for by his eloquence,
he'll calm the raging fury of the man,
and by some cleverness or skillful trick
will bring our Philoctetes back to us!
"The Simoïs will start to flow upstream,
Mount Ida will stand bare of foliage,
and Greece send war relief to Troy, before—
if my mind ever gives up on your cause—
the wit of Ajax does the Greeks some good!
"O bitter Philoctetes, it is right
that you should hate me so ferociously,
and heap your endless curses on my head,
and long, in misery, to drink my blood,
if ever chance should give me up to you,
doing to me in spades as I did you.
"Despite your enmity, I would set out
and try to bring you back with me to Troy;
if Fortune favors, I would have your bow,
just as I had that Trojan seer I captured,
just as I found the oracles, revealing
the fate of Troy, just as I carried off
the image of Minerva from its shrine
within the city of our enemy—
does Ajax now compare himself to me?
"The Fates forbade the city to be captured
without that image: where was bold Ajax then?
Whatever happened to his boastful speech?
Why was he frightened? How does Ulysses dare
to venture out beyond the sentry line,
entrusting his own safety to the night,

and facing opposition, enters Troy,
and penetrates its citadel and steals
the goddess from her altar, and then brings
the captured image past our enemies?
"And had I not accomplished all of this,
the bull-hide shield of seven thicknesses
that our Ajax carries on his left arm
would have been worn in vain, for on that night
I guaranteed our victory at Troy:
I overcame Pergama when I made it
possible to overcome the city!
"Allow me, Ajax, to express the thought
your scrunched up face and muttering convey:
'Part of his glory goes to Diomedes!'
Of course it does: nor were *you* all alone
when you braced your shield before the Grecian fleet;
you had a host beside you: I but one.
"Unless he knew that fighting has less value
in warfare than strategic capability,
and that the prize by right should not be given
merely to an indomitable arm,
Diomedes would also rise to claim it,
and lesser Ajax, and Eurypylus,
Andraemon's son, and Idomeneus,
and his own countryman, Meriones,
and Agamemnon's brother, Menelaüs,
would also seek it; all of them, however,
though strong of hand, my equals on the field,
have yielded to my insight and my counsel.
"Your arm is purposeful in war, but lacks
the wisdom that my counsel can provide;
you have mere strength, but not my intellect;
lacking my foresight, you know only *how*,
not *when* to fight; that is my special skill,

and the task which our leaders picked me for;
you represent the body, I the mind,
and as an oarsman to an admiral,
or as a GI to a general,
so much are you inferior to me,
because, in our bodies, our hands
are of far lesser value than our brains:
in them resides the vigor of our lives.
"Now you, O leaders, should award the prize
to your faithful guardian, considering
the many years which I have loyally spent
in anxious care for these concerns of ours,
as compensation for my services.
"My labor now is ended: I've removed
the obstacle of the resistant Fates,
and I have taken lofty Troy for you
by making possible the city's capture.
"Now, by the hopes that we all have in common,
and by the walls of Troy, fated to topple,
and by those gods I've recently removed
from our foe, and by whatever else
is left to do with wisdom and with daring
before Troy falls, remember all I've done!
"And if you *still* won't give the arms to me
(he pointed to the image of Minerva)—
give them to her!"
The leadership was moved,
and the outcome showed what eloquence could do:
the skillful man bore off the hero's armor,
while the other one, who had so often stood
alone against great Hector and endured
iron and fire and the wrath of Jove,
discovered a passion he could not withstand:
the undefeated man was overcome

by the anger that he turned against himself.
He seized his sword and turned to face them all:
"But surely this, at least, is mine," he said.
"Or will Ulysses take this from me too?
I must employ it now against myself,
and the blade so often stained with Trojan gore
must now be steeped in its own master's blood,
lest anyone but Ajax conquer Ajax!"
He, when he finished speaking, drove that sword
into his previously unscarred breast,
up to the hilt—and none was strong enough
to draw the weapon out, until the force
of his own blood expelled it, and the earth
was stained with its color; from patches of green turf
there sprang a purple flower, which before
had sprung from the mortal wound of Hyacinthus;
and on its petals, letters were inscribed,
appropriate both to the man and boy,
spelling a hero's name, a cry of woe.

The sorrows of Hecuba

Ulysses then set sail for the isle of Lemnos
(the realm of Thoas and Hypsipyle,
where once a famous massacre took place)
to carry back the arrows of Hercules;
and after he had brought them and their master,
Philoctetes, back to the Greek forces,
the final blow of that long war was struck. . . .
Troy was ablaze, the flames not yet subsided;
Jove's altar was still drinking the thin blood
of aged Priam, and Apollo's priestess,
drawn by her hair, raised unavailing hands
in silent supplication; Trojan women,
while they still could, embraced the images
of native gods—until triumphant Greeks

dragged their appealing plunder from the temples.
Astyanax was flung off of that tower
from which his mother would point out to him
his father on the battlefield, defending
his reputation and ancestral realm.
And now the north wind urged them to depart;
the sails flapped noisily against the masts
and the mariner had whistled up a breeze.
"Farewell, O Troy, for we are carried off,"
they cry, kissing the earth as they relinquish
their still-smoldering homes. Last to embark—
a pitiable sight—was Hecuba,
discovered at the princes' sepulchers,
clutching the tombs and kissing their dry bones;
Ulysses broke her grip and dragged her off,
but she hid Hector's ashes in her bosom,
and left locks of her white hair on his tomb,
her hair and tears a pointless offering.
There is, across the way from where Troy was,
a country that the men of Thrace inhabit;
here was the wealthy court of Polymestor,
to whom, O Polydorus, your father Priam,
entrusted you in secret to be raised
far from the fighting: a wise decision,
had he not sent you off with a great treasure,
provoking avarice and ensuring evil.
When Troy collapsed, the impious Thracian king
savagely cut the throat of his young charge,
and then, as though to show that crimes could be
eliminated just as easily
as victims are, the corpse of Polydorus
was tossed down from a cliff into the sea.
Awaiting quiet seas and a steady wind,
Agamemnon gave orders that the fleet

was to be moored along the Thracian coast;
quite unexpectedly, the ground split open,
and there emerged the ghost of great Achilles,
as large, and in his form as threatening
as in that time when, like a wild man, he
went after Agamemnon with his sword
and challenged him for his unjust behavior:

"O Greeks," he said, "do you depart for home
heedless of me? My body lies decayed,
as are the thanks you owe me for my service!
This cannot be: so that my sepulcher
may not go without honor, let my shade
be pleasured by the death of Polyxena."

He finished speaking, and the Greeks obeyed
his unforgiving ghost: torn from the arms
of her mother Hecuba, for whom the maiden
was almost the only comfort she had left,
that fierce, unfortunate, unfeminine
virgin was brought directly to the grave
and sacrificed upon that ominous tomb.

And after she had been brought to the altar,
and realized that she would be the victim
of this cruel sacrifice, not even then
did she forget herself; but when she saw
Neoptolemus waiting, blade in hand
and eyes fixed on her countenance, she said,

"The time has come to spill my noble blood;
let there be no delay: plunge your blade now
into my throat or breast," and she bared both,
"for you may rest assured: Polyxena
does not desire to live as a slave!

"My only wish is that my death somehow
could be unnoticed by my mother,
for her awareness of it spoils the joy

that I would take in it—although her life,
and not my death, should really make her tremble!

"Do not press close around me now, if what
I ask of you is just: let no man's hand
defile a maiden's honor by its touch,
lest I go to the Styx unwillingly!
My death will be more acceptable to him,
whoever he is, whom you propitiate,
if I endure it willingly. But if
any are moved by these last words of mine—
no captive maid but Priam's daughter asks!—
then let my mother have my body back
without a ransom; let her tears, not gold,
redeem my corpse for its sad funeral:
when she was able to, she gave you gold."

The tears that she was able to restrain
flowed in abundance from the eyes of those
who heard her speak; and even as he plunged
his blade into the breast she offered him,
the priest himself, though with reluctance, wept.

Her knees gave out, and she slid to the ground,
a resolute expression on her face
right to the end—and as she fell took care
to cover up those parts that should be hidden
and served the honor of her chastity.

The Trojan women took her body up,
once more lamenting another child of Priam,
the many victims given by one house;
and they mourned you, who, until yesterday,
had been the king's consort and queen-mother,
the image of an Asia in its prime—
now, even for a captive, you appear
especially unfortunate. Ulysses,
in his triumph, would surely not have wished

you to be his, except that you gave birth
to Hector, who would not have chosen *him*
to be his mother's master and her lord!
She bathed her daughter's corpse now with the tears
that she had shed so often for her country,
her children, and her husband; she poured those tears
into her daughter's wound, and kissed her face
and beat her own breast, accustomed to the gesture,
and as she plucked her hair in bloody clumps,
these words, and even more than these, she cried:
"O daughter, the last grief of your poor mother,
what else is there still left for me to lose?
The wound that you were given is my own,
lest I should ever lose a child of mine
without it being murdered—and yet you,
because you were a woman, I imagined,
would be safe from the sword—but even so,
as a woman, you too have perished by it,
killed as so many of your brothers were,
the victims of Achilles, who has bereft
the Trojan people and their helpless queen.
"But after he had fallen to the arrows
of Paris and Apollo, I said, 'Surely
Achilles is no longer to be feared!'
Now more than ever I had cause to fear him!
The very ashes in his sepulcher
despise our race, and even from the grave
we feel the enmity that he still bears us!
I have been fruitful for Achilles' sake!
"Great Troy has fallen, and the public woe
has ended in calamity—yet it *has* ended:
for me alone the story still continues,
my ship of sorrow holds its steady course.
"So very fortunate till recently,

in children, in their marriages, my husband—
now destitute, an exile, sundered from
my family's remains! Penelope
will soon display me to her women friends
on Ithaca, and tell them, as I weave
my daily quota, 'This is Priam's queen,
and noble Hector's celebrated mother.'
"Now after all the others have been lost,
you who were left to alleviate my grief
have now been sacrificed upon his tomb!
The child that I gave birth to has become
an offering made to Achilles' ghost!
Why do I linger here, unyielding? To what end
is my old age, rich only in its years?
"O cruel gods, why draw my lifetime out,
unless to show me even further grief?
For who could think that Priam could be called
fortunate after Troy had been demolished?
Only your father's death was fortunate,
my daughter, for he did not see you die,
leaving his life and kingdom both at once.
"But surely you, a princess of the blood,
would have your funeral rites as dowry
and lie in state among your ancestors?
No, this is not the fortune of our house:
your only offerings will be my tears,
your burial, upon a foreign beach!
"We have lost everything—yet there remains
what may allow me to continue living
a little while: her mother's favorite,
my youngest once, and now my only son,
my Polydorus, sent to the Thracian king
on these same shores. But why do I delay
to wash this cruel wound with water

and bathe your face, still splattered with your blood?"
She finished speaking and went down to shore,
tottering with age, and in her grief
tearing her white hair: "O women of Troy,
fetch me an urn," the luckless one commanded,
intending to draw water from the sea,
she found instead the body of her son
washed onto shore, disfigured by the open
wounds carved in it by Thracian implements.
The Trojan women screamed, but Hecuba
was silent in her grief, which had devoured
the tears and the cry that sprang up deep inside her;
she stood stone still and fixed her angry gaze
now on the ground and now upon the heavens,
and sometimes staring at her dead son's face
and sometimes, and more often, at his wounds,
as surging rage armed and instructed her.
Yet even in her fury, she behaved
as though she were still queen, and fixed her mind
and her imagination on revenge;
and as a mother lioness, whose cub
is taken from her, follows its spoor back
to find the enemy it cannot see,
so Hecuba, when anger mixed with grief,
forgot her years, but not her bravery,
and went directly to the Thracian king,
for this cruel murder had been his idea,
and asked him for an audience, pretending
that she would give him gold that she had long
kept hidden for her son. Deceived by this,
and by his customary avarice, the king
came in secret and implored her thus:
"Give your son the treasure, now, Hecuba,
for everything you give will go to him,

as everything you've so far given has,
I swear by all the gods."
She stared at him
ferociously as he foreswore himself,
and swelling with the flames of indignation,
she seized him, calling to the captive women,
and sank her fingers in his faithless eyes,
and plucked them out—for anger gave her strength—
then plunged her hands, stained with his foul blood,
into the places where his eyes had been
(for they were there no more) and plucked *them* out.
The Thracians were enraged by this disaster
which befell their king, and started to throw stones
and spears at Hecuba; growling, she snapped
at the stones they threw at her, and even though
her jaws were meant for words, she started barking
when she attempted speech. Because of this,
the place has taken (and still takes) its name
[in Greek, *Cynossema*: Sign of the Dog]
from the place where Hecuba, remembering
the evils of that distant time, would howl
across the Thracian grasslands mournfully.
The Trojans and her enemies, the Greeks,
were likewise moved by what became of her,
as were the gods in heaven, all of them,
even the one who is the bride and sister
of Jupiter, for Juno, too, denied
that Hecuba deserved to end like this.

Memnon

Although she had supported them with arms,
Aurora had no time to sympathize
when Troy and Hecuba both came to ruin.
The goddess had a care closer to home;
a private grief tormented her, the loss

of her son Memnon, whom she had just seen
Achilles murder with his deadly spear
on the Phrygian fields; and, as she watched,
the reddish color of the dawn grew pale
and clouds spread over the entire sky.
Aurora was unable to look on
as her son's body fed the final flames,
but didn't think it inappropriate,
just as she was, and with her hair unbound,
to fling her arms around the knees of Jove
and supplement her speech with flowing tears:
"Although I am inferior to all
the other gods that dwell in shining heaven
(my temples being few and far between),
I nonetheless approach you as a goddess,
but not to ask you for more festal days
on earth below, for temples or for altars
ablaze with the bright flames of sacrifice:
nevertheless, if you would just consider
all that I do (though I am just a woman),
the services I undertake for you,
when, with new light, I sever night from day,
you'd say that I deserved to be rewarded.
"But my present situation and concern
is not to ask for honors I deserve:
I come because I am bereft of Memnon,
who bravely (but in vain) bore arms for Priam,
and, still a youth, was slain by bold Achilles,
for so you wished it. Now I pray that you,
ruler supreme of all the gods in heaven,
grant him some honor, a solace for his death
and consolation for his mother's wound."
Jupiter nodded, as the towering
pyre collapsed into its leaping flames,

and thick, black smoke clouds blotted out the day,
as when a water nymph exhales a fog
that can't be penetrated by the sun;
black embers flying up accumulate
into one body, which, thickening, takes shape,
drawing warmth and animation from the fire;
lightness provides it with a pair of wings,
and birdlike at first, but very soon a bird
in fact, it flies off noisily among
innumerable sisters like itself,
all of them having the same origin.
Three times they flew around the blazing pyre,
and their mournful cries in harmony arose
and filled the air; on their fourth circuit, they
divided into two opposing camps
which waged ferocious war against each other,
employing their sharp beaks and curved talons
until they had worn out their wings and breasts;
and then, as sacrifices to the dead,
these ashy creatures fell back to the earth,
remembering the hero that they sprang from.
The unexpected offspring took their name
from their creator: they are the *Memnonides*,
or *children of Memnon*; when the sun has crossed
the zodiac, their combat is renewed:
they fight and die in mourning for their parent.
So others wept while Hecuba was barking,
but Aurora was intent on her own grief,
and even to this day she sheds her tears,
the morning dew that falls upon the world.

The daughters of Anius

Nevertheless, the Fates did not allow
the hopes of Troy to perish with the city:
Aeneas, the heroic son of Venus,

brought out the sacred objects in his arms,
and likewise sacred, the venerable burden
of his father, Anchises. These were the spoils of war
that pious man selected from his wealth,
and with his son Ascanius, he bore
in his fleet of refugees from Antandros
and from pernicious Thrace, so lately stained
with the blood of Polydorus; winds and tides
favored his voyage, and he soon arrived
at Delos, the city of Apollo, which
he entered with his cohorts.
There Anius
the king, who served Apollo as high priest,
received him in his temple and his palace
and showed him the city, with its famous shrine
containing the two trees Latona gripped
while she was giving birth to the twin gods.

Here they gave incense to the altar's flame,
then doused it with an offering of wine,
and after sacrificing cattle, burned
the entrails, as was customary, then
went back into the palace and reclined
on piles of carpets and refreshed themselves
with gifts of Ceres and with flowing wine.

Devout Anchises asked, "Priest of Apollo,
am I mistaken in my recollection,
or did you not have four daughters and a son
when I first came to visit in your city?"

Anius shook his head, bound with white ribbons,
and sadly answered him: "You are not wrong,
O greatest of heroes, for you saw me then
as the father of five children, of whom now
(such the inconstancy of human life!)
I am almost entirely bereft;

what aid can I expect from my absent son,
who holds the land of Andros (named for him)
in his father's place, and rules there as its king?

"Apollo gave him the gift of prophecy,
but Bacchus gave a gift to my four daughters
greater than they could have prayed or hoped for:
whatever any of these maidens touched,
turned into grain, or wine, or olive oil:
a profitable metamorphosis!

"When Agamemnon, the great scourge of Troy,
learned of this gift (lest you should think that we
had not experienced your trials), he
at once resorted to the use of force,
dragged the reluctant girls from my embrace
and ordered them to use their heavenly gift
to supply provisions for the Argive fleet.

"Each of them fled where she was able to:
two of the girls sought refuge in Euboea,
the other two, in Andros with their brother.
The Greeks arrived and threatened him with war
unless he gave them up: the ties that bind
in piety were overcome by fear,
and he surrendered them for punishment:
a brother's pardonable cowardice,
for he had no Aeneas to defend
his Andros, and no hero like great Hector,
who helped you to endure for ten long years.

"Now as the Greeks were forging manacles
to bind my daughters, they all raised their arms
to heaven, and together they cried out,
'O father Bacchus, deliver us from this!'

"The author of their gift delivered them—
if you can call it a delivery
to lose your human form in some strange way—

I couldn't understand then how they lost it,
nor am I able to explain it now.
But I *do* know how this evil came to end:
they put on plumage and became the birds
attending Venus, your immortal consort:
my daughters were all changed to snow-white doves."

The daughters of Orion

And there were more such stories until dinner
concluded and they sought their beds.
At daybreak,
the oracle of Phoebus bade them seek
their ancient mother and related shores;
the king presented gifts on their departure:
a scepter to Anchises, and a robe
and quiver to Ascanius his grandson;
a goblet to Aeneas which a guest
had brought back from Aionia for the king.
The precious goblet was the handiwork
of Alcon of Hyleus, who had engraved
a lengthy narrative along its side.
The scene: a city having seven gates,
by which the viewer knows that it is Thebes;
funeral services were taking place
before the city walls: at sepulchers,
flames leapt into the air from blazing pyres
and mothers with bared breasts and unbound hair
proclaimed their grief; and even water nymphs
wept at the ruin of their dried-out springs;
the trees were all bare and goats gnawed dry rocks.
But look, where in the middle of the city,
the daughters of Orion, both of them,
are exhibiting unwomanly behavior:
this one exposes her throat to the blade,
while that one bares her breast to the cast spear;

they sacrifice themselves to save their people;
then with great ceremony, they are borne
through the city's crowds, to where they are cremated.
And to prevent their family's extinction,
twin boys (whom fame has named the Coronae)
spring from the still-warm ashes of the virgins;
these lads at once join in the services
commemorating their maternal cinders.
These figures had been brilliantly depicted
around the outside of that ancient bronze;
its lip was decorated with a rough
border of gold-engraved acanthus leaves.
Nor did the Trojans offer gifts less worthy:
they gave Apollo's priest an incense box,
a saucer, and a crown of gold and gems.
From there, recalling that Teucrians
sprang from Teucer, they sailed off to Crete,
but couldn't bear for long the wrath of Jove
and left that island of a hundred cities,
eager to reach the shores of Italy.
Fierce storms of winter tossed their ships about,
and when at last they came to the deceitful
harbor of the Strophades, Aëllo,
a Harpy, terrified them with her threats.
And then to Samos, where Neritos dwells,
and Ithaca, the kingdom of Ulysses
the deceitful; they sailed past both of these,
and saw Ambracia, contested by the gods,
with its image of a judge turned into rock,
but better known now for Apollo's deeds;
they saw Dodona, of the talking oaks,
and Chaonia's bay, where once the threatened sons
of King Molossos managed to escape
the impious flames on wings that they both sprouted.

They next sought out the Phaiakhian's land,
felicitous for its abundant orchards,
and landed in Epirus at Buthrotos,
a town that was a replica of Troy,
and ruled by Helenus, a son of Priam;
thanks to the prophecies of the Phrygian seer,
they were aware of what the future held for them,
and after that, they came to Sicily.

That island has three capes that run to sea
in three directions: Pachynus is turned
to the rainy south, while Lilybaeum faces
the gentle western breezes; Pelorus
looks north and sees the Great and Lesser Bears,
two groups that never set beneath the sea.

By strength of oar and by the favoring tides,
the Teucrians arrived and beached their fleet
at nightfall on the sands of Messana:
Scylla assails the whole coast on the right,
and, on the left, unsleeping Charybdis;
the latter devours and regurgitates
the ships that she has captured, while the former
is girdled with wild dogs from the waist down.

She has a virgin's face, and, if our poets
are not to be completely disbelieved,
was once a maiden ardently pursued
by many lovers, all of whom she scorned,
finding among the sea nymphs (who adored her)
a shelter from unwanted male attentions,
where she could boast of outmaneuvered swains.

And there once, while she offered Galatea
her hair to groom, that lovelorn Nereid,
sighing repeatedly, told her this tale:

Polyphemus, Galatea, and Acis

"Without a doubt, O virgin, you attract
men of refinement, those of a better class,

whom you can brush off without any fear
of consequence; but I, although the daughter
of two immortals, Nereus and Doris,
and although guarded by a throng of sisters,
could not escape from the undesired
attentions of the Cyclops without grief."
A flood of tears kept her from saying more.

The other smoothly scrubbed away the tears
from Galatea's eyes and soothed her, saying,
"Tell me the reason for your sorrow, dear,
do not conceal it—I'm a faithful friend!"

And Galatea answered Scylla so:
"Acis, the son of Faunus and a nymph,
gave pleasure to his parents, but gave me,
a pleasure even greater, to be sure:
we were inseparable. At sixteen,
he was a gorgeous boy, whose tender cheeks
displayed the faintest down: I felt for him
exactly what the Cyclops felt for me:
incessant longing. Nor, if you had asked,
would I have been capable of telling you
whether my detestation of the Cyclops
meant more to me than did my love of Acis:
for they were equal!

"O Venus most benign,
how powerful a governance is thine!

"For see where that wild creature which the woods
are terrified to look upon, the host
no stranger ever safely sees, the one
who disregards Olympus and its gods,
now realizes what love's all about,
and as he burns with powerful desire,
entirely ignores his rocks and flocks;
you give attention now to your appearance,
Polyphemus, and now you take a rake

against your matted locks, and are well pleased
to trim your shaggy beard with a great scythe,
observing your hirsuteness in a pool
and practicing an ardent swain's expressions.
"Your love of slaughter and bloodthirstiness
now disappears, and ships can come and go
in perfect safety.
"Meanwhile, Telemus,
son of Eurymus, an unerring seer,
had landed here on Sicily, near Etna.
"He said to terrible Polyphemus,
'That eye of yours, the only one you've got,
and which you wear in the middle of your head,
is going to be taken—by Ulysses!'
"The Cyclops laughed and said, 'O foolish seer,
you are entirely mistaken here:
another has already taken it!'
"So he dismissed the one who tried in vain
to warn him, and set out with heavy heart,
walking with leaden steps along the shore
or turning back, exhausted, to his cave.
"A sloping, wedge-shaped cliff juts out to sea,
washed evenly on both sides by the waves:
the brutal Cyclops scrambled to its top
and sat down in the middle of the rock,
soon followed by his sheep, now leaderless.
"And after placing by his feet the pine
he used as walking stick—though others might
employ it as the yardarm of a ship—
he took his pipes made from a hundred reeds,
and piped away: the mountains felt it keenly,
and the waters, too; a rock concealing me,
I lay in the lap of my darling Acis,
whence I could hear, so very far away,

234

words of the song the Cyclops sang to me,
and kept them afterward within my mind:
"'O Galatea, whiter than the snowy white
flowers that decorate the privet hedge,
richer in blossoms than the meadow is,
taller, more slender than an alder tree,
brighter than crystal, more skittish than a kid,
smoother than a seashell on the shore
worn by the ceaseless motion of the waves,
more pleasing than the shade in summertime
or sun in winter, swifter than the deer,
and even more remarkable to see,
far more conspicuous than the tall plane tree;
clearer than ice, sweeter than ripe grapes,
softer than swans' down or the curdled milk,
and, if you would not always flee from me,
more beautiful than an irrigated garden.
"'Yet you, the very selfsame Galatea,
are fiercer than an untamed heifer is,
harder than oak, more feigning than the sea,
tougher than willow wands or bryony,
less movable than the rock I'm sitting on,
rougher than rapids, prouder than a peacock,
fiercer than fire, bitterer than thistles,
grumpier than a nursing mother-bear,
more unresponsive even than the ocean,
less apt to pity than a stepped-on snake,
and, finally, the worst of all your faults,
the one that I most wish to rid you of:
not only swifter than the deer pursued
by the baying pack, but even swifter than
the winds and the swiftest breezes in the air!
"'If only you would get to know me well,
you would regret your giving me the rush,

condemn yourself for holding out against me,
and do your best to keep a catch like me:
a large part of this mountain is my own;
I have my caves, cut from the living rock,
protected from excessive summer heat
and winter's chill; my apples strain their branches,
and yellow grapes are hung upon their vines
like lumps of gold, and purple ones as well:
to serve you, maiden, there will be both kinds;
and in the summer, you yourself will gather
delicious strawberries in wooded shade,
in autumn, cherries, and the sweet black plums,
and not just those, but the big yellow ones,
which have the color of fresh new wax.
"'Nor will you lack, with me as your mate,
chestnuts and fruit of the arbutus tree,
and orchards will be placed at your disposal.
"'This flock is mine entirely, and many
others are out there grazing in the valley,
many I have in the woods, and many more
are penned in stables deep within my caves;
and if you were to ask, I could not say
how many sheep are mine, for only paupers
can tally up the number of their flocks;
but don't trust me when I sing my own praises:
just look around you here and trust your eyes,
see how these sheep can scarcely get around,
with their teats hanging down between their shanks.
"'The little lambs are kept warm in their folds,
as are an equal number of small goats.
The milk I get from them is snowy white,
and part of it is kept for drinking fresh,
and the rest of it is made into my cheeses.
"'You'll get no ordinary gifts from me,

and nothing that is easily obtained,
like deer, and hares, and goats, and pairs of doves,
or a bird's nest lifted off a treetop:
on a mountainside, I found a pair of twins,
too like for you to tell one from the other—
playmates for you! Cubs of the shaggy bear!
I cried out, when I found them, "For my mistress!"
"'Come on now, Galatea, now's the time
to lift your pretty head above the waves!
Come on now, don't despise my offerings!
I have a good opinion of myself:
lately I saw my image in the water,
and my appearance pleased enormously.
"'Just look how big I am! Not even Jove—
this Jupiter that you go on about,
who you say governs heaven—is as big!
Abundant hair hangs over my fierce face
and shoulders, shading me, just like a grove;
but don't think me unsightly just because
I am completely covered in dense bristles:
unsightly is the tree that has no leaves,
the horse without a mane; birds have their plumage
and sheep are most attractive in their wool,
so facial hair and a full body beard
are really most becoming in a man.
"'In the middle of my forehead is one eye,
as large in its appearance as a shield:
what of it, then? Does not the mighty Sun
see everything that happens here on earth?
And as for eyes, he too has only one!
"'And furthermore, my father Neptune rules
your waters; I present him as a gift
to be your father-in-law—if you will only
have pity on my prayers and supplications!

"'For only you do I bow down before,
despising Jupiter and heaven too,
and his all-penetrating thunderbolt!
I fear you, Galatea, and your wrath,
far more ferocious than Jove's armaments!
"'But I could bear your scorn more patiently
if you fled everyone—though you do not:
how can you spurn the Cyclops, but love Acis,
preferring his embraces to my own?
Well, he may please himself for all of that,
but what I don't like is, he pleases *you,*
Galatea—just let me at the guy,
he'll learn that I'm as strong as I am big!
I'll tear his living gut out and I'll scatter
his body parts in fields and in your waters,
so you can mingle with his mangled limbs!
"'I burn indeed, and your offense against me
blazes within more fiercely than a fire:
I feel as though Mount Etna in eruption
has been transported into my own breast,
and none of this makes any difference
to how you feel about me, Galatea!'
"And after uttering these vain complaints,
he stood erect (for I saw everything),
and as a bull whose cow is snatched away,
unable to stand still, goes wandering
through forests and familiar fields, until
that wild one catches sight of me with Acis,
and we both unaware and fearless too:
"'I see!' he cried out, 'and I will see to it
that this fond coupling will be your last!'
And these words spoken in a frightening voice,
such as an angry Cyclops ought to have,
that left Mount Etna shaken to its core.

"In fear, I dove into the nearby waters,
while my Sicilian hero turned and fled,
crying out, 'Galatea! Help me! Please!'
and 'Help me, parents! Admit into your kingdom
the son who otherwise will be soon dead!'
"The Cyclops followed, pausing just to fling
a portion that he'd broken off the mountain,
and even though the barest corner struck him,
it nonetheless crushed Acis altogether.
I (who could do but as the Fates permitted)
caused Acis to assume ancestral powers.
"Bright purple blood streamed from beneath the rock,
and in a little while the redness faded
until it turned the color of a stream
swollen from the first rainstorms of spring,
then shortly afterward completely cleared.
"The boulder that the Cyclops threw cracked open,
and from within, there sprang a living reed
of noble size; and from the hollow rock
there came the sound of waters leaping up,
and marvelous! there suddenly emerged,
from the middle of that womb, a tender youth
whose fresh new horns were wreathed in streaming rushes,
and who, though larger than he used to be,
and with a face now of immortal blue,
was Acis, changed into a river god,
whose waters kept the name he had before."

Scylla and Glaucus

When Galatea finished with her story,
the company of Nereids dissolved
and went off swimming in the placid waters.
Not Scylla, though: the maiden did not dare
entrust her body to the liquid depths,
but wandered naked on the thirsty beach

or swam, when she was weary, in a pool
secluded and remote, to cool her limbs.
But look, where other limbs, so lately changed
(near Anthedon, a town set in Boeotia),
belonging to a strange new resident
of the deep sea, skim now across its waves:
Glaucus is here—and brought to a standstill
by his desire at first sight of her,
he says whatever comes into his mind
that he thinks might be able to prevent her
from fleeing him; but she flees anyway,
fear speeding her, until she comes to rest
atop a mountain very near the shore,
a massive mountain, facing out to sea,
which rose up till it gathered in a peak
of shaded woods that hung out over it:
here, in a place of safety, Scylla stopped,
not knowing whether he was god or monster,
admiring his color and the hair
descending past his shoulders to his back,
where at his groin began a fish's tail.
He senses her discomfiture, and says,
while leaning on a rock that stood nearby,
"Maiden, I am no monster, no wild thing;
I am, in fact, a god of these same deeps,
and of no less authority to govern
than Proteus or Triton or Palaemon.
"Before that, I was, nonetheless, a mortal,
but so bound to the ocean, to be sure,
that even then I schooled myself in it:
now I would draw in nets laden with fish,
and now, while sitting on a rock, employ
my rod and line.
"There is a strip of beach

adjacent to green meadows: on one side,
the waves, and on the other, fields,
undamaged by the grazing of horned cattle,
or depredations made by sheep or goats;
no busy bee has gathered flowers here,
no festive wreathes were ever taken hence,
and grasses never felt the sickle's sweep.
"I was the first to stop there on that turf,
while my wet fishing lines were drying out
and I examined my catch of the day,
all laid out in a line along the shore,
the fish that chance had swept into my nets
or whom credulity brought to my hooks.
"Now comes what sounds like fiction, I admit,
but what advantage would I gain by feigning?
Lying on the grass, my plunder from the surf
began to stir, and flipped from side to side,
as all at once, they strove to leave the earth
and get back to the water. While I watched,
dumbfounded and incapable of moving,
they fled, the lot of them, abandoning
the shore and their new master for the sea.
"I stood stock-still in wonder a long time,
asking myself how such a thing could be;
was it some god—or something in the grass?
'How could mere grass,' I asked, 'be strong as that?'
"I plucked some and I ground it in my teeth,
and scarcely had I gulped that unknown liquid,
when suddenly my heart began to pound,
and my whole sensibility was taken
with the desire for another element,
which I could not resist for long: 'Farewell,
O earth, which I will nevermore return to,'
I said, and plunged beneath the ocean's waves.

"The sea gods welcomed me, pronounced me fit
to join their honorable company,
and asked the Ocean and his consort, Tethys,
to take away whatever still remained
of my mortality; and this they did
first, by the recital of a hymn, nine times,
to purge me of my evil; then they bade
me to immerse myself a hundred times
in just as many rivers; when I did,
the rivers that flow on from every part
poured all their cleansing waters on my head.
"I can recall what happened up to this point,
and repeat it to you; this I recollect,
but I don't understand the rest of it.
When I awoke, my body and my mind
were both much changed from what they once had been:
I saw then for the first time my green beard,
and my long hair, which spreads across the waves,
and my broad shoulders, and my sea-blue arms
and legs which vanish in a fish's tail.
"But where's the benefit of my new form,
and that the sea gods are all pleased with me—
what point is there to my divinity,
if you have not been touched by all of this?"
And so he spoke, and had much more to say,
and would have said it, had not Scylla fled;
then he, enraged by her rejection, went
to the wondrous halls of Titan's daughter, Circe.

Glaucus

Now he who dwells among the swelling waves
left Etna, perched upon the Giant's Neck,
and left the Cyclops' fields, that were unused
to rake and plow and unbeholden to
the oxen yoked together in matched pairs;
Messana, too, he left behind, and left
the walls of Rhegium, on the far side
of that shipwrecking strait which separates
the shores of Sicily and Italy.
 From there, with mighty strokes propelling him
across the Tyrrhene Sea, Glaucus arrived
at the grass-covered hills and fabled halls
inhabited by many varied beasts,
where Circe, daughter of the Sun, held sway.
 No sooner had he seen her and exchanged
greetings, when he urgently implored her:
"Have pity on a god, I beg you, goddess,
for you alone can cure my passion—if
you find me worthy! The strength of magic herbs
is better known to no one than to me,
for they have utterly transformed my life!
 "What caused my madness? This: one glimpse of Scylla
on the Italian coast, off Sicily!
It would be much too shameful to repeat
the promises that she dismissed with scorn,
the vows and the endearments she rejected!
 "But if there is some power found in charms,
then by all means, recite a charm for me;
or, if herbs should be of greater potency,
rely on those you know as efficacious;
I am not asking to be healed and whole,
to have this burden lifted from my heart,
but that these flames should burn *her* in some part."

Such flames burned no one more than they burned Circe,
(either because of her own inclinations
or by the agency of Venus, acting
in retribution for the Sun's exposure
of her own indiscretion once, with Mars)
and who responded to his plea with this:
"You would do better to pursue someone
as ready and as willing as yourself,
someone who reciprocates your passion.
"For you were worthy once (most certainly!)
of being asked, and, take my word for it,
if only you will give a girl some hope,
you will assuredly be asked again.
"Don't think that you are lacking in appeal,
for I, a goddess, the daughter of the Sun,
the mistress of strong drugs and incantations,
I pray that you will have me! Only spurn
the one who spurns your passion, and return
the love of one who loves you: let one deed serve
two women as they each of them deserve."
Glaucus responded to her proposition:
"The leaves of trees will spring out of the ocean,
and seaweed will be found on mountain ranges,
before my love for Scylla ever changes."
The goddess was offended; even though
she could not injure him, another god
(nor did she wish to, being so in love),
yet stung by his rejection, she concocted
at once a mess of horrifying herbs
and poison potions; as she blended these,
she murmured certain charms of Hecate's,
then dressed herself in a cloak of azure hue,
and passing on through throngs of cringing beasts,
she left her palace, seeking Rhegium,

across the straits directly from Messana,
and made her way over the roiling waters
as if she walked upon the solid earth,
her bare feet dry as she skimmed the tops of waves.
There was a little pool, curved like a bow,
that Scylla found appealing for its quiet;
here she restored herself from midday heat,
when the sun was high and shadows disappeared.
Circe got here before the maiden did,
and fouled that place with poisons that produced
prodigious monsters; juice of noisome roots
she sprinkled there, and three times nine times spoke
the dark and winding words of incantation,
her lips well practiced in the magic arts.
Arriving, Scylla sinks into the pool
up to her waist, and when she first beholds
her private parts deformed into the shapes
of barking dogs, cannot believe them *her*,
and in her fear, attempts to drive them off,
and then flees from their gaping wantonness;
but what she flees is drawn along with her,
and reaching down to touch herself below,
discovers not her thighs and legs and feet,
but that those parts of her have been replaced
by gaping mouths, like those of Cerberus;
she stands on rabid dogs and on the backs
of beasts beneath her, and her private parts
are girded with a ring of monstrous shapes.
Her lover Glaucus wept at this and fled
from having any more to do with Circe,
whose use of potent herbs was too aggressive.
Scylla remained where she was standing, though,
and when the opportunity arose
for her to show the hatred she bore Circe,

she carried off Ulysses' men as plunder,
and would have done the same to the Trojan ships
had she not been transformed into a rock
before their coming—a rock that stands there still,
deep in the water, shunned by navigation.

Aeneas wanders

When the Trojans had passed Scylla and Charybdis,
and were quite near the shores of Italy,
a head wind drove them to the Libyan coast,
where Dido took Aeneas to her heart
and home, but was unable to endure
a separation from her Phrygian mate;
and on a pyre built to counterfeit
the sacred rites, she fell upon his sword:
and she, who had been tricked, tricked everyone.
  And fleeing that new city in the sands,
Aeneas once again returned to Eryx,
the royal residence of his true friend
Acestes; here, at Anchises tomb,
he honored his father with gift offerings.
  And setting out again in ships that Iris,
the messenger of Juno, almost burned,
he soon sailed past the Aeolian isles,
and the lands that reek of burning sulfur,
and the rocky islets haunted by the Sirens,
the daughters of Acheloüs; and then,
once he had lost the helmsman of his ship,
he coasted past Inareme and Prochyte,
and Pithecusae on its barren hill,
an island named for its inhabitants.
  For to be sure, the father of the gods,
enraged by all the fraud and perjury
and criminality of the Cercopians,
transformed their men into misshapen creatures,

so that they should seem unlike human beings
and yet appear quite similar as well,
with shortened limbs and flattened, pushed-back noses
and faces deeply lined with old-age furrows;
and with their bodies cloaked in yellow hair,
he sent them off to dwell in these abodes,
but not before he took from them the use
of their congenitally lying tongues,
yet left them with the power to complain,
in raucous, strident noises, of their lot.

The Sibyl

When he had sailed past these and left behind
the walls of Parthenope on his right,
there, on his left side he beheld the tomb
of Misenus, Aeolus' tuneful son,
and the fertile lowlands' sedgy marsh
on the coast of Cumae, where he stopped and entered
the cave of the superannuated Sibyl
to pray that he might journey through Avernus
for consultation with his father's shade.
  For a long time, the Sibyl kept her gaze
fixed on the ground, but when the god within
had stirred her to frenzy, she raised her eyes to his:
"It is a great thing that you ask of me,"
the Sibyl said, "O man of mighty deeds,
whose strength and piety have been essayed
by sword and fire and are well esteemed.
  "So put aside your apprehension here,
Aeneas: what you ask for will be granted;
and with me leading, you will come to know
the Elysian abodes and that extraordinary
kingdom within whose borders you will find
the shade of your dear father: nothing prevents
such access to the man of excellence."

She spoke and showed him, deep within the wood
of Proserpina, a shining golden branch
and ordered him to break it from its tree.
Aeneas did as he was told and saw
the underworld's formidable resources,
and his ancestral spirits, and the shade
of that great-spirited and venerable man,
father Anchises. He carefully observed
the laws and customs of the places there,
and learned what dangers he himself would face
in the wars to come. And afterward,
as he retraced his steps in weariness,
struck up a conversation with his guide,
to alleviate the journey's tedium.

And while they were returning through dim twilight
on that dreadful road, Aeneas said to her,
"Whether you are yourself a goddess, or
are one who is most pleasing to the gods,
you will seem always most divine to me.
I will avow that my opportunity
to tour the underworld and leave it alive
has been your gift to me; and in exchange,
when I return to where the air is fresh,
I will erect a temple and establish
a cult that will burn incense in your honor."

The Sibyl took a deep breath and responded,
"I am no goddess—and no mere mortal
is worthy of the gift of sacred incense!
But lest you err by ignorance, know that
eternal life *was* offered to me once,
if I would yield my maidenhead to Phoebus,
who, while he thought I would submit to him,
attempted to seduce me with fine gifts:
"'Select, Cumaean virgin, what you wish,
and you will have whatever it may be.'

"I pointed to a piled-up heap of sand
and asked a gift that would prove meaningless:
that I should have as many years of life
as sand grains in the pile. My words escaped
before I'd thought to say, '*unaging* years.'
He gave the years and promised endless youth
if I would let him love me—but I spurned
the gifts of Phoebus and remained a maid.

"My better days have turned their back on me,
and scant old age with palsied step draws near,
which I must suffer for a long, long time,
for seven centuries have been accomplished,
and three more yet remain to me before
my years are equal to those grains of sand:
three hundred harvestings of grape and grain.

"A time will come when many days reduce
my body to near nothing, and old age
whittles my limbs to where they scarce can bear
their meager burden; nor will I then seem
to have inspired love in a god's breast;
Phoebus himself perhaps will not remember,
or may deny that he desired me:
these are the changes I will come to bear,
but when I am no longer visible,
I will be recognized by my voice still,
according to the promise of the Fates."

So while they journeyed up that sloping road,
the Sibyl told her story to Aeneas;
they exited the underworld at Cumae,
and there Aeneas offered customary
sacrifices, then landed on the shore
that, as yet, did not bear his nurse's name.

Canto I

Dante, at the age of thirty-five, *comes to his senses to find he has wandered from the true path and is lost in a wild and trackless forest. It is shortly after sunrise and, at the end of the valley, he can see a hill lit by the sun's rays. Taking heart, he begins to climb upward toward the light, but his progress is blocked, first by a prancing leopard, then by a roaring lion, then by a ravening female wolf, or "she-wolf." This third beast so terrifies him that, despairing of scaling the heights, he is forced back down into the darkness below.*

As he retreats, he glimpses a faint figure to whom—whatever he may be, a living man or a ghost—he cries out desperately for help. The figure reveals that he is the shade of a Roman poet who sang of Aeneas, a survivor of the fall of Troy. Dante recognizes his beloved Virgil, his chief authority and poetic model. Virgil tells him that he must reach the light by another, less direct route. The she-wolf bars all access to the sun-drenched mountain, but the day will come when she will be driven back to Hell by a messianic Hound that will rid the world of her depravity. Virgil offers to be Dante's guide on the journey that will lead through Hell and Purgatory. Another, worthier guide will accompany him into Paradise. Dante is eager to undertake this pilgrimage.

Nel mezzo del cammin di nostra vita
mi ritrovai per una selva oscura,
ché la diritta via era smarrita.
Ahi quanto a dir qual era è cosa dura
esta selva selvaggia e aspra e forte
che nel pensier rinova la paura!
Tant' è amara che poco è piú morte;
ma per trattar del ben ch'i' vi trovai,
dirò de l'altre cose ch'i' v'ho scorte.

Io non so ben ridir com' i' v'intrai,
tant' era pien di sonno a quel punto
che la verace via abbandonai.
Ma poi ch'i' fui al piè d'un colle giunto,
là dove terminava quella valle
che m'avea di paura il cor compunto,
guardai in alto e vidi le sue spalle
vestite già de' raggi del pianeta
che mena dritto altrui per ogne calle.
Allor fu la paura un poco queta,
che nel lago del cor m'era durata
la notte ch'i' passai con tanta pieta.

Midway through the journey of our life
I found myself within a dark wood,
for the straight way had now been lost.
Ah, how hard it is to describe that wood,
a wilderness so gnarled and rough
the very thought of it brings back my fear.
Death itself is hardly more bitter;
but to tell of the good that I found there
I will speak of the other things I saw.

I cannot say just how I entered that wood,
so full of sleep was I at the point
when I abandoned the road that runs true.
But when I reached the foot of a hill
that rose up at the end of the valley
where fear had pierced me through to the heart,
I lifted my eyes and saw its shoulders
already bathed in the light of that planet
that leads us straight along every path.
This calmed a little the lake of my heart
that had surged with terror all through the night
that I had just spent so piteously.

E come quei che con lena affannata,
uscito fuor del pelago a la riva,
si volge a l'acqua perigliosa e guata,
cosí l'animo mio, ch'ancor fuggiva,
si volse a retro a rimirar lo passo
che non lasciò già mai persona viva.
Poi ch'èi posato un poco il corpo lasso,
ripresi via per la piaggia diserta,
sí che 'l piè fermo sempre era 'l piú basso.
Ed ecco, quasi al cominciar de l'erta,
una lonza leggera e presta molto,
che di pel macolato era coverta;
e non mi si partia dinanzi al volto,
anzi 'mpediva tanto il mio cammino,
ch'i' fui per ritornar piú volte vòlto.

Temp' era dal principio del mattino,
e 'l sol montava 'n sú con quelle stelle
ch'eran con lui quando l'amor divino
mosse di prima quelle cose belle;
sí ch'a bene sperar m'era cagione
di quella fiera a la gaetta pelle
l'ora del tempo e la dolce stagione;
ma non sí che paura non mi desse
la vista che m'apparve d'un leone.
Questi parea che contra me venisse
con la test' alta e con rabbiosa fame,
sí che parea che l'aere ne tremesse.
Ed una lupa, che di tutte brame
sembiava carca ne la sua magrezza,
e molte genti fé già viver grame,
questa mi porse tanto di gravezza
con la paura ch'uscia di sua vista,
ch'io perdei la speranza de l'altezza.
E qual è quei che volontieri acquista,
e giugne 'l tempo che perder lo face,
che 'n tutti suoi pensier piange e s'attrista;

And as a man who, gasping for breath,
has escaped the sea and wades to shore,
then turns back and stares at the perilous waves,
So too my mind, still racing in flight,
turned back to wonder at the narrow gorge
that had never left any traveler alive.
I rested a little and then resumed
my journey across that deserted slope,
so that my firmer foot was always below.
But look there—near the start of the climb
a leopard prowls, all swift and light
and covered with a rippling, spotted hide.
It was everywhere that I turned my eyes,
blocking my way at every turn, so that
again and again I was forced to go back.

The time was early morning, and the sun
was ascending the sky with those very stars
that rose along with it when Divine Love
First set those beautiful things in motion.
So the hour of day and the sweet season
were reasons for me to hope for the best
From that fierce beast with the gaudy pelt;
but not so much that I did not feel fear
at the sight of a lion that then appeared.
This one looked to be coming toward me,
his head held high and roaring with hunger
so that the very air seemed to be trembling—
And then a she-wolf, so emaciated
she seemed stricken with every kind of craving
and had already caused many to live in grief.
The very sight of this creature burdened me
with such a weight of desperate fear
that I lost all hope of attaining the height;
And as a man who eagerly racks up gains
weeps and is wretched in all of his thoughts
when the time finally comes for him to lose,

tal mi fece la bestia sanza pace,
che, venendomi 'ncontro, a poco a poco
mi ripigneva là dove 'l sol tace.

Mentre ch'i' rovinava in basso loco,
dinanzi a li occhi mi si fu offerto
chi per lungo silenzio parea fioco.
Quando vidi costui nel gran diserto,
"*Miserere* di me," gridai a lui,
"qual che tu sii, od ombra od omo certo!"
Rispuosemi: "Non omo, omo già fui,
e li parenti miei furon lombardi,
mantoani per patrïa ambedui.
Nacqui *sub Iulio,* ancor che fosse tardi,
e vissi a Roma sotto 'l buono Augusto
nel tempo de li dèi falsi e bugiardi.
Poeta fui, e cantai di quel giusto
figliuol d'Anchise che venne di Troia,
poi che 'l superbo Ilïón fu combusto.
Ma tu perché ritorni a tanta noia?
perché non sali il dilettoso monte
ch'è principio e cagion di tutta gioia?"
"Or se' tu quel Virgilio e quella fonte
che spandi di parlar sí largo fiume?"
rispuos' io lui con vergognosa fronte.
"O de li altri poeti onore e lume,
vagliami 'l lungo studio e 'l grande amore
che m'ha fatto cercar lo tuo volume.
Tu se' lo mio maestro e 'l mio autore,
tu se' solo colui da cu' io tolsi
lo bello stilo che m'ha fatto onore.
Vedi la bestia per cu' io mi volsi;
aiutami da lei, famoso saggio,
ch'ella mi fa tremar le vene e i polsi."

"A te convien tenere altro vïaggio,"
rispuose, poi che lagrimar mi vide,
"se vuo' campar d'esto loco selvaggio;

So did that restless beast make me feel.
Advancing always, she kept pushing me back,
little by little, to where the sun is mute.

While I was scrambling down to those depths
a figure presented itself to my eyes,
one who appeared to be faint through long silence.
When I saw him in that vast and trackless waste,
I cried out to him: "*Miserere mei,*
whatever you are, living man or shade!"
And he answered me: "Not a living man,
though once I was. My parents were Lombards,
both of them natives of Mantua.
I was born *sub Julio,* though late,
and lived in Rome under noble Augustus
in the time of the false and lying gods.
I was a poet, and sang of that just
son of Anchises, who came out of Troy
after proud Ilion fell in fire and ash.
But you, why do you return to woe so great?
Why not ascend this blissful mountain,
the source and cause of every kind of joy?"
"Can you be Virgil, then, that great wellspring,
that wide, spreading stream of eloquence?"
I blushed with shame as I said this to him.
"O glory and light of all other poets,
may my long study of your works repay me,
and the love that made me pore over your verse.
You are my master, you are my author.
It is from you alone that I have acquired
the beautiful style that has won me honor.
Look at the beast that makes me turn back.
Save me from her, glorious sage,
for she fills me with fear and makes my blood pound!"

"You will have to go by another road,"
he answered me when he saw my tears flow,
"if you want to escape this wilderness.

ché questa bestia, per la qual tu gride,
non lascia altrui passar per la sua via,
ma tanto lo 'mpedisce che l'uccide;
e ha natura sí malvagia e ria,
che mai non empie la bramosa voglia,
e dopo 'l pasto ha piú fame che pria.
Molti son li animali a cui s'ammoglia,
e piú saranno ancora, infin che 'l veltro
verrà, che la farà morir con doglia.
Questi non ciberà terra né peltro,
ma sapïenza, amore e virtute,
e sua nazion sarà tra feltro e feltro.
Di quella umile Italia fia salute
per cui morí la vergine Cammilla,
Eurialo e Turno e Niso di ferute.
Questi la caccerà per ogne villa,
fin che l'avrà rimessa ne lo 'nferno,
là onde 'nvidia prima dipartilla.
Ond' io per lo tuo me' penso e discerno
che tu mi segui, e io sarò tua guida,
e trarrotti di qui per loco etterno;
ove udirai le disperate strida,
vedrai li antichi spiriti dolenti,
ch'a la seconda morte ciascun grida;
e vederai color che son contenti
nel foco, perché speran di venire
quando che sia a le beate genti.
A le quai poi se tu vorrai salire,
anima fia a ciò piú di me degna:
con lei ti lascerò nel mio partire;
ché quello imperador che là sú regna,
perch' i' fu' ribellante a la sua legge,
non vuol che 'n sua città per me si vegna.
In tutte parti impera e quivi regge;
quivi è la sua città e l'alto seggio:
oh felice colui cu' ivi elegge!"

This savage beast that makes you wail
does not allow any to pass that way.
She will harry you until she takes your life.
Her nature is so depraved and vicious
that her craving can never be satisfied.
Fed, she is hungrier than before.
Many are the beasts with whom she mates,
and there will be more, until the Veltro comes,
the Hound that will put her to a painful death.
He will not feed on property or wealth,
but on wisdom, on love, and on virtue.
His birthplace will be between Feltro and Feltro,
And he will be lowly Italy's salvation,
the land for which the virgin Camilla died
along with Euryalus, Turnus, and Nisus.
He will hunt her down through every village
until he sends her back to Hell below
from where Envy first sent her into this world.
Therefore I think that it is best for you
to follow me. I will be your guide
and lead you from here to an eternal place,
Where you will listen to cries of despair
and see the ancient tormented spirits
who lament forever their second death.
And you will see the souls who are content
to stay in the fire, because they hope to arrive,
whenever it may be, among the blessed.
And then, if you wish to ascend to their side,
there will be a soul more worthy than I,
and with her I will leave you when I depart.
For the Emperor who reigns on high
wills that I, who did not obey his law,
never gain admittance into His city.
His rule is everywhere, but there is His reign,
there is His city and exalted throne.
Happy are those chosen to share His domain!"

E io a lui: "Poeta, io ti richeggio
  per quello Dio che tu non conoscesti,
    acciò ch'io fugga questo male e peggio,
che tu mi meni là dov' or dicesti,
  sí ch'io veggia la porta di san Pietro
    e color cui tu fai cotanto mesti."
Allor si mosse, e io li tenni dietro.

And I to him: "Poet, I implore you
  by that very God whom you did not know:
    help me escape this and worse ills too.
Lead me to the place you speak of, so I may go
  and look upon Saint Peter's gate, and see
    those whom you say are full of sorrow."
Then he set out, and I kept him before me.

Canto II

As all other living creatures seek their nightly rest, Dante the pilgrim alone sets forth upon his journey. The narrating poet summons his faculties and invokes the Muses' aid. And now the pilgrim, who had eagerly accepted Virgil's proposal to lead him into the realms of the afterlife, hesitates, recalling that his precursors on such a voyage, Aeneas and Saint Paul, were granted this privilege because of their respective roles as founder of Rome and apostle of Christ to the Gentiles. Dante fears his going may be temerarious. Virgil goads

Lo giorno se n'andava, e l'aere bruno
toglieva li animai che sono in terra
da le fatiche loro; e io sol uno
m'apparecchiava a sostener la guerra
sí del cammino e si de la pietate,
che ritrarrà la mente che non erra.
O muse, o alto ingegno, or m'aiutate;
o mente che scrivesti ciò ch'io vidi,
qui si parrà la tua nobilitate.

Io cominciai: "Poeta che mi guidi,
guarda la mia virtù s'ell' è possente,
prima ch'a l'alto passo tu mi fidi.
Tu dici che di Silvïo il parente,
corruttibile ancora, ad immortale
secolo andò, e fu sensibilmente.
Però, se l'avversario d'ogne male
cortese i fu, pensando l'alto effetto
ch'uscir dovea di lui, e 'l chi e 'l quale,
non pare indegno ad omo d'intelletto;
ch'e' fu de l'alma Roma e di suo impero
ne l'empireo ciel per padre eletto:

Dante's cowardice, assuring him that his journey, like Aeneas' and Paul's, has been willed in Heaven. The woman whom Dante loved in his youth, Beatrice, descended into Limbo, where the Roman poet dwells for all eternity, to urge Virgil to go to Dante's aid. Beatrice in turn was dispatched by the Virgin Mary, who sent Saint Lucy to her to tell her of Dante's need. Virgil's reassurances restore the pilgrim's resolve and ready him once more for the fray.

Day was departing, and the darkening air
was relieving the creatures who live on Earth
of all their labors. I alone was left
To gird myself for the struggle ahead,
the journey's toil and the toil of pity,
which unerring memory shall now retrace.
O Muses, O high Genius, come to my aid.
O Memory, who wrote down all that I saw,
here your nobility shall clearly be seen.

"Poet," I began, "you are my guide.
Consider whether I am strong enough
before you trust me to the deeps below.
You tell how Silvius' father, Aeneas, went,
while still in his body, to the eternal world
and was there with all his senses intact.
But that evil's constant Adversary
should show him such favor, considering both
his high legacy and who he himself was,
Makes perfect sense to a man of reason.
For he was chosen in the Empyrean
to be the father of Mother Rome and her realm;

la quale e 'l quale, a voler dir lo vero,
fu stabilita per lo loco santo
u' siede il successor del maggior Piero.
Per quest' andata onde li dai tu vanto,
intese cose che furon cagione
di sua vittoria e del papale ammanto.
Andovvi poi lo Vas d'elezïone,
per recarne conforto a quella fede
ch'è principio a la via di salvazione.
Ma io, perché venirvi? o chi 'l concede?
Io non Enëa, io non Paulo sono;
me degno a ciò né io né altri 'l crede.
Per che, se del venire io m'abbandono,
temo che la venuta non sia folle.
Se' savio; intendi me' ch'i' non ragiono."

E qual è quei che disvuol ciò che volle
e per novi pensier cangia proposta,
sí che dal cominciar tutto si tolle,
tal mi fec' ïo 'n quella oscura costa,
perché, pensando, consumai la 'mpresa
che fu nel cominciar cotanto tosta.
"S'i' ho ben la parola tua intesa,"
rispuose del magnanimo quell' ombra,
"l'anima tua è da viltade offesa;
la qual molte fiate l'omo ingombra
sí che d'onrata impresa lo rivolve,
come falso veder bestia quand' ombra.
Da questa tema acciò che tu ti solve,
dirotti perch' io venni e quel ch'io 'ntesi
nel primo punto che di te mi dolve.
Io era tra color che son sospesi,
e donna mi chiamò beata e bella,
tal che di comandare io la richiesi.
Lucevan li occhi suoi piú che la stella;
e cominciommi a dir soave e piana,
con angelica voce, in sua favella:

And both Rome and her empire, the truth to tell,
were founded to serve as the holy place,
where Saint Peter's successor now has his seat.
Aeneas, in the journey you affirm he made,
came to know things that helped him prevail
and that led as well to the mantles of popes.
Then Paul, the Chosen Vessel, went there
to bring confirmation from the other world
of the faith that leads us to salvation.
But I, why should I go there? Who permits me?
I am not Aeneas, I am not Paul.
Neither I nor anyone thinks me worthy.
And so, if I do abandon myself to this journey,
I fear it may be madness. You are wise,
you understand better than I can explain."

Like a man who unwills what he has willed
and upon second thought changes his mind
and finally gives up on the course he began,
So was I in the shadow of that slope,
for my thinking undid the enterprise
whose first steps had been so precipitous.
"If I've understood well what you have said,"
replied the shade of the great-souled Poet,
"your spirit is stricken with cowardice,
Which often so shrouds a man in doubt
that he abandons his first noble resolve,
like a beast that shies when shadows are falling.
To free you from this fear I will tell you now
why I have come and what I was told
when first I felt pangs of sorrow for you.
I was in Limbo when a Lady called me,
so blessed and so beautiful that I prayed
she allow me to be of service to her.
Her eyes outshone the stars in the sky,
and when she spoke her voice was as sweet
and soft as an angel's, as she said to me:

'O anima cortese mantoana,
di cui la fama ancor nel mondo dura,
e durerà quanto 'l mondo lontana,
l'amico mio, e non de la ventura,
ne la diserta piaggia è impedito
sí nel cammin, che vòlt' è per paura;
e temo che non sia già sí smarrito,
ch'io mi sia tardi al soccorso levata,
per quel ch'i' ho di lui nel cielo udito.
Or movi, e con la tua parola ornata
e con ciò c'ha mestieri al suo campare,
l'aiuta sí ch'i' ne sia consolata.
I' son Beatrice che ti faccio andare;
vegno del loco ove tornar disio;
amor mi mosse, che mi fa parlare.
Quando sarò dinanzi al segnor mio,
di te mi loderò sovente a lui.'
Tacette allora, e poi comincia' io:
'O donna di virtù, sola per cui
l'umana spezie eccede ogne contento
di quel ciel c'ha minor li cerchi sui,
tanto m'aggrada il tuo comandamento,
che l'ubidir, se già fosse, m'è tardi;
piú non t'è uo' ch'aprirmi il tuo talento.
Ma dimmi la cagion che non ti guardi
de lo scender qua giuso in questo centro
de l'ampio loco ove tornar tu ardi.'
'Da che tu vuo' saver cotanto a dentro,
dirotti brievemente,' mi rispuose,
'perch' i' non temo di venir qua entro.
Temer si dee di sole quelle cose
c'hanno potenza di fare altrui male;
de l'altre no, ché non son paurose.
I' son fatta da Dio, sua mercé, tale,
che la vostra miseria non mi tange,
né fiamma d'esto 'ncendio non m'assale.

'O courteous spirit of Mantua, whose fame
still endures in the world, and will endure
as long as the world itself shall last—
A friend of mine, who is not Fortune's friend,
is so entangled on the barren slope
that he has turned back from the road in fear.
From what I have heard of him in Heaven
I am afraid he may already be so lost
that I have arisen too late to help him.
Go now, and use your beautiful words
and anything needed for his deliverance.
Rescue him, so that I might be consoled.
I who send you forth am Beatrice,
come from a place where I long to return.
Love moved me to do this, love makes me speak.
When I am again before my Lord
I will praise you often in His presence.'
She fell silent then, and I responded:
'Lady of virtue, through whom alone
humankind transcends what is contained
by the heaven of least circumference,
Your command is so pleasing to me
that instant obedience would still be too late.
You have only to reveal to me your will.
But tell me the reason you have no fear
of descending into this central core
from the spacious region where you long to be?'
'Since you have such a deep desire to know,'
the Lady replied, 'I will tell you briefly
why I am not afraid to come to this place.
One should fear those things alone
that can cause one harm. Other things, no:
what causes no harm is not to be feared.
I am so made by the grace of God
that I am untouched by your sorrow and pain,
nor can I be hurt by these scorching flames.

Donna è gentil nel ciel che si compiange
di questo 'mpedimento ov' io ti mando,
sí che duro giudicio là sú frange.
Questa chiese Lucia in suo dimando
e disse:—Or ha bisogno il tuo fedele
di te, e io a te lo raccomando.—
Lucia, nimica di ciascun crudele,
si mosse, e venne al loco dov' i' era,
che mi sedea con l'antica Rachele.
Disse:—Beatrice, loda di Dio vera,
ché non soccorri quei che t'amò tanto,
ch'uscí per te de la volgare schiera?
Non odi tu la pieta del suo pianto,
non vedi tu la morte che 'l combatte
su la fiumana ove 'l mar non ha vanto?—
Al mondo non fur mai persone ratte
a far lor pro o a fuggir lor danno,
com' io, dopo cotai parole fatte,
venni qua giú del mio beato scanno,
fidandomi del tuo parlare onesto,
ch'onora te e quei ch'udito l'hanno.'
Poscia che m'ebbe ragionato questo,
li occhi lucenti lagrimando volse,
per che mi fece del venir piú presto.
E venni a te cosí com' ella volse:
d'inanzi a quella fiera ti levai
che del bel monte il corto andar ti tolse.
Dunque: che è? perché, perché restai,
perché tanta viltà nel core allette,
perché ardire e franchezza non hai,
poscia che tai tre donne benedette
curan di te ne la corte del cielo,
e 'l mio parlar tanto ben ti promette?"

Quali fioretti dal notturno gelo
chinati e chiusi, poi che 'l sol li 'mbianca,
si drizzan tutti aperti in loro stelo,

There is in Heaven a gracious Lady
with such pity for the plight to which I send you
that the strict decree above has been broken.
This Lady summoned Lucy and said to her:
"Your faithful one now stands in need of you,
and I deliver him into your care."
And Lucy, an enemy of everything cruel,
arose and came to me where I sat
with venerable Rachel, and said to me:
"Beatrice, true glory of God,
why do you not go to that man's aid
who left the common crowd for love of you?
Do you not hear his pitiful lament
or see how he is threatened by death
in the flood that outswells even the sea?"
No one on Earth was ever so quick
to gain an advantage or escape from harm
as I was then upon hearing these words,
And down I came from my blessed throne,
placing my trust in your noble speech,
which honors you and all who have heard it.'
When Beatrice had finished speaking to me
she averted her eyes that shone with tears,
which made me all the more eager to come.
And just as she wished, I came to you
and rescued you from the beast that hindered
the short path up the beautiful mountain.
What is this, then? Why do you hang back?
Why do you nurse such cowardice?
Why are you not bold, daring, and free,
When three such blessed Ladies in Heaven
are concerned for you, and when my words
are a pledge to you of so great a good?"

As little flowers, drooping and closed
in the chill of night, straighten their stems
and open up when the sun shines on them,

tal mi fec' io di mia virtude stanca,
  e tanto buono ardire al cor mi corse,
    ch'i' cominciai come persona franca:
"Oh pietosa colei che mi soccorse!
  e te cortese ch'ubidisti tosto
    a le vere parole che ti porse!
Tu m'hai con disiderio il cor disposto
  sí al venir con le parole tue,
    ch'i' son tornato nel primo proposto.
Or va, ch'un sol volere è d'ambedue:
  tu duca, tu segnore e tu maestro."
    Cosí li dissi; e poi che mosso fue,
intrai per lo cammino alto e silvestro.

So too my courage, which had ebbed away;
  and so much good spirit rushed into my heart
    that I said to him, like a man set free:
"How compassionate she who came to my aid,
  and how courteous you, who when you heard
    the true words she spoke, so quickly obeyed!
And now your words have restored my soul
  and made me so eager to come with you
    that my first intent is once again my goal.
Let us go now, for though we are two,
  we have one will. You are my master and guide."
    Those were my words, and when he withdrew
I followed him into the desolate divide.

Canto III

The inscription on the Gate of Hell *is explained by Virgil, who takes Dante by the hand and leads him in. A hideous babel of cries, articulate and inarticulate, strikes their ears. Virgil explains that here, in this the Vestibule of Hell, the Uncommitted, rejected alike by Hell proper and by Heaven, are punished, along with the neutral angels, who sided neither with God nor with Satan. Now, naked, bloody, and pricked on by stinging insects, they pursue a meaningless banner wherever it may lead. They do not merit the pilgrim's attention. Among them Dante recognizes the man "who through cowardice made the Great Refusal."*

'Per me si va ne la città dolente,
per me si va ne l'etterno dolore,
per me si va tra la perduta gente.
Giustizia mosse il mio alto fattore;
fecemi la divina podestate,
la somma sapïenza e 'l primo amore.
Dinanzi a me non fuor cose create
se non etterne, e io etterno duro.
Lasciate ogne speranza, voi ch'intrate'.

Quest parole di colore oscuro
vid'ïo scritte al sommo d'una porta;
per ch'io: "Maestro, il senso lor m'è duro."
Ed elli a me, come persona accorta:
"Qui si convien lasciare ogne sospetto;
ogne viltà convien che qui sia morta.
Noi siam venuti al loco ov' i' t'ho detto
che tu vedrai le genti dolorose
c'hanno perduto il ben de l'intelletto."

Farther along, a crowd of dead souls is gathering on the shore to be ferried over the swamp of Acheron. Despite Virgil's remonstrance, Charon the demon boatman refuses to carry Dante across because he is alive. Before Charon can return, another grieving flock of sinners has assembled. Virgil explains that all those who die in a state of mortal sin instinctively come here, spurred by Divine Justice. Just then, an earthquake occurs and a crimson flash lights up the darkness. Dante loses his senses and falls to the ground.

THROUGH ME IS THE WAY TO THE CITY OF WOE.
THROUGH ME IS THE WAY TO SORROW ETERNAL.
THROUGH ME IS THE WAY TO THE LOST BELOW.
JUSTICE MOVED MY ARCHITECT SUPERNAL.
I WAS CONSTRUCTED BY DIVINE POWER,
SUPREME WISDOM, AND LOVE PRIMORDIAL.
BEFORE ME NO CREATED THINGS WERE
SAVE THOSE ETERNAL, AND ETERNAL I ABIDE.
ABANDON ALL HOPE, YOU WHO ENTER.

These words I saw etched in shadow
above a gate, and I said: "Master,
the meaning of these lines is hard for me."
And he, like one who always knows what to say,
"All fear and doubt must be forgotten now.
Here must all cowardice be laid to rest.
We have come to the place where I foretold
you would see the souls of the wretched damned
who have lost the good of the intellect."

E poi che la sua mano a la mia puose
con lieto volto, ond' io mi confortai,
mi mise dentro a le segrete cose.
Quivi sospiri, pianti e alti guai
risonavan per l'aere sanza stelle,
per ch'io al cominciar ne lagrimai.
Diverse lingue, orribili favelle,
parole di dolore, accenti d'ira,
voci alte e fioche, e suon di man con elle
facevano un tumulto, il qual s'aggira
sempre in quell' aura sanza tempo tinta,
come la rena quando turbo spira.
E io ch'avea d'orror la testa cinta,
dissi: "Maestro, che è quel ch'i' odo?
e che gent' è che par nel duol sí vinta?"

Ed elli a me: "Questo misero modo
tegnon l'anime triste di coloro
che visser sanza 'nfamia e sanza lodo.
Mischiate sono a quel cattivo coro
de li angeli che non furon ribelli
né fur fedeli a Dio, ma per sé fuoro.
Caccianli i ciel per non esser men belli,
né lo profondo inferno li riceve,
ch'alcuna gloria i rei avrebber d'elli."
E io: "Maestro, che è tanto greve
a lor che lamentar li fa sí forte?"
Rispuose: "Dicerolti molto breve.
Questi non hanno speranza di morte,
e la lor cieca vita è tanto bassa,
che 'nvidïosi son d'ogne altra sorte.
Fama di loro il mondo esser non lassa;
misericordia e giustizia li sdegna:
non ragioniam di lor, ma guarda e passa."

E io, che riguardai, vidi una 'nsegna
che girando correva tanto ratta,
che d'ogne posa mi parea indegna;

And when he had placed his hand on mine
with a cheerful look from which I took comfort,
he led me among the things that are hidden.
Here sighs and wailing and lamentation
echoed so loud through the starless air
that when I first heard them it made me weep.
A welter of language, of horrible tongues,
accents of anger, cries of woe,
voices shrill and hoarse, and beating hands
Swirled together in unceasing tumult
through that ancient, timeless, tainted air,
like sand when a cyclone whirls it around.
Horror shrouded my head, and I asked:
"Master, what is this sound I hear, and who
are these people so routed by pain?"

He answered me: "This is the wretched state
of the sorrowing souls who passed through life
avoiding infamy but unworthy of praise.
Mingled with them is the cowardly band
of angels who neither rebelled against God
nor were loyal to Him, but to themselves alone.
Heaven rejects them to preserve its beauty
and deep Hell will not have them, for fear
that the damned below might win some glory."
I asked him: "Master, what pains them so
that it makes them lament in grief like this?"
And he answered: "I will be brief.
Those who are here have no hope of death,
and their blind existence is so debased
that they are envious of every other fate.
The world does not allow them to be known;
mercy and justice alike disdain them.
They are of no account. Look and pass on."

And when I looked again, I saw a banner
whirling around the circumference so fast
that it seemed it could not bear to rest.

e dietro le venía sí lunga tratta
  di gente, ch'i' non averei creduto
    che morte tanta n'avesse disfatta.
Poscia ch'io v'ebbi alcun riconosciuto,
  vidi e conobbi l'ombra di colui
    che fece per viltade il gran rifiuto.
Incontanente intesi e certo fui
  che questa era la setta d'i cattivi,
    a Dio spiacenti e a' nemici sui.
Questi sciaurati, che mai non fur vivi,
  erano ignudi e stimolati molto
    da mosconi e da vespe ch'eran ivi.
Elle rigavan lor di sangue il volto,
  che, mischiato di lagrime, a' lor piedi
    da fastidiosi vermi era ricolto.

E poi ch'a riguardar oltre mi diedi,
  vidi genti a la riva d'un gran fiume;
    per ch'io dissi: "Maestro, or mi concedi
ch'i' sappia quali sono, e qual costume
  le fa di trapassar parer sí pronte,
    com' i' discerno per lo fioco lume."
Ed elli a me: "Le cose ti fier conte
  quando noi fermerem li nostri passi
    su la trista riviera d'Acheronte."
Allor con li occhi vergognosi e bassi,
  temendo no 'l mio dir li fosse grave,
    infino al fiume del parlar mi trassi.

Ed ecco verso noi venir per nave
  un vecchio, bianco per antico pelo,
    gridando: "Guai a voi, anime prave!
Non isperate mai veder lo cielo:
  i' vegno per menarvi a l'altra riva
    ne le tenebre etterne, in caldo e 'n gelo.
E tu che se' costí, anima viva,
  pàrtiti da cotesti che son morti."
    Ma poi che vide ch'io non mi partiva,

And behind the banner there followed
  a long train of people, so many,
    I had not thought death had undone so many.
Some of them I recognized, and among these
  I picked out the shade of that man
    who through cowardice made the Great Refusal.
I knew in a flash of certainty
  that these were the sorry lot who displeased
    both God Himself and His enemies.
These wretches, who never truly lived,
  were naked and pricked from head to toe
    by swarms of horseflies and wasps, whose bites
And stings streaked their faces with blood
  that mingled with their tears and streamed down
    to be lapped at their feet by loathsome worms.

Then I raised my eyes to look beyond them
  and saw a crowd on the shore of a river,
    prompting me to ask: "Master, now tell me
Who these people are and why they seem—
  as it appears to me in this faded light—
    so eager to cross to the other side?"
And he said to me: "You will be told
  all about this when we halt our steps
  on the dismal shore of the Acheron."
And so, eyes lowered and full of shame,
  afraid that my words had offended him,
    I kept from talking until we reached the river.

There we saw, coming toward us in a boat,
  an old man with shriveled white hair
    crying out, "Cursed are you, evil souls!
Do not hope to see Heaven ever!
  I come to take you to the other shore,
    into eternal darkness, heat, and cold.
And you, over there, you living soul,
  move away now from those who are dead."
    When he saw that I didn't move, he said:

disse: "Per altra via, per altri porti
verrai a piaggia, non qui, per passare:
più lieve legno convien che ti porti."
E 'l duca lui: "Caron, non ti crucciare:
vuolsi così colà dove si puote
ciò che si vuole, e più non dimandare."
Quinci fuor quete le lanose gote
al nocchier de la livida palude,
che 'ntorno a li occhi avea di fiamme rote.
Ma quell' anime, ch'eran lasse e nude,
cangiar colore e dibattero i denti,
ratto che 'nteser le parole crude.
Bestemmiavano Dio e lor parenti,
l'umana spezie e 'l loco e 'l tempo e 'l seme
di lor semenza e di lor nascimenti.
Poi si ritrasser tutte quante insieme,
forte piangendo, a la riva malvagia
ch'attende ciascun uom che Dio non teme.
Caron dimonio, con occhi di bragia
loro accennando, tutte le raccoglie;
batte col remo qualunque s'adagia.
Come d'autunno si levan le foglie
l'una appresso de l'altra, fin che 'l ramo
vede a la terra tutte le sue spoglie,
similemente il mal seme d'Adamo
gittansi di quel lito ad una ad una,
per cenni come augel per suo richiamo.
Così sen vanno su per l'onda bruna,
e avanti che sien di là discese,
anche di qua nuova schiera s'auna.

"Figliuol mio," disse 'l maestro cortese,
"quelli che muoion ne l'ira di Dio
tutti convegnon qui d'ogne paese;
e pronti sono a trapassar lo rio,
ché la divina giustizia li sprona,
sì che la tema si volve in disio.

"By another way, other ports, not here,
you will find passage across the shore.
It is a lighter craft that must carry you."
And my guide said to him: "Do not vex yourself,
Charon. This is willed where there is power
to do what is willed. Now question us no more."
At this the ferryman's grizzled jaws relaxed,
though his eyes were set in wheels of fire
as he poled his boat across the bruised swamp.
Those exhausted, naked souls turned pale
and their teeth started to chatter with fear
as soon as they heard Charon's cruel words.
They cursed God and they cursed their parents,
cursed the human race, the place and time
and seed of their conception and birth.
Then all together, with loud lamentation,
they drew near to that malignant shore
that awaits the man who does not fear God.
The demon Charon, eyes glowing like coals,
beckoned to them and collected them all,
beating those who lingered with the blade of his oar.
As leaves in autumn take flight and fall
one after the other, until the branch
sees all of its tattered colors on the ground,
So too did these, Adam's evil seed,
cast themselves one by one from that shore
when the sign was given, like a hawk to its lure.
And so they go, over the umber water,
but before they disembark on the other bank,
a new crowd gathers on the nearer side.

"My son," my gracious master explained,
"All those who die in the wrath of God
come together here from every land,
Ready and willing to cross the river,
for Divine Justice so spurs them on
that their very fear becomes desire.

Quinci non passa mai anima buona;
e però, se Caron di te si lagna,
ben puoi sapere omai che 'l suo dir suona."

Finito questo, la buia campagna
tremò sí forte, che de lo spavento
la mente di sudore ancor mi bagna.
La terra lagrimosa diede vento,
che balenò una luce vermiglia
la qual mi vinse ciascun sentimento;
e caddi come l'uom cui sonno piglia.

No virtuous soul ever comes this way,
and so, if Charon complains of you,
you understand now what he means to say."

When he had finished, the darkling plain
quaked so fearfully that even now
the memory soaks me with sweat again.
From the tear-drenched ground up rose a wind
that flashed a crimson light so terrible
it overpowered my senses and mind,
And like a person seized with sleep, I fell.

Canto IV

Roused from his swoon *by a clap of thunder, the pilgrim finds himself on the brink of the abyss. At Virgil's bidding, the two poets descend into the First Circle, Limbo. Here, where the unbaptized reside, there are no loud lamentations, only sighs of yearning and regret. This is the place to which Virgil, through no fault of his own, is condemned, along with many others, to live in longing for the salvation he knows he cannot have because he was born before Jesus Christ came into the world to save humankind. In answer to the pilgrim's question, Virgil says that, exceptionally, many Old Testament figures were removed from Limbo by a victorious liberator and taken up to Paradise shortly after his own*

Ruppemi l'alto sonno ne la testa
un greve truono, sí ch'io mi riscossi
come persona ch'è per forza desta;
e l'occhio riposato intorno mossi,
dritto levato, e fiso riguardai
per conoscer lo loco dov' io fossi.
Vero è che 'n su la proda mi trovai
de la valle d'abisso dolorosa
che 'ntrono accoglie d'infiniti guai.
Oscura e profonda era e nebulosa
tanto che, per ficcar lo viso a fondo,
io non vi discernea alcuna cosa.

"Or discendiam qua giú nel cieco mondo,"
cominciò il poeta tutto smorto.
"Io sarò primo, e tu sarai secondo."
E io, che del color mi fui accorto,
dissi: "Come verrò, se tu paventi
che suoli al mio dubbiare esser conforto?"

arrival. The pilgrims make their way through the throng of souls to where a flame lights up the surrounding darkness. This is where those who achieved fame in the non-Christian world are honored. Virgil is greeted by his fellow poets—Homer, Horace, Ovid, and Lucan—and Dante is welcomed as the sixth in their number. Together they enter a noble castle on whose lawns the heroic spirits of the past, as well as the Muslim Saladin, are assembled, watched over by the countless philosophers and scientists of antiquity and of the Arabic Middle Ages. Leaving the other poets and the light behind, Dante and Virgil press on into darkness.

A clap of thunder rumbled in my head
and broke through my sleep, so that I woke
with a start, as if someone had shaken me.
I got to my feet and turned my rested eyes
in every direction, gazing intently
to make out the place where I found myself.
The truth was that I stood on the brink
of the chasm of grief, the abyss of pain
that holds the sound of infinite sorrow.
It was so dark and deep and full of mist
that although I stared down into its depths
there was nothing at all that I could discern.

"Let us descend into the blind world below,"
the Poet began, his face deathly pale.
"I will lead the way, and you will follow."
I saw my guide's pallor, and I asked:
"How should I come if you are afraid,
since I look to you when I am in doubt?"

Ed elli a me: "L'angoscia de le genti
che son qua giú, nel viso mi dipigne
quella pietà che tu per tema senti.
Andiam, ché la via lunga ne sospigne."
Cosí si mise e cosí mi fé intrare
nel primo cerchio che l'abisso cigne.

Quivi, secondo che per ascoltare,
non avea pianto mai che di sospiri
che l'aura etterna facevan tremare;
ciò avvenia di duol sanza martíri,
ch'avean le turbe, ch'eran molte e grandi,
d'infanti e di femmine e di viri.
Lo buon maestro a me: "Tu non dimandi
che spiriti son questi che tu vedi?
Or vo' che sappi, innanzi che piú andi,
ch'ei non peccaro; e s'elli hanno mercedi,
non basta, perché non ebber battesmo,
ch'è porta de la fede che tu credi;
e s' e' furon dinanzi al cristianesmo,
non adorar debitamente a Dio:
e di questi cotai son io medesmo.
Per tai difetti, non per altro rio,
semo perduti, e sol di tanto offesi
che sanza speme vivemo in disio."

Gran duol mi prese al cor quando lo 'ntesi,
però che gente di molto valore
conobbi che 'n quel limbo eran sospesi.
"Dimmi, maestro mio, dimmi, segnore,"
comincia' io per volere esser certo
di quella fede che vince ogne errore:
"uscicci mai alcuno, o per suo merto
o per altrui, che poi fosse beato?"
E quei che 'ntese il mio parlar coverto,
rispuose: "Io era nuovo in questo stato,
quando ci vidi venire un possente,
con segno di vittoria coronato.

And he said: "The anguish of the people
here below has painted my face
with the pity that you mistake for fear.
Now let us go, for the long journey calls."
So he entered, and had me enter
the First Circle that rings the abyss.

Here was no lamentation, or none
that could be heard, but only sighs,
sighs that made the timeless air tremble,
Sighs of sadness, but not of torment,
that arose from crowds many and large,
throngs of infants, women, and men.
My good master said to me: "Do you not wonder
what spirits are these you see before you?
I would have you know, before you go farther,
That they did not sin. But if they earned merit,
it did not suffice without the rite of baptism,
the portal to the faith that you observe;
And if they preceded Christianity,
they did not give the worship owed to God.
I myself am counted one of these.
For these defects, and for no other fault,
we are lost, but afflicted only so far
that we live in longing without any hope."

My heart beat with sorrow when I heard this,
for I realized that people of outstanding worth
were forever suspended in that Limbo.
"Tell me, Master, tell me, sir," I began,
eager to be absolutely sure
of the faith that conquers every error,
"Did anyone ever go forth from here
by his own merit or that of another
to be blessed later?" He knew what I meant
And answered: "I was new to this state
when I witnessed a powerful being descend
crowned with the insignia of victory.

Trasseci l'ombra del primo parente,
d'Abèl suo figlio e quella di Noè,
di Moïsè legista e ubidente;
Abraàm patrïarca e Davíd re,
Israèl con lo padre e co' suoi nati
e con Rachele, per cui tanto fé,
e altri molti, e feceli beati.
E vo' che sappi che, dinanzi ad essi,
spiriti umani non eran salvati."

Non lasciavam l'andar perch' ei dicessi,
ma passavam la selva tuttavia,
la selva, dico, di spiriti spessi.
Non era lunga ancor la nostra via
di qua dal sonno, quand' io vidi un foco
ch'emisperio di tenebre vincia.
Di lungi n'eravamo ancora un poco,
ma non sí ch'io non discernessi in parte
ch'orrevol gente possedea quel loco.
"O tu ch'onori scïenzïa e arte,
questi chi son c'hanno cotanta onranza,
che dal modo de li altri li diparte?"
E quelli a me: "L'onrata nominanza
che di lor suona sú ne la tua vita,
grazïa acquista in ciel che sí li avanza."

Intanto voce fu per me udita:
"Onorate l'altissimo poeta;
l'ombra sua torna, ch'era dipartita."
Poi che la voce fu restata e queta,
vidi quattro grand' ombre a noi venire:
sembianz' avevan né trista né lieta.

Lo buon maestro cominciò a dire:
"Mira colui con quella spada in mano,
che vien dinanzi ai tre sí come sire:

He plucked from here our first parent's shade,
the shade of Abel and the shade of Noah,
and that of Moses, obedient lawgiver,
Of the patriarch Abraham, and David king,
Israel along with his father and sons
and with Rachel, for whom he did so much,
And many others. He made them blessed;
and before these, I would have you know,
no human soul had achieved salvation."

We did not stop walking while he spoke
but proceeded steadily through a forest,
a forest, I mean, of thronging souls.
We had not gone very far from the spot
where I had slept, when I saw a fire rising
triumphant over a hemisphere of shadow.
We were still a little distance away
but close enough that I could dimly discern
the gloried people who possessed this place.
"O Poet who honors knowledge and art,
who are these whose honor is so great,
that it sets them apart from all the rest?"
And he said to me: "Their glory and fame
that resound among you in your life above
win grace in Heaven that advances them here."

As he finished I heard another voice saying:
"Honor the Poet most exalted!
His shade, which had departed, now returns."
After the voice had fallen silent and still,
I saw four great shades drawing near to us
with an air that seemed neither joyful nor sad.

At this my good master began to speak:
"Observe the one with the sword in his hand
leading the other three as their lord.

quelli è Omero poeta sovrano;
  l'altro è Orazio satiro che vene;
    Ovidio è 'l terzo, e l'ultimo Lucano.
Però che ciascun meco si convene
  nel nome che sonò la voce sola,
    fannomi onore, e di ciò fanno bene."

Cosí vid' i' adunar la bella scola
  di quel segnor de l'altissimo canto
    che sovra li altri com' aquila vola.
Da ch'ebber ragionato insieme alquanto,
  volsersi a me con salutevol cenno,
    e 'l mio maestro sorrise di tanto;
e piú d'onore ancora assai mi fenno,
  ch'e' sí mi fecer de la loro schiera,
    sí ch'io fui sesto tra cotanto senno.
Cosí andammo infino a la lumera,
  parlando cose che 'l tacere è bello,
    sí com' era 'l parlar colà dov' era.
Venimmo al piè d'un nobile castello,
  sette volte cerchiato d'alte mura,
    difeso intorno d'un bel fiumicello.
Questo passammo come terra dura;
  per sette porte intrai con questi savi:
    giugnemmo in prato di fresca verdura.
Genti v'eran con occhi tardi e gravi,
  di grande autorità ne' lor sembianti:
    parlavan rado, con voci soavi.

Traemmoci cosí da l'un de' canti,
  in loco aperto, luminoso e alto,
    sí che veder si potien tutti quanti.
Colà diritto, sovra 'l verde smalto,
  mi fuor mostrati li spiriti magni,
    che del vedere in me stesso m'essalto.
I' vidi Eletra con molti compagni,
  tra ' quai conobbi Ettòr ed Enea,
    Cesare armato con li occhi grifagni.

That is Homer, the sovereign poet.
  Next comes Horace, the satirist,
    Ovid is third, and behind him Lucan.
Since each of them shares with me the title
  announced just now by the solitary voice,
    they do me honor, and in that they do well."

And so I saw assembled the noble school
  of that lord of highest poetry
    that soars like an eagle above the rest.
After they had talked among themselves awhile
  they turned to me with a gesture of welcome
    that made my master break into a smile.
And then they showed me more honor still,
  for they made me one of their company,
    so that I was sixth in that flight of wisdom.
In this way we went on into the light
  talking of things better left in silence now,
    just as it was good to speak of them then.
We came to the foot of a noble castle
  girded seven times by towering walls
    themselves encircled by a beautiful stream.
This we crossed as if on solid ground,
  and I passed through the seven gates with the sages.
    We came into a meadow green with fresh grass
Where there were people with grave and solemn eyes
  and great authority in their looks.
    They seldom spoke, and their voices were soft.

Then we drew to one side into a place apart
  that was high and open and full of light,
    so we could see them all, each and every one.
There in plain view on the enameled green
  the spirits of the great were shown to me.
    To have seen them still exalts my soul.
I saw Electra with many companions,
  among whom I knew Aeneas and Hector,
    and Caesar, armed with flashing falcon eyes.

Vidi Cammilla e la Pantasilea;
da l'altra parte vidi 'l re Latino
che con Lavina sua figlia sedea.

Vidi quel Bruto che cacciò Tarquino,
Lucrezia, Iulia, Marzïa e Corniglia;
e solo, in parte, vidi 'l Saladino.
Poi ch'innalzai un poco piú le ciglia,
vidi 'l maestro di color che sanno
seder tra filosofica famiglia.
Tutti lo miran, tutti onor li fanno:
quivi vid' ïo Socrate e Platone,
che 'nnanzi a li altri piú presso li stanno;
Democrito che 'l mondo a caso pone,
Dïogenès, Anassagora e Tale,
Empedoclès, Eraclito e Zenone;
e vidi il buono accoglitor del quale,
Dïascoride dico; e vidi Orfeo,
Tulïo e Lino e Seneca morale;
Euclide geomètra e Tolomeo,
Ipocràte, Avicenna e Galïeno,
Averoís che 'l gran comento feo.

Io non posso ritrar di tutti a pieno,
però che sí mi caccia il lungo tema,
che molte volte al fatto il dir vien meno.
La sesta compagnia in due si scema:
per altra via mi mena il savio duca,
fuor de la queta, ne l'aura che trema.
E vegno in parte ove non è che luca.

I saw Camilla and Penthesilea,
and on the other side King Latinus
who sat with his daughter Lavinia.

I saw that Brutus who drove out Tarquin;
Lucretia, Julia, Marcia, and Cornelia;
and apart by himself I saw Saladin.
When I lifted my eyes a little higher
I saw the master of those who know
seated with his brood of philosophers.
All gaze upon him and do him honor.
There I saw Socrates, and Plato too,
closest to him and before all the others;
Anaxagoras, Thales, and Diogenes;
Democritus, who attributes the world to chance;
Heraclitus, Zeno, and Empedocles.
And there too I saw the great herbalist,
Dioscorides, and also Orpheus,
Cicero, Linus, Seneca the moralist,
Euclid, and Ptolemy, the heavens' surveyor,
Hippocrates, Avicenna, and Galen,
Averroës too, the great commentator.

Hurried along by my poem's long intent
I cannot portray all those who were there,
and my words often fall short of the event.
The band of six now dwindled to a pair,
and my sage guide led me along other lines
out of the silence into the trembling air,
And I came to a place where nothing shines.

Canto V

Dante and Virgil descend *from the First to the Second Circle. At the entrance, they find the half-human, half-bestial judge of all Hell, Minos, from whom the arriving sinners receive their wordless sentence. When the individual sinner has confessed his or her guilt, Minos wraps his tail around his body, indicating by the number of coils the circle to which the shade's sin condemns it. Minos attempts to dissuade the living Dante from entering, but Virgil silences him. In the darkness of the circle can be heard the roar of a whirlwind and the cries of its hapless victims, the Lustful, who in life allowed themselves to be carried away by the winds of passion. Among those borne upon and buffeted by the wind, Virgil points out a number of famous adulteresses and adulterers from history and legend. Already seized with pity, Dante desires to speak to a pair of shades who are swept along inseparably. Like homing doves, they glide toward him as the wind pauses. One of them, a woman, tells Dante where they were from, what inspired their noble love, and how they died a violent death. Dante, who has recognized Francesca da Rimini, the adulterous wife of Gianciotto Malatesta, asks her how she and her lover first discovered their sexual attraction for one another. By reading together the Arthurian romance of Lancelot and Guinevere, she answers. The book played the same role as Galahalt, the literary adulterers' go-between. Overcome with pity, Dante faints.*

Cosí discesi del cerchio primaio
giú nel secondo, che men loco cinghia
e tanto piú dolor, che punge a guaio.
Stavvi Minòs orribilmente, e ringhia:
essamina le colpe ne l'intrata;
giudica e manda secondo ch'avvinghia.
Dico che quando l'anima mal nata
li vien dinanzi, tutta si confessa;
e quel conoscitor de le peccata
vede qual loco d'inferno è da essa;
cignesi con la coda tante volte
quantunque gradi vuol che giú sia messa.
Sempre dinanzi a lui ne stanno molte:
vanno a vicenda ciascuna al giudizio,
dicono e odono e poi son giú volte.
"O tu che vieni al doloroso ospizio,"
disse Minòs a me quando mi vide,
lasciando l'atto di cotanto offizio,

And so I descended from the First Circle
down to the Second, which confines less space
but much more pain, spurring tortured cries.
There stands Minos the Terrible, snarling.
He judges each sinner at the entrance
and sentences him by coiling his tail.
What I mean is that when the ill-born soul
comes before him it confesses completely,
and Minos, that connoisseur of sin,
Sees what its just place in Hell should be
and winds his tail around himself as many times
as the number of the circle that he assigns.
They stand in crowds and go one by one,
each to its judgment. They confess, they hear,
and then they are hurled into the pit below.
When I caught his eye, Minos set to one side
the high duties of his magistracy. "You there,"
he said, "who approach our grim hospitality,

"guarda com' entri e di cui tu ti fide;
non t'inganni l'ampiezza de l'intrare!"
E 'l duca mio a lui: "Perché pur gride?
Non impedir lo suo fatale andare:
vuolsi cosí colà dove si puote
ciò che si vuole, e piú non dimandare."

Or incominciàn le dolenti note
a farmisi sentire; or son venuto
là dove molto pianto mi percuote.
Io venni in loco d'ogne luce muto,
che mugghia come fa mar per tempesta,
se da contrari venti è combattuto.
La bufera infernal, che mai non resta,
mena li spirti con la sua rapina;
voltando e percotendo li molesta.
Quando giungon davanti a la ruina,
quivi le strida, il compianto, il lamento;
bestemmian quivi la virtù divina.
Intesi ch'a cosí fatto tormento
enno dannati i peccator carnali,
che la ragion sommettono al talento.

E come li stornei ne portan l'ali
nel freddo tempo, a schiera larga e piena,
cosí quel fiato li spiriti mali
di qua, di là, di giú, di sú li mena;
nulla speranza li conforta mai,
non che di posa, ma di minor pena.
E come i gru van cantando lor lai,
faccendo in aere di sé lunga riga,
cosí vid' io venir, traendo guai,
ombre portate da la detta briga;
per ch'i' dissi: "Maestro, chi son quelle
genti che l'aura nera sí gastiga?"

Beware of entering and watch whom you trust.
Do not be deceived by the gate's wide mouth."
And my guide said to him: "Why do you cry out?
Do not impede his journey ordained on high,
for this is willed where the power abides
to do what is willed. Question us no more."

Now the eternal note of sadness began
to make itself felt to me, and I came to a place
where lamentation assaulted my ears,
A place where all light is dumb but that sounds
like the sea howling in a hurricane
when opposing blasts wrestle on the deep.
There an infernal wind that never rests
whirls the damned spirits around and around
with stinging blasts that torture them in flight.
When they reach the shattered precipice
the cries, the shrieks, the lamentations rise;
there they blaspheme the Power Divine.
I came to understand that those condemned
to this torment were the souls of the lustful
who put rational thought below carnal desire.

As flocks of starlings beat their wings and fly
in the cold of the year, crowding the air,
so too that wind drove these accursed souls
Upward and downward and this way and that,
without hope of comfort or even lesser pain,
without hope of repose forevermore.
And as cranes fall into long lines in the sky,
chanting their rounds as they wing their way on,
so too I saw coming, with songs of grief,
Shadows blown on by the force of that wind.
And I asked: "Master, who are these people,
and why does the black air punish them so?"

"La prima di color di cui novelle
tu vuo' saper," mi disse quelli allotta,
"fu imperadrice di molte favelle.
A vizio di lussuria fu sí rotta,
che libito fé licito in sua legge,
per tòrre il biasmo in che era condotta.
Ell' è Semiramís, di cui si legge
che succedette a Nino e fu sua sposa:
tenne la terra che 'l Soldan corregge.
L'altra è colei che s'ancise amorosa,
e ruppe fede al cener di Sicheo;
poi è Cleopatràs lussurïosa.
Elena vedi, per cui tanto reo
tempo si volse, e vedi 'l grande Achille,
che con amore al fine combatteo.
Vedi París, Tristano"; e piú di mille
ombre mostrommi e nominommi a dito,
ch'amor di nostra vita dipartille.

Poscia ch'io ebbi 'l mio dottore udito
nomar le donne antiche e ' cavalieri,
pietà mi giunse, e fui quasi smarrito.
I' cominciai: "Poeta, volontieri
parlerei a quei due che 'nsieme vanno,
e paion sí al vento esser leggeri."
Ed elli a me: "Vedrai quando saranno
piú presso a noi; e tu allor li priega
per quello amor che i mena, ed ei verranno."
Sí tosto come il vento a noi li piega,
mossi la voce: "O anime affannate,
venite a noi parlar, s'altri nol niega!"
Quali colombe dal disio chiamate
con l'ali alzate e ferme al dolce nido
vegnon per l'aere, dal voler portate;
cotali uscir de la schiera ov' è Dido,
a noi venendo per l'aere maligno,
sí forte fu l'affettüoso grido.

"The first of those whose stories you long
to learn," my guide began, "was an empress
with dominion over many tribes and tongues.
She was so abandoned to sensual vice
that she made lust legitimate in her laws
to expunge the shame that she had incurred.
She is Semiramis. We read of her
that as widow of Ninus she ascended his throne
and held the land that the Sultan now rules.
Beside her is she who cut short her own life
for love unfaithful to Sychaeus' ashes.
Next to her is the lascivious Cleopatra.
Look now at Helen, about whom so many
seasons of ill revolved, and great Achilles,
who in his final hour did battle with love.
See Paris and Tristan!" A thousand shades
or more he pointed out and named,
each severed by love from our mortal life.

After I had listened to my teacher name
these fair ladies of old and their champions,
I was seized with pity, bewildered, and lost.
And I began: "Poet, I would gladly
speak to those two who go together
and seem to move so light on the wind."
He answered me: "Wait until you see them move
closer to us. Then implore them by the love
that leads them on, and they will come to you."
As soon as the wind had whirled them nearer
I shouted to them: "O troubled souls,
come speak with us, if no one forbids it."
As doves summoned by their own desire
steady their wings and come through the air,
drawn by love to their sweet nesting place,
So glided these spirits from Dido's side
and came to us through the poisoned air,
so powerful was my heartfelt cry.

"O animal grazïoso e benigno
che visitando vai per l'aere perso
noi che tignemmo il mondo di sanguigno,
se fosse amico il re de l'universo,
noi pregheremmo lui de la tua pace,
poi c'hai pietà del nostro mal perverso.
Di quel che udire e che parlar vi piace,
noi udiremo e parleremo a voi,
mentre che 'l vento, come fa, ci tace.
Siede la terra dove nata fui
su la marina dove 'l Po discende
per aver pace co' seguaci sui.
Amor, ch'al cor gentil ratto s'apprende,
prese costui de la bella persona
che mi fu tolta; e 'l modo ancor m'offende.
Amor, ch'a nullo amato amar perdona,
mi prese del costui piacer sí forte,
che, come vedi, ancor non m'abbandona.
Amor condusse noi ad una morte.
Caïna attende chi a vita ci spense."
Queste parole da lor ci fuor porte.

Quand' io intesi quell' anime offense,
china' il viso, e tanto il tenni basso,
fin che 'l poeta mi disse: "Che pense?"
Quando rispuosi, cominciai: "Oh lasso,
quanti dolci pensier, quanto disio
menò costoro al doloroso passo!"
Poi mi rivolsi a loro e parla' io,
e cominciai: "Francesca, i tuoi martíri
a lagrimar mi fanno tristo e pio.
Ma dimmi: al tempo d'i dolci sospiri,
a che e come concedette amore
che conosceste i dubbiosi disiri?"

E quella a me: "Nessun maggior dolore
che ricordarsi del tempo felice
ne la miseria; e ciò sa 'l tuo dottore.

"O living soul, so gracious and kind
to brave the black air and visit us,
who dyed the Earth the color of blood—
If the King of the Universe were our friend
we would pray to Him to grant you peace,
since you have taken pity on our woe.
Whatever it pleases you to speak or hear,
that will we listen to or speak ourselves,
while the wind is quiet, as the wind is now.
The city where I was born lies on the shore
where the river Po comes down to the sea
with all its tributaries to rest in peace.
Love, which kindles quickly in the gentle heart,
impassioned this man with my beautiful form
taken from me in a way that still wounds.
Love, which excuses no beloved from loving,
filled me with passion so strong for this man,
that, as you see, it has not left me yet.
Love led us both to share in one death.
Caïna awaits him who snuffed out our life."
These words drifted upon the wind to us.

When I had heard these wounded souls, I bowed
my head and kept it low, until the Poet
finally asked me, "What are you brooding on?"
When I could speak again, I answered, "Ah,
how many sweet thoughts, how much desire
drove these lovers to this sorrowful pass!"
Then turning to the lovers I spoke again.
"Francesca, the suffering you endure
moves me to weep in pity for your pain.
But tell me this. In that time of sweet sighs,
how, by what means, did Love grant to you
the knowledge of your hesitant desires?"

And she answered: "There is no greater sorrow
than to recall a time of happiness
in a time of misery, as your teacher knows.

Ma s'a conoscer la prima radice
 del nostro amor tu hai cotanto affetto,
  dirò come colui che piange e dice.
Noi leggiavamo un giorno per diletto
 di Lancialotto come amor lo strinse;
  soli eravamo e sanza alcun sospetto.
Per piú fiate li occhi ci sospinse
 quella lettura, e scolorocci il viso;
  ma solo un punto fu quel che ci vinse.
Quando leggemmo il disïato riso
 esser basciato da cotanto amante,
  questi, che mai da me non fia diviso,
la bocca mi basciò tutto tremante.
 Galeotto fu 'l libro e chi lo scrisse:
  quel giorno piú non vi leggemmo avante."

Mentre che l'uno spirto questo disse,
 l'altro piangëa; sí che di pietade
  io venni men cosí com' io morisse.
E caddi come corpo morto cade.

But if you have so great a desire
 to learn what first made us fall in love,
  I will tell it as one who weeps and tells.
One day we two were reading for pleasure
 of Love's mastery over Lancelot.
  We were alone, and suspected nothing.
As we read the story our eyes would meet
 and our faces pale at each other's glance,
  but at one point only did we taste defeat.
When we read how the longed-for smile was kissed,
 the smile of Guinevere, by her great lover—
  this man, with whom I keep eternal tryst,
Trembling all over, placed his lips on mine.
 That book and its author were our Galahalt,
  And that day we read not another line."

While this spirit spoke, the one at her side
 wept with such a piteous sound
  that my senses failed, and as if I had died
My body fell like a corpse to the ground.

Canto XXIV

As he reacts to the changing weather *of Virgil's facial expressions, first betokening anxiety, then resolution, Dante is like the peasant who at first takes the hoarfrost for snow, but quickly rejoices when the frozen dew melts in the February sun. Arriving at the ruined bridge, Virgil takes Dante into his arms and together they climb laboriously out of the Sixth Bolgia. Once out, Dante is not allowed to linger and catch his breath. As they cross the next bridge, over the murky Seventh Bolgia, an angry voice is heard uttering indistinguishable words in the darkness below. Approaching closer, they see that on the opposite side the bolgia is teeming with exotic reptiles while naked human figures, their hands bound by snakes, run among them. A serpent bites one of these figures in the neck, and he instantly crumbles to dust, only to spring up again, just as the Phoenix is said to rise from its ashes. Though dazed, when interrogated by Virgil he reveals, with a show of violence, that he is Vanni Fucci, a Black Guelph from Pistoia. Dante presses him further, to find out what sin he is guilty of. Ashamed, the sinner admits he was a thief and, to avenge his humiliation by Dante, prophesies the ultimate defeat of Dante's party, the White Guelphs.*

In quella parte del giovanetto anno
che 'l sole i crin sotto l'Aquario tempra
e già le notti al mezzo dí sen vanno,
quando la brina in su la terra assempra
l'imagine di sua sorella bianca,
ma poco dura a la sua penna tempra,
lo villanello a cui la roba manca,
si leva, e guarda, e vede la campagna
biancheggiar tutta; ond' ei si batte l'anca,
ritorna in casa, e qua e là si lagna,
come 'l tapin che non sa che si faccia;
poi riede, e la speranza ringavagna,
veggendo 'l mondo aver cangiata faccia
in poco d'ora, e prende suo vincastro
e fuor le pecorelle a pascer caccia.

Cosí mi fece sbigottir lo mastro
quand' io li vidi sí turbar la fronte,
e cosí tosto al mal giunse lo 'mpiastro;
ché, come noi venimmo al guasto ponte,
lo duca a me si volse con quel piglio
dolce ch'io vidi prima a piè del monte.

When the year is young, and the sun
is warming his locks under Aquarius
and the nights are almost as short as the days,
When frost copies on the woods and fields
the likeness of her wintry sister,
but the quill she draws with soon becomes blunt,
Then the peasant whose fodder is running low
gets up in the morning, looks out, and sees
the fields all white. He slaps his thigh,
Goes back inside, and grumbles for a while,
worries, frets, doesn't know what to do;
but then he goes back out and hope returns
When he sees how quickly the face of the world
has changed its expression. He takes his crook
and drives his sheep out to hunt for pasture.

My master likewise caused me dismay
when I saw his brow so anxious and troubled,
but just as quickly a remedy appeared.
For when we came to the shattered bridge
my guide turned to me with that gentle look
that I saw first at the foot of the mountain.

Le braccia aperse, dopo alcun consiglio
  eletto seco riguardando prima
    ben la ruina, e diedemi di piglio.
E come quei ch'adopera ed estima,
  che sempre par che 'nnanzi si proveggia,
    cosí, levando me sú ver' la cima
d'un ronchione, avvisava un'altra scheggia
  dicendo: "Sovra quella poi t'aggrappa;
    ma tenta pria s'è tal ch'ella ti reggia."
Non era via da vestito di cappa,
  ché noi a pena, ei lieve e io sospinto,
    potavam sú montar di chiappa in chiappa.
E se non fosse che da quel precinto
  piú che da l'altro era la costa corta,
    non so di lui, ma io sarei ben vinto.
Ma perché Malebolge inver' la porta
  del bassissimo pozzo tutta pende,
    lo sito di ciascuna valle porta
che l'una costa surge e l'altra scende;
  noi pur venimmo al fine in su la punta
    onde l'ultima pietra si scoscende.
La lena m'era del polmon sí munta
  quand' io fui sú, ch'i' non potea piú oltre,
    anzi m'assisi ne la prima giunta.

"Omai convien che tu cosí ti spoltre,"
  disse 'l maestro; "ché, seggendo in piuma,
    in fama non si vien, né sotto coltre;
sanza la qual chi sua vita consuma,
  cotal vestigio in terra di sé lascia,
    qual fummo in aere e in acqua la schiuma.
E però leva sú; vinci l'ambascia
  con l'animo che vince ogne battaglia,
    se col suo grave corpo non s'accascia.
Piú lunga scala convien che si saglia;
  non basta da costoro esser partito.
    Se tu mi 'ntendi, or fa sí che ti vaglia."

After thinking it over a moment or two
  and examining the rubble, he spread
    his arms out and wrapped them around me.
And, like a person who plans every move
  and seems to see everything in advance,
    while he was lifting me up toward the top
Of one great rock he was already mapping
  the handhold to follow, saying, "Grab that one next,
    but test it to see if it will bear your weight."
It was no route for those wearing thick cloaks,
  for we, light as he was and I with his support,
    could hardly make it from one ledge to another.
And except for the fact that on that embankment
  the slope was shorter than on the other side—
    I don't know about him, but I would have been beat.
But because Malebolge all slopes inward
  to the bottom of the central pit,
    each of the valleys is situated
So that one side towers over the other.
  At long last, however, we reached the point
    where the last stone breaks off from the edge.
I had so little breath left in my lungs
  after the ascent, I could go no farther,
    and I sat down as soon as I got to the top.

"You're going to have to stop being so lazy,"
  my master said. "No one attains fame
    propped on down pillows or under coverlets,
And without fame you will waste your life
  and leave no more of yourself on Earth
    than smoke in the air or foam on water.
So stop gasping and get up! Conquer your breath
  with the spirit that wins all of its battles
    if it doesn't surrender to the weight of its body.
There is a longer ladder yet to be climbed.
  It is not enough to have left those souls behind.
    If you understand me, do something about it!"

Leva'mi allor, mostrandomi fornito
meglio di lena ch'i' non mi sentia,
e dissi: "Va, ch'i' son forte e ardito."

Su per lo scoglio prendemmo la via,
ch'era ronchioso, stretto e malagevole,
ed erto piú assai che quel di pria.
Parlando andava per non parer fievole;
onde una voce uscí de l'altro fosso,
a parole formar disconvenevole.
Non so che disse, ancor che sovra 'l dosso
fossi de l'arco già che varca quivi;
ma chi parlava ad ira parea mosso.
Io era vòlto in giú, ma li occhi vivi
non poteano ire al fondo per lo scuro;
per ch'io: "Maestro, fa che tu arrivi
da l'altro cinghio e dismontiam lo muro;
ché, com' i' odo quinci e non intendo,
cosí giú veggio e neente affiguro."
"Altra risposta," disse, "non ti rendo
se non lo far; ché la dimanda onesta
si de' seguir con l'opera tacendo."

Noi discendemmo il ponte da la testa
dove s'aggiugne con l'ottava ripa,
e poi mi fu la bolgia manifesta:
e vidivi entro terribile stipa
di serpenti, e di sí diversa mena
che la memoria il sangue ancor mi scipa.
Piú non si vanti Libia con sua rena;
ché se chelidri, iaculi e faree
produce, e cencri con anfisibena,
né tante pestilenzie né sí ree
mostrò già mai con tutta l'Etïopia
né con ciò che di sopra al Mar Rosso èe.
Tra questa cruda e tristissima copia
corrëan genti nude e spaventate,
sanza sperar pertugio o elitropia:

I got up then, pretending not to be
nearly as winded as I felt, and said,
"Go ahead now. I'm strong and determined."

We took the way that led up the ridge,
a tortuous path hedged in by rocks,
and far steeper than the last one we crossed.
I was talking as I went, so I would not seem
so exhausted, when a voice, ill suited
for forming words, came out of the ditch.
I don't know what it said, being as yet
at the crown of the arch that crosses there,
but the one that spoke seemed driven to rage.
I turned my gaze below, but my eyes could not pierce
the shroud of darkness down to the bottom,
so I said, "Master, would you please go down
To the next bank? Let's descend the wall,
for from this point I can't understand what I hear,
and when I look down there I can't see a thing."
"The only reply," he said, "that I will give
is just to do it, for a proper request
should be met with action performed in silence."

We came down at the end of the bridge
where it abuts the eighth embankment,
and the ditch's contents were revealed to me.
I saw within it a terrifying mass
of serpents, snakes of so many strange kinds
that the memory of it still chills my blood.
Libya can boast of nothing like this,
for rich as it is in trail-scorchers and dart snakes,
plow-adders, line-winders, and two-headed asps,
It has never had, with Ethiopia thrown in,
and all of the lands along the Red Sea,
so many, or such evil vipers as these.
And amid this cruel and hideous swarm
people were running, naked and panicked,
with no place to hide and no magic stone.

con serpi le man dietro avean legate;
quelle ficcavan per le ren la coda
e 'l capo, ed eran dinanzi aggroppate.
Ed ecco a un ch'era da nostra proda,
s'avventò un serpente che 'l trafisse
là dove 'l collo a le spalle s'annoda.
Né O sí tosto mai né I si scrisse,
com' el s'accese e arse, e cener tutto
convenne che cascando divenisse;
e poi che fu a terra sí distrutto,
la polver si raccolse per sé stessa
e 'n quel medesmo ritornò di butto.
Cosí per li gran savi si confessa
che la fenice more e poi rinasce,
quando al cinquecentesimo anno appressa;
erba né biado in sua vita non pasce,
ma sol d'incenso lagrime e d'amomo,
e nardo e mirra son l'ultime fasce.
E qual è quel che cade, e non sa como,
per forza di demon ch'a terra il tira,
o d'altra oppilazion che lega l'omo,
quando si leva, che 'ntorno si mira
tutto smarrito de la grande angoscia
ch'elli ha sofferta, e guardando sospira:
tal era 'l peccator levato poscia.
Oh potenza di Dio, quant' è severa,
che cotai colpi per vendetta croscia!

Lo duca il domandò poi chi ello era;
per ch'ei rispuose: "Io piovvi di Toscana,
poco tempo è, in questa gola fiera.
Vita bestial mi piacque e non umana,
sí come a mul ch'i' fui; son Vanni Fucci
bestia, e Pistoia mi fu degna tana."
E ïo al duca: "Dilli che non mucci,
e domanda che colpa qua giú 'l pinse;
ch'io 'l vidi omo di sangue e di crucci."

Their hands were bound behind their backs with snakes
whose heads and tails transfixed their loins
and were tied in knots in front of their bellies.
A serpent suddenly shot after one
who was near our bank and buried its fangs
at the knot that joins the neck to the shoulders.
An *o* or an *i* was never written as fast
as that soul caught fire and burned to a crisp,
reduced to nothing but a pile of ashes;
But when he was undone on the ground like this,
the dust reassembled all by itself
and instantly resumed its previous form.
In the same way, learned men say,
the Phoenix dies and is born again
on the evening of its five hundredth year.
It does not feed on grasses or grain,
but on tears of incense and on amomum,
and its last nest is feathered with nard and myrrh.
Like someone who falls without knowing how,
either because some devil drags him down
or because he is seized with paralysis,
And when he gets up he looks around stunned,
completely bewildered by the great anguish
he is suffering, and then stares ahead sighing—
So too that sinner when he rose to his feet.
Oh, the power of God! What stern severity
that showers down blow upon blow in vengeance!

My guide then asked him who he was,
to which he answered: "Not long ago
I poured down from Tuscany to this savage throat.
A bestial life, not a human one, pleased me,
mule that I was. I am Vanni Fucci,
the beast, and Pistoia was my chosen lair."
I said to my guide: "Tell him not to leave,
and ask him what sin got him down here,
for I knew him as a bloody, violent man."

E 'l peccator, che 'ntese, non s'infinse,
ma drizzò verso me l'animo e 'l volto,
e di trista vergogna si dipinse;
poi disse: "Piú mi duol che tu m'hai colto
ne la miseria dove tu mi vedi,
che quando fui de l'altra vita tolto.
Io non posso negar quel che tu chiedi;
in giú son messo tanto perch' io fui
ladro a la sagrestia d'i belli arredi,
e falsamente già fu apposto altrui.
Ma perché di tal vista tu non godi,
se mai sarai di fuor da' luoghi bui,
apri li orecchi al mio annunzio, e odi.
Pistoia in pria d'i Neri si dimagra;
poi Fiorenza rinova gente e modi.
Tragge Marte vapor di Val di Magra
ch'è di torbidi nuvoli involuto;
e con tempesta impetüosa e agra
sovra Campo Picen fia combattuto;
ond' ei repente spezzerà la nebbia,
sí ch'ogne Bianco ne sarà feruto.
E detto l'ho perché doler ti debbia!"

The sinner heard me, and did not dissemble.
In fact, he turned all his attention toward me
and blushed with bitter shame. Then he said:
"It causes me more pain that you have caught me
in the misery where you see me now
than I felt when I left the other life.
I have no choice but to answer your question.
They put me so far down here in Hell
because I stole from the church's treasury
And let the blame fall on an innocent man.
But so that you may not triumph in this sight
if you ever get out of this desolate place,
Open your ears now to what Vanni Fucci says:
Pistoia first rids herself of the Blacks,
then Florence changes her people and her ways.
But from Val di Magra Mars will awaken
a lightning bolt wrapped in threatening clouds,
and a sudden and bitter storm will break
As they rush to combat on Campo Piceno,
from where suddenly the mist and fog will be rent
so that every White will feel the blow.
And I tell you this to make you lament."

Canto XXV

Pistoian thief Vanni Fucci *makes an obscene gesture leveled at God and is silenced, his arms bound by two snakes. He flees before the Centaur Cacus can catch up with him. Dante and Virgil's ensuing exchange is interrupted by the appearance of three shades who are looking for a lost companion. One of them is assailed by a six-legged reptile, which clings to him until their two forms, human and reptilian, fuse into a monstrous hybrid, which slowly squirms away.*

Al fine de le sue parole il ladro
le mani alzò con amendue le fiche,
gridando: "Togli, Dio, ch'a te le squadro!"
Da indi in qua mi fuor le serpi amiche,
perch' una li s'avvolse allora al collo,
come dicesse 'Non vo' che piú diche';
e un'altra a le braccia, e rilegollo,
ribadendo sé stessa sí dinanzi,
che non potea con esse dare un crollo.

Ahi Pistoia, Pistoia, ché non stanzi
d'incenerarti sí che piú non duri,
poi che 'n mal fare il seme tuo avanzi?

Per tutt' i cerchi de lo 'nferno scuri
non vidi spirto in Dio tanto superbo,
non quel che cadde a Tebe giú da' muri.
El si fuggí che non parlò piú verbo;
e io vidi un centauro pien di rabbia
venir chiamando: "Ov' è, ov' è l'acerbo?"
Maremma non cred' io che tante n'abbia,
quante bisce elli avea su per la groppa
infin ove comincia nostra labbia.

A second serpent darts at one of the other two, pierces his navel, and falls to the ground. As smoke pours from the wound and the serpent's mouth, they begin, slowly and uncannily, to exchange shapes at a distance, until the serpent has become a man and the man a serpent. Dante recognizes the only thief in the group whose human form, at least for now, has not been stolen.

When he had finished speaking, the thief
raised his hands and made figs with both fists,
crying out, "Take them, God. These are for you!"
And that is when snakes and I became friends,
for one of them coiled around his neck
as if to say, "You will speak no more,"
And another snake constricted his arms,
lashing them so firmly in front
that he could not even wiggle them.

Ah, Pistoia, Pistoia! Why don't you decree
your own incineration, since you are more
evil than even your founders could be?

In all of Hell, through all its dark circles,
I saw no spirit so arrogant toward God,
not even he who fell from the walls of Thebes.
Vanni Fucci fled without another word.
Then I saw a Centaur come up, shouting with rage,
"Which way did he go? Where's the crude one?"
Maremma's swamps can't have as many reptiles
as crawled along this Centaur's back
up to where our human torso begins;

Sovra le spalle, dietro da la coppa,
con l'ali aperte li giacea un draco;
e quello affuoca qualunque s'intoppa.
Lo mio maestro disse: "Questi è Caco,
che, sotto 'l sasso di monte Aventino,
di sangue fece spesse volte laco.
Non va co' suoi fratei per un cammino,
per lo furto che frodolente fece
del grande armento ch'elli ebbe a vicino;
onde cessar le sue opere biece
sotto la mazza d'Ercule, che forse
gliene diè cento, e non sentí le diece."

Mentre che sí parlava, ed el trascorse,
e tre spiriti venner sotto noi,
de' quai né io né 'l duca mio s'accorse,
se non quando gridar: "Chi siete voi?"
per che nostra novella si ristette,
e intendemmo pur ad essi poi.
Io non li conoscea; ma ei seguette,
come suol seguitar per alcun caso,
che l'un nomar un altro convenette,
dicendo: "Cianfa dove fia rimaso?"
per ch'io, acciò che 'l duca stesse attento,
mi puosi 'l dito su dal mento al naso.

Se tu se' or, lettore, a creder lento
ciò ch'io dirò, non sarà maraviglia,
ché io che 'l vidi, a pena il mi consento.

Com'io tenea levate in lor le ciglia,
e un serpente con sei piè si lancia
dinanzi a l'uno, e tutto a lui s'appiglia.
Co' piè di mezzo li avvinse la pancia
e con li anteriör le braccia prese;
poi li addentò e l'una e l'altra guancia;

And on his shoulders just behind his neck
a dragon crouched with outstretched wings,
ready to breathe fire on whomever it met.
My master said: "That is Cacus,
who beneath the rock of Mount Aventine,
time after time made a lake of blood.
He does not travel in his brothers' company,
on account of the cunning theft he made
of the great herd that pastured near his lair.
It was for this his crooked ways were ended
by Hercules' club, who dealt him perhaps
a hundred blows, though he felt only ten."

While he spoke, the Centaur galloped past,
and three spirits came up from below
unnoticed by either my guide or me
Until they cried out: "Who are you two?"
At this we broke off our conversation
and gave our attention to them alone.
I did not know them, but it happened,
as it often turns out by coincidence,
that one of them had cause to name another,
Saying, "Where in Hell can Cianfa be?"
When I heard this, I alerted my leader
by placing a finger over my lips.

If, Reader, you are slow to believe
what I'm about to say, it will be no surprise,
for I, who saw it, hardly believe it myself.

While I kept my wide open eyes on them
a six-legged serpent suddenly shot up
onto one's chest and clamped on tight.
It clasped his belly with its middle feet
and with its forefeet took hold of his arms,
then stuck its fangs into both of his cheeks;

li diretani a le cosce distese,
e miseli la coda tra 'mbedue
e dietro per le ren sú la ritese.
Ellera abbarbicata mai non fue
ad alber sí, come l'orribil fiera
per l'altrui membra avviticchiò le sue.
Poi s'appiccar, come di calda cera
fossero stati, e mischiar lor colore,
né l'un né l'altro già parea quel ch'era:
come procede innanzi da l'ardore,
per lo papiro suso, un color bruno
che non è nero ancora e 'l bianco more.
Li altri due 'l riguardavano, e ciascuno
gridava: "Omè, Agnel, come ti muti!
Vedi che già non se' né due né uno."
Già eran li due capi un divenuti,
quando n'apparver due figure miste
in una faccia, ov' eran due perduti.
Fersi le braccia due di quattro liste;
le cosce con le gambe e 'l ventre e 'l casso
divenner membra che non fuor mai viste.
Ogne primaio aspetto ivi era casso:
due e nessun l'imagine perversa
parea; e tal sen gio con lento passo.

Come 'l ramarro sotto la gran fersa
dei dí canicular, cangiando sepe,
folgore par se la via attraversa,
sí pareva, venendo verso l'epe
de li altri due, un serpentello acceso,
livido e nero come gran di pepe;
e quella parte onde prima è preso
nostro alimento, a l'un di lor trafisse;
poi cadde giuso innanzi lui disteso.
Lo trafitto 'l mirò, ma nulla disse;
anzi, co' piè fermati, sbadigliava
pur come sonno o febbre l'assalisse.

It spread its hind feet onto his thighs
and inserted its tail right in between them
bending it upward to touch the small of his back.
Ivy has never clung to a tree
the way this horrible beast entwined
its own limbs around the other's body.
And then, as if they were made of hot wax,
they stuck together, and as their colors mixed
neither one seemed what it had been at first.
It was just the way a dark color moves
before a flame across a sheet of paper
not yet charred black, though the white dies away.
The other two spirits were looking on,
and each cried, "Look at you change, Agnello!
Already you are neither two nor one!"
But the two heads had by now become one,
and then we saw the two profiles merging
into one face, where both were lost.
Two arms were fashioned out of four limbs;
the thighs, the legs, the belly, the chest
became body parts never seen before.
Each former feature was blotted out;
the perverse figure was double and none,
and such as it was, it moved on at a crawl.

As a lizard darts like quicksilver through hedges
under the Dog Star's terrible scourge,
and flashes like lightning if it crosses the road,
So too a small fiery serpent appeared,
purple and black like crushed peppercorns,
and made for the bellies of the other two.
It transfixed one of them in that part
through which we receive our first nourishment,
then fell down before him, stretched on the ground.
The soul it had pierced gazed down on it
but said nothing, just stood there and yawned
as if drowsy with sleep or weak with fever.

Elli 'l serpente e quei lui riguardava;
l'un per la piaga e l'altro per la bocca
fummavan forte, e 'l fummo si scontrava.

Taccia Lucano omai là dov' e' tocca
del misero Sabello e di Nasidio,
e attenda a udir quel ch'or si scocca.
Taccia di Cadmo e d'Aretusa Ovidio,
ché se quello in serpente e quella in fonte
converte poetando, io non lo 'nvidio;
ché due nature mai a fronte a fronte
non trasmutò sí ch'amendue le forme
a cambiar lor matera fosser pronte.

Insieme si rispuosero a tai norme,
che 'l serpente la coda in forca fesse,
e 'l feruto ristrinse insieme l'orme.
Le gambe con le cosce seco stesse
s'appiccar sí, che 'n poco la giuntura
non facea segno alcun che si paresse.
Togliea la coda fessa la figura
che si perdeva là, e la sua pelle
si facea molle, e quella di là dura.
Io vidi intrar le braccia per l'ascelle,
e i due piè de la fiera, ch'eran corti,
tanto allungar quanto accorciavan quelle.
Poscia li piè di rietro, insieme attorti,
diventaron lo membro che l'uom cela,
e 'l misero del suo n'avea due porti.
Mentre che 'l fummo l'uno e l'altro vela
di color novo, e genera 'l pel suso
per l'una parte e da l'altra il dipela,
l'un si levò e l'altro cadde giuso,
non torcendo però le lucerne empie,
sotto le quai ciascun cambiava muso.
Quel ch'era dritto, il trasse ver' le tempie,
e di troppa matera ch'in là venne
uscir li orecchi de le gote scempie;

He eyed the serpent; the serpent eyed him.
Smoke poured out from his wound and from
the reptile's mouth, and the two smokes met.

Let Lucan fall silent, where his poem tells
of putrefied Sabellus and swollen Nasidius,
and let him wait for what my poem will let fly.
Let Ovid fall silent, for if in his verse
he transforms Cadmus into a snake
and Arethusa into a babbling fountain,
I am not envious, for he never transmuted
two different natures face to face, so that their forms
readily interchanged their substances.

Their transformation had a strange symmetry:
a fork developed in the tail of the reptile
while the wounded man's feet were welded together.
His calves and thighs were stuck fast to each other,
adhering so firmly it became impossible
to see any sign of a seam or juncture,
While the snake's cloven tail took on the shape
that the other had lost, and its skin grew soft
as the skin of the other grew scaly and tough.
I saw the man's arms shrink into his armpits,
and the reptile's forefeet, which had been short,
grow longer in proportion to the other's loss.
Its two hind feet then twisted together
and became the member that men conceal,
while the wretch's own manhood grew feet and claws.
The smoke enveloped both of the figures
with a new color, propagating hair
on one part while stripping hair from another.
One rose up and the other fell down,
but neither turned aside those baleful eyes
even as their muzzles underneath were changing.
The one standing erect contracted his face
up toward the temples, and from the leftover skin
ears were extruded from the smooth, flat cheeks.

ciò che non corse in dietro e si ritenne
di quel soverchio, fé naso a la faccia
e le labbra ingrossò quanto convenne.
Quel che giacëa, il muso innanzi caccia,
e li orecchi ritira per la testa
come face le corna la lumaccia;
e la lingua, ch'avëa unita e presta
prima a parlar, si fende, e la forcuta
ne l'altro si richiude; e 'l fummo resta.
L'anima ch'era fiera divenuta,
suffolando si fugge per la valle,
e l'altro dietro a lui parlando sputa.
Poscia li volse le novelle spalle,
e disse a l'altro: "I' vo' che Buoso corra,
com' ho fatt' io, carpon per questo calle."

Cosí vid' io la settima zavorra
mutare e trasmutare; e qui mi scusi
la novità se fior la penna abborra.
E avvegna che li occhi miei confusi
fossero alquanto e l'animo smagato,
non poter quei fuggirsi tanto chiusi,
ch'i' non scorgessi ben Puccio Sciancato;
ed era quel che sol, di tre compagni
che venner prima, non era mutato;
l'altr' era quel che tu, Gaville, piagni.

The excess mass that did not shift around back
provided material for a nose on the face
and to thicken the lips to proportionate size.
The one that lay prone elongated his snout
and retracted his ears back into his head,
the way that snails draw in their horns.
And just as his tongue, which had been intact
and capable of speech, now split apart,
so too the forked tongue fused, and then the smoke cleared.
The soul that had become a wild animal
ran off hissing down the valley floor,
and the other, who could speak now, spat as it ran.
Then he turned his new shoulders back on it
and said to the third, "I want Buoso to run
along this road on all fours, as I have done!"

So I saw the baggage in the seventh hold
transform and transmute; the utter strangeness
explains why my quill could not be controlled.
And although my vision was in disarray
and my mind was somewhat bewildered,
these souls could not so easily sneak away
That I could not make out among the three
Puccio Sciancato. It was this one alone
who remained unchanged. The other was he
For whom you, village of Gaville, still groan.

Canto XXVI

After ironically congratulating Florence *for the distinction c having so many thieves in Hell, Dante cautiously proceeds with his exploratioi of the Eighth Bolgia. As he leans precariously from the bridge, the sight he see below reminds him of a swarm of fireflies on a summer night. Moving over th floor of the bolgia, in fact, he sees countless tongues of flame, which he realize conceal within them the souls of the sinners. One flame that particularly attract his attention is split in a forked tongue. Within it, says Virgil, are not one bu*

Godi, Fiorenza, poi che se' sí grande
che per mare e per terra batti l'ali,
e per lo 'nferno tuo nome si spande!
Tra li ladron trovai cinque cotali
tuoi cittadini onde mi ven vergogna,
e tu in grande orranza non ne sali.
Ma se presso al mattin del ver si sogna,
tu sentirai, di qua da picciol tempo,
di quel che Prato, non ch'altri, t'agogna.
E se già fosse, non saria per tempo.
Cosí foss' ei, da che pur esser dee!
ché piú mi graverà, com' piú m'attempo.

Noi ci partimmo, e su per le scalee
che n'avea fatto i borni a scender pria,
rimontò 'l duca mio e trasse mee;
e proseguendo la solinga via,
tra le schegge e tra ' rocchi de lo scoglio
lo piè sanza la man non si spedia.
Allor mi dolsi, e ora mi ridoglio
quando drizzo la mente a ciò ch'io vidi,
e piú lo 'ngegno affreno ch'i' non soglio,

two Greek heroes, Ulysses (or Odysseus) and Diomedes, two of the warriors most responsible for the defeat and destruction of Troy. In the Odyssey*, a sequel to the* Iliad*, Ulysses was also, like Aeneas and like Dante, a famous exile and a wanderer and a seeker. No wonder Dante is eager to hear how his journeying ended. At Virgil's request, the overreaching Ulysses describes how he persuaded his comrades to follow him on his final and most ambitious (and fatal) voyage.*

Rejoice, O Florence, for so great have you grown
that your wingspan extends over land and sea,
and even through Hell your name is known.
Among the thieves I found five who were
your citizens, which fills me with shame
and hardly lifts you to heights of honor.
But if dreams we have near morning are true,
you will feel, before too much time goes by,
what Prato, and others, crave for you.
Were it done now, it would be none too soon,
and would that it were, since it must be done
and will weigh on me more as my life wears on.

We left that place, and my leader climbed
the same stairs that the jutting stones had made
for our descent. Then he hoisted me up,
And we made our solitary way
through the rocks and along the splintered ridge
where the foot could not advance without the hand.
I grieved then, and I grieve again now
when I turn my mind to what I saw there,
and now I rein in my native genius

perché non corra che virtù nol guidi;
sí che, se stella bona o miglior cosa
m'ha dato 'l ben, ch'io stessi nol m'invidi.

Quante 'l villan ch'al poggio si riposa,
nel tempo che colui che 'l mondo schiara
la faccia sua a noi tien meno ascosa,
come la mosca cede a la zanzara,
vede lucciole giú per la vallea,
forse colà dov' e' vendemmia e ara:
di tante fiamme tutta risplendea
l'ottava bolgia, sí com' io m'accorsi
tosto che fui là 've 'l fondo parea.
E qual colui che si vengiò con li orsi
vide 'l carro d'Elia ál dipartire,
quando i cavalli al cielo erti levorsi,
che nol potea sí con li occhi seguire,
ch'el vedesse altro che la fiamma sola,
sí come nuvoletta, in sú salire:
tal si move ciascuna per la gola
del fosso, ché nessuna mostra 'l furto,
e ogne fiamma un peccatore invola.
Io stava sovra 'l ponte a veder surto,
sí che s'io non avessi un ronchion preso,
caduto sarei giú sanz' esser urto.
E 'l duca, che mi vide tanto atteso,
disse: "Dentro dai fuochi son li spirti;
catun si fascia di quel ch'elli è inceso."
"Maestro mio," rispuos' io, "per udirti
son io piú certo; ma già m'era avviso
che cosí fosse, e già voleva dirti:
chi è 'n quel foco che vien sí diviso
di sopra, che par surger de la pira
dov' Eteòcle col fratel fu miso?"

Rispuose a me: "Là dentro si martira
Ulisse e Dïomede, e cosí insieme
a la vendetta vanno come a l'ira;

To keep it from running where virtue won't lead,
so that if a kind star or something yet better
has endowed me with wit, I might not abuse it.

In the season when he who lights the world
lingers, hiding his face least from us,
and at twilight the fly yields to the mosquito,
A shepherd resting on a hill will see
swarms of fireflies twinkling along the valley
where perhaps he plows, perhaps gathers grapes—
With so many flames was the entire Eighth Trench
aglow, as I realized when I reached the point
where I could see all the way to the bottom.
And as the prophet who was avenged by bears
saw Elijah's chariot when it took flight,
the horses rising straight up to heaven
Faster than his eyes could ever follow,
so that all he could see was a little cloud
of shooting flame ascending the sky,
So too each flame moved along the gullet
of this trench, for not one betrayed its theft,
though each stole away a sinner inside.
I was standing on the bridge, leaning out to see,
and had I not caught hold of a pier of rock
I would have fallen below without a push.
And my guide, seeing me so intent,
explained, "The spirits are inside the fires.
Each robes himself with that which burns him."
"Master," I replied, "hearing you say so
makes me certain, but I had already thought
that this was the case and was about to ask:
Who is in that fire so cleft at the top
that it seems it could have risen from the pyre
where Eteocles and his brother were laid?"

He answered me: "Ulysses and Diomedes
are tormented there, eternal comrades
in punishment as once they were in wrath.

e dentro da la lor fiamma si geme
l'agguato del caval che fé la porta
60 onde uscí de' Romani il gentil seme.
Piangevisi entro l'arte per che, morta,
Deïdamìa ancor si duol d'Achille,
63 e del Palladio pena vi si porta."
"S'ei posson dentro da quelle faville
parlar," diss' io, "maestro, assai ten priego
66 e ripriego, che 'l priego vaglia mille,
che non mi facci de l'attender niego
fin che la fiamma cornuta qua vegna;
69 vedi che del disio ver' lei mi piego!"
Ed elli a me: "La tua preghiera è degna
di molta loda, e io però l'accetto;
72 ma fa che la tua lingua si sostegna.
Lascia parlare a me, ch'i' ho concetto
ciò che tu vuoi; ch'ei sarebbero schivi,
75 perch' e' fuor greci, forse del tuo detto."

Poi che la fiamma fu venuta quivi
dove parve al mio duca tempo e loco,
78 in questa forma lui parlare audivi:
"O voi che siete due dentro ad un foco,
s'io meritai di voi mentre ch'io vissi,
81 s'io meritai di voi assai o poco
quando nel mondo li alti versi scrissi,
non vi movete; ma l'un di voi dica
84 dove, per lui, perduto a morir gissi."

Lo maggior corno de la fiamma antica
cominciò a crollarsi mormorando,
87 pur come quella cui vento affatica;
indi la cima qua e là menando,
come fosse la lingua che parlasse,
90 gittò voce di fuori e disse: "Quando
mi diparti' da Circe, che sottrasse
me piú d'un anno là presso a Gaeta,
93 prima che sí Enëa la nomasse,

Within their flame they lament the Wooden Horse,
the stratagem that opened the gates of Troy
through which the noble seed of Rome set forth. 60
Trapped within they lament the craft by which
Deidamia still mourns Achilles in death,
and for the stolen Palladium they pay the price" 63
"If they are able to speak from within
those burning tongues, I pray you, Master,
and multiply my prayer a thousand times, 66
Do not refuse to let me wait here until
the horned flame comes near. You see
how strongly desire inclines me toward it." 69
And he said to me: "Your prayer
is praiseworthy, and so I grant it.
But see that you restrain your tongue 72
And let me do the talking. I understand
just what you want, but because they were Greeks
they might be scornful of what you would say." 75

When the double flame came close enough
that it seemed to my guide the right time and place,
I heard him speak in a manner like this: 78
"O you who are paired within one fire,
if I deserved anything of you while I lived,
deserved anything of you either great or small, 81
When in the world I wrote high poetry,
stop for a moment, and let one of you tell
where he wandered lost and met his death." 84

The greater horn of that ancient flame
began to quiver and murmur low
as if it were a candle vexed by the wind; 87
And then, wagging its tip back and forth
as if it were a speaking tongue, the flame
flung out a voice and said, "When I left 90
Circe, who had held me back
a year or more on her isle near Gaeta,
before Aeneas gave it that name, 93

né dolcezza di figlio, né la pieta
del vecchio padre, né 'l debito amore
lo qual dovea Penelopè far lieta,
vincer potero dentro a me l'ardore
ch'i' ebbi a divenir del mondo esperto
e de li vizi umani e del valore;
ma misi me per l'alto mare aperto
sol con un legno e con quella compagna
picciola da la qual non fui diserto.
L'un lito e l'altro vidi infin la Spagna,
fin nel Morrocco, e l'isola d'i Sardi,
e l'altre che quel mare intorno bagna.
Io e' compagni eravam vecchi e tardi
quando venimmo a quella foce stretta
dov' Ercule segnò li suoi riguardi
acciò che l'uom piú oltre non si metta;
da la man destra mi lasciai Sibilia,
da l'altra già m'avea lasciata Setta.
'O frati,' dissi, 'che per cento milia
perigli siete giunti a l'occidente,
a questa tanto picciola vigilia
d'i nostri sensi ch'è del rimanente
non vogliate negar l'esperïenza,
di retro al sol, del mondo sanza gente.
Considerate la vostra semenza:
fatti non foste a viver come bruti,
ma per seguir virtute e canoscenza.'
Li miei compagni fec' io sí aguti,
con questa orazion picciola, al cammino,
che a pena poscia li avrei ritenuti;
e volta nostra poppa nel mattino,
de' remi facemmo ali al folle volo,
sempre acquistando dal lato mancino.
Tutte le stelle già de l'altro polo
vedea la notte, e 'l nostro tanto basso,
che non surgëa fuor del marin suolo.

Neither the sweet thought of my son, nor reverence
for my old father, nor the love I owed
Penelope and that would have made her glad
Could overcome my burning desire
for experience of the wide world above
and of men's vices and their valor.
I put forth on the deep, open sea
with one ship only, and a skeleton crew
of companions who had not deserted me.
I saw one coast, then another, as far as Spain,
as far as Morocco; I saw Sardinia
and the other islands lapped by the waves.
My crew and I were old and slow
when we pulled into the narrow straits
where Hercules had set up his pillars
To mark where men should not pass beyond.
I had left Seville on the starboard side
and off the port left Ceuta behind.
'Brothers,' I said, 'who through a hundred
thousand perils have reached the West,
do not deny to the last glimmering hour
Of consciousness that remains to us
experience of the unpeopled world
that lies beyond the setting sun.
Consider the seed from which you were born!
You were not made to live like brute animals
but to live in pursuit of virtue and knowledge!'
This little speech steeled my crew's hearts
and made them so eager for the voyage ahead
I could hardly have restrained them afterward.
We swung the stern toward the morning light
and made our oars wings for our last, mad run,
the ship's left side always gaining on the right.
All of the stars around the opposite pole
now shone in the night, while our own was so low
it did not rise above the ocean's roll.

Cinque volte racceso e tante casso
  lo lume era di sotto da la luna,
    poi che 'ntrati eravam ne l'alto passo,
quando n'apparve una montagna, bruna
  per la distanza, e parvemi alta tanto
    quanto veduta non avëa alcuna.
Noi ci allegrammo, e tosto tornò in pianto;
  ché de la nova terra un turbo nacque
    e percosse del legno il primo canto.
Tre volte il fé girar con tutte l'acque;
  a la quarta levar la poppa in suso
    e la prora ire in giú, com' altrui piacque,
infin che 'l mar fu sovra noi richiuso."

Five times had we seen it wax and wane,
  the light on the underside of the moon,
    since we began our journey on the main,
And then a mountain loomed in the sky,
  still dim and distant, but it seemed to me
    I had never seen any mountain so high.
We shouted for joy, but our joy now
  turned into grief, for a whirlwind roared
    out of the new land and struck the ship's prow.
Three times it spun her around in the water,
  and the fourth time around, up the stern rose
    and the prow plunged down, as pleased Another,
Until above us we felt the waters close."

Canto XXVII

The flame containing Ulysses and Diomedes *moves away, and a other flame approaches. Moving like a tongue and forming words, it asks the ne comers for news of Romagna. Is the shade's homeland in peace or at war? W Virgil's encouragement, Dante replies that hostilities in the region are tempor ily suspended in a kind of armed truce. Asked who he is, the spirit in the flame whom the early commentators identify as the mercenary captain Guido Montefeltro—agrees to tell his story, so confident is he that his interlocutor c never go back on earth to reveal what he is about to learn. Guido made a car*

Già era dritta in sú la fiamma e queta
per non dir piú, e già da noi sen gia
con la licenza del dolce poeta,
quand' un'altra, che dietro a lei venía,
ne fece volger li occhi a la sua cima
per un confuso suon che fuor n'uscia.
Come 'l bue cicilian che mugghiò prima
col pianto di colui, e ciò fu dritto,
che l'avea temperato con sua lima,
mugghiava con la voce de l'afflitto,
sí che, con tutto che fosse di rame,
pur el pareva dal dolor trafitto;
cosí, per non aver via né forame
dal principio nel foco, in suo linguaggio
si convertïan le parole grame.
Ma poscia ch'ebber colto lor vïaggio
su per la punta, dandole quel guizzo
che dato avea la lingua in lor passaggio,
udimmo dire: "O tu a cu' io drizzo
la voce e che parlavi mo lombardo,
dicendo 'Istra ten va, piú non t'adizzo,'

as a cunning military strategist but decided late in life to save his soul by becoming a Franciscan friar. When the pope found out that he was now an obedient member of the Church, he summoned the friar to him and asked for his military counsel against the rival Colonna family. Guido, at first reluctant, agreed when Pope Boniface VIII offered him preemptive absolution. When Guido died, however, and Saint Francis came to carry his soul into Heaven, a theologically informed demon from Hell claimed it instead, pointing out that the astute Guido had been hoodwinked, since one cannot unwill a sin and then go on to commit it.

The flame, which was no longer speaking now,
stood erect and quiet, and with the consent
of the gentle Poet, moved away from us
When another one that followed behind
called our attention to its flickering crown
by the confused sound that issued from it.
As the Sicilian bull (whose first sound was the cry
of the artisan—and it served him right—
who molded and filed the statue's form)
Used to bellow with the voice of its victim,
and so seemed itself, though it was hollow bronze,
to be transfixed with the worst kind of pain—
So too these wretched and muffled words,
having no way out of their fiery source,
were converted into the language of fire.
But when they found their way to the flame's peak
they gave to it the same vibration
they had received from the tongue that spoke them,
And we heard it say: "You, to whom I direct
my voice, I heard just now a trace of Lombard
when you said, 'Be off now, I press you no more.'

perch' io sia giunto forse alquanto tardo,
non t'incresca restare a parlar meco;
vedi che non incresce a me, e ardo!
Se tu pur mo in questo mondo cieco
caduto se' di quella dolce terra
latina ond' io mia colpa tutta reco,
dimmi se Romagnuoli han pace o guerra;
ch'io fui d'i monti là intra Orbino
e 'l giogo di che Tever si diserra."

Io era in giuso ancora attento e chino,
quando il mio duca mi tentò di costa,
dicendo: "Parla tu; questi è latino."
E io, ch'avea già pronta la risposta,
sanza indugio a parlare incominciai:
"O anima che se' là giú nascosta,
Romagna tua non è, e non fu mai,
sanza guerra ne' cuor de' suoi tiranni;
ma 'n palese nessuna or vi lasciai.
Ravenna sta come stata è molt' anni:
l'aguglia da Polenta la si cova,
sí che Cervia ricuopre co' suoi vanni.
La terra che fé già la lunga prova
e di Franceschi sanguinoso mucchio,
sotto le branche verdi si ritrova.
E 'l mastin vecchio e 'l nuovo da Verrucchio,
che fecer di Montagna il mal governo,
là dove soglion fan d'i denti succhio.
Le città di Lamone e di Santerno
conduce il lïoncel dal nido bianco,
che muta parte da la state al verno.
E quella cu' il Savio bagna il fianco,
cosí com' ella sie' tra 'l piano e 'l monte,
tra tirannia si vive e stato franco.
Ora chi se', ti priego che ne conte;
non esser duro piú ch'altri sia stato,
se 'l nome tuo nel mondo tegna fronte."

Although I may have arrived a little late,
may it not irk you to stop and speak with me.
You see that I am not irked, and I am on fire!
If it is only recently that you fell
into this blind world from sweet Italy's land,
from where I bring with me all my guilt,
Tell me if Romagna is at peace or war,
for I was from the mountains between Urbino
and the ridge from which the Tiber springs."

I was still bent down, intent on the flame,
when my master gave my ribs a nudge
and said, "You speak; this one is Italian."
My answer to him was already well rehearsed,
and without further delay I began,
saying, "O soul, hidden down there,
Your Romagna is not, nor ever has been,
without strife in its tyrannous rulers' hearts,
but when I left she was not openly at war.
Ravenna is now as she has been for years.
The Eagle of Polenta broods over her
so as to cover Cervia with its wings.
The land that endured the long ordeal
and reduced the French knights to a bloody heap
finds itself again beneath the green claws.
Verruchio's mastiffs, both the old and the young,
who dealt so harshly with Montagna,
bore holes with their teeth as they always have done.
The Little Lion of the White Den rules
the cities on the Lamone and the Santerno
and changes sides from summer to winter.
And the town whose side the Savio bathes—
just as it straddles mountain and plain,
so too it lives between tyranny and freedom.
And now, I ask you, tell us who you are.
Do not refuse one who has not refused you,
so may your name in the world be proud."

Poscia che 'l foco alquanto ebbe rugghiato
al modo suo, l'aguta punta mosse
di qua, di là, e poi diè cotal fiato:
"S'i' credesse che mia risposta fosse
a persona che mai tornasse al mondo,
questa fiamma staria sanza piú scosse;
ma però che già mai di questo fondo
non tornò vivo alcun, s'i' odo il vero,
sanza tema d'infamia ti rispondo.
Io fui uom d'arme, e poi fui cordigliero,
credendomi, sí cinto, fare ammenda;
e certo il creder mio venía intero,
se non fosse il gran prete, a cui mal prenda!,
che mi rimise ne le prime colpe;
e come e *quare,* voglio che m'intenda.
Mentre ch'io forma fui d'ossa e di polpe
che la madre mi diè, l'opere mie
non furon leonine, ma di volpe.
Li accorgimenti e le coperte vie
io seppi tutte, e sí menai lor arte,
ch'al fine de la terra il suono uscie.
Quando mi vidi giunto in quella parte
di mia etade ove ciascun dovrebbe
calar le vele e raccoglier le sarte,
ciò che pria mi piacëa, allor m'increbbe,
e pentuto e confesso mi rendei;
ahi miser lasso! e giovato sarebbe.
Lo principe d'i novi Farisei,
avendo guerra presso a Laterano,
e non con Saracin né con Giudei,
ché ciascun suo nimico era cristiano,
e nessun era stato a vincer Acri
né mercatante in terra di Soldano,
né sommo officio né ordini sacri
guardò in sé, né in me quel capestro
che solea fare i suoi cinti piú macri.

After the flame had roared for a while
in its own way, the sharp point flickered
to and fro, and then breathed out these words:
"If I believed that my answer were made
to one who might ever return to the world
this flame would be still and quiver no more;
But since, if what I hear is true, no one
has ever returned alive from this abyss,
I answer you without fear of disgrace.
I was a man of arms, but thereafter wore,
to make amends, the cord of a Franciscan,
and my trust in this would have been rewarded,
If not for the Great Priest—and may he suffer!
He sent me back to my old sinful ways,
and I want you to hear me tell how and why.
While I still had the form of flesh and bones
my mother gave me, my actions were not
like those of the lion, but of the fox.
I knew all the tricks, every subterfuge,
and I practiced the art of deception so well
that my fame spread to the ends of the Earth.
But when I saw that I had arrived
at that stage of life when it befits a man
to lower his sails and coil up his ropes,
What had pleased me before began then to grieve.
I repented, confessed, and turned to God,
and—oh, wretched me!—it would have worked,
But the Prince of the Latter-Day Pharisees
had a war on his hands near the Lateran.
He was not fighting Saracens or Jews;
His enemies were Christians, down to a man,
not one of whom had gone to conquer Acre
or get rich as a trader in the Sultan's land.
This Prince who had no regard for his office,
for his own holy orders or my friar's cord
(that used to make those who wore it grow lean),

Ma come Costantin chiese Silvestro
d'entro Siratti a guerir de la lebbre,
così mi chiese questi per maestro
a guerir de la sua superba febbre;
domandommi consiglio, e io tacetti
perché le sue parole parver ebbre.
E' poi ridisse: 'Tuo cuor non sospetti;
finor t'assolvo, e tu m'insegna fare
sí come Penestrino in terra getti.
Lo ciel poss' io serrare e diserrare,
come tu sai; però son due le chiavi
che 'l mio antecessor non ebbe care.'
Allor mi pinser li argomenti gravi
là 've 'l tacer mi fu avviso 'l peggio,
e dissi: 'Padre, da che tu mi lavi
di quel peccato ov' io mo cader deggio,
lunga promessa con l'attender corto
ti farà trïunfar ne l'alto seggio.'
Francesco venne poi, com' io fu' morto,
per me; ma un d'i neri cherubini
li disse: 'Non portar; non mi far torto.
Venir se ne dee giú tra ' miei meschini
perché diede 'l consiglio frodolente,
dal quale in qua stato li sono a' crini;
ch'assolver non si può chi non si pente,
né pentere e volere insieme puossi
per la contradizion che nol consente.'
Oh me dolente! come mi riscossi
quando mi prese dicendomi: 'Forse
tu non pensavi ch'io löico fossi!'
A Minòs mi portò; e quelli attorse
otto volte la coda al dosso duro;
e poi che per gran rabbia la si morse,
disse: 'Questi è d'i rei del foco furo';
per ch'io là dove vedi son perduto,
e sí vestito, andando, mi rancuro."

This Prince sought me out. As Constantine
sent for Sylvester from up on Soracte
to cure his leprosy, this Prince sent for me
To doctor the fever of his pride.
He asked my counsel, and I stayed quiet,
for he sounded as if he were crazy or drunk.
Then he spoke again: 'Do not mistrust me.
I absolve you in advance, so now you teach me
how to throw Penestrino to the ground.
I can lock and unlock Heaven, as you know.
There are two keys, a pair whose value
my predecessor did not seem to understand.'
The arguments became so weighty
that silence seemed the worse of two paths,
and I said, 'Father, since you absolve me
Of the sin into which I now must fall—
long on promise but short on delivery—
that's how to triumph upon your High Seat.'
When I died, Francis came for my soul,
but one of the black angels said to him,
'Hands off this one, don't do me wrong!
Down he goes to the ranks of my slaves,
for he gave a liar's counsel, and since that time
I have been waiting to clutch him by the hair.
He who does not repent cannot be absolved,
nor can one repent a thing while he wills it,
for that is a contradiction in terms.'
Ah me, in my sorrow! What a shock it was
when he seized me and said, 'It may surprise you
to learn that the devil is a logician!'
He took me to Minos, and Minos coiled his tail
eight times around his hard, scaly back,
and then bit it in his rage and pronounced,
'This sinner gets the fire befitting a thief.'
And so I am lost where you see me here,
and robed like this I go in bitter grief."

Quand' elli ebbe 'l suo dir cosí compiuto,
 la fiamma dolorando si partio,
  torcendo e dibattendo 'l corno aguto.
Noi passamm' oltre, e io e 'l duca mio,
 su per lo scoglio infino in su l'altr' arco
  che cuopre 'l fosso in che si paga il fio
a quei che scommettendo acquistan carco.

It spoke no more, and when it fell silent
 the sorrowful flame took its leave of us,
  Tossing its flickering horn as it went.
We moved on then, my guide and I, along
 the rocky cliff and to the arch that soared
  over the next ditch, where all those belong
Who pay for the sin of sowing discord.

Canto XXXII

The poet balks *at trying to put into words the horror of the final circle of Hell and invokes the aid of the Muses. The bottom of the pit is a frozen lake of ice in which the final group of sinners, the Traitors—to family, homeland, guests, and benefactors—are immersed up to the neck. Dante is warned to tread carefully lest he step on someone. In the first sector, Caïna, the sinners' heads are bent down, allowing their tears to fall and freeze on their faces. Dante observes two heads jammed close facing one another. He calls out to them, asking who they are, and they look up but do not answer. When they look back down, they butt heads like goats. Another shade, Camiscion dei Pazzi, reveals that they are the fratricidal Alberti brothers from the Bisenzio valley and names several others who betrayed their relatives. The pilgrim and his guide move on to the next sector, Antenora, where Traitors to their homeland are punished. Somehow, Dante kicks one of them in the face. He refuses to tell Dante his name, despite a promise of fame. Bocca degli Abati, whose treachery cost the Guelphs the victory at Montaperti, is betrayed by Buoso da Duera, true to treacherous form; but in reply Bocca outs him too and several other traitors. The canto ends with two more shades eternally—but still more brutally—on top of one another. One of them is gnawing on the other's head. Dante asks why.*

S'ïo avessi le rime aspre e chiocce,
come si converrebbe al tristo buco
sovra 'l qual pontan tutte l'altre rocce,
io premerei di mio concetto il suco
piú pienamente; ma perch' io non l'abbo,
non sanza tema a dicer mi conduco;
ché non è impresa da pigliare a gabbo
discriver fondo a tutto l'universo,
né da lingua che chiami mamma o babbo.
Ma quelle donne aiutino il mio verso
ch'aiutaro Anfione a chiuder Tebe,
sí che dal fatto il dir non sia diverso.
Oh sovra tutte mal creata plebe
che stai nel loco onde parlare è duro,
mei foste state qui pecore o zebe!

Come noi fummo giú nel pozzo scuro
sotto i piè del gigante assai piú bassi,
e io mirava ancora a l'alto muro,
dicere udi'mi: "Guarda come passi:
va sí, che tu non calchi con le piante
le teste de' fratei miseri lassi."

If I could write the harsh and grating rhymes
appropriate to that mouth of sorrow
upon which rests the bedrock of the world,
I would press out more fully all the juice
of my poem's concept, but since I cannot,
I begin to speak with some trepidation.
This is not something to be treated lightly—
to describe the bottom of the universe—
nor for a tongue that cries Mama and Papa.
But may those same Ladies aid my verse
who helped Amphion raise the wall of Thebes,
so that the telling does not diverge from the fact.
And you, O misbegotten souls beyond the rest,
crowded in this place too hard for words,
better had you been born as sheep or goats!

We were much farther down now, on the floor
of the dark pit, well below the Giant's feet,
and I was still staring up at the high wall
When I heard a voice say to me, "Watch out
where you walk so you don't step on the heads
of the broken, worn out brothers down here!"

Per ch'io mi volsi, e vidimi davante
e sotto i piedi un lago che per gelo
avea di vetro e non d'acqua sembiante.
Non fece al corso suo sí grosso velo
di verno la Danoia in Osterlicchi,
né Tanaï là sotto 'l freddo cielo,
com' era quivi; che se Tambernicchi
vi fosse sú caduto, o Pietrapana,
non avria pur da l'orlo fatto cricchi.
E come a gracidar si sta la rana
col muso fuor de l'acqua, quando sogna
di spigolar sovente la villana,
livide, insin là dove appar vergogna
eran l'ombre dolenti ne la ghiaccia,
mettendo i denti in nota di cicogna.
Ognuna in giú tenea volta la faccia;
da bocca il freddo, e da li occhi il cor tristo
tra lor testimonianza si procaccia.
Quand' io m'ebbi dintorno alquanto visto,
volsimi a' piedi, e vidi due sí stretti,
che 'l pel del capo avieno insieme misto.

"Ditemi, voi che sí strignete i petti,"
diss' io, "chi siete?" E quei piegaro i colli;
e poi ch'ebber li visi a me eretti,
li occhi lor, ch'eran pria pur dentro molli,
gocciar su per le labbra, e 'l gelo strinse
le lagrime tra essi e riserrolli.
Con legno legno spranga mai non cinse
forte cosí; ond' ei come due becchi
cozzaro insieme, tanta ira li vinse.
E un ch'avea perduti ambo li orecchi
per la freddura, pur col viso in giúe,
disse: "Perché cotanto in noi ti specchi?
Se vuoi saper chi son cotesti due,
la valle onde Bisenzo si dichina
del padre loro Alberto e di lor fue.

I turned around and saw stretched out,
beneath my feet, a lake frozen hard
with a surface more like glass than water.
Never did the Danube in Austria
or the Don under its cold and distant sky
freeze with a sheet of winter ice as thick
As there was here, for if the Alp Tambura
had fallen on it, or Pietrapana,
it would not have creaked, even at the edge.
And as frogs lie in a pond and croak
with just their muzzles out of the water
when the peasant girl has dreams of gleaning,
So the sorrowful shades were up to their necks in ice,
their cheeks blue that should have blushed with shame,
and their teeth clacking like the beak of a stork.
Their faces were turned downward; their mouths
gave testimony to the cold they felt,
and their eyes to the grief in their broken hearts.
For a moment I looked in every direction,
then I glanced down and saw two heads
so close to each other that their hair was tangled.

"Tell me, you two who are chest to chest,"
I said, "Who are you?" They bent their necks back,
and when they had lifted their faces toward me,
Their eyes, until now moist only within,
welled up with tears that flowed over their lips
and froze, locking their faces in an icy grip
More tightly than a clamp has ever bound boards.
This enraged them so much that like two goats
they started to butt their foreheads together.
Another, who had lost both his frostbitten ears,
said to me, with his face still cast down,
"Why are you staring so hard at us?
If you want to put names to these two heads,
the valley the Bisenzio runs through belonged
to their father Alberto, and to them.

D'un corpo usciro; e tutta la Caina
  potrai cercare, e non troverai ombra
    degna piú d'esser fitta in gelatina:
non quelli a cui fu rotto il petto e l'ombra
  con esso un colpo per la man d'Artù;
    non Focaccia; non questi che m'ingombra
col capo sí, ch'i' non veggio oltre piú,
  e fu nomato Sassol Mascheroni;
    se tosco se', ben sai omai chi fu.
E perché non mi metti in piú sermoni,
  sappi ch'i' fu' il Camiscion de' Pazzi;
    e aspetto Carlin che mi scagioni."

Poscia vid' io mille visi cagnazzi
  fatti per freddo; onde mi vien riprezzo,
    e verrà sempre, de' gelati guazzi.
E mentre ch'andavamo inver' lo mezzo
  al quale ogne gravezza si rauna,
    e io tremava ne l'etterno rezzo;
se voler fu o destino o fortuna,
  non so; ma, passeggiando tra le teste,
    forte percossi 'l piè nel viso ad una.
Piangendo mi sgridò: "Perché mi peste?
  se tu non vieni a crescer la vendetta
    di Montaperti, perché mi moleste?"
E io: "Maestro mio, or qui m'aspetta,
  sí ch'io esca d'un dubbio per costui;
    poi mi farai, quantunque vorrai, fretta."
Lo duca stette, e io dissi a colui
  che bestemmiava duramente ancora:
    "Qual se' tu che cosí rampogni altrui?"
"Or tu chi se' che vai per l'Antenora,
  percotendo," rispuose, "altrui le gote,
    sí che, se fossi vivo, troppo fora?"
"Vivo son io, e caro esser ti puote,"
  fu mia risposta, "se dimandi fama,
    ch'io metta il nome tuo tra l'altre note."

They were born from one body. You may search
  all of Caïna and not find a shade
    worthier than these to be glazed in aspic;
Not the one whose chest and shadow were pierced
  with one hard thrust from Arthur's hand; not Focaccia;
    not this one here, my perpetual shadow,
Whose head completely encumbers my view.
  His name was Sassol Mascheroni,
    and if you are Tuscan you know who he was.
And so you won't make me talk any more,
  know that I was Camiscion dei Pazzi.
    I wait for Carlino to exonerate me."

After that I saw a thousand faces
  purple and shivering like dogs. It still makes me
    shudder at frozen fords, as I always will.
And while we were on our way to the center
  where all gravity pools, and I was
    trembling and shivering in the timeless cold,
Whether it was willed, fated, or mere chance
  I do not know, but picking my way among the heads,
    I happened to kick one of them in the face.
He moaned and cried out, "Why are you
  grinding me with your heel? If you didn't come here
    to better avenge Montaperti, why give me grief?"
And I said to my master, "Wait here for me.
  I want to clear up a doubt about this one,
    and then we can hurry as much as you wish."
My leader stopped, and I said to the shade,
  who was still cursing and swearing at me,
    "Who are you to be bawling out others?"
"No, who are you," he answered, "going through
  Antenora kicking others in the face,
    which would be too much to bear if you were alive?"
"I am alive," was my reply, "and if fame
  has any appeal, it might be worth it to you
    if I put your name in my notes somewhere."

290

Ed elli a me: "Del contrario ho io brama.
Lèvati quinci e non mi dar piú lagna,
ché mal sai lusingar per questa lama!"
Allor lo presi per la cuticagna
e dissi: "El converrà che tu ti nomi,
o che capel qui sú non ti rimagna."
Ond' elli a me: "Perché tu mi dischiomi,
né ti dirò ch'io sia, né mosterrolti
se mille fiate in sul capo mi tomi."

Io avea già i capelli in mano avvolti,
e tratti glien' avea piú d'una ciocca,
latrando lui con li occhi in giú raccolti,
quando un altro gridò: "Che hai tu, Bocca?
non ti basta sonar con le mascelle,
se tu non latri? qual diavol ti tocca?"
"Omai," diss' io, "non vo' che piú favelle,
malvagio traditor; ch'a la tua onta
io porterò di te vere novelle."
"Va via," rispuose, "e ciò che tu vuoi conta;
ma non tacer, se tu di qua entro eschi,
di quel ch'ebbe or cosí la lingua pronta.
El piange qui l'argento de' Franceschi:
'Io vidi,' potrai dir, 'quel da Duera
là dove i peccatori stanno freschi.'
Se fossi domandato 'Altri chi v'era?'
tu hai dallato quel di Beccheria
di cui segò Fiorenza la gorgiera.
Gianni de' Soldanier credo che sia
piú là con Ganellone e Tebaldello,
ch'aprì Faenza quando si dormia."

Noi eravam partiti già da ello,
ch'io vidi due ghiacciati in una buca,
sí che l'un capo a l'altro era cappello;
e come 'l pan per fame si manduca,
cosí 'l sovran li denti a l'altro pose
là 've 'l cervel s'aggiugne con la nuca:

And he said, "What I crave is just the reverse.
Get out of here and stop bothering me.
Down in this pit your flattery falls flat."
I took him by the hair at the nape of his neck
and said, "Either you tell me your name
or you're not going to have any hair left here."
He said to me, "You can pull out every last hair
and I still won't let you know who I am,
even if you bash my head a thousand times."

I had already twisted his hair in my hand
and yanked out more than one or two clumps
while he howled and kept his eyes turned down,
When someone cried, "What's with you, Bocca?
Don't you make enough noise clattering your teeth
without howling too? What devil has got you?"
"Now," I said, "I don't care if you speak any more,
you damned traitor. To your eternal shame,
I will tell the world the truth about you."
"Go away," he answered, "and say what you want,
but if you do get out of here, don't hold back
about the one with the ready tongue just now.
He's bemoaning here the silver of the French.
'I saw,' you can say, 'the one from Duera
down where the sinners stay fresh on the ice.'
And if you are asked who else was there,
right by your side is the Beccheria
whose throat was slit by the Florentines.
Gianni de' Soldanieri is a little farther on,
I think, with Ganelon and Tebaldello,
who opened Faenza while it slumbered in dreams."

We had already taken our leave of that shade
When I saw in one hole a pair frozen so close
that the head of one was the other's hood.
As a hungry man works on a crust of bread,
the upper one's teeth were in the lower one's skull
where the brain meets the nape at the back of the head.

non altrimenti Tidëo si rose
le tempie a Menalippo per disdegno,
che quei faceva il teschio e l'altre cose.
"O tu che mostri per sí bestial segno
odio sovra colui che tu ti mangi,
dimmi 'l perché," diss' io, "per tal convegno,
che se tu a ragion di lui ti piangi,
sappiendo chi voi siete e la sua pecca,
nel mondo suso ancora io te ne cangi,
se quella con ch'io parlo non si secca."

And like Tydeus, who was driven by spite
to gnaw on Melanippus' severed head,
this one chewed on the bone and the stuff inside.
"O you who show in so bestial a way
your hatred for him whom you devour,
tell me why," I said, "and if what you say
Shows that your grievance is just and right,
then, knowing you and his sin, I will try
to pay you back in the world of light,
If the tongue I speak with does not go dry."

Canto XXXIII

The shade on top, *a fellow Tuscan, turns from his cannibalistic meal to respond to Dante. It will not be easy for him to retell his grief, but he will steel himself to do so, as long as it brings opprobrium upon his former victimizer, now his victim. He is Count Ugolino; his hated rival, the Archbishop Ruggieri. While it is common knowledge that Ugolino died in Ruggieri's prison, now Dante will hear the cruel details of his death. Confined in the Tower of Hunger with his children, they each dreamed a dream foreshadowing their fates. The next day the door of the tower was nailed shut, and they were left to starve. His sons died first, leaving him, blinded by denutrition, to grope over their dead bodies. Finally famine proved more powerful than grief. The author adds Pisa, the new Thebes, to his anathemas. Leaving Antenora for Ptolomaea, where the Traitors who violated the laws of hospitality are punished, they find them with their heads bent back, so that their tears freeze over their eyes, denying grief its expression. An icy wind blows, burning Dante's face. A sinner begs the passersby to prize the frozen tears from his eyes. Asking him who he is, Dante makes an ambiguous promise. The traitor is Fra Alberigo, who treacherously slew his guests, causing his soul to be carried off to Hell before his body died, a "privilege" granted to the shades in Ptolomaea. Next to him is the soul of the Genoese traitor Branca Doria. His body too remains up on earth, occupied by a demon who eats and drinks and sleeps and puts on clothes. Dante does not liberate his eyes; and betraying the betrayer he considers to be an act of courtesy.*

La bocca sollevò dal fiero pasto
quel peccator, forbendola a' capelli
del capo ch'elli avea di retro guasto.
Poi cominciò: "Tu vuo' ch'io rinovelli
disperato dolor che 'l cor mi preme
già pur pensando, pria ch'io ne favelli.
Ma se le mie parole esser dien seme
che frutti infamia al traditor ch'i' rodo,
parlare e lagrimar vedrai insieme.
Io non so chi tu se' né per che modo
venuto se' qua giú; ma fiorentino
mi sembri veramente quand' io t'odo.
Tu dei saper ch'i' fui conte Ugolino,
e questi è l'arcivescovo Ruggieri:
or ti dirò perché i son tal vicino.
Che per l'effetto de' suo' mai pensieri,
fidandomi di lui, io fossi preso
e poscia morto, dir non è mestieri;

Lifting his mouth from his savage meal,
the sinner wiped it on the hair of the head
he had just been chewing on from behind,
And he began, "You want me to renew
a desperate sorrow, the very thought of which
wrings my soul before I even begin to speak.
But if my words prove to be the seeds
whose harvest is infamy for the traitor I gnaw,
you will see me weep and speak though my tears.
Who you are I do not know, nor how
you have come down here, but you seem,
when I hear your voice, to be a Florentine.
You need to know I was Count Ugolino,
and this is the Archbishop Ruggieri.
Now I will tell you why we are such close neighbors.
The details of how my trust was betrayed
by his dark conspiracies, how I was taken
and put to death, there is no need to recount,

però quel che non puoi avere inteso,
  cioè come la morte mia fu cruda,
    udirai, e saprai s'e' m'ha offeso.
Breve pertugio dentro da la Muda,
  la qual per me ha 'l titol de la fame,
    e che conviene ancor ch'altrui si chiuda,
m'avea mostrato per lo suo forame
  piú lune già, quand' io feci 'l mal sonno
    che del futuro mi squarciò 'l velame.
Questi pareva a me maestro e donno,
  cacciando il lupo e ' lupicini al monte
    per che i Pisan veder Lucca non ponno.
Con cagne magre, studïose e conte
  Gualandi con Sismondi e con Lanfranchi
    s'avea messi dinanzi da la fronte.
In picciol corso mi parieno stanchi
  lo padre e ' figli, e con l'agute scane
    mi parea lor veder fender li fianchi.
Quando fui desto innanzi la dimane,
  pianger senti' fra 'l sonno i miei figliuoli
    ch'eran con meco, e dimandar del pane.
Ben se' crudel, se tu già non ti duoli
  pensando ciò che 'l mio cor s'annunziava;
    e se non piangi, di che pianger suoli?
Già eran desti, e l'ora s'appressava
  che 'l cibo ne solëa essere addotto,
    e per suo sogno ciascun dubitava;
e io senti' chiavar l'uscio di sotto
  a l'orribile torre; ond' io guardai
    nel viso a' mie' figliuoi sanza far motto.
Io non piangëa, sí dentro impetrai:
  piangevan elli; e Anselmuccio mio
    disse: 'Tu guardi sí, padre! che hai?'
Perciò non lagrimai né rispuos' io
  tutto quel giorno né la notte appresso,
    infin che l'altro sol nel mondo uscío.

But what you cannot possibly know—
  how cruel my death was—that you will hear,
    and judge for yourself if he has wronged me.
The mew for hawks that because of me
  has come to be known as the Tower of Hunger,
    and in which others are yet to be imprisoned,
Had already shown me through its narrow slit
  several waxing moons, when a terrible dream
    tore aside the veil that shrouded the future.
This man, in my dream, was a master of the hunt,
  tracking a wolf and its cubs across the mountain
    that blocks Lucca from the Pisans' view.
Driving trained bitches that were lean and eager,
  he had Gualandi out in front of him,
    along with Sismondi and Lanfranchi,
And after a mere sprint both father and sons
  bore the look of exhaustion, and how real
    the fangs seemed that made shreds of their flanks.
When I awoke, a little before dawn,
  I heard my children, who were imprisoned with me,
    crying in their sleep and asking for bread.
You are cruelty incarnate if you are not
  grieving now at what my heart told me,
    and if this does not make you weep, what does?
They were awake now, and the hour approached
  when our food was usually brought to us,
    and we each were anxious because of our dreams.
Then I listened as the nails were driven into the door
  of that horrible tower, and I looked upon
    the faces of my children without a word.
I did not weep; I had turned to stone inside.
  They wept, and my poor little Anselm said,
    'What a look you have, Father. What is the matter?'
I shed no tear at that, nor spoke a word
  all that day or the following night,
    until the sun next came out into the world.

Come un poco di raggio si fu messo
nel doloroso carcere, e io scorsi
per quattro visi il mio aspetto stesso,
ambo le man per lo dolor mi morsi;
ed ei, pensando ch'io 'l fessi per voglia
di manicar, di súbito levorsi
e disser: 'Padre, assai ci fia men doglia
se tu mangi di noi: tu ne vestisti
queste misere carni, e tu le spoglia.'
Queta'mi allor per non farli piú tristi;
lo dí e l'altro stemmo tutti muti;
ahi dura terra, perché non t'apristi?
Poscia che fummo al quarto dí venuti,
Gaddo mi si gittò disteso a' piedi,
dicendo: 'Padre mio, ché non m'aiuti?'
Quivi morí; e come tu mi vedi,
vid' io cascar li tre ad uno ad uno
tra 'l quinto dí e 'l sesto; ond' io mi diedi,
già cieco, a brancolar sovra ciascuno,
e due dí li chiamai, poi che fur morti.
Poscia, piú che 'l dolor, poté 'l digiuno."

Quand' ebbe detto ciò, con li occhi torti
riprese 'l teschio misero co' denti,
che furo a l'osso, come d'un can, forti.

Ahi Pisa, vituperio de le genti
del bel paese là dove 'l sí suona,
poi che i vicini a te punir son lenti,
muovasi la Capraia e la Gorgona,
e faccian siepe ad Arno in su la foce,
sí ch'elli annieghi in te ogne persona!
Che se 'l conte Ugolino aveva voce
d'aver tradita te de le castella,
non dovei tu i figliuoi porre a tal croce.
Innocenti facea l'età novella,
novella Tebe, Uguiccione e 'l Brigata
e li altri due che 'l canto suso appella.

As soon as a slender ray of light streamed
into that dismal stone cell, I could see
in their four faces the reflection of my own,
And bit both my hands for grief. My children,
thinking I did this driven by hunger,
rose up in an instant and cried out to me,
'Father, it would give us much less pain
if you fed on us. It was you who clothed us
in this pitiable flesh, and you should strip it away!'
Then I calmed myself, to spare them more grief.
That day and all the next we stayed silent.
Ah, hard Earth, could you not have swallowed us?
After we had come to the fourth day, Gaddo
threw himself down outstretched at my feet,
saying, 'Father, Father, why don't you help me?'
There he died, and as sure as you see me,
I saw the other three drop, one by one,
between the fifth and sixth day. Then I began,
Blind by now, to grope over their corpses,
and for two days called them when they were dead.
Then starvation finished what sorrow could not."

When he had said this, his eyes looking away,
he seized the wretched skull again in his teeth,
and like a dog ground away at the bone.

Ah, Pisa! Disgrace of all the fair lands
where *sì* is heard, since your neighbors
won't take your punishment into their hands,
Let Capraia and Gorgona shift themselves around
into the Arno's mouth and make a dam
so that every last one of your citizens is drowned!
Even if you thought that Count Ugolino
betrayed you along with your walls and castles,
you should not have tortured his children too,
Like a modern Thebes. Their youthful years
made Uguiccione and Brigata innocent,
and the other of whom my reader hears.

Noi passammo oltre, là 've la gelata
ruvidamente un'altra gente fascia,
non volta in giú, ma tutta riversata.
Lo pianto stesso lí pianger non lascia,
e 'l duol che truova in su li occhi rintoppo,
si volge in entro a far crescer l'ambascia;
ché le lagrime prime fanno groppo,
e sí come visiere di cristallo,
rïempion sotto 'l ciglio tutto il coppo.
E avvegna che, sí come d'un callo,
per la freddura ciascun sentimento
cessato avesse del mio viso stallo,
già mi parea sentire alquanto vento;
per ch'io: "Maestro mio, questo chi move?
non è qua giú ogne vapore spento?"
Ond' elli a me: "Avaccio sarai dove
di ciò ti farà l'occhio la risposta,
veggendo la cagion che 'l fiato piove."

E un de' tristi de la fredda crosta
gridò a noi: "O anime crudeli
tanto che data v'è l'ultima posta,
levatemi dal viso i duri veli,
sí ch'ïo sfoghi 'l duol che 'l cor m'impregna,
un poco, pria che 'l pianto si raggeli."
Per ch'io a lui: "Se vuo' ch'i' ti sovvegna,
dimmi chi se', e s'io non ti disbrigo,
al fondo de la ghiaccia ir mi convegna."
Rispuose adunque: "I' son frate Alberigo;
i' son quel da le frutta del mal orto,
che qui riprendo dattero per figo."
"Oh," diss' io lui, "or se' tu ancor morto?"
Ed elli a me: "Come 'l mio corpo stea
nel mondo sú, nulla scïenza porto.
Cotal vantaggio ha questa Tolomea,
che spesse volte l'anima ci cade
innanzi ch'Atropòs mossa le dea.

296

We walked on farther, to where the glacier
wraps another group in its rough sheet,
their faces not bent downward, but all upturned.
Their very weeping prevents their weeping,
and their grief, which cannot escape their eyes,
turns inward to increase their suffering,
For the first tears congeal into a knot
and then, like an eyeglass made of crystal, they fill
all of the socket beneath the brow.
And now, although my face was numb
with the bitter cold and had no more feeling
than if it had become a hard callus,
It seemed to me as if I felt a wind,
and I asked, "Master, who makes this wind blow?
Has not every vapor here been laid to rest?"
He answered me, "You will soon be where
your eye itself will answer the question
as to the cause of these gusts of wind."

Then one of the damned in the crust of ice
cried out to us, "O souls so cruel
that you are condemned to the last station,
Lift from my eyes these frozen veils, so that
I may vent a little the pain that cramps
my heart, before my tears freeze solid again."
And so I told him, "If you want my help,
tell me who you are, and if I do not ease your pain,
may I be sent down to the bottom of the ice."
He answered then, "I am Fra Alberigo,
the one with the fruit from the garden of Evil,
and here I am more than repaid, date for fig."
"Oh," I said to him, "are you already dead?"
He answered, "Of my body's condition
in the world above I have no idea.
This circle Ptolomaea has the privilege
that many times a soul falls into its depth
before Atropos has severed its thread,

E perché tu piú volontier mi rade
le 'nvetrïate lagrime dal volto,
sappie che, tosto che l'anima trade
come fec' ïo, il corpo suo l' è tolto
da un demonio, che poscia il governa
mentre che 'l tempo suo tutto sia vòlto.
Ella ruina in sí fatta cisterna;
e forse pare ancor lo corpo suso
de l'ombra che di qua dietro mi verna.
Tu 'l dei saper, se tu vien pur mo giuso:
elli è ser Branca Doria, e son piú anni
poscia passati ch'el fu sí racchiuso."
Io credo," diss' io lui, "che tu m'inganni;
ché Branca Doria non morí unquanche,
e mangia e bee e dorme e veste panni."
"Nel fosso sú," diss' el, "de' Malebranche,
là dove bolle la tenace pece,
non era ancora giunto Michel Zanche,
che questi lasciò il diavolo in sua vece
nel corpo suo, ed un suo prossimano
che 'l tradimento insieme con lui fece.
Ma distendi oggimai in qua la mano;
aprimi li occhi." E io non gliel' apersi;
e cortesia fu lui esser villano.

Ahi Genovesi, uomini diversi
d'ogne costume e pien d'ogne magagna,
perché non siete voi del mondo spersi?
Ché col peggiore spirto di Romagna
trovai di voi un tal, che per sua opra
in anima in Cocito già si bagna,
e in corpo par vivo ancor di sopra.

And, so that you may be all the more willing
to scrape the icy tears from my face,
know this: the instant a soul has made a betrayal,
As I did, its body becomes the possession
of a demon, who inhabits and governs it
until its allotted time comes around.
The soul plunges down into this arctic cistern.
Perhaps the body of the shade wintering
here behind me still appears above on Earth.
You ought to know, if you have just come down.
He is Ser Branca Doria, and many years have passed
since he was locked up in cold storage like this."
"I think you are lying to me," I said.
Branca Doria is far from dead. He eats
and drinks and sleeps and puts on clothes."
"In the Malebranche's ditch above," he said,
"where the sticky tar is boiling hot
Michel Zanche had not yet arrived
When this one here left a devil in charge
of his own body, as did a kinsman
who joined him in that treacherous murder.
Now reach out and open my eyes for me."
But I was content to leave them frozen shut,
for to be rude to him was courtesy.

Ah, men of Genoa, of so little worth!
Indecent, foul, and full of corruption,
why have you not yet been driven from Earth?
For with a shade from Romagna, none more vile,
I saw one of you who has plunged his soul
into Cocytus' ice, and all the while
On Earth he seems to be alive and whole.

Canto XXXIV

The pilgrims reach the fourth and final zone *of Cocytus, Judecca, where Virgil warns Dante that they are at last about to see Dis, king of Hell and embodiment of evil. In fact, squinting ahead, Dante perceives something that looks like a giant sail-driven windmill, towering above the ice, in which the last sinners can be seen to be totally immersed. Half dead with fear, Dante views the three-faced monster, whose arms alone dwarf the mythical Giants Nimrod, Ephialtes, and Antaeus, the last of whom handed them down into the Ninth Circle in Canto XXXI. In each of his three mouths, this rebel against God mangles one of Christian and Roman history's greatest traitors, Judas, Brutus, and Cassius. Now that they have seen everything Hell has to show, Virgil tells Dante to hang onto him tightly and begins to clamber down the gruesome Dis' hairy sides. When he reaches the leviathan's haunches, he inverts his position and begins to ascend, leading Dante to believe that they are going back up. Eventually, however, they scramble down onto solid ground and Virgil explains that they have passed through the center of the Earth. Following a cave hollowed out by an underground stream, they now make their way to the surface and emerge from the darkness of Hell to see the stars.*

"*Vexilla regis prodeunt inferni*
verso di noi; però dinanzi mira,"
disse 'l maestro mio, "se tu 'l discerni."
Come quando una grossa nebbia spira,
o quando l'emisperio nostro annotta,
par di lungi un molin che 'l vento gira,
veder mi parve un tal dificio allotta;
poi per lo vento mi ristrinsi retro
al duca mio, ché non lí era altra grotta.
Già era, e con paura il metto in metro,
là dove l'ombre tutte eran coperte,
e trasparien come festuca in vetro.
Altre sono a giacere; altre stanno erte,
quella col capo e quella con le piante;
altra, com' arco, il volto a' piè rinverte.
Quando noi fummo fatti tanto avante,
ch'al mio maestro piacque di mostrarmi
la creatura ch'ebbe il bel sembiante,
d'innanzi mi si tolse e fé restarmi,
"Ecco Dite," dicendo, "ed ecco il loco
ove convien che di fortezza t'armi."

"*Vexilla regis prodeunt inferni*
toward us," my master said. "Look straight ahead
and see if you can make him out."
Like a windmill turning on the horizon
when a thick fog drifts and settles in
or when our hemisphere turns toward night,
Such a structure I now seemed to see;
then I took shelter behind my leader's back,
for there was no other way to block the wind.
I was now (and I shudder to put this into verse)
where the shades hung completely engulfed,
showing through the ice like straw through glass.
Some are lying sideways, some stand upright,
one with his head, another with feet on top,
and another bent over double like a bow.
And when we had made our way forward far enough
that it pleased my master to reveal to me
the creature who had been so beautiful once,
He stepped to one side and had me stop,
saying, "Behold Dis. And there is the place
where you must steel your soul to the utmost."

Com' io divenni allor gelato e fioco,
nol dimandar, lettor, ch'i' non lo scrivo,
però ch'ogne parlar sarebbe poco.
Io non mori' e non rimasi vivo;
pensa oggimai per te, s'hai fior d'ingegno,
qual io divenni, d'uno e d'altro privo.

Lo 'mperador del doloroso regno
da mezzo 'l petto uscia fuor de la ghiaccia;
e piú con un gigante io mi convegno,
che i giganti non fan con le sue braccia:
vedi oggimai quant' esser dee quel tutto
ch'a cosí fatta parte si confaccia.
S'el fu sí bel com' elli è ora brutto,
e contra 'l suo fattore alzò le ciglia,
ben dee da lui procedere ogne lutto.
Oh quanto parve a me gran maraviglia
quand' io vidi tre facce a la sua testa!
L'una dinanzi, e quella era vermiglia;
l'altr' eran due, che s'aggiugnieno a questa
sovresso 'l mezzo di ciascuna spalla,
e sé giugnieno al loco de la cresta:
e la destra parea tra bianca e gialla;
la sinistra a vedere era tal, quali
vegnon di là onde 'l Nilo s'avvalla.
Sotto ciascuna uscivan due grand' ali,
quanto si convenia a tanto uccello:
vele di mar non vid' io mai cotali.
Non avean penne, ma di vispistrello
era lor modo; e quelle svolazzava,
sí che tre venti si movean da ello:
quindi Cocito tutto s'aggelava.
Con sei occhi piangëa, e per tre menti
gocciava 'l pianto e sanguinosa bava.
Da ogne bocca dirompea co' denti
un peccatore, a guisa di maciulla,
sí che tre ne facea cosí dolenti.

Do not ask, Reader, how frozen and faint
I became then, for I cannot write it down;
every word known to man would not be enough.
I did not die, and yet I was no longer alive.
Imagine, if you can, what I became,
deprived of death and bereft of life.

The emperor of the world of pain
stood out of the ice up to his chest,
and I am bigger standing beside a Giant
Than a Giant would be beside one of his arms.
You can see how huge the whole must be
for a part such as this to fit into place.
If he was as beautiful once as now he is
hideous, and arched his brow against his Maker,
well may he be the source of all woe.
How great a sense of wonder overcame me
when I saw three faces arranged on his head.
One was in the front, as red as cinnabar,
And the other two were aligned with this one
just over the middle of each shoulder,
and all of them fused at the crown of his head.
The one on the right was a pale yellow,
while the left one was as dark a color
as those who live beyond the Nile's cataracts.
Under each face grew a pair of wings
of a size that matched this portentous bird.
I never saw sails so large catch the wind at sea.
They had no feathers, but were bald like the wings
of the darkling bat, and he beat them slowly,
so that three winds blew away from him,
And this was why all Cocytus was frozen.
He wept from six eyes, and over three chins
the tears dripped down with bloody slaver.
In each mouth he chewed upon a sinner
with teeth like a harrow that scutches flax,
and so he kept three in constant agony.

A quel dinanzi il mordere era nulla
verso 'l graffiar, che talvolta la schiena
rimanea de la pelle tutta brulla.

"Quell' anima là sú c'ha maggior pena,"
disse 'l maestro, "è Giuda Scarïotto,
che 'l capo ha dentro e fuor le gambe mena.
De li altri due c'hanno il capo di sotto,
quel che pende dal nero ceffo è Bruto:
vedi come si storce, e non fa motto!;
e l'altro è Cassio, che par sí membruto.
Ma la notte risurge, e oramai
è da partir, ché tutto avem veduto."

Com' a lui piacque, il collo li avvinghiai;
ed el prese di tempo e loco poste,
e quando l'ali fuoro aperte assai,
appigliò sé a le vellute coste;
di vello in vello giú discese poscia
tra 'l folto pelo e le gelate croste.
Quando noi fummo là dove la coscia
si volge, a punto in sul grosso de l'anche,
lo duca, con fatica e con angoscia,
volse la testa ov' elli avea le zanche,
e aggrappossi al pel com' om che sale,
sí che 'n inferno i' credea tornar anche.
"Attienti ben, ché per cotali scale,"
disse 'l maestro, ansando com' uom lasso,
"conviensi dipartir da tanto male."
Poi uscí fuor per lo fóro d'un sasso
e puose me in su l'orlo a sedere;
appresso porse a me l'accorto passo.

Io levai li occhi e credetti vedere
Lucifero com' io l'avea lasciato,
e vidili le gambe in sú tenere;

For the sinner in front to be chewed alive
was nothing compared to the claws that flayed him,
so at times his back was utterly stripped of skin.

"The soul up there who is punished the most,"
my master said, "is Judas Iscariot,
who has his head within and flails his legs outside.
Of the other two, with their heads below,
the one who hangs from the black snout is Brutus.
See how he writhes and never says a word.
The other is Cassius, so powerful in stature.
But night is coming on again, and it is time
for us to depart, for we have seen all there is."

Then, as he wanted, I clasped him around the neck,
and he, gauging the timing and distance,
made his move when the wings opened wide,
And caught hold of the great shaggy flanks.
From one clump of matted hair to another
and down through frozen crusts he descended,
And when we had come to where the thigh
turns within the socket of the hip, my leader,
straining with the weight and near exhaustion,
Brought his head around to where his legs had been,
and struggled with the hair like someone climbing
so that I thought we were going back to Hell.
"Hold tight, for it is by such stairs as these,"
my master said to me, gasping for breath,
"that we must depart from evil so great."
At last he climbed through a vent in the rock,
perched me on its edge, and then with a careful stride
brought himself over to where I sat on the rim.

I raised my eyes, expecting I would see
Lucifer as I had left him below, but instead
I saw him with legs stretched out above,

e s'io divenni allora travagliato,
la gente grossa il pensi, che non vede
qual è quel punto ch'io avea passato.
"Lèvati sú," disse 'l maestro, "in piede:
la via è lunga e 'l cammino è malvagio,
e già il sole a mezza terza riede."
Non era camminata di palagio
là 'v' eravam, ma natural burella
ch'avea mal suolo e di lume disagio.

"Prima ch'io de l'abisso mi divella,
maestro mio," diss' io quando fui dritto,
"a trarmi d'erro un poco mi favella:
ov' è la ghiaccia? e questi com' è fitto
sí sottosopra? e come, in sí poc' ora,
da sera a mane ha fatto il sol tragitto?"
Ed elli a me: "Tu imagini ancora
d'esser di là dal centro, ov' io mi presi
al pel del vermo reo che 'l mondo fóra.
Di là fosti cotanto quant' io scesi;
quand' io mi volsi, tu passasti 'l punto
al qual si traggon d'ogne parte i pesi.
E se' or sotto l'emisperio giunto
ch'è contraposto a quel che la gran secca
coverchia, e sotto 'l cui colmo consunto
fu l'uom che nacque e visse sanza pecca;
tu haï i piedi in su picciola spera
che l'altra faccia fa de la Giudecca.
Qui è da man, quando di là è sera;
e questi, che ne fé scala col pelo,
fitto è ancora sí come prim' era.
Da questa parte cadde giú dal cielo;
e la terra, che pria di qua si sporse,
per paura di lui fé del mar velo,
e venne a l'emisperio nostro; e forse
per fuggir lui lasciò qui loco vòto
quella ch'appar di qua, e sú ricorse."

And if I became confused, well then,
let the dull minds out there that fail to see
the point I had passed be the judge of that.
"Up on your feet," the master said to me.
"The way is long and the road not easy,
and the sun is climbing past the third hour."
It was no great palatial hall where we were,
but more of a kind of natural dungeon
with a rough floor and a lack of light.

"Before I tear myself away from the abyss,
O my master," I said when I had risen,
"talk to me and clear up my confusion.
Where is the ice? And how did Lucifer there
get stuck upside down? And how did the sun
transit so quickly from evening to dawn?"
And he said, "You imagine that you are still
on the other side of the center, where I
caught hold of the hair of the Evil Worm
Who pierces the world. You remained on that side
as long as I was descending. But when I pivoted
you passed the point to which all weights are drawn.
And now you are beneath the hemisphere
opposite the one that arches over
the great land mass, under whose zenith
The Man was slain who was born and lived without sin;
and your feet are resting upon a little round
that forms the other face of Judecca.
Here it is morning when it is evening there,
and Lucifer, whose pelt formed a ladder for us,
is in the same position as he was before.
He fell down from Heaven on this side of Earth,
and the land withdrew behind a veil of ocean
and fled to the north, toward our hemisphere;
And the Earth that once filled the empty space
where we are standing, perhaps to escape him,
rushed upward to form what now looms above us."

Luogo è là giú da Belzebú remoto
tanto quanto la tomba si distende,
che non per vista, ma per suono è noto
d'un ruscelletto che quivi discende
per la buca d'un sasso, ch'elli ha roso,
col corso ch'elli avvolge, e poco pende.
Lo duca e io per quel cammino ascoso
intrammo a ritornar nel chiaro mondo;
e sanza cura aver d'alcun riposo,
salimmo sú, el primo e io secondo,
tanto ch'i' vidi de le cose belle
che porta 'l ciel, per un pertugio tondo.
E quindi uscimmo a riveder le stelle.

There is a region below, stretching underground
as far from Beelzebub as his tomb is deep,
not known by sight, but only by the sound
Of a rivulet winding down through a tunnel
that it has eroded from the solid rock
as it flows in its gently sloping channel.
Up this hidden way my guide and I now went
to return again to the world of light,
and without thought of rest we made the ascent,
He leading the way and I following,
until the beautiful things that Heaven bears
appeared above through a round opening,
And we came out again and saw the stars.

Breinigsville, PA USA
07 January 2011
252866BV00002B/263-348/P

9 781609 278694